The Creole Archipelago

EARLY AMERICAN STUDIES

Series editors
Daniel K. Richter
Kathleen M. Brown
Max Cavitch
Emma Hart

Exploring neglected aspects of our colonial, revolutionary, and early national history
and culture, Early American Studies reinterprets familiar themes and events in fresh ways.
Interdisciplinary in character, and with a special emphasis on the period from
about 1600 to 1850, the series is published in partnership
with the McNeil Center for Early American Studies.

A complete list of books in the series is available from the publisher.

The Creole Archipelago

Race and Borders in the Colonial Caribbean

Tessa Murphy

PENN

UNIVERSITY OF PENNSYLVANIA PRESS

PHILADELPHIA

Published by
University of Pennsylvania Press
Philadelphia, Pennsylvania 19104-4112
www.upenn.edu/pennpress

Printed in the United States of America on acid-free paper
10 9 8 7 6 5 4 3 2 1

A catalogue record for this book is available
from the Library of Congress
ISBN 978-0-8122-5338-2

Contents

Introduction

Islands Beyond Empires

Although their destination lay more than twenty miles away, the vessel's experienced seafarers knew exactly where they were going. They had rowed their *canóa*—a long, narrow vessel, made from the trunk of a single hollowed-out tree—across the channel just the day before.[1] Now, they made use of the strong ocean current to sweep the dugout canoe back from the northwest coast of Ioüànalao—an island now known as St. Lucia—to the southern tip of Ioüánacaéra, or Martinique.[2] With the coast of the 436-square-mile island they called home just visible on the horizon, the rowers had no need for compasses or charts to guide their four-hour journey through the Caribbean Sea. They made landfall on the first stretch of sand they could reach, swimming alongside their dugout canoe as they pulled it ashore in a shallow bay. Announcing their arrival by blowing on the conch shell they kept in their canoe for this very purpose, the rowers were welcomed home by their *hvéitinocou,* fellow residents of the village, eager for news from the neighboring island.[3]

The short ocean journey between Ioüànalao and Ioüánacaéra was just one of many voyages these able seafarers, who refer to themselves as Kalinago, regularly made along the chain of soaring islands that compose the eastern Caribbean archipelago.[4] From Camáhogne (Grenada) in the south, rowers could stop to rest, take on water, or find provisions at any of the small Grenadine islands that stretch out like stepping stones to Iouloúmain (St. Vincent), some fifty-five miles to the north. From there, rowers who wanted to continue north to Ioüànalao, Ioüánacaéra, Oüáitoucoubouli (Dominica), Caloucaéra (Guadeloupe), and beyond could use the islands' volcanic peaks, which rise to heights of 4,800 feet above the Caribbean Sea, to guide their journeys.[5] As they ranged along the chain of volcanic islands, each one visible from the next, to trade, raid, harvest provisions, fish, and hunt turtles and small game, the seafarers forged maritime routes designed to maximize the abundant natural resources of the archipelago.[6]

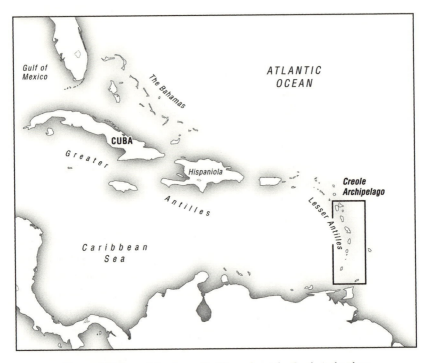

Figure 1. This map of the circum-Caribbean shows the Creole Archipelago
stretching from Guadeloupe in the north to Grenada in the south.

Kalinagos could not have predicted how profoundly their versatile maritime technology would shape the development of the colonial Caribbean.
Using canáoa to retain dominion over areas that sailing ships could not reach,
such as windy shores and rocky coasts, in the seventeenth century Kalinagos
successfully prevented Europeans from establishing sovereignty over Dominica,
St. Lucia, St. Vincent, and Tobago and impeded the development of the French
colony of Grenada. Later, as Europeans, Africans, and their descendants appropriated canáoa, which they also called *pirogues, periaguas,* or *pettiaugers,* they
began to encroach on these Kalinago domains.[7] By leaving European colonies
to establish themselves in neighboring islands, these multiracial, multilingual
settlers both extended and evaded key features of the societies from which they
came, forging an interconnected creolized community that would repeatedly
complicate European colonization of the Caribbean: a "Creole Archipelago."
     People who initially settled on the small islands that constituted Kalin-
ago domains established plantations, but they produced provisions, coffee,
and cacao, rather than the sugar prized in larger neighboring colonies such as

Martinique. Like their neighbors, they too forced enslaved people of African descent to work their plantations, but many of these captives had been born in the Americas rather than in Africa. And enslaved and free residents of the islands maintained commercial, familial, and religious networks, but these networks connected them to nearby port cities such as Saint-Pierre, Martinique, rather than to distant European capitals. Crucially, people who established themselves beyond the boundaries of colonial rule developed shared understandings of who could wield power in these maritime borderlands—understandings that were often at odds with those of colonial authorities. Free people of Indigenous, European, African, or mixed ancestry, many of whom settled in the islands precisely to avoid the restrictions imposed on them in surrounding colonies, insisted on their right to exercise authority as heads of household, members of the Catholic Church, and the owners of land and enslaved people.

People who asserted this authority repeatedly found themselves forced to engage with the very colonial officials whose rule they sought to skirt or selectively engage with. And yet, despite their frequent attempts to evacuate or assert control over this interconnected maritime world, it was not until the global reordering of the Seven Years' War (1756–1763) that the British and French crowns managed to establish sovereignty over the entire archipelago. Crown officials who were dispatched to the eastern Caribbean in the wake of the war introduced sweeping reforms, drawing on prevailing understandings of political economy in their efforts to integrate the new colonies into existing empires as rapidly and as rationally as possible. As Kalinagos, white and free Black planters, and enslaved people contested attempts to transform this Caribbean frontier into a center of sugar production, British and French authorities responded with experimental arrangements and accommodations. Despite securing legal and political privileges that exceeded those of their counterparts elsewhere in the British and French empires, however, existing residents of the archipelago repeatedly sought a return to the autonomy they enjoyed before 1763. When they failed to achieve this return through diplomatic means, some turned to violence. Capitalizing on the disturbances that rippled out of the American War of Independence and the French and Haitian Revolutions, broad coalitions of Indigenous, enslaved, white people, and free people of color repeatedly rose up against colonial rule in the eastern Caribbean. Yet the insurrections that rocked the region during the 1790s owed less to revolutionary currents emanating from Europe than to locally rooted desires to retain Indigenous dominion, protect the customary rights of free people of color, and escape the labor regime associated with sugar production. These insurrections ultimately ended in the expulsion or execution of thousands of longtime residents of the eastern Caribbean archipelago, as colonial authorities abandoned their decades-long attempts to assimilate the creolized society that had taken shape beyond the borders of early sugar colonies.

The history sketched here—of an interconnected maritime world that became a center of broader imperial experimentation and contestation—remains little known. Even the islands on which this book focuses—Dominica, Grenada, St. Lucia, St. Vincent, and Tobago—are largely absent from histories of the seventeenth- and eighteenth-century Caribbean, much less the wider Atlantic World.[8] As Haitian scholar Michel-Rolph Trouillot noted, such "absences are neither neutral nor natural"; instead, the lack of scholarly attention to this region both reflects and reinforces how histories of the Caribbean generally take shape.[9] Individual islands enter the historical record at the moment of European colonization, and colonial agents and their present-day successors created and continue to maintain the archive associated with each island's history. Recovering the history of islands that remained uncolonized for long stretches of time, or that were contested by multiple polities, necessitates drawing on an array of archival, archaeological, cartographic, and ethnolinguistic sources to reconstruct the world that emerged at the interstices of competing European and Indigenous powers. It also requires a clear understanding of the watery geography that helped shape this borderland world, and of how people capitalized on this geography to forge and maintain everyday lives and communities that differed from what was available to them in surrounding colonial spaces.

Approaching the colonial Caribbean as its inhabitants did—as an interconnected region rather than a set of discrete territories—allows us to understand the islands' intertwined social, economic, and political trajectories in ways that existing imperial or national histories often fail to convey. As a growing body of work on the Caribbean, Atlantic, and Pacific demonstrates, ordinary people, not just empires or nation-states, forged geographic imaginaries, and these imaginaries in turn shaped the geopolitical, economic, and social possibilities that they perceived to be available to them.[10] For people who relied on water to get from place to place, to provide food, to link them with allies and protect them from enemies, the sea did not present the frightening prospect that it did to the Europeans who authored the archives on which historians largely rely.[11] Throughout the Caribbean, generations of people—Kalinagos, Africans, Europeans, and their descendants—used canáoa to approach the sea not as a barrier but as a conduit. Doing so allowed them to create a lived geography that did not align with the borders imposed by distant crowns. Attempts to assimilate this distinctive region into existing empires prompted experimentation and diplomatic contestation before giving way to violence, as colonial designs clashed with longstanding practices. Eschewing imperial formulations such as the British West Indies or the French Antilles, this book foregrounds how physical geography and human activity worked to forge and maintain a shared social, economic, and political space in the eastern Caribbean. By shifting the vantage point from which the Lesser Antilles are usually examined, *The Creole Archipelago* reorients understandings of their place in early American and Atlantic history. Rather than a scattering of European outposts overseas, the islands come into view as a center of broader contests over Indigenous dominion, racial belonging, economic development, and colonial subjecthood.

Defining the Creole Archipelago

The imperial or national frameworks typically employed to analyze Caribbean history are at odds with the geographic realities that shaped daily life in the region. The pervasive misconception that islands constitute discrete economic and political units with clearly defined borders rendered colonial officials, as well as later historians, ill equipped to recognize and grapple with the many elements of island life that extended to other shores.[12] By emphasizing how individuals used maritime routes to forge connections across islands and therefore across multiple Indigenous and European domains, the framework of a Creole Archipelago provides a different means of engaging with early American and Atlantic history.[13] Rather than using the records of a single empire to analyze how that empire viewed and governed a given colony and its inhabitants, an archipelagic approach assembles the traces of people who are present in, but rarely the focus of, religious, commercial, diplomatic, cartographic, and visual records held in repositories across the Americas and Europe. While even this multisited approach often entails what historian Marisa Fuentes calls "narrat[ing] the fleeting glimpses" these archives yield, it nonetheless provides a different perspective on how people thought about, navigated, related to, and remade the world in which they lived.[14] Instead of highlighting the myriad ways that European empires became entangled, *The Creole Archipelago* invites us to focus on the many residents of early America whose lives only occasionally intersected with European structures of power, and to foreground how they experienced and made sense of their evolving world.[15]

The Creole Archipelago thus refers to both a physical space—a chain of small volcanic islands, each visible from the next, that stretches 280 miles from Guadeloupe in the north to Grenada in the south—and a hybrid community that emerged as people who were born and spent their lives in this space engaged in exchange, interaction, accommodation, and contestation. Although scholars have applied the terms "Creole" and "Archipelago" to a variety of contexts, here they are used in their original sense: creole from the Latin *creare*, meaning to produce or create, and archipelago from the Greek *arkhi* and *pelagos*, meaning "chief sea," in reference to the Mediterranean.[16] Approaching the Caribbean as a body of water, albeit one in which there are many islands, allows us to foreground how different groups of people interacted with this aquatic space and what kind of worlds they created as a result of their quotidian interactions.[17]

The meaning of the term "Creole" evolved considerably from its first appearance in the early modern Iberian Atlantic world, variously referring to Europeans born in the Americas, enslaved people born in the Americas, and people of Afro-European ancestry—whether free or enslaved—born in the Americas, as well as the vernaculars and institutions they created.[18] Common across all these definitions is the importance of place in determining belonging. Both colonial contemporaries and later scholars distinguished between people who came to the Americas from elsewhere and those who were born and spent their lives in the region, even if they were all part of the same empire or nation. Thus, Creoles were defined not necessarily by mixed heritage but by what historian Cécile Vidal describes as their "distance from the territorial center of the nation . . . and their nearness with other nations, [which] held the potential to shape them into different people."[19]

Indigenous Americans are rarely included in understandings of creolization.[20] This is due in no small part to the fact that when Indigenous nations incorporate other peoples, languages, and practices into their communities, colonizers often cast them as no longer Indigenous, thereby denying Indigenous claims to land or sovereignty.[21] As anthropologist Patrick Wolfe has shown, this highly "restrictive racial"—and, I would argue, cultural—"classification of Indians straightforwardly furthered the logic of elimination" underlying settler colonialism.[22] Yet scholars need not accept or perpetuate a logic that serves to dispossess, and even disavow the very existence of, Indigenous peoples throughout the Americas. As historian Melanie Newton argues, resituating "indigeneity as a key site of struggle" provides a means of integrating Indigenous people into Caribbean history while also highlighting "new ways to expose colonial forms of knowledge and power."[23] Anthropologist Nancie Solien Gonzalez has shown that Kalinagos adopted "rapid change as a survival technique," profoundly shaping and borrowing from the hybrid culture that emerged through processes of interaction and exchange in the eastern Caribbean.[24] Many formed families and communities with fugitives from slavery, a process of ethnogenesis that gave rise to Black Caribs and ultimately to the Garifuna people of present-day Central America.[25] By refusing to accept the notion that Indigenous people who engage in adaptation and incorporation cease to be Indigenous, we can better appreciate how processes of creolization allowed Kalinagos to remain important, if little-acknowledged, political, military, and economic actors up to the present day.

Although island residents never used the term Creole Archipelago, the region's interconnected geography was not lost on observers, who noted that the islands "compose a chain in the form of a half circle, with Grenada and Guadeloupe at the two ends."[26] Nor were the regional orientations and resultant loyalties of the archipelago's inhabitants unknown to colonial authorities, who regularly complained that the priorities of island residents were at odds with broader imperial projects.

The fact that the goals of distant crowns did not always align with colonists' actions or desires is hardly surprising; historians emphasize how the development of creole identities and institutions generated imperial ruptures throughout the Americas.[27] Yet the geography of the eastern Caribbean allowed these differences to multiply, preventing the consolidation of imperial hegemony in the region until at least the late eighteenth century. The ability to use canáoa to move independently between islands—and thus between what political scientist James C. Scott terms state and nonstate spaces—allowed residents of the Creole Archipelago to extend certain features of colonial society while skirting others.[28] As individuals sought to avoid the obligations of subjecthood such as paying taxes or obeying laws that limited their autonomy or authority, they removed themselves to neighboring islands that crown officials struggled to control. Yet the proximity of these islands to centers of colonial rule also allowed free residents of the Creole Archipelago to engage with states as needed, regularly paddling or sailing to the French colonies of Martinique and Guadeloupe to partake in the rites of the Catholic Church, obtain goods, and sell the cacao, coffee, cotton, and foodstuffs produced by the people they held in slavery on their small plantations.

Life in the Creole Archipelago was far from peaceful. Contests over land produced bloodshed and relegated some groups, such as Kalinagos, to smaller or more marginal areas. Far more people lived and died in slavery than found freedom in the region, as white and free planters of color extended colonial practices of slaveholding beyond the boundaries of colonial rule. The absence of legal institutions such as courts meant that residents of the islands developed their own means of distributing justice, and available evidence, though scant, suggests they were often brutal. Colonial authorities who sought to control these embryonic settlements sometimes razed them to the ground, and free and enslaved residents were vulnerable to pirate attacks and kidnapping. Yet the process of interacting, whether on friendly or hostile terms, also produced some of the defining features of the Creole Archipelago. Kalinago agricultural practices, such as manioc cultivation, were adapted and expanded to include new crops from Europe, Africa, and elsewhere in the Americas. French emerged as a lingua franca allowing individuals to communicate, trade, and form alliances. Coercive and consensual relationships produced people of mixed race, whose presence accelerated the creation of familial, cultural, and political ties.[29] People of Afro-European ancestry assumed important roles in this creolized society as members of the Catholic Church, heads of household, participants in community militias, and the owners of land and enslaved people.[30]

As in mainland North America, people who settled beyond the borders of individual colonies shared many of the same goals as those who remained within them: they wanted to own property, establish families, and exercise autonomy.[31] The difference was that people who settled in borderlands, whether on islands or on the mainland, often did so because they lacked the economic or social capital to achieve these goals. By moving to spaces where land was free, trade was unrestricted, and laws limiting the possibilities of people of color were unevenly observed or enforced, residents of the Creole Archipelago succeeded in forging lives increasingly unavailable to them in nearby colonies.

Colonial agents sent to assimilate the islands into existing empires when they were ceded to France and Great Britain at the end of the Seven Years' War therefore encountered a society that both resembled and differed from neighboring colonial spaces. The Creole Archipelago was a slave society, but it was one in which Indigenous people claimed dominion over large swaths of land; enslaved people, many of whom were born in the Americas, labored on small, mixed-agriculture plantations rather than sugar estates; free people of color exercised authority; and planters had few ties to distant metropoles. Attempts to integrate this society prompted innovation and negotiation, transforming the archipelago into a center of broader experiments in political economy. By carefully reconstructing the economic, social, and informal political features of the world that residents of this island chain created and maintained for more than a century, this book highlights the unintended by-products of early modern colonization and considers how they in turn shaped and complicated later imperial projects. What motivated people to venture beyond colonial boundaries, and what did they do once there? How did crown authorities attempt to remake, reform, or erase the practices of people who settled outside the sphere of their rule, and how did their attempts inform broader imperial strategies? What were the consequences of the lengthy contest between the rationalizing, centralizing impulses of eighteenth-century empires and the autonomous actions of people who sought to evade those very impulses?

An analysis that situates the Creole Archipelago at its center highlights the range of possibilities available to individuals and groups within this relatively small geographic space and considers the factors that led them to choose one possibility over another. Looking outward from this little-studied island chain shows how key phenomena in early modern global history—the growth of transatlantic economies, the changing shape of empires, and the rise of revolutionary movements—were both experienced and shaped by people all too often left out of imperial histories.[32]

Situating the Creole Archipelago in Space

Early modern European sailors designated Caribbean islands as windward or leeward according to the island's location relative to the prevailing winds that propelled their ships. Yet these wind-based designations fail to capture how people who relied on paddle-powered vessels such as canáoa navigated the same waters. Although no Caribbean colony developed in isolation, interisland linkages were particularly pronounced in the eastern Caribbean.[33] The Lesser Antilles—so called in order to distinguish the islands from the much larger Greater Antilles to the north—form a crescent-shaped arc that stretches more than 500 miles from the Virgin Islands in the north to Grenada, just north of South America, in the south. Islands vary in size from 650-square-mile Guadeloupe to Saba, just 5 square miles. While the Lesser Antilles account for only 3 percent of total land area in the Caribbean, they are home to a variety of ecosystems, from moorlands to rainforests to mangrove swamps.[34] These environments result in considerable biodiversity, allowing the islands' Indigenous

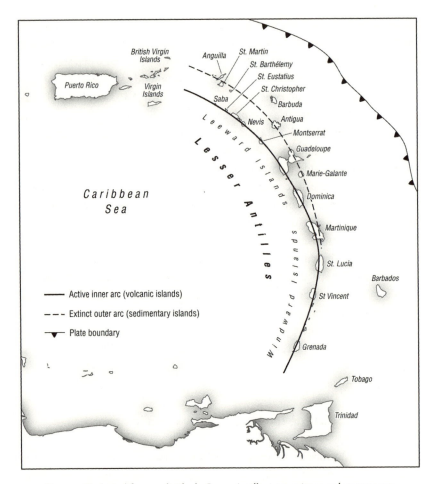

Figure 2. Geological features divide the Lesser Antilles into an inner and an outer arc.
Windward and leeward distinctions reflect the islands' positions relative to prevailing winds.

inhabitants to maximize natural resources by ranging through the region to
fish and hunt turtles, manatees, and the now-extinct monk seal and by creating gardens on otherwise uninhabited islands where they could take refuge in
the event of storms or attacks.[35]

Geological features divide the Lesser Antilles into an inner and an outer
arc. The former is composed of a continuous chain of volcanic peaks, which
rise to heights of more than 4,800 feet. This mountainous landscape con-
trasts markedly with that found on the flatter coral limestone outer arc, where
islands such as Antigua and Barbuda boast maximum elevations ranging from

just 72 to 1,300 feet.[36] The islands of Barbados, Trinidad, and Tobago, which lie east and southeast of the Lesser Antillean chain, constitute a separate geological subregion, which is not volcanic and is therefore generally flatter.

In addition to affecting rainfall and vegetation within each territory, the Lesser Antilles' topographic features shape how individuals navigate between islands.[37] Each island of the inner arc lies no more than 25 miles from the next, allowing the mountainous peaks of one landmass to be seen from the one previous; as a modern guide to the region notes, "navigation becomes a matter of picking a peak and steering for it."[38] In contrast, Barbados lies approximately 110 miles east of the volcanic chain, meaning that seafarers cannot rely on visual cues to travel to and from the 166-square-mile island. While Barbados' location in the open Atlantic made it accessible to European sailors, it was less frequented by seafarers in canóa and was reportedly uninhabited when Europeans first arrived there.[39]

European sailors dubbed the southernmost part of the Lesser Antilles—Martinique, St. Lucia, St. Vincent, and Grenada—the Windward Islands. Owing to their more sheltered position relative to the winds, Europeans referred to the more northerly islands of the Lesser Antilles, including Dominica and Guadeloupe, as the Leeward Islands, and these designations persist to the present day. For seafarers whose vessels can be propelled by paddles, however, the distance between landmasses is much more salient than any wind-based distinctions. The channel dividing the northernmost Windward Island of Martinique from the southernmost Leeward Island of Dominica is only twenty-five miles wide, and seventeenth- and eighteenth-century travelers remarked that they could reach the more northerly island by pirogue after four to five hours at sea; the return journey took roughly one hour longer.[40] Travelers departing the northern coast of St. Lucia could reach southern Martinique, some twenty-one miles away, in approximately four hours, while voyagers crossing the twenty-three-mile channel between St. Vincent and St. Lucia spent about five hours at sea.[41] By relying on oars or sails as conditions dictated, Indigenous, free, and enslaved people throughout the circum-Caribbean used versatile watercraft to develop routes that authorities found difficult to police.[42]

Differences in maritime technology also influenced settlement and trade patterns. Europeans labeled the coasts of each island as leeward or windward, again in reference to prevailing winds. The windward coasts of the Lesser Antilles, located on the eastern sides of the islands bordering the Atlantic Ocean, are generally fringed by rough seas; the western or leeward coasts, which face the Caribbean Sea, are much calmer. While Europeans established ports on sheltered leeward shores, they noted that people who relied on nimble, paddle-powered vessels were not as dissuaded by the windier conditions on the islands' Atlantic sides. "They laugh when we would shiver in fear," noted a seventeenth-century French missionary, recounting in amazement how Kalinagos took particular pleasure in body surfing on Dominica's windward coast, "where the sea is much rougher and the rivers much more rapid."[43]

Human relationships to geography continued to shape the development of the Creole Archipelago throughout the colonial era. As Europeans established plantations and port towns on calmer leeward coasts, Kalinagos in the Lesser Antilles, like Indigenous people and Maroons throughout the Americas, increasingly concentrated their settlements in areas that Europeans found difficult to access.[44] By settling on rougher windward coasts or in mountainous areas, Kalinagos maintained spaces of dominion amid growing European encroachment.

As in other parts of the colonial Americas, the intensification of plantation production soon prompted other people to encroach on Indigenous domains.[45] Once again, geography played an important role in shaping possibilities. Enslaved Africans used pirogues to escape to nearby islands, where they established themselves in areas they could defend.[46] Planters, in contrast, were motivated to find lands where they could establish estates for themselves or their children, many of whom were mixed-race. While residents of Barbados relocated to more distant English outposts in Carolina, Jamaica, and even Surinam, French subjects in Guadeloupe and Martinique made the short ocean journey to islands they could glimpse from the colonies' shores.[47] This regional diaspora selectively disseminated features of French colonial society— including Catholicism, the French language, plantation production, and the exploitation of enslaved Africans—just beyond the boundaries of French sovereignty. Yet the people who carried these features into neighboring islands did not replicate other elements of French colonial life, such as the expulsion of Indigenous people or the severing of ties between Euro- and Afro-descended family members. The world they created was thus both a product of and an inherent challenge to neighboring colonial societies.

The Creole Archipelago took shape because the physical geography of the Lesser Antilles did not conform to the imagined geography of empire. In larger islands such as Hispaniola and Cuba, the centralizing forces of plantation production propelled people into less-sought-after lands within established colonies.[48] But in the small space of the eastern Caribbean, people who could not or did not want to participate in sugar production instead settled just outside sugar islands. While this regional migration allowed them a degree of autonomy they could not secure under colonial rule, the society they created remained deeply embedded in the trade networks and religious and social structures of neighboring colonies. Over the course of the eighteenth century, residents of the Creole Archipelago created communities that repeatedly challenged the nature and extent of European colonialism, helping to spur reforms, experiments, and ultimately war.

Situating the Creole Archipelago in Time

The framework of a Creole Archipelago provides a means of examining colonization and its unintentional by-products in tandem. Histories of the Caribbean typically trace the development of a single colony or imperial formation such as Jamaica or the British West Indies, showing how capital, merchants, and planters radically transformed sparsely populated outposts into centers of plantation production.[49] As subjects of a single crown, united by their pursuit of wealth, their desire to maintain control over an enslaved majority, and their strong economic, familial, and cultural ties to the metropole, free residents of the colonial Caribbean are often presented as fundamentally different from their peers on the American main.[50] Yet in many respects, the interconnected archipelago of the eastern Caribbean more closely resembles borderland regions of the mainland Americas than isolated colonies like Barbados.

Although the Creole Archipelago emerged in a particular place and time because of broader historical forces, it had much in common with other spaces of contestation and accommodation that took shape at the edges of competing European and Indigenous sovereignties in the Americas, such as the Great Lakes region or the American Southwest.[51] Like the terrestrial borderlands more familiar to historians, the eastern Caribbean was, to borrow the words of historians Pekka Hämäläinen and Samuel Truett, an "area of cross-cultural interaction at the edges of empires," one where Indigenous people did not merely play European powers off one another but actively shaped and limited what these powers were able to do.[52] It was a space in which regular interactions and exchanges between a diversity of peoples gave rise to roles and relationships that deviated from those sanctioned by colonial law, allowing legitimate interracial families and influential people of color to exercise influence.[53] It was also a place of violence, one where individuals wielded power without being restrained by a colonial state.[54] As in other parts of the Americas, the transition from borderlands to formal colonies in the eastern Caribbean involved considerable interimperial rivalry and ultimately sparked profound transformations.[55] Yet as in other early modern borderlands, the agents of distant crowns proved unable to control the archipelago and its inhabitants to the extent they had envisioned, allowing key features of the society forged outside of and in response to empires to persist within them.[56]

As this broad characterization of borderlands suggests, historians can find them virtually anywhere they look, which in turn threatens to minimize their utility as an interpretive framework. Yet scholars who use borderlands as a means to capture what more traditional imperial or national histories miss suggest a number of ways that this framework can be refined to help expand and diversify current understandings of early America. Among these are turning to a broader range of sources; moving beyond Indigenous-settler dynamics to include other historical actors, particularly people of African descent; and looking past familiar terrestrial borders in search of other places where people met, comingled, and competed.[57] A borderlands perspective on the colonial Caribbean therefore provides a more nuanced understanding of power relations in the region. Rather than a set of discrete territories quickly mastered by powerful crowns, the archipelago comes into view as a site where overlapping Indigenous, African, and European polities alternately dominated, vied, and coalesced with one another.

Responding to borderlands historians' call to revisit the archives and methodologies that typically inform colonial history is essential to diversifying present understandings of the Caribbean and its place in early American and Atlantic history. A tendency to use colonial correspondence and trade records to chart the development of plantations and port towns means that Indigenous people feature very little in Caribbean history beyond the early colonial era.[58] Yet eighteenth-century Catholic parish registers testify to the continued presence of Kalinagos, whose participation in baptismal rites furnished them with written proof of their children's free birth. Maps betray Indigenous influence on settlement and trade patterns throughout the region, while bilingual dictionaries simultaneously illustrate the transmission of Indigenous knowledge to Europeans and hint at Kalinago worldviews.

Enslaved people are similarly silenced in colonial archives, becoming most visible when they threaten or undermine the system that produced those archives, such as during insurrections.[59] Yet Fuentes' call to read *along the bias grain* to eke out extinguished and invisible but no less historically important lives" serves as a forceful reminder that enslaved peoples' muted presence in more mundane records can inadvertently testify to their central place in the societies that produced such records.[60] Free people in slave societies rarely bothered to mention who was paddling their pirogues, ferrying their goods to market, or forging the paths that allowed surveyors to produce maps of the colonies precisely *because* enslaved people were so ubiquitous in and central to these societies. While acknowledging these silences fails to yield individual biographies, it nonetheless builds on the work of historians who emphasize the presence and experiences of enslaved people outside of the plantation contexts in which they are most often examined.[61]

An archipelagic, borderlands approach to Caribbean history also provides a salient reminder that, in the words of historian Alison Games, a single place or region "tends to look very different when viewed from different vantages and within different imperial or commercial frameworks."[62] In early Spanish records, the Lesser Antilles appear as peripheral islands peopled by *indios caribes*: man-eating savages whose barbarism made them eligible for enslavement.[63] In seventeenth-century British archives, the same islands come into focus as fertile commons where English sailors could take on wood and water and as sites of refuge for people fleeing slavery in the English colony of Barbados.[64] In eighteenth-century French correspondence, the islands are alternately cast as dens of disorder and contraband and as essential outlets for a growing colonial population.[65] While even triangulating these myriad views fails to illuminate the full story of the tens of thousands of people who lived and labored in the archipelago, it suggests the potential pitfalls of using a single linguistic or imperial archive to understand the history of places that took shape at the confluence of multiple powers.

The history detailed here builds on studies of entangled empires, which examine "interconnected societies" to gauge how they mutually influenced one another.[66] But the book's emphasis on creolization also encourages historians to decenter empires as the poles around which ordinary people organized their daily lives. As Shannon Dawdy argues in her study of "rogue colonialism" in French New Orleans, "colonialism frequently creates conditions that foster not only cultures of resistance, but also . . . an environment that encouraged many people to refashion themselves and to collectively invent new institutions" and practices.[67] By carefully reconstructing when, where, how, and why these new practices emerged, *The Creole Archipelago* shows how they persisted alongside and competed with those subsequently introduced by colonial authorities, sparking little-studied ideological and practical contests that reverberated well beyond the islands' borders.

Scholars of the Caribbean have long cautioned against treating the region's past as merely the "overseas history" of individual European crowns.[68]

Centering the Creole Archipelago reminds us that very big things—debates over sovereignty, attempts to rationalize and improve plantation production and trade, and contests about who could be a colonial subject and on what grounds—happened in relatively small places throughout the Atlantic World. By highlighting the role of Indigenous Americans, enslaved and free people of color, and middling colonists in shaping these broader historical phenomena, this book encourages a reconsideration of the geographic and temporal vantage points from which they are usually examined and provides a new means of integrating the Caribbean into studies of early America and the broader Atlantic World.

*   *   *

By focusing on an interconnected region and the diversity of people who forged lives in this region, *The Creole Archipelago* reveals a lengthy contest between attempts to establish control and the desire of individuals and groups to evade, undermine, or selectively engage with that control. Although the book focuses on a chain of islands that eventually became part of the French and British empires, it does not seek to provide a comprehensive comparison of imperial strategies. Instead, focusing on a part of the early Americas where Indigenous, European, and locally rooted powers competed and coexisted for generations suggests the need to decenter empire in order to understand the region in a way that would have made sense to those who lived there.

The book's first two chapters provide a counterpoint to histories of Indigenous disappearance and enslavement in the colonial Caribbean by emphasizing how Kalinagos limited European settlement and the spread of sugar monoculture in the seventeenth- and early eighteenth-century Lesser Antilles.[69] Warfare between Kalinagos and Europeans resulted in formal recognition of Indigenous dominion over Dominica and St. Vincent, and the agreement that St. Lucia and Tobago would not be colonized by the English or French. Although Grenada was claimed by France in 1649, its location at the far reaches of the archipelago left it vulnerable; sparsely settled, the island lacked the administrative apparatus usually afforded to French colonies and was poorly integrated into France's mercantilist trade system.[70] By the last decades of the seventeenth century, however, as the turn to sugar production prompted the consolidation of large estates in Martinique and Guadeloupe, free and enslaved Africans, Europeans, and their descendants began to migrate to Grenada and to nearby Kalinago domains.[71] As they modified and extended Kalinago practices of interisland provisioning and trade, these multiracial, multilingual free and forced migrants developed regional economic, religious, and social networks that depended on and contributed to—yet remained beyond the effective control of—nearby colonies.[72] By 1763, Dominica, Grenada, St. Lucia, and St. Vincent were home to several thousand Kalinagos, at least 6,500 free people of European and African descent, and more than 30,000 enslaved people, many of them born in the Caribbean.[73]

The growth of the plantation complex repeatedly threatened to erase the distinctive world of the Creole Archipelago, as English and French officials eyed the islands as potential sugar colonies. But it was not until the global reordering of the Seven Years' War that metropolitan authorities gained the power to assimilate the islands into existing empires. The book's next three chapters focus on the decade immediately following the war to show how newly imposed political, economic, and legal boundaries affected this creole society. Great Britain's victory in the war allowed King George III to harness some of the last available lands in the Caribbean; at the 1763 Treaty of Paris, Dominica, Grenada, St. Vincent, and Tobago were ceded to Britain, while St. Lucia became a French colony. The archipelago came into view as a laboratory of empire, as both British and French officials drew on shared understandings of political economy in their attempts to transform the islands into productive plantation colonies.[74] Yet imperial designs failed to account for the realities of daily life in the region, as different groups of people capitalized on the proximity of competing regimes to evade and contest crown designs. Thousands of existing island residents who spoke a different language, practiced a different religion, and in some cases were a different race forced European officials to grapple with who could be a colonial subject, and on what terms.[75] Enslaved people responded to the introduction of sugar planting with desertion and violence, while settler encroachment on Kalinago lands led to the eruption of all-out war in 1772. Examining repeated instances of diplomatic and armed conflict that predate the Age of Revolutions shows that the contests that shook the region in the 1790s took shape decades earlier, as various residents of the Creole Archipelago attempted to preserve key elements of their existing society under new colonial regimes.

The book's final chapters reframe seemingly contingent or external events by nesting them in these longstanding regional realities. Broader contests such as the American War of Independence and the French Revolution extended into the Lesser Antilles, resulting in repeated conquests and occupations of the islands.[76] Although these disruptions originated far outside the region, local factors were key in shaping how people responded to them. For Catholics, free people of color, and enslaved and Indigenous people, repeated intra- and inter-imperial wars presented new opportunities to exercise power, assert title to land, and seek opportunities under a different political regime. Analyzing two little-studied insurgencies that paralyzed the eastern Caribbean in the mid-1790s—Fedon's Rebellion in Grenada and the Second Carib War in St. Vincent—*The Creole Archipelago* situates them as part of a much longer struggle between imperial attempts to rationalize and centralize colonial rule and local desires to continue exercising customary rights first forged outside of empire.

These conflicts resulted in the exile of thousands of people, as authorities brought their experiment in incorporating new colonial subjects to an abrupt and violent end. Although many of the people who created and maintained the Creole Archipelago were forcibly removed hundreds of miles beyond the region's borders, this book shows that the small corner of the Caribbean from which they came—like many seemingly small places throughout the early Americas—was a key site of broader contests over agricultural and trade practices, understandings of subjecthood and racial belonging, and the exercise of legitimate authority in the eighteenth-century Atlantic World.

Chapter 1

Kalinago Dominion and the Shape
of the Eastern Caribbean

The man was "tired of living among his people." Eager to find new lands, he "embarked his whole family" in their canáoa, a dugout vessel as much as sixty feet long and capable of carrying fifty to sixty people.[1] The family traveled for many days; rather than depending on sails, they used large wooden paddles to propel their boat north from the river basin into the open sea.[2] After navigating along a chain of islands—some small and rocky, others with peaks that disappeared from view into the clouds above—they came ashore in a small cove, its sand blackened by the volcano above. With its many shallow bays to land canáoa, dense rainforests for shelter from attack, and plenty of rivers providing water, fish, and *mannatoüi*, or manatees, the lush green island was the perfect place for the man and his family to call home. They named their mountainous new homeland Oüáitoucoubouli meaning "tall is her body," but for generations, as their numbers grew and they spread out across the constellation of islands to the north and south, the man's descendants continued to refer to themselves by the name of their adventurous ancestor: Kalinago.[3]

The origin story that Indigenous inhabitants of Oüáitoucoubouli, or Dominica, related to French Dominican missionary Jean Baptiste Du Tertre when he visited the island in the 1640s aligns with modern archaeological findings, which suggest that humans migrated from South America to the Caribbean as long as eight thousand years ago.[4] More important than the story's veracity, however, is the insight it offers on how the Caribbean's Indigenous inhabitants understood the geography and history of the region. The people who called themselves Kalinago recognized that while different islands had different names—Caloucaéra, or Guadeloupe, immediately to the north of Dominica, and Ioüánacaéra, Ioüànalao, Iouloúmain, and Camáhogne (Martinique, St. Lucia, St. Vincent, and Grenada), forming a crescent-shaped arc to the south—all were part of an interconnected archipelago.[5] Men and women who used canoes to travel through Caribbean waters therefore treated islands not as bounded spaces but as part of a broader region, regularly navigating along the island chain to gather provisions, to trade, and to visit and exchange information with people in neighboring *carbets*, the large communal houses that served as the center of Kalinago social and political life.[6]

By the time that missionaries like Du Tertre began to document the history and language of Kalinago people in the mid-seventeenth century, the Natives' relationship to the region had begun to change. Kalinago practices of interisland travel and exchange evolved in the period after 1492, as European incursions prompted population loss and dispersal.[7] Father Pacifique de Provins, a member of the Capuchin order who, like Du Tertre, visited Dominica in the 1640s, noted that the island "is only inhabited by some assembled savages who [were] chased by Christians from the mainland as well as from neighboring islands that they stole from them."[8] Du Tertre echoed the views of his fellow missionary, characterizing Dominica's Kalinago inhabitants as "the leftovers of the innumerable barbarians that the Spanish Christians exterminated."[9] These and other comments from early French voyagers reveal how Iberian conquest of the Caribbean in the fifteenth and sixteenth centuries shaped the perceptions and practices of subsequent European colonizers.[10] Aware of the tales of Spanish destruction that gave rise to the Black Legend, French missionaries like Provins sought to portray their own relations with Indigenous peoples in a more positive light. Yet their chronicles offer insight on more than just European responses to the actions of other colonizers. They also reveal that far from being an isolated or static group, the people that Europeans dubbed "savages" had generations of experience with conquerors and colonists from across the Atlantic. These experiences affected many facets of Indigenous society in the Caribbean, as individuals and groups secured new trade goods and relationships, developed new means of communication, fled or migrated to establish new settlements, and forged new political, military, and personal alliances. They also shaped relations between Natives and newcomers. As English and French settlers began to establish colonies in the Lesser Antilles in the middle decades of the seventeenth century, the people they encountered drew on a range of commercial, military, and diplomatic strategies to maintain spaces of autonomy and dominion amid growing European encroachment.

The aqueous geography of the eastern Caribbean archipelago facilitated this autonomy, as Kalinagos used waterways to escape colonial expansion, form alliances with other Indigenous people, launch attacks on Europeans, and continue to engage in established patterns of interisland travel and trade.[11] The epidemics, warfare, and Spanish slaving missions that reduced the Indigenous populations of the Greater Antillean islands on which Europeans first settled were documented by contemporary chroniclers and informed the work of subsequent historians, whose estimates of the Caribbean's population before the arrival of Europeans range from 60,000 to almost 8 million people on the island of Hispaniola alone.[12] Yet a growing body of archaeological and historical evidence demonstrates that inhabitants of the Lesser Antilles, who had less contact with Europeans and whose settlements were smaller and more dispersed, were affected differently than their counterparts to the north.[13] Although the number of Kalinagos diminished in the centuries after the arrival of Europeans, the Caribbean's Indigenous inhabitants did not disappear. While some remained in islands claimed by Europeans, others migrated to the South American mainland or to mountainous islands, such as Dominica, where they could better defend themselves from further incursion.[14] In the early colonial era, these islands became Indigenous strongholds, as Kalinagos from neighboring islands concentrated their numbers there.[15] Owing to their ability to use waterways to quickly move between islands, Kalinagos continued to engage settlers in lengthy diplomatic and military contests over territory, trade, and the expansion of slavery and plantation production in the eastern Caribbean throughout the seventeenth and eighteenth centuries.[16] The forcible transportation of almost five thousand Black Caribs off the island of St. Vincent in 1797, along with the creation of a reservation in Dominica in 1903, testifies to the continued presence of people who identify as Indigenous to the Caribbean long after their ancestors were supposedly rendered extinct.[17]

Despite their absence from many histories of the Caribbean, close examination of surviving missionary and travelers' accounts, parish records, government correspondence, censuses, and maps reveals that Indigenous people shaped the imperial geography, economy, and society of the Lesser Antilles until at least the end of the eighteenth century.[18] Refining their strategies as they drew on prior experiences with different groups of settlers, Kalinagos used a combination of diplomacy and force to actively limit European settlement of the region and hinder the establishment of plantations.[19] In 1660, a treaty between French, English, and Kalinago signatories formally acknowledged Indigenous dominion over the islands of Dominica and St. Vincent, and a number of subsequent treaties, including the 1748 treaty of Aix-la-Chapelle, reaffirmed the limits of European sovereignty in the early modern Americas.

Recognizing how Kalinagos shaped Caribbean colonization provides an important corrective to prevailing histories that ignore or silence the influence and even the presence of the region's Indigenous peoples and offers a new understanding of why islands that settlers prized as potential plantation colonies remained beyond the reach of European rule until the mid-eighteenth century.[20] In addition to acting as spaces of Kalinago dominion, islands that lay outside the sphere of European empires in the colonial Caribbean served as attractive sites of refuge for people who were marginalized by the advance of the plantation complex.[21] By the first decades of the eighteenth century, fugitives from slavery, free people of color, and small planters increasingly migrated to islands formally recognized as Kalinago territories, giving rise to diverse, Creolized communities. Yet it was Indigenous action—not imperial disinterest—that inadvertently allowed for the creation of these sites of refuge. In their determination to maintain spaces of dominion amid increasing foreign incursion, Kalinagos helped forge an archipelago in which some of the most profitable colonies in the Americas were interspersed with islands that remained outside of European empire.

Long before the arrival of Europeans, the Caribbean's Indigenous inhabitants developed versatile maritime technologies that allowed them to forge commercial, political, and military networks that stretched across islands, elaborating an interconnected geography that larger wind-powered vessels could not replicate. As they adapted to an evolving geopolitical landscape, Kalinagos deployed military and diplomatic strategies that enabled them to preserve features of this interconnected world in the face of growing European encroachment. The 1660 treaty that formally recognized Kalinago territories in the Lesser Antilles sheds light on how Europeans responded to Indigenous claims to dominion and reveals how Indigenous people formed new alliances and concentrated their settlements in order to maintain this dominion, even as it was increasingly challenged by the growth of slavery and the plantation complex. Recovering the place that Kalinagos sought to secure within the evolving hierarchy of the colonial Caribbean counters depictions of Indigenous people as passive victims of economic and territorial expansion and testifies to their role in creating spaces and societies that evolved outside the sphere of European rule—ones that would frustrate later imperial projects.

Indigenous Geographies of the Eastern Caribbean

Both archaeological and historical records confirm that the Indigenous peoples of the circum-Caribbean approached the region as part of a larger, interconnected space. As experienced seafarers, swimmers, and even surfers, Kalinagos treated waterways not as barriers but as thoroughfares, using dugout canoes to travel, trade, and raid across long distances.[22] Ignoring the ways that this versatile maritime technology allowed people to range over large areas, the first Europeans in the Caribbean instead assigned the region's Indigenous inhabitants to broad categories based on the islands in which they encountered them. The peaceable Arawak were said to reside in Greater Antillean islands such as Hispaniola, while the bellicose, allegedly man-eating Carib circulated through the smaller Lesser Antillean islands.[23] Despite the simple binary imposed by Europeans, archaeological excavations illustrate that the Indigenous Caribbean constituted a "cultural mosaic" populated by a diversity of peoples.[24] Linguistic evidence demonstrates that Arawakan languages were spoken throughout the region, undermining European notions of a clear dichotomy between the inhabitants of the Greater and Lesser Antilles.[25] The possibility of assigning the Caribbean's Indigenous peoples to one of two categories is further complicated by the fact that they did not lead insular lives. As they used canoes to travel as far away as the South American main, Indigenous inhabitants of the circum-Caribbean elaborated "a vast, pan-regional network system" that belied European attempts to impose clear territorial divisions.[26]

European contemporaries almost never referred to the people they encountered in the Lesser Antilles as Kalinago. Missionaries, colonial officials, and settlers instead used the term Carib, or Caraïbe, or the generic term "Indian," or they signaled what they perceived to be their inherent superiority to their Native neighbors by labeling them *sauvage*: wild, untamed, or savage beings. Yet as Dominican missionary Raymond Breton's 1665 Franco-Kalinago dictionary reveals, "the words Galibi and Carib were names that the Europeans gave them, and . . . their real name was Callinago . . . they distinguish themselves only by the words Oubaóbanum [and] Balouébanum, that is to say, of the islands or of the mainland."[27] Although terms used in historical sources have been retained, the term "Kalinago" is used to refer to the people Europeans encountered when they began settling the eastern Caribbean in the seventeenth century, as well as their descendants. Eschewing European labels in favor of a term by which the region's inhabitants identified themselves honors the wishes of their descendants, while also placing historical Kalinagos on an equal analytical footing with the French, English, and other European subjects with whom they engaged in trade, diplomacy, and war.[28]

Like the Europeans they encountered, Kalinagos were not a static or timeless people. Throughout the pre-contact era, Indigenous areas of settlement and trade, as well as political and military alliances, evolved in response to the availability of natural resources and the presence of competing polities.[29] The arrival of Europeans put further pressures on existing adaptations, as Kalinagos responded to the introduction of new people, diseases, and technologies. Beginning in the late fifteenth century, European incursions triggered substantial migrations among the populations of the circum-Caribbean.[30] In the ensuing decades, the Indigenous inhabitants of individual islands increasingly relocated to areas not occupied by Europeans, such as the islands' mountainous interiors or rougher Atlantic coasts.[31] They also migrated to islands that posed practical challenges to European colonization, concentrating their settlement on mountainous, densely forested islands such as Dominica and St. Vincent.

These interisland migrations contributed to the erasure of Kalinagos from the written sources on which historians of the colonial Americas usually rely. A 1671 census records only 72 "sauvages mestis et capouis" living in all of the Lesser Antillean islands to which France laid claim: 51 in Guadeloupe, 19 in Saint Christophe, and 2 in Saint Croix, with Martinique and Grenada notably absent from the count.[32] By 1683, that number increased to 106, including 61 in Martinique, and as of 1685 officials reported a total of 116 free and 138 enslaved "Caribs" across France's Caribbean colonies.[33] The discrepancy between these figures requires explanation; it is likely that officials who were primarily interested in the plantation economy neglected to count people who did not contribute to its growth.[34] It is also possible that colonial authorities reclassified some Kalinagos as members of other groups, such as mulattoes in order to facilitate or justify their enslavement.[35] But the changing numbers of Kalinagos in colonial censuses also points to continued interisland movement. As Kalinagos used their versatile vessels to navigate the eastern Caribbean chain, their contact with colonial authorities remained intermittent, but they did not disappear. A close reading of European documents instead suggests that Kalinago understandings of the Caribbean's maritime geography allowed them to retain spaces of autonomy and dominion long after many historians presume that they ceased to shape the geopolitics of the region.

European Incursions and Evolving Political Geography

Although Kalinagos successfully prevented early Iberian incursions in the Lesser Antilles, challenges to Indigenous dominion increased as other European powers began to settle the region.[36] Following the appointment of Cardinal Richelieu as King Louis XIII's Chief Minister in 1624 and the ascension of Charles I to the English throne in 1625, the respective crowns of France and England began to devote greater resources to Atlantic commerce and colonization. In 1625, King Charles I granted the Leeward Island of St. Christopher (now St. Kitts) to Thomas Warner, and the following year, France's *Compagnie de l'Isle de Saint-Christophe* also began to settle the sixty-five-square-mile island.[37] Examining Kalinago responses to these settlements reveals how their strategies changed as the number of foreigners in the eastern Caribbean grew.

Kalinago residents of St. Christopher—a place they called *Liamuiga*, "fertile island," in reference to its importance as a provisioning site—had little tolerance for the growing number of newcomers.[38] In a vivid illustration of the ways that earlier encounters influenced Kalinago responses to European incursion, Du Tertre wrote that "the devil persuaded" Kalinagos that foreigners "had come to the island to cruelly massacre them, like they had killed their ancestors in all the lands that they occupied."[39] Preconceived notions about the likely actions of the other side shaped both European and Kalinago strategies, with disastrous consequences for the latter group. Joining forces in what Du Tertre later tried to justify as a defensive action, in 1626 French and English settlers massacred dozens of Kalinagos, driving the survivors from the island and dividing St. Christopher into two European colonies.[40]

Although Europeans reported that the 1626 attack succeeded in expelling all Kalinagos from St. Christopher, the decision to share the island between English and French settlers testifies to the continued strength of the Lesser Antilles' Indigenous inhabitants in the early colonial era. Unable to adequately protect themselves from Kalinagos, the subjects of rival European crowns were forced to ally against what they perceived to be a shared threat.[41] The need for a defensive alliance between the competing nations persisted for decades, demonstrating how Kalinagos helped shape the imperial geography of the Caribbean: until St. Christopher was ceded to Great Britain by the 1713 Treaty of Utrecht, the French controlled the eastern and western coasts of the island, while the English held the middle.[42]

Settlement patterns elsewhere in the Lesser Antilles further illustrate how European vulnerability to Kalinagos influenced early colonization of the

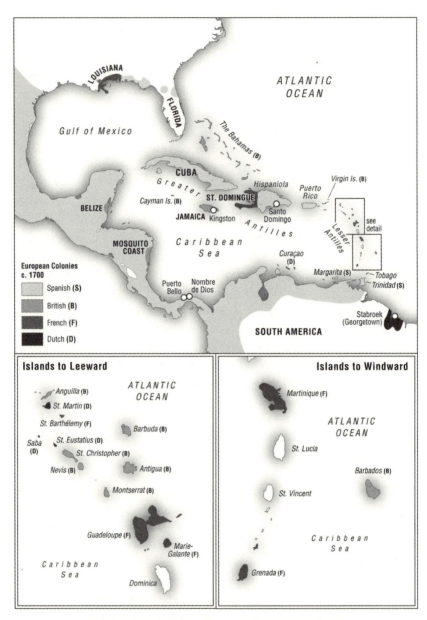

Figure 3. By 1700, Spain was forced to share space with English,
French, Dutch, and Indigenous powers in the Caribbean.

region. The English colony of Barbados, which was reportedly uninhabited at the time of English arrival, was chosen in part for its strategic location more than one hundred miles east of Kalinago strongholds.[43] While Barbados soon flourished, English colonies in the Leeward Islands initially languished due to repeated Indigenous raids.[44]

French settlers who established colonies in Guadeloupe and Martinique in 1635 similarly discovered that the islands' inhabitants were loath to tolerate their new neighbors. Drawing on earlier experiences, settlers in Martinique—many of whom had previously lived in the first French Caribbean colony on St. Christopher—initially took pains to avoid Kalinagos. By living in close proximity to their fort and agreeing not to go hunting alone, the French revealed their continued vulnerability. They also sought reinforcements, strengthening their position with the help of a regiment from St. Christopher. As the number of armed French settlers on the calmer western side of Martinique grew, Kalinagos began to relocate, concentrating their numbers on the island's rougher eastern coast or migrating to neighboring islands such as Dominica. They did not go quietly, however. Du Tertre reported that as Kalinagos abandoned villages close to areas of French settlement, they set "fire to all the huts, and [dug] up all the foodstuffs," adopting a scorched-earth policy that they would continue to pursue well into the eighteenth century.[45] As noted by Jacques Bouton, a Jesuit missionary who participated in the initial French settlement of Martinique, by 1640 the island's Indigenous inhabitants "separated" themselves by retreating to areas bordered "by inaccessible hills." "We see them rarely, and only when they come by sea to trade," Bouton wrote, indicating that Kalinagos removed themselves to parts of the island accessible only by canáoa, allowing them to exercise autonomy at a remove from their new neighbors.[46] By 1645—just ten years after the French first arrived in Martinique—Capuchin missionary Provins reported that the colony was shared between one thousand French settlers and approximately four hundred Kalinagos, "who have their separate district."[47]

Missionary accounts like those of Du Tertre, Bouton, and Provins likely served as the basis for the first published map of Martinique, which provides a clear visual representation of this separation of territory.[48] The map, which dates to 1652, shows several French settlements, churches, and plantations along the island's western or leeward coast. By including these features on a published map illustrating the progress of French settlement, the mapmaker highlighted French success in taming the leeward side of the island, which borders the calmer Caribbean Sea and is therefore better suited to transatlantic trade.[49] The rougher windward or Atlantic coast of Martinique, on the eastern side of the island, is considerably less marked. The lack of names assigned to the island's eastern bays and inlets does not indicate emptiness, however. Instead, the area is labeled as the *Cabesterre ou demeure des sauvages*: the place where the "savages," or Kalinagos, live. A line separating the *demeure des sauvages* from the *demeure des François* cuts across the island's mountainous center, suggesting a clear division of space not unlike that elaborated by the French and English in Saint Christopher.

Sharing space in this nascent French colony accomplished both practical and ideological goals. By demarcating which half of Martinique was inhabited by Kalinagos and which by the French, the mapmaker provided a clear visual representation of where Europeans could safely establish settlements and where their plantations would be more vulnerable to Kalinago attack. By illustrating that the French respected the autonomy of their "savage" neighbors, the mapmaker also implicitly contrasted French benevolence with the actions of rival Europeans, who both figuratively and literally erased Indigenous people from their domains. Although the lack of annotation on the eastern half of the map suggests that the French were not well informed about the land over which their Native neighbors continued to hold dominion, the mapmaker notes that the carbet, or Kalinago village, indicated on the map by a series of small dwellings, is the "place where the Caribs make their assemblies."

These assemblies became increasingly important in the mid-seventeenth century, as Kalinagos planned and coordinated attacks on the growing number of settlers in their midst. Du Tertre reported that in 1636, just one year after the French arrived in Martinique, the island's Kalinago residents, "not believing themselves strong enough . . . to entirely chase the French from the island . . . called to their aid those of Dominica, St. Vincent, and Guadeloupe." Allying with the inhabitants of surrounding islands, they "composed a corps of 1,500 men, [and] presented themselves at the fort." While this impressive show of military strength failed to dislodge French settlers in Martinique—after being fired on by a cannon, the Kalinago warriors "ran with incredible speed back to their pirogues, and took to the sea"—the coordinated attack illustrates both the facility and the continued importance of interisland movement during the initial era of European settlement.[50]

The 1636 military engagement between French and Kalinago forces in Martinique illustrates a number of other key points. First, earlier experiences with colonists elsewhere in the Caribbean taught Kalinagos that Europeans were unlikely to leave of their own accord; it was therefore important to try to expel them while they were still few in number. Second, the presence of

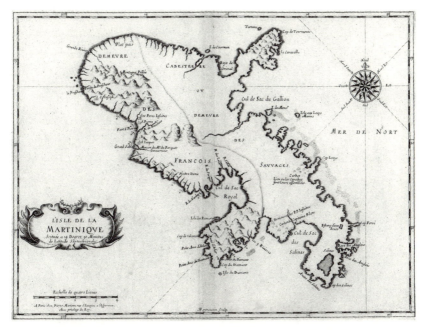

Figure 4. *L'isle de la Martinique* (Paris: Pierre Mariette, c. 1652). This map of
Martinique, published in Paris in the mid-seventeenth century, neatly divides the
island into French and Indigenous zones. The windward side is labeled as the dwelling
place of the "sauvages," or Kalinagos. Courtesy John Carter Brown Library.

foreign polities encouraged Indigenous people from different parts of the
circum-Caribbean to cooperate. As the number of Europeans in the Lesser
Antilles grew, Indigenous leaders increasingly relied on interisland alliances to
counter foreign incursion. By organizing as broader groups, Kalinagos fought
to preserve a degree of dominion, economic and military influence in islands
that Europeans increasingly claimed as their own.[51]

In addition to withdrawing to areas of individual islands not settled by
Europeans, such as windward coasts, Kalinagos responded to foreign incursions by concentrating their settlements in other islands. The case of Guadeloupe illustrates this broader trend. French colonization of Guadeloupe,
which also began in 1635, was initially characterized by deadly warfare between
Natives and settlers.[52] According to Du Tertre, in 1640, "after many discus-
sions of the sort that we can have with people who express themselves more
by signs than by words, and who have no more reason than brutes," Kalinago
and French residents of Guadeloupe reached a verbal treaty.[53] The missionary
reported that "promises were reciprocally made . . . to never again do each

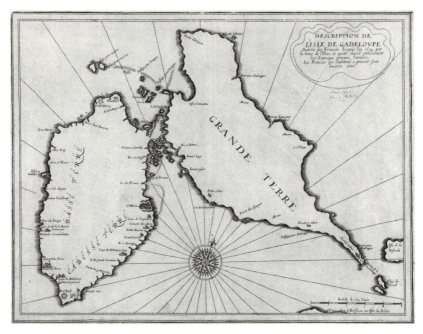

Figure 5. *Description de l'Isle de Gadeloupe* [sic]... (Paris: I. Boisseau, 1648).
This published map of Guadeloupe provides scant detail about Grande Terre, a
silence that suggests that French settlers had not managed to establish themselves
in the eastern side of the colony. Courtesy John Carter Brown Library.

other any wrong, and to treat each other from this point forward as good
friends."[54] News of the peace soon attracted more French settlers to the colony,
reigniting Kalinago resentment.[55] Yet the increased number of armed French
settlers in the island prevented Kalinagos from mounting an effective defense
against this invasion. Instead, Du Tertre reported that Kalinagos withdrew to
the relative safety of nearby Dominica, some twenty-nine miles to the south,
"leaving [only] the most industrious among them to spy on the French, to
observe their conduct, and to learn their weaknesses."[56]

The 1648 map of Guadeloupe above, which was created little more than a
decade after the French first settled the island, supports Du Tertre's assertion
that Kalinagos withdrew to take refuge elsewhere. A note on the map indicates
that "having entirely *chassé* the savages called Caribs, the French who inhabit
the island presently number about 2000."

A verb that can be translated as "chased" or "hunted," *chassé* as used to
describe French actions toward Kalinagos in Guadeloupe hints at the way
colonization of the island was pursued. As in Martinique, French settlers

concentrated their efforts on the leeward side of the colony, where calmer waters provided better shelter for their large sailing vessels. Like the "demeure des sauvages" in Martinique, the eastern half of the map shows little evidence of European settlement, and the lack of French place names on the part of the island known as Grande Terre suggests that colonists remained unsure of the geographic features of a territory whose Indigenous inhabitants they had only recently chased or hunted out. Although the mapmaker likely intended the map to illustrate French success over "the savages," Du Tertre's comment suggests that Kalinago withdrawal was also strategic. By leaving a few individuals to "learn the weaknesses" of the French, Kalinagos sought to ensure that they would be better informed about the practices of the newcomers, allowing them to more effectively combat any future incursions.

Reexamining colonial documents such as maps and censuses shows that while Kalinagos increasingly evaded contact with Europeans, they did not disappear. As Bouton noted as early as the 1640s, "we cannot say [what] their number [is], because they are in continual visits with those of Dominica and other islands."[57] Making use of established maritime routes, Kalinagos continued to move between islands, traversing spaces that were now claimed as settler domains. Withdrawing to places like Dominica allowed Kalinagos to concentrate both their population and their military, diplomatic, and economic power in specific territories, while also forming alliances with those who already lived there; as Breton wrote, Kalinagos who withdrew from Guadeloupe to Dominica "ignited the spirits of the others, who were already disposed to war."[58] Early defeats in St. Christopher, Martinique, and Guadeloupe influenced Indigenous responses to European colonization elsewhere in the Lesser Antilles. Informed by their experiences in these islands, Kalinagos worked to prevent the implantation of similar settlements in Dominica, St. Lucia, St. Vincent, and Tobago and created a contested space in the peripheral French colony of Grenada—strategies that would serve them well in subsequent negotiations with both the French and the English.

Contested Territory: Grenada as Rival Ground

Contests over Grenada reflect the continued evolution of Kalinago responses to European incursion in the latter half of the seventeenth century and highlight the role of Indigenous people in limiting the growth of the plantation complex in certain areas of the Caribbean, even as it accelerated elsewhere.[59] French claims to Grenada date to 1649, when a small contingent of settlers from Martinique was sent to the island. Although Jacques Dyel, the Governor du Parquet, attempted to negotiate a division of territory between Grenada's French and Indigenous residents, the island's existing inhabitants responded to the growing number of foreigners by launching attacks.[60] The anonymous account of a French settler who participated in the initial colonization of Grenada vividly illustrates Kalinago suspicion of the newcomers. Displaying a clear sense of dominion over the island, soon after du Parquet's arrival, Kalinago leaders in Grenada approached the governor and asked him "why he had set foot in their land, and had started a settlement there without their permission."[61] Recognizing the settlers' position of weakness relative to the far more numerous Kalinagos, du Parquet reportedly assured the emissaries that he and his men would protect them from attack and that they hoped to live in peace. Although Kalinagos agreed to form a defensive alliance against common English and South American enemies, they warned the French that "they should content themselves with the land that they made available to them, and not settle elsewhere" in the island.[62] Perhaps envisioning a division of territory not unlike that first attempted in Martinique, Kalinago residents of Grenada consciously sought to restrict French settlement to a specific area, where they could benefit from French military strength without relinquishing their own dominion.

Despite this agreement, the first decade of French colonization in Grenada was marked by warfare.[63] Grenada's location between the South American main and the rest of the Lesser Antillean chain to the north ensured that other Indigenous inhabitants of the region, who used the island as a stopping-off point during their lengthy voyages by sea, were also invested in maintaining the territory as a non-European domain. As a result, Kalinagos in Grenada were able to secure reinforcements from neighboring islands and from South America. Putting aside any existing animosities, Kalinagos sought the support of "either the Galibi or the Arawak or the Ouaro, or others," to mount a common defense against the French.[64] Aided by Indigenous allies, Kalinagos in Grenada launched a series of attacks that kept the French "entrenched in their fort, without daring to leave it."[65]

Grenada's significance in the broader struggle between Kalinago and European forces is reflected in the number of combatants who participated in this contest: on several occasions throughout the 1650s, dozens of pirogues collectively bearing more than a thousand Kalinago warriors descended on the island.[66] Cognizant that existing inhabitants of individual islands lacked both the soldiers and the arms to rout settlers on their own, Indigenous residents of various territories increasingly worked together to prevent further European incursion.[67] The maritime technology that allowed Kalinagos to forge a shared space across geographic boundaries now helped them confront newly created imperial borders, as they used canoes to prevent foreigners from gaining a foothold in Grenada. Europeans were acutely aware of the advantage offered by the Kalinagos' small, versatile vessels, "that go by sail and by oar." As an official explained, "the King's ships are not suited for [an] expedition" against Kalinagos, as "large vessels . . . will not take a single pirogue in ten years."[68] Lacking protection against coordinated Indigenous attacks, French settlement in Grenada remained precarious; twenty years after the island was claimed by the French, authorities reported that it was home to just 98 French households and 229 enslaved people.[69] The census taker failed to count Kalinagos, assigning Grenada's Indigenous inhabitants a "null value" that should not be mistaken for evidence of their disappearance.[70]

Despite Kalinagos' absence or erasure from a document designed to measure and illustrate French colonial power, other evidence reveals how Indigenous people shaped the colonization of Grenada. In a testament to the initial success of Kalinago strategies of regional cooperation, in 1657 French officials in Grenada attempted to sue for peace with all Indigenous inhabitants of the eastern Caribbean, not just those in the island. Negotiations in Grenada were therefore attended by Kalinago residents of the colony as well as by Kalinago representatives from St. Vincent and Dominica. To mark their mutual pledge of peace, the French presented Kalinago leaders with "hatchets, blades, and knives," while Kalinagos brought the French "three beautiful turtles, a rich caret, and lizards." More than mere gifts, the French interpreted these tokens as "signs of the acceptance and ratification of [peace by] all the other Caribs and Galibis of all the adjacent islands."[71] Arguing that Kalinagos "all dress the same way, wear the same colors, [speak] the same language, bear the same arms, [and] have the same interests," the anonymous French settler in Grenada reasoned that these commonalities rendered it impossible to treaty with the inhabitants of only one island. The belief that "a peace could not be good if it is only with a few individuals" led European and Kalinago representatives to reach a verbal accord that would be respected by all parties.[72]

This episode of interisland negotiation reveals that while coordinated military attacks left the strongest impression in the writings of Europeans, they constituted only one of several strategies on which Kalinagos drew in order to shape the imperial geography of the eastern Caribbean. By engaging in verbal negotiations with French officials, Indigenous leaders sought to restrict foreign settlement to specific islands or parts of islands, while continuing to exercise dominion over the remaining land. In the mid-seventeenth century, neither side was in a position to dominate the other. Instead, in the early colonial era Kalinagos and settlers also relied on diplomacy to establish and maintain their respective claims to the archipelago.

The Growth of the Plantation Complex and the Limits of Shared Space

The acceleration of plantation production and the accompanying increase of settlers and enslaved people soon led Europeans to seek a more formal division of space in the Lesser Antilles. In the 1650s, repeated episodes of war throughout the region laid the groundwork for the first written treaty between Kalinago and European signatories, which in 1660 divided the archipelago into mutually agreed-on English, French, and Kalinago domains that would persist for a century. More than two decades after Europeans began to invade Kalinago domains, colonists were still vulnerable to attack, and attempts to settle neighboring islands repeatedly ended in disaster.[73] A close reading of the first extant example of a written treaty between the three groups reveals that Caribbean colonization was not determined by Europeans alone.[74] Kalinago visions of the region included a separate space for Indigenous people. In the mid-seventeenth century, this was a vision that Europeans were forced to recognize.

By the 1650s, sugar began to replace tobacco as the leading export from Martinique.[75] The change in crops was accompanied by a shift in the nature and scale of labor in the colony, as planters increasingly exploited enslaved Africans instead of French indentured workers.[76] According to Du Tertre, "the Savages soon made use of these slaves to begin their uprisings anew." Reasoning that enslaved people could not be prevented from escaping "as long as the Savages give them shelter, or give them pirogues to go elsewhere," French settlers in Martinique became increasingly resolved not to share the island with people who might make common cause with their captives.[77] Seeking to avenge a Kalinago attack on three French settlers who had ventured into Indigenous territory on Martinique's east coast, in 1658 the island's militia raised six hundred men to launch an assault on the "demeure des sauvages." Dispatching two hundred men by boat and four hundred by land, including the respective superiors of the Jesuit and Dominican orders, French forces descended on Kalinago strongholds on the windward side of Martinique. After a brief battle, Kalinagos "embarked in their pirogues, some retreating to

St. Vincent and others to Dominica, and by the end of 1658, the French were in peaceable possession of the whole island of Martinique."[78]

Despite claiming to have driven Kalinagos from Martinique, French settlers remained uneasy. Alleging that following their expulsion, Kalinagos "assassinated several notable planters" in the colony and "subtracted as many as five hundred slaves, whom they transported wherever they wished," in 1660 French colonial authorities sought to broker a written treaty with Indigenous leaders.[79] The treaty was signed March 31, 1660, between English, French, and Kalinago representatives assembled at the home of Charles Hoüel, governor of Guadeloupe. The French and English signatories were empowered by the governors of their respective colonies, while the Kalinagos were represented by "fifteen of the most notable . . . of the Caribs" from Dominica and St. Vincent and "those who formerly lived in the said island of Martinique"; Kalinago representatives from Grenada were notably absent.[80] In addition to identifying more than a dozen Kalinago men afforded positions of authority within their respective communities, Hoüel sought to ensure that the promises of these representatives would be honored by all Indigenous inhabitants of the region. Through interpreter Jean Jardin, a French subject who spoke and understood "the language of the savages," Governor Hoüel "asked the said Caribs whether they had the power to treaty for themselves and in the name of all the others of the said islands [of] St. Vincent and Dominica." The Kalinago signatories confirmed that "having spoken to the largest part of the said savages, who consented" to the terms of peace, they were in a position to represent Kalinagos from both islands.[81]

Although the treaty is written in French and adheres to European diplomatic conventions, the content of the document makes clear that it was the product of negotiation by all three parties. Each nation—English, French, and Kalinago—was represented by leaders mentioned by name, with each group of signatories representing a broader group animated by specific and clearly articulated concerns. The terms of the treaty hint at the years of violence and failed diplomacy that motivated all three parties to broker a formal peace. After noting that "the said island of Martinique has been engaged in war with the savages for the last six years, which has caused great misfortunes by the murders fires and kidnapping of slaves committed by the said savages," the signatories mutually agreed that "the said French and English nations . . . and the said Caribs of the said islands St. Vincent Dominica and those who formerly lived in the said island of Martinique will live in peace, all acts of hostility ceasing."[82] While this passage explicitly attributes the crimes of murder, arson, and kidnapping to "savage" Kalinagos, it also reveals that Europeans were far from blameless in the lengthy conflict to which the treaty refers. The mention that some of the Kalinago signatories "formerly lived in the said island of Martinique" hints at considerable Kalinago migration and resettlement occasioned by European colonization, while other parts of the text allude to further aggressions on the part of Europeans. One of the Kalinago signatories—referred to only by the title of Baba, signifying his role as chief or "father" of his people—requested that his nephews, "who had been taken by one Billaudel" of Martinique, be returned to him. In assenting to his request, the English and French representatives relied on the advice of the Jesuit missionaries who attended the negotiations. The Jesuits reasoned that "it was not only just but necessary to undertake the said restitution, as it would be a means to confirm and maintain the peace."[83] Returning the Baba's nephews therefore served as a hostage release intended to ensure future good-will between parties.

The missionaries also expressed their hope that returning the Baba's nephews would help accomplish another goal outlined in the treaty: Kalinago conversion to Christianity. Kalinago representatives were asked whether "they wished to learn how to pray to God like [the French] and allow the said missionary fathers to instruct them."[84] In agreeing that a missionary named Father Beaumont could continue to reside among them in Dominica, Kalinago representatives stipulated that missionaries should be the only Europeans of "one or the other [English or French] nation to inhabit the two islands of St. Vincent and Dominica, which are all that remain for [the Kalinagos'] retreat."[85] No other foreigners would be allowed to settle in the considerably diminished territory over which Kalinagos retained formal dominion.

Although French officials assented to this clause as a first step in the Kalinagos' conversion into Christians—and perhaps subsequently into allies and trading partners—an analysis of the treaty from a Kalinago perspective suggests a far different goal. By conceding that a single foreigner could maintain his existing residence in Dominica, Kalinago representatives attempted to ensure their continued dominion over an island in which increasing numbers of their people now congregated. Aware that they would not be able to return to their carbets in islands now formally recognized as French and English colonies, Kalinagos assented to the treaty in an attempt to ensure that their communities in islands not settled by Europeans would remain undisturbed. A small number of outsiders who had shown themselves willing to learn the Kalinago language and customs, such as Father Beaumont, Father Breton, and perhaps Jean Jardin, could be tolerated; a large number of settlers could not. By agreeing to create separate European and Indigenous domains, Kalinagos conceded that islands such as St. Christopher and Martinique had been lost to Europeans. Adopting the tools of the colonizers, Kalinagos relied on a written diplomatic agreement to preserve the islands of Dominica and St. Vincent as "all that remain for their retreat."

Despite this formal division of territory, missionary accounts betray traces of Kalinago presence in Martinique long after they were supposedly expelled, testifying to Kalinagos' continued interactions with both Europeans and Africans and their role in shaping the colonial Caribbean. In 1694, Jean Baptiste Labat, a Dominican missionary who arrived in Martinique the same year and would go on to spend more than a decade running a sugar plantation in the colony, journeyed to Robert, on the island's east coast. There he was welcomed at the carbet of a Kalinago man named Rose, a Christian convert who along with his wife had "ten or twelve children," and who had given the area—Pointe Rose—its name. At the time of Labat's visit, Rose was hosting almost thirty Kalinagos for the funeral of a fellow Kalinago from St. Vincent; the mourners were awaiting the arrival of the deceased's family before burial could take place.[86] After enjoying a midday feast of fish and crab, Labat accepted Rose's offer to have his eldest son and several other Kalinago men help pilot the missionary's canoe along the rough Atlantic coast to his next destination. As the seven enslaved people who accompanied Labat "and the three Caribs took turns swimming as they wished," the motley group of travelers covered the four leagues between Pointe Rose and Cul de Sac François in just two hours, all without taking on "a single drop of water" in their agile Kalinago vessel.[87] The French missionary's vivid account of an afternoon spent in the company of Africans and Indigenous Americans at the turn of the eighteenth century confirms that the 1660 treaty did not result in the Kalinagos' total expulsion from Martinique. Instead, Indigenous people interacted with settlers and enslaved people while continuing to exercise dominion over parts of the colony that the newcomers found difficult to access, and Kalinago practices of interisland travel and exchange established long before the journeys of Columbus persisted well into the colonial era.

As he journeyed through the Lesser Antilles in 1700, Labat also commented on the scale and characteristics of Kalinago domains in neighboring islands, providing a glimpse of an increasingly creolized world at the fringes of European settlement. Labat speculated that there were no more than two thousand Kalinagos in Dominica, one thousand fewer than the number reported by Provins some sixty years before.[88] Although "all of the old Caribs that [Labat] saw still knew how to make the sign of the Cross, and [say] the Christian prayers in their language, and even a few in French," few could actually communicate in the foreign tongue; instead, Labat relied on a Frenchman who had taken refuge among the Kalinagos to act as an interpreter.[89] In addition to harvesting crops that predated European arrival in the Americas, such as manioc, Kalinagos in Dominica raised pigs and poultry—livestock that accompanied European invasion of the region.[90] Despite living in proximity to European settlements and integrating items introduced by Europeans into their daily lives, Kalinagos maintained their own domain. More than sixty years after French and English colonizers began to establish permanent settlements in the eastern Caribbean archipelago, Indigenous people preserved territories outside the sphere of European rule—ones where European languages, religion, and authority were known but did not predominate.

"Le Centre de la République Caraïbe": Kalinago Responses to the Plantation Complex

Although historians often credit the 1660 treaty with ushering in an era of peace in the Lesser Antilles, subsequent events demonstrate that diplomacy failed to end hostilities.[91] Nowhere was the tenuous nature of this détente more keenly felt than in Grenada. Unlike Guadeloupe and Martinique, Grenada was not included in the 1660 negotiations, and the sparsely populated French colonial outpost remained a frequent target of coordinated attack by Kalinagos.[92]

Successive leaders of France's Windward Island colonies—an administrative unit that grouped Guadeloupe, Martinique, and Grenada under a single governor-general headquartered in Martinique—despaired of ever brokering peace with the region's Indigenous inhabitants. "There is no way to reason with people without faith and without religion, who are more like beasts than men," wrote Governor-General Jean-Charles de Baas-Castelmore in 1674, suggesting that the French should instead enslave or wage war against Kalinagos.[93] Although a separate peace, which stipulated that Kalinagos from surrounding domains "could not go inhabit the island of Grenada" was reached in February 1678, French claims to Grenada remained tenuous in the face of Indigenous opposition.[94]

A comparison of extant population figures for France's three Windward Island colonies highlights the extent to which Kalinago defense of Grenada helped limit foreign settlement of the island. Despite benefiting from the protection of French officials, Grenada's population remained anemic compared to that of other French colonies. In 1671, the 436-square-mile island of Martinique counted 4,326 free inhabitants and 6,582 enslaved people; Grenada, while considerably smaller at just 133 square miles, counted only 283 free and 222 enslaved people. This disparity was even more pronounced thirty years later: by 1700, Martinique had 21,640 total residents and Guadeloupe 10,929; Grenada's population, both free and enslaved, totaled just 870.[95] Although land grants were available in the colony, the persistent threat of Indigenous attack, coupled with the island's location at the far reaches of France's realm and its neglect on the part of French officials, meant that only a small number of settlers could be enticed to Grenada.

Grenada's small settler population also affected the island's economy. By limiting the number of foreigners who could settle in their domain, Kalinagos helped prevent the expansion of plantation production to France's southernmost Caribbean colony. The latter half of the seventeenth century witnessed the triumph of sugar in Martinique, as the majority of arable land in the island became devoted to the production of this lucrative export.[96] By 1686—just fifty years after Martinique was first settled by the French—the island boasted 168 sugar plantations.[97] Guadeloupe lagged somewhat behind, with ninety sugar plantations as of 1686. Yet in the same year Grenada, which was settled by experienced colonists from Martinique more than thirty-five years earlier, was not yet home to a single sugar plantation. French settlers in Grenada had no hospital, only a single church, and a total of eighteen horses to transport the wealthiest colonists to the island's only town, Fort Royal.[98]

Only in 1687 did Grenada's planters successfully begin producing sugar. 1687 marked a sugar boom throughout France's Lesser Antillean colonies, as the number of plantations in Martinique rose from 168 to 184 in the space of a single year.[99] Almost four decades after Grenada was first settled, planters in the island also founded the colony's first four *sucreries*. Yet even this belated experiment proceeded on shaky ground, as Kalinago attacks intensified in the 1690s.[100] By 1700, the number of sugar plantations in Grenada decreased from four to three, and there was no refinery in which to process the island's cane.[101] While Grenada's slow development owed in part to lack of investment and distance from centers of transatlantic trade, colonists and officials also complained about the effects of an Indigenous population hostile to the establishment of plantations. "A perpetual tradition, passed from father to son, means that [Kalinagos] will always be very dangerous in spirit," wrote a Grenada official at the turn of the century. The Kalinago threat would not disappear on its own, the official reasoned; if the French wanted to successfully colonize Grenada, they would need to make themselves the Kalinagos' "masters."[102]

The desire to "master" Kalinagos became more pressing as the growth of the plantation complex propelled increasing numbers of Europeans and Africans into Indigenous domains. By the late seventeenth century, as English and French colonies in the Lesser Antilles transitioned to sugar monoculture, the consolidation of large estates in the hands of a small elite diminished the amount of available land and foreclosed the possibility that former indentured servants, or *engagés*, could join the planter class.[103] While land scarcity in Barbados drove aspiring planters to other English colonies such as Carolina, French subjects in Martinique and Guadeloupe had fewer options.[104] The icy wilderness of New France held little attraction for those who dreamed of establishing sugar estates, and few planters could be enticed to the distant and vulnerable settlement of Grenada. French colonists who lacked the means to participate in the sugar industry instead established themselves at its margins. In regions of Martinique and Guadeloupe where soil quality, altitude, or annual rainfall inhibited the growth of sugarcane, engagés and their descendants established small, mixed-agriculture plantations that provisioned neighboring estates.[105] In addition to growing food such as manioc and plantains, these small planters invested in secondary export crops like cacao and cotton. By the late seventeenth century, some began to extend this plantation system beyond the boundaries of French sovereignty. Abandoning areas of Martinique and Guadeloupe where cultivation was difficult, smallholders opted for more fertile lands freely available in nearby islands. In addition to replicating the mixed agriculture they already practiced, settlers took advantage of tropical forests in St. Lucia, St. Vincent, Dominica, and Tobago to bring much-needed wood to French colonies. Proximity to Martinique or Guadeloupe allowed individuals who relocated to neighboring islands to maintain economic and social ties they had forged in French colonies, as they regularly used pirogues to return to their home parishes to sell their wares and to partake in social and religious celebrations.

The growing number of French subjects residing outside the sphere of French rule soon attracted the attention of rival colonial powers. As Colonel Edwyn Stede, English governor of Barbados, reported in 1689, "the French . . . took great liberty to hunt, fish, and fowl" in St. Lucia, St. Vincent, and Dominica. Stede's concern was both practical and geopolitical. It was "a thing of great importance both to [English] honour and interest," he argued, not to allow the French crown to establish a foothold in the islands. The "above one hundred . . . families of French" in St. Lucia by 1689 engaged in farming,

fishing, and timbering, which "afforded them no small supplies for the maintenance of the people at Martinique, as did also those islands furnish them
with wood and timber." Despite the tenuous nature of their settlements—after
discovering the settlers in St. Lucia, Stede "sent all the people away to Martinique . . . then burnt their houses and destroyed their . . . plantations"—the
people Stede deemed "troublesome and encroaching neighbors" increasingly
ventured into Kalinago domains, as they sought to benefit from resources
available just beyond the boundaries of French rule.[106]

In addition to free settlers, enslaved Africans took advantage of the proximity of islands that lay outside the sphere of colonial rule. During his travels
through the Lesser Antilles in 1700, Father Labat noted that "a very large
number of fugitive slaves, most of them from Barbados," lived in St. Vincent,
having arrived in the island in vessels that carried them westward across the
open sea.[107] Although the Jesuit missionary was at a loss to explain why Kalinagos initially tolerated the presence of fugitives from slavery in an island he
characterized as "the center of the Carib Republic," he speculated that the
growing population of Maroons, "which greatly surpasses that of the Caribs,"
would force Kalinagos "to one day find another island" in which to live.[108]

Labat's comment about the growing number of non-Native people who
had taken refuge in the "center of the Carib Republic" by the turn of the
eighteenth century was corroborated by François-Roger Robert, intendant of
France's Windward Islands from 1695 until 1702. In a discussion of the possibility of capturing the Black inhabitants of St. Vincent in order to sell them into
slavery, Robert speculated that in addition to arriving from Barbados, many of
St. Vincent's African inhabitants settled there "a long time ago, [when] a vessel
loaded with slaves wrecked" off the island's coast. The shipwreck's survivors "were
humanely received by the Caribs," and soon "many of these negroes married the
daughters of Caribs, and from thence their numbers grew."[109] Robert's account
offers conflicting information about the relationship between Kalinago people
and others who had come to reside in their domains. While the intendant stated
that "the Caribs of the island would like for the negroes who have established
themselves there to be removed," he also noted that "many of these negroes are
allied with the Caribs and live together" peaceably.[110] While some Kalinagos
formed familial, social, and perhaps military alliances with refugees from sugar
plantations, others remained wary of or openly hostile to the newcomers.

The intendant's description of the multiethnic society evolving in dangerous proximity to the heart of France's Caribbean colonies offered a new
Kalinago origin story. In the respective accounts of both Robert and Labat, the

Indigenous people who used diplomacy and violence to carve out an autonomous existence amid European encroachers were being subsumed. In their place were "Black Caribs": people who had little right to freedom, much less title to the lands on which they lived. In the ensuing decades, this rhetorical transformation would have very real consequences, as Europeans used the story of a shipwrecked slaving vessel to justify usurping lands guaranteed to Kalinagos by earlier treaties.[111] At the turn of the eighteenth century, however, the story served a different purpose: Robert used the example of Afro-Kalinago cooperation to remind settlers that Indigenous people posed a threat to the expansion of the plantation complex and that St. Vincent's inhabitants would not tolerate the presence of Frenchmen among them. Kalinagos "would rather see two thousand negroes established in their island," he warned, "than to see just fifty armed Frenchmen disembark" there.[112] Having successfully asserted dominion over a small number of islands, Kalinagos were demonstrably unwilling to allow colonists to infringe on their territory. Yet as the respective accounts of Labat and Robert show, by the turn of the eighteenth century Kalinagos were increasingly sharing space with others who sought to escape the expansion of the plantation complex. Their awareness of how plantation production accelerated settlement led them to violently oppose the creation of sugar estates in Grenada and to entertain alliances with other people who sought to live beyond the reach of European rule.

Seeking a Place in Plantation Society:
Kalinago Responses to the Rise of Slavery

In the first decades of the eighteenth century, the continued growth of sugar production in France's Windward Island colonies directly affected Kalinago dominion in two important ways. The first was the diminishing availability of land in French colonies, which increasingly drove settlers to neighboring islands. Owing to French practices of partible inheritance, planter families divided their estates among growing numbers of heirs.[113] Claiming that they would soon be unable to sustain their children, in the early eighteenth century planters in Martinique began to petition colonial authorities for land in other islands, such as Tobago.[114] More immediately alarming to Kalinagos, however, was the dramatic growth of the enslaved population in neighboring colonies. As Martinique grew to become the leading producer of sugar in the early-eighteenth-century Caribbean, slavers trafficked thousands of people from West Africa to the 436-square-mile island; between 1700 and 1720 alone, more than twenty-one thousand Africans disembarked in Martinique.[115] In addition to observing and interacting with growing numbers of enslaved people as they continued to trade and travel to the colonies, Kalinagos encountered fugitives from slavery in their own territories, as Maroons sought refuge in neighboring islands.[116] As the economic and demographic growth of neighboring plantation colonies rendered the possibility of maintaining a separate domain increasingly difficult, Kalinagos took steps to ensure that their own liberty would not be infringed on. Turning once again to a familiar tool of negotiation, in 1719 St. Vincent's Kalinago inhabitants negotiated a treaty designed to maintain the security of themselves and their land, as well as to ensure that both enslaved and free people would respect their autonomy.

Persistent land scarcity, coupled with a desire to engage in interisland trade, prompted increasing numbers of French subjects in Martinique to move to neighboring islands in the first decades of the eighteenth century. While settlers who used pirogues to travel between islands helped supply French colonies with timber and food, the fact that they did so with little supervision attracted the ire of French authorities. The desire to keep French subjects under surveillance grew more pressing in the wake of an uprising by colonists centered in southwestern Martinique, just across the channel from St. Lucia. Responding to harsh measures designed to curb the informal trade that had flourished during the War of Spanish Succession (1701–1714), in 1717 members of Martinique's militia successfully ousted the island's unpopular colonial administrators.[117] The governor-general subsequently sent to enforce order in France's Windward Island colonies, the Marquis de Feuquières, who served from 1717 to 1727, was particularly anxious to rein in the "bad subjects" whose desire for "libertinage" motivated them to establish themselves in St. Lucia, St. Vincent, and Dominica.[118] While the governor-general expressed concerns about illegal commerce, noting that residents of the islands traded with pirates and even built ovens to provide interlopers with fresh bread, he also worried about the nature of societies being constructed beyond the reach of French law. Characterizing emigrants as a threat to "the commerce of the islands and the interests of the King and the planters," de Feuquières declared that "faithless" subjects who failed to evacuate neighboring islands would be subject to "a hard and tireless war."[119]

While complaints about unruly subjects pepper all colonial correspondence, people who could independently travel between colonial and surrounding Indigenous domains posed particular problems. The short distances between islands—St. Lucia is twenty-one miles south of Martinique, while Dominica lies approximately twenty-five miles north of Martinique and twenty-nine miles south of Guadeloupe—meant that individuals could undertake journeys independently, and the sheltered bays that dotted the islands' western coasts made it impossible to police embarkations.[120] French administrators recognized the mobility offered by pirogues as a threat, and a 1721 law banned residents of Grenada from owning vessels capable of carrying more than three passengers. Colonists who owned larger pirogues were obliged to keep them chained inside their dwellings when not in use or be forced to compensate the owner of any enslaved people who used the vessel to abscond to other territories.[121] Lawmakers were acutely aware of the disadvantages of banning watercraft "so necessary in an island for fishing, for transporting goods and people from one area to another and from their plantations to the parish [town]," yet frequent references to the ban in the ensuing years suggest that enforcement of the ordinance was at least attempted, if not successfully.[122] Despite attempting to limit the use of pirogues, patrol regional commerce, and forbid the settlement of neighboring islands, by the early decades of the eighteenth century, French authorities claimed that there was little they could do to keep settlers and enslaved people from using Indigenous watercraft to circulate through the Lesser Antillean archipelago. With St. Lucia and Dominica visible across the channels separating French colonies from spaces that remained outside the sphere of European rule, people who sought to escape the purview of the crown could simply move elsewhere.

Kalinagos did not fail to notice the growing numbers of settlers, enslaved people, and fugitives from slavery in their midst. Acutely aware of the ways that the plantation complex which had taken root in neighboring colonies was also affecting their domains, in 1719 Kalinago representatives brokered a new agreement with authorities in Martinique. Although the 1719 treaty was not enacted, its content sheds light on the evolution of Kalinago-European relations and suggests that Kalinagos were aware of the racial hierarchy developing in conjunction with the plantation system. Asserting that they had "the authority to represent the body of the nation," a number of Kalinago men from St. Vincent agreed to recognize the King of France as their sovereign. In exchange, the Kalinago representatives made a number of stipulations. They formally reasserted their title to the island and insisted that it would not be permitted "for any Frenchman . . . to run off with" their lands. They further stipulated that the French teach them how to use arms and ammunition and promise to assist them against "the negroes their enemies."[123]

Kalinago leaders were preoccupied with more than just their internal security. Other articles of the treaty reveal that they sought to assert themselves on equal footing with French subjects born in the islands, ensuring that they would not be enslaved or mistreated. They insisted that they be exempt from the capitation tax—a benefit that officials afforded to "Creoles native to the colonies"—and that the justice system established for French subjects would also apply to them.[124] Most revealing is article seven of the 1719 treaty, which stipulates that the same punishment visited on enslaved people who assaulted whites would be applied if an enslaved person harmed a Kalinago person.[125] With these simple stipulations, Kalinagos sought to protect against the growing number of Maroons in St. Vincent, while also ensuring that their position in the rapidly evolving colonial hierarchy of the eastern Caribbean would resemble that of white Creoles, not of enslaved Africans. The vision of Franco-Kalinago cooperation elaborated in this treaty represents a clear Kalinago attempt to avoid being reduced to the position of enslaved people and to retain a measure of the dominion they established by means of a similar treaty almost sixty years earlier.

Kalinagos' ability to broker such treaties diminished as the plantation complex grew and planters consolidated their power and authority. The map of Martinique excerpted here reveals how the colony evolved as planters turned to sugar production, expanding the territory on which they settled and thrusting growing numbers of enslaved Africans into Indigenous domains. A notation on the map indicates that in 1718, the colony's first wind-powered mill for processing sugar was erected near Robert, just north of the place where Kalinagos once "made their assemblies."[126] By the middle decades of the eighteenth century, the side of the island once reserved as the "demeure des sauvages" was home to the highest number of sugar mills in Martinique's three regions, with 6 mills powered by wind, 20 by water, and 101 by cattle all marked on the eastern half of the map.[127] Eager to showcase the progress of French settlement in the island, the mapmaker made no note of Kalinagos. Yet close examination of this European map betrays traces of the long contest between Natives and settlers in the eastern Caribbean archipelago. Northwest of Cul de Sac François is Batterie à Massacre, Massacre Fort, the site of the assault that resulted in Kalinago expulsion from Martinique and that helped prompt the 1660 treaty that formally divided the Lesser Antilles into European and Indigenous domains.

The demographic and economic changes that accompanied the rise of sugar production led to similar Indigenous erasures in other colonial documents. In the early eighteenth century, French and English colonial correspondence increasingly grouped Dominica and St. Vincent alongside St. Lucia and Tobago as neutral islands, ignoring earlier treaties that acknowledged them as Kalinago territories. The rhetorical transformation of islands once recognized

Figure 6. Detail of *Carte de l'Isle de la Martinique* (Paris: Dezauche, 1779). Details from
this mid-eighteenth-century map of Martinique reveal how the rise of sugar production
affected the island's Kalinago inhabitants. While certain locations, such as Pointe à la Rose,
bear the names of former Kalinago leaders, plantations also dot the side of Martinique
formerly recognized as an Indigenous domain. Courtesy John Carter Brown Library.

as Kalinago domains into neutral spaces opened the possibility that the islands
could become home to other groups. As the century progressed, growing
numbers of poor and middling white planters, free people of color, fugitives
from slavery, and others who did not fit into a plantation society rooted in
strict economic and racial hierarchies took refuge in these purportedly neutral
territories, giving rise to diverse, creolized communities—ones that officials
would subsequently struggle to assimilate into European empires.

*   *   *

Despite the absence or erasure of Indigenous people from many of the documents authored by Europeans, closer reading of these colonial texts reveals
that the Caribbean's Indigenous inhabitants continued to exercise diplomatic
and military power long after they were supposedly exterminated, expelled, or

enslaved. Drawing on their knowledge of the Caribbean's aqueous geography in order to establish themselves in places Europeans found difficult to access, form interisland alliances, and launch attacks, Kalinagos shaped the development of the eastern Caribbean archipelago well into the colonial era. As Kalinagos contested and countered colonization, they modified and limited European territorial, economic, and political projects in ways that are not often acknowledged by historians. Although the rise of the plantation complex increasingly marginalized Kalinagos, forcing them to share space with settlers, enslaved people, and Maroons, they drew on generations of experience with colonizers to negotiate their place in the evolving political and racial hierarchy of the early Americas. By fighting to ensure that certain islands would remain outside of European empire in the colonial Caribbean, Kalinagos were instrumental in forging a diverse society that stretched across islands: a Creole Archipelago.

Chapter 2

Creating the Creole Archipelago

Marianne Dorival had made the journey before, but this trip posed new challenges. The young woman had given birth just five weeks earlier, at her home in Ouassigany, near the southwest tip of St. Vincent. Now Marianne was returning to Martinique so that the baptism of her infant son, Etienne André, could be celebrated in the island of her birth.[1] Marianne and her husband, Etienne Lefort, likely embarked in a pirogue piloted by enslaved seafarers early in the morning, to avoid the strongest rays of the late June sun.[2] Traveling through the calmer waters along the western coast of the eighteen-mile-long island they called home, the young couple might have stopped to rest for the night after crossing the twenty-three-mile channel separating St. Vincent from St. Lucia to the north. By June 29, 1733, they passed St. Lucia and arrived at their destination: the coastal village of Les Anses d'Arlet, southwest Martinique, almost one hundred miles north of their home in St. Vincent. Named for the Kalinago leader who once held dominion over the *anses* or coves that sheltered the travelers' pirogue, the village was now home to approximately 300 white settlers, 200 free people of color, and the roughly 1,500 people they held in slavery.[3] There, in the Church of St. Henri, a Capuchin priest inscribed the baptism of Marianne and Etienne's infant son in the same register that contained a record of the couple's marriage in the church three years earlier.[4]

Marianne's voyage from the Kalinago territory of St. Vincent to the French colony of Martinique was just one of many short ocean journeys regularly undertaken by residents of the eastern Caribbean archipelago. Throughout the colonial era, the aqueous geography that allowed Kalinagos to evade and attack Europeans continued to facilitate the independent movement of people, goods, and information across porous maritime borders. By the eighteenth century, however, people who used pirogues to navigate between islands were not necessarily Indigenous.[5] Instead, as the century progressed, growing numbers of colonial subjects like Marianne migrated outside the sphere of French rule and established themselves in the Kalinago territories of Dominica and St. Vincent and the neutral islands of St. Lucia and Tobago. As the islands became home to thousands of settlers and the enslaved people over whom they claimed ownership, contemporaries began to refer to all four islands as neutral. Equating Kalinago domains with islands that were frequently contested between European powers elided their status as Indigenous territories and raised the possibility that these fertile lands might be claimed by a distant crown.[6]

Reconstructing the lives of migrants like Marianne sheds light on a little-known phenomenon: the development of slave societies beyond the boundaries of European rule in the colonial Americas. Historians have long recognized that growing settler populations led people to venture beyond colonial borders in mainland North America.[7] Yet the tendency to examine islands as discrete, bounded entities means that similar migratory processes in the colonial Caribbean have been largely overlooked. Owing to land scarcity, natural disasters that affected the economic prospects of small planters, and increasingly onerous legislation targeting free people of color, in the mid-eighteenth century, thousands of French subjects left Martinique and Guadeloupe and settled in the neighboring islands of Dominica, St. Lucia, and St. Vincent; a small number went as far as Tobago. As they settled in places like Ouassigany, white and free people of color encroached on Kalinago territories, relegating the islands' Indigenous inhabitants to rougher windward coasts. Claiming lands for themselves on the calmer leeward sides of the islands, settlers ordered the enslaved people they brought with them to fell trees, clear lands, and plant provisions and export crops such as coffee and cacao. As the size and productivity of these settlements grew, they attracted the attention of French and British authorities. Despite repeated attempts to evacuate the islands, however, crown officials were unable to assert control over settler societies outside their sphere of sovereignty. As people like Marianne forged economic and social connections that bypassed imperial circuits, they elaborated a lived geography that stretched across colonial, Kalinago, and purportedly neutral territories in the eastern Caribbean archipelago, belying the notion of islands as naturally bounded spaces subordinate to the control of a single power.[8]

Like Marianne, many people who migrated to St. Vincent, St. Lucia, Dominica, or Tobago in the early eighteenth century were Creole, meaning that they were born in the Americas. Most were from the lower or middling classes of the plantation society that had taken root in Martinique and Guadeloupe by the late seventeenth century. Many were people of Afro-European ancestry, whose ties to white family members were increasingly circumscribed by prejudice and by law. Crucially, almost all were Catholics, whose continued participation in the rites of baptism, marriage, and burial left a written record of the familial and social links they maintained even after they left the formal sphere of French rule.[9]

Both the size of these settlements and the challenges they were seen to pose to colonial legal, economic, and racial norms grew as the eighteenth century progressed. By the end of the Seven Years' War (1756–1763), almost 5,000 free settlers—both whites and free people of color—shared space with at least 1,400 Kalinagos in Dominica, St. Lucia, and St. Vincent, while a small number of people carved out a living fishing and turtling in Tobago. These settlers laid claim to more than 17,000 enslaved people, whose forced labor annually yielded more than three million pounds of coffee and one million pounds of cacao, along with large quantities of food.[10] Although colonial officials attempted to control settlement, levy taxes, and enforce order in the islands, they were frequently unsuccessful. By establishing themselves in places where formal institutions of European rule such as courts, governors, and assemblies did not reach, people like Marianne were able to evade some of the impositions of empire, such as capitation taxes and racially biased legislation. Yet their migration outside the sphere of imperial rule also extended many features of French colonial society, including Catholicism, plantation production, and racialized slavery, into islands formally recognized as neutral or as Indigenous domains.

Focusing on the eastern Caribbean archipelago in the middle decades of the eighteenth century demonstrates how the consolidation of the plantation complex in French and English colonies affected neighboring territories, as imperial developments reverberated beyond borders in both mainland and island America. For Kalinagos, the presence of free and enslaved people past agreed-on boundaries threatened the dominion they fought to secure in decades prior. For settlers like Marianne, the islands promised possibilities increasingly unavailable to them in crowded plantation colonies: the chance to claim ownership over land and people, form legitimate families, and exercise certain rights such as the right to create contracts. For enslaved people, life outside of sugar colonies meant more autonomy but also more responsibility, as they performed a variety of tasks in dangerous proximity to the people who held them in bondage. For European crowns, the islands alternately seemed like sources of raw materials, potential satellite colonies, and sites of lawlessness and disorder. Understanding how different groups of people conceived of islands that lay outside of empire in the colonial Caribbean provides insight on what compelled them to go there and what they sought to accomplish in this increasingly contested archipelago. Focusing on the unintended by-products of colonial development affords new insight on how peripheries contributed to the shape of empires and suggests the shortcomings of histories that trace the development of individual Caribbean colonies.

The Growth of Creolized Communities: The 1720s to the 1750s

Settlement of the Creole Archipelago accelerated in the middle decades of the eighteenth century. While the English crown initially tried to establish claims to several neutral and Kalinago islands, the geography of the eastern Caribbean hindered access to territories that lay at least one hundred miles from the English colony of Barbados. Instead, owing to persistent land scarcity, natural disasters that affected the economic prospects of small planters, and legislation targeting free people of color, French subjects from Guadeloupe and Martinique increasingly relocated to neighboring islands as the century wore on. Once there, they developed practices that sometimes replicated but were sometimes at odds with those found in the colonies from which they had come. Although French governors continued to complain about the establishment of settlements beyond the reach of their authority, they recognized that neighboring islands helped sustain people experiencing hardship in the colonies, while also preventing other crowns from establishing a foothold in surrounding islands. As a result, they did little to prevent settlers like Marianne Dorival from venturing beyond the watery borders of French rule.

English subjects also sought to make use of resources outside the sphere of crown rule, but geography inhibited their ability to do so to the same extent as their French counterparts. While sailors from Barbados could reach St. Lucia or St. Vincent in approximately one day's journey, traveling back to the English colony without the benefit of prevailing winds could take as long as four to six days.[11] The one-hundred-mile journey across the open sea also necessitated the use of a wind-powered vessel, as opposed to the Kalinago canoes adopted by French colonists, which could be rowed through the waters between Martinique and surrounding islands in as little as four hours. While English subjects fished and cut timber on the islands' coasts, they failed to establish permanent settlements.[12]

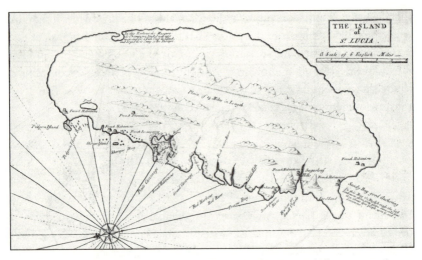

Figure 7. *The Island of St. Lucia*, c. 1725. This sketch of St. Lucia, which accompanied
Uring's published account, reveals both Kalinago and French presence on the
leeward coast of the island. Courtesy John Carter Brown Library.

The most famous such failure occurred in 1722–1723, when Nathaniel
Uring was appointed deputy governor of St. Lucia. Arriving on the island in
December 1722 with four hundred men, Uring immediately encountered several Frenchmen already there and others who "came from *Martinico* in a small
Canoa."[13] The facility with which people from Martinique traveled to and from
the neighboring island belied English visions of St. Lucia as a dependency of
Barbados. French officials issued an order commanding Uring and his men to
evacuate St. Lucia the very day they landed, and by January 1723 "a body of
1400 [French] Men had been landed [in] the Night" on the island's Windward
coast.[14] On January 8, 1723, less than a month after Uring's arrival, English and
French representatives agreed to a mutual evacuation of St. Lucia.[15]

Despite the brevity of Uring's stay on the island, his published account
provides a glimpse of the society taking shape beyond the boundaries of
French rule. A map of St. Lucia included in his *Relation of the Late Intended
Settlement*—which, like earlier French maps of Martinique and Guadeloupe,
provides far more detail about the calmer leeward coast of the island than
its rougher windward side—shows a small cluster of "Indian hutts" in the
southwest, at the foot of St. Lucia's imposing "Sugarloaf hills," or volcanic
peaks. Far more numerous, however, are the "French habitations" that dot the
island's leeward side. Uring's map reveals that by the 1720s, French subjects

who ventured beyond the sphere of colonial rule were not just cutting timber or growing provisions. Instead, they had begun to engage in export agriculture: just north of the "Indian hutts" is a "Cocoa walk," or rows of cacao trees planted for harvest.

The 1723 evacuation ordered in response to Uring's voyage was just one of many issued for St. Lucia, Dominica, St. Vincent, and Tobago in the early decades of the eighteenth century, yet the islands' permanent populations continued to grow.[16] Unlike Uring's attempt to plant an English colony on St. Lucia, however, such settlement often occurred without crown oversight, much less sponsorship. Instead, individuals like Marianne ventured outside the sphere of imperial rule in order to serve their own interests—interests that alternately supported and undermined those of the colonies they left. Like "rogue colonists" who "pushed colonial frontiers in their own self-interest" in contemporaneous Louisiana, most people who migrated to surrounding islands did so in search of opportunities.[17] The fact that they migrated as families suggests that their settlements were not transient, nor were their motivations solely economic. Instead, in the mid-eighteenth century, individuals like Marianne responded to the growth of the plantation complex and resultant land scarcity in French colonies by pursuing possibilities beyond their borders.

Describing a landing he made in northern St. Lucia in February 1732, the Marquis de Champigny, governor-general of France's Windward Island colonies, reported that the island was home to hundreds of smallholders. Noting that "most of these people are from Diamant"—the same southwestern Martiniquan parish where Marianne was born—Champigny attributed their relocation to "the poor quality of the soil . . . and the dryness that reigns" there. "These planters produce foodstuffs and raise poultry, a few have planted cotton," which he reported that they regularly transported, along with small quantities of wood, back to Martinique to sell.[18] Although ferrying goods from foreign territories to French colonies violated the recently promulgated *Exclusif*—a pair of royal edicts, issued in 1717 and 1727, that sought to promote trade within the French empire by placing strict limits on foreign commerce—Champigny recognized that this illicit activity helped provision Martinique while also providing small planters with a much-needed economic outlet.[19]

The governor-general's 1732 visit to St. Lucia coincided with a period of increased migration to the island. A 1727 earthquake, coupled with a blight on cacao throughout the Lesser Antilles—the number of cacao trees in Martinique fell from an all-time high of 13.5 million in 1726 to just 360,000 by

1734—ruined many small planters.[20] Rather than replanting their fragile crops in what was by Champigny's admission poor soil, planters "decided to abandon [Martinique] and go to neighboring islands."[21] Alarmed by the desertion of hundreds of people, particularly young men who could serve in the militia, the marquis attempted to encourage small planters to stay in Martinique by distributing coffee seeds, which had only recently been introduced to the Caribbean.[22] Authorities also exempted cacao planters from paying the annual capitation tax on themselves, as well as on their enslaved and indentured laborers, for a period of four years "in order to give them the means to recover their losses and encourage them to create new plantations."[23]

Despite these efforts, attempts to retain small planters in Martinique met with limited success. By the 1730s, the respective populations of Grenada, St. Lucia, Dominica, and St. Vincent, while still considerably smaller than those of established colonies in the Lesser Antilles, were significant.

The figures below are striking for several reasons. The effects of imperial neglect, coupled with persistent fears of Kalinago attack, reveal themselves in the population of Grenada. Despite being a colony of France, the island counted only slightly more free inhabitants than did the Kalinago territory of Dominica, while Martinique, which is approximately three times the size of Grenada, counted more than thirteen times the number of enslaved people and almost eighteen times the number of settlers. Although Grenada was a French colony, in the early eighteenth century it exhibited many of the features that characterized the Creole Archipelago, including the continued influence of Indigenous people, small settler and enslaved populations, and a higher percentage of people of color among the free population.

The fact that these population counts were archived by France's Ministry of the Marine betrays the extent to which colonial administrators monitored the purportedly neutral and Kalinago territories in their midst.[24] French officials generated a census of St. Vincent in 1732; of Dominica in 1730, 1731, 1743, 1745, and 1753; and of St. Lucia in 1730 and 1732 and then with some regularity from 1745 until 1763.[25] These censuses were primarily intended to gauge the extent of settlement in the islands, which explains why Kalinagos were not always counted. Despite this bias, surviving enumerations quantify the observations of people like Champigny: despite repeated orders to evacuate the islands, a growing number of French subjects used "pirogues or canoes" to leave the colonies "in defiance of the prohibitions" issued against such behavior.[26]

Table 1. Populations of Martinique, Grenada, St. Lucia,
Dominica, and St. Vincent, c. 1730

	Martinique	Grenada	St. Lucia	Dominica	St. Vincent
Kalinago/"Sauvages"	No data	24	37	419	No data
White People					
Men	5,205	257	100	150	172
Women	2,762	141	6	58	34
Girls "eligible for marriage"	1,625	50	2	11	17
Boys under 12	2,868	132	17[a]	74	32
Girls under 12	2,509	126		58	29
Total white population	14,969	706	125	351	284
Free People of Color					
Men	318	38	No data	12	19
Women	658	53	52	10	18
Children	519	20	74	8	66
Total population of people of color	1,495	111	126	30	103
People of color as percentage of settler population	9.08	13.59	50.20	7.87	26.61
Enslaved People					
Men	20,118	1,683		266	318
Women	15,664	965	137[a]	45	83
Children	16,849	1,235	38	84	66
Elderly or infirm people	4,386	492		No data	No data
Total enslaved population	57,017	4,375	175	395	467
Total free population	16,464	841	288	800	387
Total Population	**73,481**	**5,216**	**463**	**1,195**	**854**

Sources: No enumerations for Tobago before 1770 are extant. Figures for Martinique are offered as a point of comparison; the data date from 1738 and are sourced from Etienne Rufz, *Études Historiques et Statistiques sur la population de la Martinique, Vol. I* (Saint-Pierre, Martinique: Imprimerie de Carles, 1850), 212. Other data are from ANOM DPPC G1 498 N. 47 (Grenada, 1731); N. 82 (Dominica, 1730); N. 92 (St. Vincent, 1732); and ANOM DPPC G1 506 N. 3 (St. Lucia, 1730).

[a] The census for St. Lucia counted "white children" and "working slaves" without regard to sex.

More than a decade after Champigny first aired his concerns, authorities found the situation little improved. In 1744, Martinique's governor, André Martin de Poinsable, noted that the number of planters in St. Lucia and Dominica "increased each day." Like earlier administrators, Poinsable complained that settlers "were drawn there by nothing more than a love of independence." Poinsable was particularly incensed that unqualified men were acceding to positions of power outside the sphere of colonial rule. In Dominica, "le Maus, a petty merchant, was at ease acting as judge," Poinsable complained, and as a result, "murders and assassinations frequently occur in these neutral islands and continue to go unpunished."[27] Although Poinsable's comment repeats a familiar refrain about the lawless nature of people who lived beyond the jurisdiction of European rule, his letter also suggests that by the mid-eighteenth century, islands once recognized as Kalinago domains were increasingly home to creolized settler societies. By agreeing to vest authority in individuals like le Maus, settlers who ventured outside the sphere of French sovereignty began to construct economic and social hierarchies recognized by other members of their community.

Rather than suppressing these alternative hierarchies, French administrators sought to harness them in the service of the crown. In 1739, officials in Martinique reported that one Sieur le Grand had made himself so "loved and respected" in his role as "commander, intendant, and judge" in Dominica that "the inhabitants submit to his decisions with the same resignation as if he were vested with the necessary powers." Better still, le Grand rendered "all of his services freely, without asking anything of the inhabitants, and without having any appointments" from the French crown or otherwise.[28] Recognizing that such submission was best cultivated locally, the general of Martinique began appointing militia officers in the surrounding islands in the 1740s and 1750s.[29] Officials reasoned that it was necessary to do so in order to make "the French, [previously] left to themselves, understand that they have one religion, one Prince, and laws." Once these officers established order, however, they were to "indicate which [existing] inhabitants they judged the most capable of commanding the others."[30] Rather than imposing French rule on neighboring islands directly, officials sought to make the goals and practices of "rogue colonists" align with their own.[31] Recognizing that surrounding islands provided an outlet for small planters who could not participate in the sugar industry that increasingly dominated French colonies, authorities sought to profit from the growth of creolized communities without openly violating the terms of earlier Euro-Indigenous treaties.

"Without Aspiring to the Same Prerogatives as Whites": Race in the Creole Archipelago

Many of the people over whom the crown attempted to establish authority had left French colonies precisely to evade their laws. Far from being guilty of the "murders and assassinations" alleged by colonial officials, however, these men and women were free people of African ancestry who sought to escape the increasingly restrictive legislation to which they were subjected. Whereas people of color were reported to constitute approximately 9 percent of the free population of Martinique by 1730, they represented almost 27 percent of the settler population in St. Vincent in the same period.[32] In St. Lucia, the proportion of free people of color was even greater, amounting to slightly more than half of the settler population in 1730. By settling in spaces where laws limiting the economic and social possibilities of people of African descent did not reach, free people of color exercised an important role in shaping slave societies outside of empire.

Although much of the research on free people of color in the French Atlantic focuses on Saint-Domingue or Louisiana, many of the regulations pertaining to people of African ancestry were initially elaborated in France's first Caribbean colonies in the Lesser Antilles.[33] In 1669—three decades before the establishment of a French settlement in Louisiana, and before the rise of sugar production in Saint-Domingue—the governor-general of the Windward Islands declared that children born to enslaved women and *maistres de cazes*, or masters of households, would be free, and their mothers "confiscated for the profit of the poor."[34] The 1685 *Code Noir,* France's first comprehensive attempt to regulate the position of enslaved and free Black people, therefore elaborated on existing practices in the Lesser Antilles: Article IX of the code stipulated that a married man who fathered a child with an enslaved woman "be deprived of the slave and the children, and that she and they be confiscated for the profit of the [royal] hospital." If the man was unmarried, however, Article IX specified that he should marry the enslaved woman, "who by this means will be manumitted and the children rendered free and legitimate."[35] Although the article was rarely if ever enforced, its existence speaks to the early emergence of mixed-race families in the Lesser Antilles and indicates one of the means by which people of African descent attained freedom. Affirming the normalcy of this practice, in 1681 a visitor to Martinique noted that planters who did not free their mixed-race children at birth normally did so when sons reached the age of twenty and daughters fifteen.[36] The Code Noir also stipulated that an enslaved person could be freed by an act of manumission, or by being named the executor of his master's estate or the guardian of his children.

By the early eighteenth century, these practices created growing populations of free people of African and Afro-European ancestry in the Lesser Antilles—populations that alarmed a colonial elite intent on linking Blackness with enslavement.[37] In 1683, the governor of Martinique expressed his belief that "mulattoes *whose birth is a product of vice*" should not enjoy the same legal and social standing as whites.[38] By explicitly linking the very existence of people of mixed race to acts of illicit sex, such statements denied free people of color a legitimate place in colonial society.[39] These discriminatory attitudes accompanied legislation designed to limit the social and economic advancement of people of color in the Lesser Antilles. In 1726, Martinique's Superior Council registered an edict from King Louis XV stipulating that "notwithstanding articles 56, 57, and 59" of the Code Noir, which stated that free people of color were to enjoy the same rights, privileges, and immunities as French subjects, "freed slaves, free blacks, their children and descendants" would no longer be eligible to inherit goods or property from whites.[40] While similar legislation was extended to French Louisiana, the same law did not apply in Saint-Domingue, where mixed-race children continued to inherit sizeable estates from their white fathers, allowing them to join the planter class.[41] Whereas free people of color in Saint-Domingue exercised considerable influence until at least the end of the Seven Years' War, by the late 1720s their counterparts in the Lesser Antilles and in Louisiana were already subject to laws designed to sever ties of family or friendship with whites and relegate them to a lower place in society.[42] In 1726, Martinique's legal code was updated to specify that all free people of color—whether manumitted or born free—could be condemned to enslavement if they harbored a fugitive from slavery.[43] The same penalty applied if a person of color violated sumptuary laws by dressing in clothing that "rivaled the luxury" of whites.[44] Free birth, legitimacy, and economic standing no longer guaranteed that a person would not be reduced to slave status; by the third decade of the eighteenth century, color increasingly dictated a person's place in France's Lesser Antillean colonies.

In the early 1730s, the collection of a head tax from which only island-born whites were exempt further alienated free people of color in Martinique and Guadeloupe. The collection of the *droit de capitation* imposed on French colonial subjects and the people over whom they claimed ownership sparked debates throughout the early colonial era; government correspondence reflects confusion about whether a 1671 exemption for "male and female Creoles native to the islands" applied to free people of color.[45] Militia captains tasked with creating parish censuses regularly enumerated whites and free people of color separately, imposing a head tax on the latter group alone.[46] In 1724, a royal decree lent official sanction to this practice, and the 1730 royal tax code revised the 1671 ordinance to declare that only "*white* Creoles" were exempt from capitation.[47] Justifying the crown's decision, France's Minister of the Marine reasoned that people of color "should consider themselves lucky to enjoy freedom, without aspiring to the same prerogatives as white creoles."[48]

The minister's dismissal of people of color as "lucky" to be free highlights the increasingly tenuous place of people of African descent in the early-eighteenth-century Lesser Antilles. In contrast to Saint-Domingue, where laws limiting the possibilities for free people of color were not routinely enforced until the last decades of the eighteenth century, in France's first sugar colonies the horizons of free people of color began narrowing by the 1720s.[49] Discriminatory laws and attitudes motivated some to seek spaces where their ancestry would not limit the possibilities available to them. By establishing themselves beyond the authority of the French crown, free people of color exercised greater influence in processes of racial formation, as they participated in defining the terms of social, economic, and political inclusion in their community.[50] In direct response to the head tax, which began to be levied in 1733, free people of color began leaving Martinique for St. Lucia, Dominica, and St. Vincent. As Léo Elisabeth's painstaking examination of surviving censuses and parish registers shows, almost five hundred free people of color— more than 40% of free people of color in Martinique—disappeared from the French colony in a single year.[51]

Rather than indicating the complete disappearance of all free people of color in a given parish, these dramatic population changes offer insight on racial attitudes in early-eighteenth-century Martinique.[52] Militia captains tasked with creating the enumerations could have simply declined to note the race of neighbors, friends, or extended family members on whom they did not wish to impose further taxes, while some free people of color, particularly women married to white men, were assimilated to the category of white.[53] Increases in the number of free people of color in some parishes point to the possibility of internal migrations; some of the individuals who left Sainte-Marie, on Martinique's east coast, might have relocated north to Marigot. Even when accounting for internal migrations and misrepresentations, however, these figures suggest a considerable exodus of free people of color from Martinique in the early 1730s.

Table 2. Change in Reported Population of Free
People of Color in Martinique, 1732–1733

Parish	1732	1733	Change
Fort-Royal	113	115	+2
Case-Pilote	25	38	+13
Lamentin	35	23	−12
Trou-au-chat	21	0	−21
Rivière-Salée	64	74	+10
Les Anses d'Arlet	139	98	−41
Diamant	69	46	−23
Sainte-Luce	57	35	−22
Rivière-Pilote	27	0	−27
Marin	0	0	0
Salines	4	0	−4
François	17	0	−17
Vauclin	9	0	−9
Robert	20	0	−20
Saint-Pierre	318	137	−181
Le Precheur	23	12	−9
Carbet	55	54	−1
Sainte-Marie	15	0	−15
Trinité	83	30	−53
Marigot	4	9	+5
Grand Anse	16	5	−11
Basse-Pointe	24	0	−24
Macouba	28	0	−28
Total	**1,152**	**676**	**−476**

Source: Data from Elisabeth, *La Société martiniquaise*, 307.

The regional dimensions of this emigration are significant. The southwestern Martiniquan parishes of Diamant, Les Anses d'Arlet, and Ste. Luce, from which a total of eighty-six free people of color disappeared from the census between 1732 and 1733, lie a mere twenty-one miles north of St. Lucia; as an official later noted, "the distance from St. Lucia to Martinique, which is only 7 leagues, means that those who wish to decamp can make use of pirogues or canoes to go to the island."[54] The sixty-one individuals collectively enumerated as leaving the northern parishes of Basse-Pointe, Le Prêcheur, and Macouba would have similarly only had to travel across the narrow channel separating Martinique from Dominica, twenty-five miles to the north.

This proximity meant that people who moved to neighboring islands did not have to sever their connections with French colonies, even as they evaded the restrictions they faced there. Surviving parish registers for Martinique and Guadeloupe reveal that residents of surrounding islands continued to travel to their communities of origin to celebrate Catholic rites long after they left the sphere of French rule.[55] On September 17, 1735, Rose Jallais and Charles Mire brought their one-month-old son, Jean Baptiste, from their home in Dominica to be baptized in Trois-Rivières, southern Guadeloupe.[56] In July 1734, Pierre Delat and his wife Marie Elizabeth Potier, who like Marianne Dorival were identified as residents of St. Vincent, brought their infant son to be baptized in Les Anses d'Arlet. Baby Prospert had been born in St. Vincent just two weeks earlier, but his parents wasted no time in bringing him to southern Martinique for baptism.[57] The fact that all three sets of parents braved these ocean journeys with their newborns suggests that they viewed travel between the islands as a largely unremarkable endeavor. A desire to publicly celebrate the sacrament of baptism, and to obtain the documents that served as proof that their children had been baptized as free people, continued to draw them back to their former parishes.[58]

Residents of the Creole Archipelago also traveled to Martinique and Guadeloupe to celebrate marriage. On July 30, 1742, Jean Baptiste La Verge La Feuillée and Catherine Adenet married in Basse-Pointe, northeast Martinique. Although the groom was identified in the parish register as a resident of southern Dominica, he crossed the channel separating the Kalinago territory from the French colony in order to wed his bride in her home parish.[59] Jean Cevet, a native of Fort Royal, Martinique, who had lived for several years in Tobago, undertook an even longer journey when he married a woman named Marie Rose in her home village of Les Anses d'Arlet in 1734.[60] As these journeys illustrate, the decision to leave Martinique and settle in another island did not require individuals to abandon ties to the French colony. Instead, people who settled in Dominica, St. Lucia, St. Vincent, and Tobago maintained their existing connections with French subjects while avoiding the problems that would have affected them had they remained under French rule: like many people who quit Martinique, Jean Cevet and Marie Rose were described as "mulatto."[61]

The exodus of free people of color accelerated the growth of creolized communities outside of empire. A 1730 survey of St. Lucia indicates a total population of 463 people in the island, including 100 men bearing arms, 37 "Sauvages," or Kalinagos, and 175 enslaved people.[62] In the same year, Dominica was slightly more populated, with 395 enslaved people and 381 settlers, along with 419 Kalinagos. The census also counted the number of canoes in the island—fifty—suggesting how residents of Dominica communicated with surrounding islands.[63] By 1745—more than ten years after the passage of the capitation tax, and the next year for which enumerations of both islands are available—Dominica and St. Lucia had experienced considerable growth. St. Lucia's settler population of 882 was outnumbered by 2,573 enslaved people, while Dominica counted 1,152 free and 1,880 enslaved people. In a testament to Indigenous marginalization in the face of growing settler populations, Kalinagos were not enumerated in the 1745 census of either island.[64]

These settler populations were increasingly self-reproducing. In 1745, Dominica counted almost 200 boys and 184 girls under the age of twelve and 109 *filles à marier*, or girls over twelve deemed eligible for marriage, along with 435 adult men and 207 adult women. St. Lucia's slightly smaller settler population counted 339 adult men and 145 women, along with 132 girls, 175 boys, and 91 filles à marier.[65] This means that by the mid-eighteenth century, 43 percent of the free population of Dominica and 45 percent of that of St. Lucia was composed of children and unmarried adolescents—a considerably higher percentage than in contemporaneous Martinique.[66] As free residents of the Creole Archipelago developed a self-reproducing population, they also elaborated a society that differed from surrounding colonies in terms of racial composition, economic basis, and social norms.

In St. Lucia, free children of African descent initially outnumbered their white counterparts; in 1730, the island counted just seventeen white children compared to seventy-four "children born to free mulatresses, métisses, or negresses."[67] By 1745, the St. Lucia census enumerated 243 white children and 155 free children of color. It is more difficult to ascertain the number of free children of color in Dominica. Although enumerations taken in 1730 and 1731 distinguished between whites and free people of color, subsequent population counts for Dominica grouped all free people together without noting race.[68]

The absence of distinction with regard to color hints at the different meaning of race outside the sphere of colonial rule. By declining to explicitly note the race of spouses and children in the households of male settlers, local militia captains who created the censuses implicitly afforded legitimacy to all free families, emphasizing social belonging over racial exclusion.[69] In settlements that were vulnerable to attack from English, French, and Indigenous forces, the ability to participate in defending the community was paramount. Although the race of women and children in St. Lucia was usually noted, in the mid-eighteenth century free adult men were explicitly grouped as "married men and bachelors bearing arms, whites as well as free blacks and mulattoes."[70] The reluctance to privilege race as a primary marker of status is especially striking given that census takers in Martinique began to enumerate free people of color and whites separately by the late seventeenth century.[71] Although French colonial practice dictated that people be classified according to race, those who assumed positions of authority in the Creole Archipelago were not beholden to the same laws, nor to the same ideologies.

A nominative census taken in St. Lucia in 1745 further illustrates how race operated beyond the boundaries of colonial rule. Unlike the previous population count for St. Lucia, which dates to 1732, or contemporaneous enumerations for the Kalinago territory of Dominica, which tally the number of people in specific categories such as "white men" or "children," this more detailed list takes the form of a militia muster roll. In addition to offering unparalleled insight on St. Lucia's settler population, the existence of such rolls for 1745–1747 and 1756–1760 testifies to the French state's increased involvement in the neighboring neutral island during times of war, such as the War of Jenkin's Ear (1739–1748) and the Seven Years' War.[72] The muster rolls provide the name of each head of household, along with their marital status, number of children, and number of enslaved men, women, and children. Among those listed is Jean Baptiste Leveillé. Although no category for Indigenous people appeared on a separate population count of St. Lucia produced in the same year, Leveillé was described in the muster roll as "Carib," suggesting that while many Kalinagos lived apart from settlers and thus avoided being counted, others assimilated into settler society in the Creole Archipelago. Leveillé and his wife, whose name—like that of other wives on the muster roll—was not noted, lived with their eight children, along with two enslaved women and one enslaved child. Not far from the Leveillé family, in northwest St. Lucia,

Charlotte and Claire Grandval, described as free *mulatresses*, lived with two free children, along with five enslaved men, five enslaved women, and six enslaved children.[73] The Leveillé and Grandval households would be unusual in neighboring colonies, but in St. Lucia they were not uncommon. In regions of the Atlantic World where colonial law could not be reliably enforced, free people of African and Indigenous ancestry retained greater control over their familial, social, and economic lives.

They also participated in the institution of slavery—a participation increasingly denied to nonwhite people in the colonial Caribbean. Of the 2,573 enslaved people in St. Lucia in 1745, 91 were owned by Alexandre Nouet, identified in the militia muster roll as *mulâtre*. The number of enslaved people owned by Nouet was second only to that of a white planter named Dubuq Letang, who laid claim to 109. Although the enumerator's qualification of Nouet as mulatto suggests that his position as a member of St. Lucia's elite was not accepted without comment, the extent of his human capital testifies to a level of wealth that would have been difficult for him to achieve as a person of color in Martinique. The Nouets may have established themselves in St. Lucia for economic reasons, or they may have migrated in response to discrimination they faced owing to their unusual family: in the 1747 muster roll, Nouet is described as *capre*, a term used for the offspring of one Black and one mulatto parent. His wife is described as *blanche*, or white.[74]

While not entirely unheard of, marriage between white women and free men of African descent in the French Atlantic grew increasingly rare as the eighteenth century progressed.[75] Although people of African descent constituted a demographic majority throughout the colonial Caribbean, in French colonies whiteness remained the norm, and administrators would therefore not explicitly note that an individual was white: if his or her name was not followed by a descriptor such as mulâtre or *nègre*, the implication was that the person was of exclusively European ancestry.[76] By writing that the wife of a capre man was blanche, the person who created the 1747 St. Lucia muster roll deliberately called attention to their union. He also explicitly noted marriages between white men and women of color, which were much more common in St. Lucia than in neighboring French colonies. Whereas in Martinique, interracial marriages constituted just 0.2 percent of documented cases between 1730 and 1759, in the 1747 nominative census of St. Lucia, 5 of 103 married men for whom no racial descriptor is given—an omission that implies that they were afforded the status of whiteness—are listed as being married to a woman of color.[77]

Although these interracial marriages did not go unremarked, the fact remains that people of color such as Alexandre Nouet were able to form legitimate interracial families and attain positions of economic and concomitant social prestige in St. Lucia. This would have been much more difficult—if not impossible—to achieve in neighboring colonies, where the boundaries between Black and white were increasingly policed. While historian Marisa Fuentes rightfully cautions against celebrating "agency which depended on the subjugation of others," Nouet's visible role as a prosperous planter, the legitimate husband of a white woman and father of their twelve children, and the owner of almost one hundred enslaved people testifies to the importance of free people of color in shaping the Creole Archipelago.[78] By migrating in search of opportunities, Nouet and many others undermined the racial hierarchy on which plantation colonies were built. The challenge that powerful free people of color were seen to pose to neighboring colonial societies would only increase as the population of the Creole Archipelago, as well as their economic and social connections with colonial subjects, strengthened in the mid-eighteenth century.

"*Toute la force d'un habitant*": Slavery in the Creole Archipelago

The growing connections between colonial subjects and residents of neighboring islands owed in large part to the growth of slavery outside of empire. By the 1740s, Grenada, Dominica, St. Vincent, and St. Lucia met the definition of slave societies: enslaved people constituted a demographic majority, slavery served as the basis of the economy, and the institution of slavery dictated social relations throughout the archipelago.[79] Although documents in which enslaved people reflect on the realities of their bondage are not extant, surviving records hint at how their lives differed from those of people in surrounding colonies. Most enslaved people in the Creole Archipelago lived on small plantations, and many were born and spent their entire lives there. Rather than growing sugar, they engaged in a variety of tasks such as tending livestock, raising provisions, and cultivating coffee and cacao; although this task-based system resulted in some degree of flexibility, it also left enslaved people responsible for their own sustenance as well as that of the people who held them in slavery. The smaller size of plantations meant that rather than living in slave villages, enslaved people lived in dangerous proximity to those who held them in bondage. Although this proximity may have allowed some people to gain *relative*, de facto freedoms," for most it meant vulnerability to physical and sexual violence unrestrained by colonial law.[80] While analyses of Caribbean slavery tend to privilege large plantation or urban settings, attention to the Creole Archipelago reveals that slave societies also took shape outside of empire. For people enslaved in these societies, the everyday violence of bondage operated on a particularly intimate scale.

With almost twice the number of enslaved people as St. Lucia and more than ten times that of Dominica by 1730, Grenada's status as a French colony meant that planters in the island had a degree of access to the transatlantic slave trade not shared by their counterparts who settled outside of mercantilist networks. Despite this access, the scarcity of laborers in Grenada remained a frequent source of complaint for planters. Describing a visit to the island in 1717, the governor-general of France's Windward Islands bemoaned Grenada's lack of enslaved labor. "Slaves constitute all the power of the planter, and by extension of all the colonies," he explained. "They are very expensive in Grenada because slave ships never go there, so [planters] are obliged to buy slaves secondhand or in Martinique, and these are most often nothing more than the scraps of a cargo."[81] The governor-general's complaint reveals how the enslaved populations of Grenada, Dominica, St. Lucia, and St. Vincent evolved differently from those of surrounding colonies. Rather than being trafficked directly from Africa, enslaved people often arrived via neighboring colonies, while others were born in the Caribbean.

For the period before 1760, the *Voyages* transatlantic slave trade database lists only ten vessels whose primary place of landing was Grenada; in total, these ships disembarked just under 2,000 captives, the vast majority during the 1750s.[82] Two ships collectively disembarked 183 Africans in St. Lucia during the same period, while 1,456 enslaved people on six separate ships were landed in Tobago, all of them by Dutch traders during their failed bid to colonize the island in the mid-seventeenth century.[83] The database lists no voyages that disembarked enslaved people in Dominica or St. Vincent before 1763. In contrast, Barbados received an estimated 281,071 African captives during the same period, Martinique more than 117,000, and Guadeloupe 15,825.

Despite the relative paucity of transatlantic slavers calling at Grenada and neighboring islands, the archipelago's enslaved population continued to grow. By 1745, St. Lucia counted 2,573 enslaved people, or more than ten times the number of Africans reported to have disembarked in the island by that time. Grenada, which by 1745 had received fewer than 1,200 captives from transatlantic slaving vessels, reported an enslaved population of 8,748—seven times

Table 3. Number of Enslaved Africans Trafficked
to the Lesser Antilles, 1650–1760

	St. Lucia (Neutral)	Tobago (Neutral)	Grenada (French)	Guadeloupe (French)	Martinique (French)	Barbados (English)
1651–1675	0	1,456	200	2,535	7,386	23,340
1676–1700	0	0	0	432	8,041	73,170
1701–1725	122	0	401	1,696	35,593	84,052
1726–1750	0	0	250	802	64,964	62,296
1751–1760	61	0	1,050	10,360	26,598	33,680
Total	183	1,456	1,910	15,825	117,212	281,071

Source: Slave Voyages: Trans-Atlantic Slave Trade Database, https://slavevoyages.org/voyages/9XZ8Fed8

the number trafficked from Africa—and Dominica 1,880.[84] While still small when compared to the more than 55,000 enslaved people in Martinique by 1736, these figures testify to an active regional commerce in human beings in the eastern Caribbean.[85] "It is absolutely impossible to prevent this commerce," complained the Marquis de Feuquières, "unless we have an armed frigate that constantly patrols the neighboring islands." Reporting on the sale of some 300 enslaved people illegally disembarked at Dominica by Dutch traders in 1721, the governor-general explained, "The illegal ship arrives laden with slaves, sails in full view of St. Pierre under a Dutch flag, but close enough so as to be noticed and recognized by the merchants of the town, and then goes to Dominica where it lays anchor. The following night, all the merchants who are in the habit of conducting this business send their boats, some with money, others with sugar, cacao and indigo to barter, according to their means, for the slaves that they wish to buy, and they then disembark the slaves in their usual bays."[86]

De Feuquières' description sheds light on a common practice: sailing under a foreign flag, smugglers signaled their presence to potential purchasers both in French Martinique and in neighboring islands.[87] Although de Feuquières was most concerned about French subjects in Martinique obtaining captives without paying duties to the crown, planters in any of the surrounding islands could engage in this illicit commerce. After amassing specie or goods to exchange for human beings, planters transported them back to "their usual bays" in the pirogues they used to navigate around and between islands.[88] A language of contraband developed over the course of several decades allowed planters like Nouet to increase their captive labor force and expand their production, all while bypassing the mercantilist restrictions imposed by European crowns.

While there were far fewer enslaved people in the Creole Archipelago than in neighboring sugar colonies, their impact on the economy, culture, and daily life of the region was no less important, and they constituted a growing majority throughout the islands. By the 1750s, 75 percent of people in Dominica and 80 percent of people in St. Lucia were enslaved.[89] Grenada, which by 1755 counted eighty-seven sugar mills, had a demographic profile similar to that of other sugar colonies: as in contemporaneous Jamaica and Saint-Domingue, enslaved people constituted approximately 90 percent of Grenada's total population.[90]

Enslaved people in the Creole Archipelago lived and labored in much smaller groups than their counterparts in sugar colonies. In Jamaica, the median number of enslaved people on sugar estates rose from 99 in 1741 to 204 by 1774, and the largest plantations in the colony counted more than 500 enslaved laborers.[91] Estates in Martinique were smaller, with an average of 55 enslaved people on sugar plantations and 12 on coffee plantations by midcentury.[92] In contrast, as of 1760 the 3,812 enslaved people in St. Lucia were dispersed across 327 properties, and the majority of proprietors on the island laid claim to fewer than 10 enslaved people each. Only one household, composed of the minor children of the late Alexandre Nouet, enslaved more than 100 people: the Nouet children, whose race was not noted in the 1760 enumeration, laid claim to 74 adults and 55 children, or 42 more captives than the next largest proprietor in the island. Some slaveholders, such as Fereol Dugard, who lived in Soufrière, at the foot of St. Lucia's volcanic peaks, claimed a single enslaved person. Despite the relatively small number of captives in each household, slavery was ubiquitous throughout the Creole Archipelago, and both whites and people of color participated: by 1760, *mulatresses libres* Claire and Charlotte Grandval claimed ownership of 14 enslaved adults and 8 enslaved children, while their neighbors, *nègre libre* René Brisefert and his wife and 5 children, claimed 7 enslaved adults and 2 enslaved children. Illustrating the centrality of slavery in St. Lucia, only 44 households, or less than 12 percent of households in the island in 1760, reported owning no enslaved people.[93]

Many of the people held in slavery in the Creole Archipelago were children. While children constituted approximately 22 percent of people trafficked from Africa in the eighteenth century, by midcentury they accounted for closer to 30 percent of the enslaved population in the eastern Caribbean, and enslaved children outnumbered enslaved women in all islands.[94] The

Table 4. Enslaved Populations of Dominica, St. Lucia, and Grenada, 1730s–1750s.

	Dominica 1730	Dominica 1743	Dominica 1753	St. Lucia 1730	St. Lucia 1745	St. Lucia 1756	Grenada 1730	Grenada 1745	Grenada 1755
Men	266	626			1116		1683	3396	4733
Women	45	488			647		965	2333	3525
Adults			2327	137		2517			
Children	84	606	970	38	707	1294	1235	2550	3783
Elderly and Infirm		160	233		103	209	492	469	367
Total	395	1,880	3,530	175	2,573	4,020	4,375	8,748	12,408

Sources: ANOM DPPC G1/498 N. 47, 50, 52 (Grenada censuses 1731, 1745, 1755); ANOM DPPC G1/498 N. 82, 85, 86 (Dominica censuses, 1730, 1745, 1753); ANOM DPPC G1/506 N. 3, 4 (St. Lucia censuses 1732, 1745, 1756).

larger percentage of children owed in part to the regional trade on which planters relied; as Gregory O'Malley notes in his study of the intercolonial slave trade, "the sick, the very young, and the old attracted the least interest from slaveholders" in sugar colonies and as a result were more likely to be trafficked elsewhere.[95] Yet plantation inventories, while scarce, suggest that many of the children enslaved in the Creole Archipelago were born there. Of thirty-five enslaved people younger than thirteen living on Bois Cotlette, southern Dominica, in 1765, twenty-six—almost three-quarters (74 percent) of children on the plantation—were listed as Creole. In total, more than 40 percent of the plantation's enslaved inhabitants were born in the Americas, including forty-six-year-old Martha and forty-year-old "mulatto wench" Lucrece.[96] The inventory of a nearby Dominica plantation reveals an even stronger degree of creolization; of eighty-five people on the one-hundred-acre Desgommiers Estate, forty-three were identified as Creole.[97]

The considerable percentage of island-born children hints at the daily lives of enslaved people on these Dominica plantations and perhaps in the Creole Archipelago more broadly. In the seventeenth century, French planters with limited access to the transatlantic slave trade encouraged marriage among enslaved people "so as to have children," and the number of children on Bois Cotlette suggests that this practice persisted in islands rarely visited by transatlantic traders.[98] Unfortunately, surviving documents offer little insight on familial relations among people enslaved outside of empire; muster rolls and censuses simply tally the number of enslaved men, women, and children, while plantation inventories provide the names, ages, and, in rare instances, place of origin of enslaved people.

Yet even these simple documents offer some glimpse of the everyday violence that underlay slave societies, whether on a large or a small scale. Rather than grouping enslaved people according to family or household, the Bois Cotlette plantation inventory lists all adult men, followed by all adult women, and then all children in descending age order, making it impossible to determine relationships between individuals. By failing to recognize familial ties forged between captives, the people who made this list revealed that they viewed enslaved laborers primarily as commodities—a child's age, and therefore her capacity to work, was paramount. They also viewed enslaved women as objects of sexual predation: several children listed as "yellow," such as three-year-old Mary Clara and three-month-old Eulalia, as well as five-year-old "Creol Mustie" Emilia, were the offspring of unspecified enslaved women and white men. The fact that these children appear on a list of enslaved people indicates that their white fathers kept them in bondage and failed to acknowl-edge paternity.[99]

The smaller scale of slavery in the Creole Archipelago increased daily interactions between captives and slaveholders, producing relations distinct from those found on larger plantations. Unlike wealthy planters who absented themselves from their estates to enjoy their riches in the metropole, in the east-ern Caribbean most proprietors were resident on their plantations.[100] Rather than employing managers, these planters directed the labor of their enslaved workforce themselves.[101] As a planter from Dominica flattered himself, this practice meant that he "familiarizes himself more with his Negroes, inspiring their emulation, their zeal and their talents."[102] Enslaved people likely felt very differently about laboring under the eye of those who held them in bondage, as "small holdings . . . permitted less cultural autonomy," and increased the supervision to which enslaved people were subjected.[103] On smaller planta-tions considerably removed from centers of administrative power, people who claimed ownership over others could exert physical, sexual, and psychological violence with little fear of recourse.

The scale of slavery also affected how labor was organized. Whereas enslaved people on large plantations were assigned to work gangs according to age and ability, and performed time-sensitive labor such as harvesting or grinding sug-arcane according to a coordinated schedule, on smaller plantations work was usually organized according to tasks that enslaved people were expected to com-plete within a given day, week, or season.[104] Rather than following the strict schedule of work gangs, in the Creole Archipelago enslaved people cultivated provisions, tended livestock, raised crops such as coffee and cacao, and ferried these crops to neighboring islands by pirogue—all work that could be accom-plished independently or in small groups.[105] Task work entailed less supervision and generated a greater degree of autonomy, as enslaved people traveled from provision grounds to pastures to ports to complete different tasks.[106] Enslaved people could also take advantage of the more flexible nature of task-based labor to negotiate for compensation if they exceeded their assigned tasks.[107] But task work also meant more responsibility, as enslaved people had to enrich those who claimed ownership over them while also ensuring that all of their own needs were met. Such work could also be solitary and lonely, and the smaller scale of slavery prevented the development of villages where people could socialize away from the watchful eyes of those who held them in bondage. Did fifty-year-old Masselina, the only one of eighty-six enslaved people on Bois Cotlette described as "Ardah," have anyone with whom she could speak her native language?[108] Did the single enslaved person claimed as the property of Fereol Dugard regularly interact with anyone other than his or her captor?

While some enslaved people could use regular interactions with their captors to extract concessions, those who lived and labored in proximity to the people who held them in bondage were also particularly vulnerable to their whims. In the absence of legal codes, enslavers relied on other means to establish and display mastery over other human beings, exercising unrestrained violence on their captives.[109] People whose own position in plantation society could be called into question by their race, such as Nouet, may have asserted their authority not through negotiation or concession but through force. Records for Grenada offer chilling insight on how enslavers wielded power at a remove from crown authority. Planters in the peripheral colony, which was administered as a dependency of Martinique, complained that laws requiring them to send people to the larger colony to be prosecuted and punished meant that they could not "use the fear of immediate punishment to constrain" enslaved people.[110] In a 1743 letter, officials in Martinique reminded planters in Grenada that they were not allowed to display the severed heads of fugitives, suggesting that this violent demonstration of state terror would have persisted were it not restrained by French authorities.[111]

While the large number of free people of color in the Creole Archipelago indicates that some enslaved people succeeded in finding ways to escape their bondage, the overwhelming majority of people in the islands spent their lives as captives. Although plantations were smaller than elsewhere in the Caribbean, by the mid-eighteenth century, Dominica, Grenada, St. Lucia, and St. Vincent had transitioned from societies with slaves to slave societies. Reconstructing the features of these societies, including the early emergence of an island-born enslaved population, the persistence of diversified economies, and the presence of planters of color, testifies to the development of slave societies outside of empire in the colonial Caribbean and hints darkly at the intimate nature of the violence that underlay these societies.

Cabotage and Contraband: Trade in the Creole Archipelago

Goods produced in the slave societies of the Creole Archipelago played an important role in the economic development of France's Windward Islands, highlighting the role of island hinterlands in shaping the colonial Caribbean. Islands in which the production of export crops did not monopolize the majority of available land served as breadbaskets for neighboring sugar colonies, as enslaved people used pirogues to ferry provisions to secluded bays. By raising food and livestock that was discreetly sold in Guadeloupe and Martinique, residents of the Creole Archipelago helped sustain free and enslaved people throughout the eastern Caribbean, while also increasing the amount of land that French planters could devote to the production of sugar.

Cabotage, or coastal commerce carried out in small boats, was an essential mode of informal trade throughout the Caribbean.[112] Most islands had few roads; instead, enslaved people ferried goods between plantations and port towns within a given colony. This legal intraisland trade also lent itself to interisland contraband, as people used small watercraft to avail themselves of resources in neighboring territories.[113] Contraband trade helped address problems of food scarcity in sugar colonies, where planters eager to make a profit through exports neglected to allocate provision grounds.[114] The problem was less pronounced in larger colonies such as 4,240-square-mile Jamaica, where enslaved people could find space to cultivate gardens. In colonies such as Martinique, at 436 square miles, or Barbados, just 166 square miles, arable land was scarce. Although French planters were required by law to have three acres planted in provisions such as yams or manioc for every thirty enslaved people on an estate, such laws were rarely enforced.[115]

By the mid-eighteenth century, officials in Guadeloupe and Martinique reported that much of the food necessary to sustain the populations of the respective colonies came from surrounding islands. In an encrypted letter to his superiors in France, the governor-general of the Windward Islands, Maximin de Bompar, responded to a 1751 ordinance attempting to limit the interisland trade that supplied these goods. Colonists in Martinique, Bompar explained, depended on "manioc, poultry, cattle for the butchers etc." produced in neighboring islands; to forbid this trade "would not only reduce these planters to despair, but would also destroy a considerable branch of our commerce."[116] By admitting the importance of economic activity carried out beyond his purview, Bompar testified to the growing importance of neighboring islands in supporting the French colonial economy.

Land surveys archived by France's Ministry of the Marine confirm that planters in the Creole Archipelago devoted more land to food cultivation as the eighteenth century progressed. Growing provisions was an attractive option for small planters who could afford few enslaved laborers; contemporaries reported that a single person could cultivate a *quarré* of manioc, which yielded twenty barrels of flour.[117] In St. Lucia, an island with a total area of just 240 square miles, the amount of land planted in manioc expanded from 321 quarrés in 1744 to 530 quarrés in 1759, or from 1,023 to 1,690 acres producing more than 10,000 barrels of manioc flour.[118] Planters in Dominica also increased their production of provisions in the mid-eighteenth century. In 1730, the island had 30,000 *pieds*, or less than one acre, planted in plantains and 18 quarrés (57 acres) in yams. Fifteen years later, production of plantains in Dominica surpassed that of St. Lucia, with approximately nine acres planted, while land devoted to yams totaled 62 quarrés, or almost 200 acres. As of 1749, Dominica also boasted 1,020 acres planted in manioc; by 1759, that quantity increased to 1,745 acres, meaning that an island just north of Martinique's main port, Saint-Pierre, produced almost 11,000 barrels of manioc flour each year.[119] Although a lack of enumerations prevents an analysis of changes in food production in St. Vincent, a census of the 150-square-mile island dating to 1732 reports 210,850 pieds, or a little more than five acres, devoted to plantains, and 249 quarrés—almost 800 acres—planted in yams.[120] Taken together, these figures indicate that as early as 1730—just before the moment at which substantial migration to Dominica, St. Lucia, and St. Vincent occurred—the amount of land dedicated to food production in the islands closest to Martinique and Guadeloupe totaled more than 2,000 acres. Along with livestock—by 1745, Dominica counted 500 pigs, 1,021 goats, and almost 700 sheep, while St. Lucia boasted almost 1,000 pigs and more than 1,600 goats and sheep—these crops sustained free and enslaved people in the Creole Archipelago as well as in nearby French colonies.[121]

With maritime routes for secreting people and provisions to neighboring French colonies already well established, planters in the Creole Archipelago also began to invest in export commodities such as coffee. Coffee does not require the flat expanses of land necessary to grow sugar, and planters throughout the Caribbean were pleased to discover that the crop flourished with the cooler temperatures and heavier rainfall of the tropical highlands.[122] Contemporaries reported that two quarrés, or approximately six and a half acres, planted in coffee could be tended by three laborers. Once the plants began bearing fruit, they yielded approximately one *livre* of coffee per pied.[123] In 1744, St. Lucia had 105,220 pieds planted in coffee; by 1760, that number increased to 1,419,000 pieds, or 34 acres, for a yield of almost 1.5 million livres of beans.[124] Dominica's rainy climate and mountainous topography also lent itself to the cultivation of coffee, and by 1753, 1,185,000 pieds of the 290-square mile island were planted in coffee, along with 953,000 pieds in cacao and 261,000 pieds in cotton.[125] Planters in St. Lucia also invested heavily in cotton production.

Not enumerated in the 1744 census of the island, by 1759 planters reported 333 quarrés, or approximately 1,062 acres, planted in cotton.[126] Given that each quarré yielded approximately 1,200 French livres of cotton, the amount of cotton grown in St. Lucia represented a significant return for planters.[127]

Sugar is notably absent from these enumerations. While planters in St. Lucia briefly attempted to grow sugarcane, their experiment appears to have failed: settlers reported 46 quarrés (146 acres) planted in cane in 1747, but that number fell to 31 quarrés (99 acres) the following year, and no sugar was reported in the enumeration for 1756, the next year for which data is available.[128] Only the French colony of Grenada had the enslaved workforce, machinery, and access to European markets necessary to produce the capital- and labor-intensive crop. The last French census of Grenada, created in 1755, noted 87 sugar plantations in the island. While this is considerably fewer than the 350 sugar estates in Martinique in the same year, it confirms that the population and productivity of Grenada, like that of Dominica, St. Lucia, and St. Vincent, increased markedly in the middle decades of the eighteenth century.[129]

This increased production in turn benefited French colonial trade, as merchants eager to export commodities to the metropole under the protections of the Exclusif regularly sent small vessels to surrounding islands in order to "load them up with exclusively foreign goods that they then deposit either into their ships or into their stores."[130] The mercantilist logic of the Exclusif dictated that only the produce of French colonies should be shipped to the metropole; planters who transported crops from Dominica, St. Lucia, and St. Vincent to Martinique and Guadeloupe not only enriched themselves, they also discreetly added to the balance of transatlantic commerce between France and its colonies. Despite officials' complaints about their inability to control economic activity in surrounding islands, they were aware that neighboring territories played an important role in provisioning—and even enriching—their colonies.

Enrichment served as a strong incentive for French subjects and officials to ignore or even engage in illicit commerce. As was the case elsewhere in the colonial Americas, those who stood to profit from this commerce remained tight-lipped about any illegal activities. "Regardless of the inquiries and the expenditures that we make, a lack of informants means we cannot discover the source of the contraband," complained the governor of Guadeloupe, who identified colonists' complicity as a key part of the problem. "Without one or two armed ships commanded by naval officers *who are not creole* it is impossible to prevent [this] commerce," he explained.[131] The governor's complaint is telling: ties between French subjects in Martinique and Guadeloupe and their former neighbors or business associates who migrated to surrounding islands continued to facilitate economic relationships. Officials found it especially difficult to control the behavior of island-born residents, who used their knowledge of maritime routes to engage in cabotage between colonies and surrounding nonimperial spaces.

As the fruits of the settlers' captive labor grew, so did the level of attention they attracted. British authorities jealous of the interisland trade estimated that by the 1760s, almost three million pounds of coffee and one million pounds of cacao annually left Dominica, St. Lucia, and St. Vincent for France—figures that align with production estimates given in French censuses, and which indicate that contraband trade grew more sophisticated as the eighteenth century wore on.[132] While much of this produce enriched French merchants, representatives of the Ministry of the Marine complained that residents of neighboring islands also traded with the subjects of different crowns. "The Spanish from Margarita and Cumana, even from Caracas come in little boats to [buy] the cacao" of planters in St. Vincent, French officials explained, while "the Dutch take all their coffee, and little or none comes to Martinique."[133]

Although French administrators were aware of the increasingly ambitious activities undertaken in neighboring islands, they lacked the motivation to sever the economic connections linking their colonies to the Kalinago and neutral islands that had also become home to large numbers of non-Indigenous people. The maritime routes that connected the eastern Caribbean archipelago allowed settlers, enslaved people, and goods to circulate across geographic and imperial boundaries, giving rise to creolized societies with strong economic, social, and religious ties to neighboring French colonies.

The Seven Years' War and the End of Neutrality

As residents of the Creole Archipelago became increasingly entangled in the economic and political fabric of the wider Atlantic world, British colonial officials began to protest the growing number of settlers in these purportedly Kalinago or neutral spaces. Yet mid-eighteenth-century attempts to dislodge island residents—many of whom had resided there for decades and some of whom had never lived anywhere else—met with consternation. "What rights do [the English] have to Dominica and St. Vincent? Did they not recognize by the treaties that these islands belong to the Caribs Indigenous to the land?"

wrote the governor-general of the French Windward Islands in 1750. The governor's passing reference to Indigenous land rights—the only such invocation of Kalinago dominion in the many debates surrounding the islands in the mid-eighteenth century—quickly gave way to his real concern: the fate of the thousands of people who had already violated said treaties by establishing themselves in Kalinago domains. Protesting the proposed removal of settlers in Dominica, St. Lucia, St. Vincent, and Tobago, he appealed to his superiors' sense of humanity, imploring them to consider "what will happen to the families established in the four islands where they live in comfort, and where the fortune of their children is assured? What will happen to them if they lose the basis of their subsistence, as well as their slaves?" Invoking the scarcity of land that drove many small planters from French colonies earlier in the century, he averred that it would be impossible to find areas of Martinique or Guadeloupe in which to settle evacuees.[134] "These poor people will therefore die of misery," he wrote dramatically.[135]

The logistics of evacuating the islands continued to be debated throughout the 1750s, but by the end of the decade both French and British authorities had far more serious concerns. The extension of the Seven Years' War to the Caribbean disrupted the fragile entente that colonial officials and residents of the Creole Archipelago developed during decades of peace. While the Lesser Antilles did not witness combat during the first two years of the war, battles elsewhere in the Atlantic severely disrupted shipping routes and caused food shortages in several colonies.[136] Trade between France and its Lesser Antillean colonies fell precipitously before ceasing almost entirely following the 1759 British conquest of Guadeloupe.[137]

The outbreak of global war highlighted the ambiguous political status of territories increasingly referred to as neutral—not Kalinago—islands. "The island of St. Vincent is neutral," reasoned Governor-General Le Vassor de La Touche in 1761, "and in consequence . . . the French who are there . . . should be seen and treated as neutral." Like Marianne Dorival, many of the people who lived in St. Vincent came from French colonies. By migrating to a space that the governor-general deemed neutral, such people should "be immune from all vexation and violence from the [French] King's enemies." If, however, British forces were to attack the island, La Touche argued that these same settlers were obliged to take up arms in service to the French crown; anyone who failed to do so would be "regarded ipso facto as disobedient and in rebellion."[138] The governor-general's understanding of neutrality presented St. Vincent as a space where French subjects could live without becoming embroiled in interimperial conflicts, but where they retained an obligation to serve their sovereign if the conflict came to their shores.

Residents of St. Vincent and other Kalinago or neutral islands did not necessarily share La Touche's line of reasoning. While the governor-general was pleased to report that residents of St. Lucia promised to take up arms against the British, he was dismayed that "most of the planters" in St. Vincent, "even the principal among them," were disposed to listen to the "specious propositions" of British troops who sought to occupy the island.[139] In contrast, St. Vincent's Kalinago leaders offered "to send three thousand of their people to support Martinica, and . . . harras [sic]" British troops, signaling that they preferred to ally with the French against possible British invasion, and suggesting that Europeans severely underestimated the number of Kalinagos in the island.[140] While settlers in Dominica initially agreed to the strict terms of neutrality imposed by British commodore John Moore, to whom they sold supplies, by 1759 they were requesting food and ammunition from Martinique and were also fitting out French privateers.[141] This range of responses to interimperial war indicates that residents of the Creole Archipelago did not have a single or unified relationship with a specific crown. Instead, people who settled outside the sphere of European rule sought to forge alliances that would best serve themselves and their families.

Although French forces attempted to defend Dominica, the island fell to British troops on June 7, 1761, after just five hours of fighting.[142] Making use of Dominica's "abundance of livestock, poultry and vegetables of all sorts," British forces then used the island as a staging ground from which to launch other attacks, capturing Martinique in February 1762 and Grenada, St. Lucia, and St. Vincent over the course of the following month.[143] French officials reported that St. Lucia had "only 37 soldiers, of which 4 deserted the moment the enemy arrived." Grenada had "even fewer" French troops, and La Touche lamented that members of the militia in both islands preferred to stay home rather than help mount a defense.[144] The reluctance of island residents to defend against British conquest suggests that many would have preferred to maintain their neutrality, but the Seven Years' War foreclosed this possibility. As the following chapters explore, the 1763 Treaty of Paris prompted the assimilation and transformation of islands that formerly evolved outside the sphere of European empire, and the ensuing decades wrought unprecedented political, demographic, economic, and social changes in the eastern Caribbean. Despite momentous transformations, however, the culture and connections developed by free, enslaved, and Indigenous residents of the Creole Archipelago would not be easily undone by imperial reforms, no matter how ambitious.

*   *   *

Tracing the development of the Creole Archipelago in the middle decades of the eighteenth century demonstrates how, when, and why the interisland connections first forged by Kalinagos were harnessed by a variety of people. Although Kalinagos did not disappear, as the eighteenth century progressed they increasingly found themselves sharing space with individuals and families pushed to the margins of Caribbean plantation society by their race, socio-economic status, and hunger for opportunity. As the number of settlers grew, islands once recognized as Kalinago were increasingly characterized as neutral, a characterization that elided Indigenous dominion while acknowledging the existence of societies that regularly interacted with—while remaining just outside the sphere of—European empires. These societies shared many features with neighboring French colonies, including enslaved majorities, economies centered on plantation production, and a commitment to observing Catholic rites. Yet islands that evolved outside of empire in the colonial Caribbean also differed from surrounding colonies in terms of the power wielded by Indigenous people and free people of color, the early emergence of an island-born enslaved population, and the presence of Creole colonists whose loyalties lay not with a distant European crown but with extended family, friends, and associates scattered across the constellation of islands at the edge of the Americas. Pushed beyond colonial boundaries by their race, hunger for land, and pursuit of opportunities, thousands of people forged a slave society that contributed to, yet remained just beyond the reach of, European crowns. In the face of sweeping imperial reforms introduced after the Seven Years' War, important features of that society would endure.

Chapter 3

Colonizing the Caribbean Frontier

Marie Catherine La Verge La Feuillée watched anxiously as the ship sailed into port in Roseau, Dominica, in June 1765. Born in Le Prêcheur, northern Martinique, in 1723, Marie Catherine moved to Dominica while the island was formally recognized as a Kalinago or neutral domain.[1] Together with her husband, Nicolas Crocquet de Belligny, a fellow native of Martinique, Marie Catherine accumulated over one hundred acres of land in Dominica. She and Nicolas forced at least eighty-five enslaved people, most of them also born in the Americas, to work that land, producing coffee that enriched the couple and their twelve children.[2] But by 1765, the family's future in Dominica was uncertain. As a result of Great Britain's victory in the Seven Years' War (1756–1763), at the 1763 Treaty of Paris, King George III acquired the Kalinago and neutral islands of Dominica, St. Vincent, and Tobago, along with the former French colony of Grenada, while France acquired St. Lucia. Eager to harness the productive potential of what were collectively referred to as the Southern Caribbee or Ceded Islands, Great Britain's Board of Trade immediately began designing sweeping plans for how to develop the new colonies.[3] More than two years later, in 1765, agents tasked with implementing key elements of these plans—the Commissioners for the Sale and Disposal of Lands in the Ceded Islands—began to arrive. As the commissioners disembarked in Roseau—which they insisted should now be called Charlottetown, in honor of their queen—Marie Catherine wondered how the imperial designs these men brought with them would affect the lives that she and thousands of other residents of the Creole Archipelago had forged outside the boundaries of European empire.

While historians acknowledge that the period after the Seven Years' War was one of widespread imperial reform, focusing on the eastern Caribbean archipelago provides an opportunity to examine these reforms on a small scale, in order to appreciate how they affected people like Marie Catherine, the many individuals she held in bondage, and Kalinagos living outside of plantation regimes.[4] The ways that the British and French crowns responded to the altered geopolitical landscape of the postwar era differed in many respects, yet both crowns approached the Lesser Antilles as a site for reforms and experiments in political economy.[5] Informed by experiences administering plantation colonies elsewhere in the Americas, British and French administrators harnessed a range of expertise in order to develop the islands as rapidly and as rationally as possible.[6] Despite their small size, in the latter half of the eighteenth century the Lesser Antilles were home to wide-ranging experiments in creating and administering plantation colonies, ruling over a diversity of colonial subjects, and maximizing productivity. These experiments encountered considerable obstacles, as imperial visions of orderly colonial development confronted the realities of daily life in this interconnected archipelago. Yet close attention to the surveying, settlement, and economic development of the British Ceded Islands and French St. Lucia suggests important similarities between crowns whose strategies and priorities—particularly in the latter half of the eighteenth century—are often assumed to diverge. While Chapters 4 and 5 explore how these imperial designs reverberated in the lives of existing settlers and enslaved and Indigenous people, this chapter emphasizes how the eastern Caribbean served as a laboratory in which both the British and the French crowns enacted and experimented with broader imperial designs.[7]

As she watched the commissioners disembark in Roseau, Marie Catherine likely had some inkling of how the political geography, demography, and economy of the Creole Archipelago, as well as the region's broader relationship to European empires, was about to change. Instead of being linked by pirogues to French colonies visible from their shores, the Ceded Islands were now politically and economically tied to far-flung British possessions such as Jamaica, more than a thousand miles away, and from there to a dramatically expanded British empire. These ties would in turn shape who lived in the islands, and what their lives were like while there. In the ten years immediately following the 1763 Treaty of Paris, hundreds of settlers from Britain and from existing British colonies, most of them white men unaccompanied by wives or children, purchased large plots of land on a chain of islands with a total area of approximately seven hundred square miles—five hundred square miles smaller than Rhode Island. Hoping to grow rich and return to Great Britain to enjoy their wealth, these planters invested heavily in sugar production, consolidating the smaller coffee and cacao plantations that dotted the islands into large estates. While former French subjects in Grenada retained title to their lands, people who had claimed plots in Dominica and St. Vincent while they were Kalinago domains, including Marie Catherine's husband Nicolas, could only obtain leases from the Commissioners for the Sale of Lands.[8] In the ensuing years, these leaseholders, both whites and free people of color, would agitate for the same rights as their propertied neighbors, generating contests over subjecthood that are the focus of Chapter 4.

Attempts to engineer ideal plantation colonies in the eastern Caribbean also had significant consequences across the Atlantic, as France and Great Britain, along with Bourbon Spain, increased their participation in the transatlantic slave trade in the post–Seven Years' War era.[9] In the decade after 1763, European slavers trafficked more than eighty thousand West Africans to new towns in the Ceded Islands, turning formerly illicit ports into centers of regional and transatlantic commerce in human lives.[10] While many survivors of the Middle Passage were subsequently sold elsewhere in the Americas, in the space of a single decade at least thirty-seven thousand were forced to remain in the new colonies, dwarfing the population of thirty thousand enslaved people scattered across the archipelago before the treaty and altering the languages, cultures, and labor regimes on the region's growing plantations.[11] As thousands of enslaved people labored to convert forested lands into cane fields, they encroached on Kalinago domains. While Chapter 5 explores how Kalinagos and enslaved people responded to the expansion of sugar production, this chapter emphasizes the centrality of the transatlantic slave trade to British and French plans for rebuilding their respective empires. Although this traffic would come under attack in the ensuing decades, immediately after the Seven Years' War European powers shared a belief that trading in enslaved Africans was essential to regaining imperial wealth. The human costs of this trade were largely ignored as officials sought to increase commerce with West Africa while simultaneously maximizing the economic productivity of the Ceded Islands, altering the new colonies' place in broader transatlantic systems.

The commissioners who sailed into Roseau in June 1765, as well as the French surveyors who arrived in St. Lucia in the same period, publicly signaled the respective crowns' designs for their new colonies. By settling lands with loyal subjects, the commissioners would foster a resident population to protect the colonies in the event of future war while also joining the interests of planters and merchants to those of the state. Tropical commodities produced in the islands would enrich settlers while also quickly generating the capital needed to service wartime debts. The tens of thousands of enslaved people forced to produce these commodities would require supplies from elsewhere in the empires, such as salt fish from North America, while obtaining African captives would simultaneously stimulate the shipping industry, train thousands of sailors, and encourage the trade in metropolitan manufactures on the West African coast. Rather than choosing between two seemingly divergent systems—one that privileged commercial networks and another in which settlers represented imperial interests overseas—in the eastern Caribbean the French and British crowns did both. As Chapters 4 and 5 explore in detail, these imperial designs encountered considerable obstacles. For people like Marie Catherine, who watched from shore, the commissioners' arrival marked the beginning of contests that would endure for decades, as distant crowns exercised newfound authority to engineer spaces that had previously evolved outside of empire. For the agents of those crowns, however, the islands represented a promising new frontier—one in which the commissioners themselves proved eager to invest.

Expertise and Imperial Designs After the Seven Years' War

The end of the Seven Years' War heralded the start of new contests over the shape of empire. British forces conquered many French possessions during the conflict, including Canada, Senegal, Guadeloupe, Martinique, and Grenada, and the decision of which territories to restore to France therefore rested with King George III. Although France entered negotiations from a position of weakness, the new secretary of the Marine, the duc de Choiseul, began devising plans to rebuild French power even before the war came to an end.[12] Both crowns consulted a range of experts to inform the policies they each pursued, and peace negotiations testify to an in-depth consideration of the shape the respective empires should take.[13] While Great Britain had more power and resources to realize its vision of empire, British and French administrators, along with their Spanish counterparts, recognized that colonies in the circum-Caribbean could simultaneously serve economic, military, and territorial goals.[14] They therefore sought to add to their West Indian possessions in order to increase the production of plantation commodities, create new markets for metropolitan manufactures, service wartime debts, and settle the islands with subjects on whom they could depend.

Historians seeking to understand how France reimagined empire in the wake of the Seven Years' War often turn to debates over Canada. Choiseul's

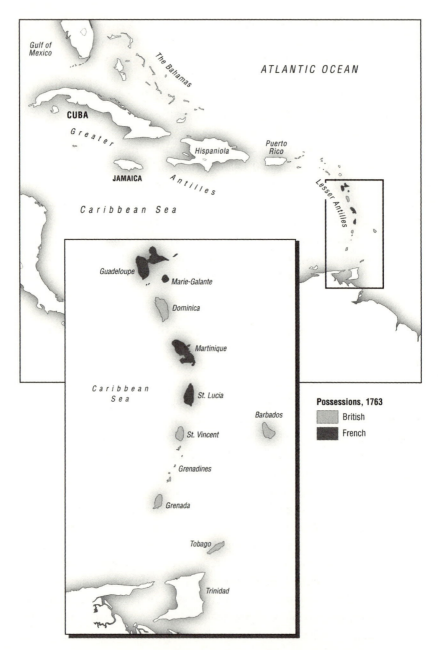

Figure 8. After the 1763 Treaty of Paris, Great Britain established control over Dominica, St. Vincent, Grenada, and Tobago, while France gained St. Lucia and maintained control of Guadeloupe and Martinique.

willingness to relinquish claims to territory in mainland North America in exchange for the restoration of Guadeloupe and Martinique is cited as an example of his vision for a new imperial system, one centered on trade rather than territory.[15] Yet as Pernille Røge persuasively argues, this vision was not restricted to that of a narrow mercantilist empire; instead, French designs for a mainland American colony in Guiana, as well as debates about whether to establish settlement colonies in West Africa, testify to broader plans to wed economic and military reform to enlightened experimentation in France's remaining overseas territories.[16] Choiseul's designs for St. Lucia exemplify these plans. While small, the island was "vital for French trade" and as a site of maritime defense; if St. Lucia should fall into British hands, the most profitable of France's Lesser Antillean colonies, Martinique, would be vulnerable to attack.[17] Although Choiseul initially insisted that earlier treaties recognizing Kalinago dominion over Dominica and St. Vincent be respected, he later agreed that the islands could be ceded, provided that St. Lucia be afforded to France.[18] In exchange for the restoration of Guadeloupe and Martinique and British recognition of French claims to St. Lucia, King Louis XV agreed to abandon all pretensions to St. Vincent, Dominica, and Tobago and to cede Grenada to Great Britain. By affording military protection to Martinique, providing lands on which French subjects displaced by the war could settle, and contributing to the balance of French trade, St. Lucia promised to contribute to Choiseul's strategies for imperial reorganization in the face of greater British power.

Representatives of the British crown were even more optimistic about the role that Grenada, Dominica, St. Vincent, and Tobago could play in the newly expanded empire. Using the press as a vehicle for the promotion and dissemination of broader political agendas, individuals and institutions vaunted the promise of the new territories.[19] William Young, Commissioner for the Sale and Disposal of Lands, was among them. Although Young spent less than a decade in the Ceded Islands, retiring to England in 1773, his activities in the archipelago offer insight on how the new colonies fit into broader visions of empire in the wake of the Seven Years' War. By the time of his death in 1788, Young laid claim to almost nine hundred enslaved people whose forced labor sustained his four Caribbean plantations: one in Antigua, one in Tobago, and two in St. Vincent. Yet his investments cost him dearly: when Young died, his son, William Young, Jr., inherited debts of over £110,000.[20] Young's considerable investment in the Ceded Islands—both economic and ideological—is emblematic of how imperial officials and investors sought to integrate formerly neutral and Kalinago domains into existing empires. People like Young knew little about the interconnected Creole society established by people like Marie Catherine La Verge La Feuillée. Instead, they saw the islands as blank spaces to be colonized and cultivated—ones where the plantation complex could be expanded and improved.

In his 1764 pamphlet *Considerations which may tend to promote the settlement of our new West-India Colonies*, Young outlined how land grants, liberal trade regulations, and easy access to capital would rapidly transform the Ceded Islands into profitable sugar colonies.[21] Such strong endorsements about the potential benefits of the new colonies were necessary, as plans to develop the archipelago also met with vocal criticism. Planters in existing British West Indian colonies, fearful that a greater supply of sugar would lead to a decrease in market price, were suspicious of new competitors. They also expressed concern that the emigration of small planters to the new territories would deplete their militias, leaving a tiny white minority more vulnerable to enslaved insurgency.[22] Seeking to allay such fears, Young presented the Ceded Islands as blank slates where the mistakes of the past could be avoided. Settlement would be carefully regulated, Young explained, and great care be taken to avoid the "many inconveniences [that] are found to have occurred in [other] new colonies."[23]

One such "inconvenience" related to the availability of enslaved people, who Young argued "should be immediately supplied as they may happen to fall off."[24] In the mid-eighteenth century, French philosophers known as *economistes* or physiocrats began to explore the possibility of creating plantation colonies without the use of enslaved labor.[25] Yet as Pernille Røge acknowledges, physiocrats "were far less forceful in their attacks on slavery than they were in their relentless efforts to liberalise commerce," and their unsuccessful experiments with free labor in the circum-Caribbean failed to furnish alternative models of colonization.[26] In the British empire, sustained public attacks on West Indian slavery and the slave trade would not emerge until the abolitionist movement gained strength in the 1780s.[27] Instead, in the immediate wake of the Seven Years' War, agents of the French, British, and Spanish crowns largely subscribed to the idea that slavery and the slave trade would enrich their empires.[28] After negotiating for the restoration of France's trade post at Gorée, the French crown opened the slave trade to all French merchants. In the ensuing decade, 543 French slaving voyages trafficked more than 175,000 captives from West Africa, most of them to Saint-Domingue.[29]

British visions of postwar prosperity also rested on the continued exploitation of African labor. *Candid and Impartial Considerations on the Nature of the*

Sugar Trade, a 1763 pamphlet supported by Prime Minister Lord Bute, high-lighted how the trade in West African people stimulated various segments of the British economy.[30] From shipping and insurance to textiles and firearms, "in the main, very little that is not our own growth or manufacture" could be traded for or used by West Africans.[31] Challenges to the slave trade would gain strength in the coming decades, but in the period immediately after 1763, European crowns viewed traffic in human lives as essential to rebuilding empires struggling under the weight of wartime debts.

Attention to imperial designs reveals that in both France and Great Brit-ain, crown officials and a variety of interested parties elaborated visions in which new Caribbean colonies wedded military, territorial, and commercial goals, while also providing an opportunity to improve on existing practices of plantation production. Heavily researched plans for the settlement and development of the Ceded Islands testify to the importance of these small territories in evolving understandings of political economy after the Seven Years' War.

Signaling Sovereignty:
Surveyors in the Eastern Caribbean

Before these plans could be enacted, the islands needed to be surveyed. Brit-ish and French administrators began to take stock of what each crown had gained in the Caribbean even before the Treaty of Paris was signed, as naval officers who helped conquer the islands assessed the present situation and future potential of the new colonies. British officers generated reports on the islands' respective size, climate, topography, and economy, and the Board of Trade wasted no time in using their findings to shape policy. How many free people currently lived in each territory? How many enslaved people did they claim? What crops did they grow, and in what quantity? Most important, what *could* they grow? Implicit throughout the detailed and lengthy question-naires is a desire for expansion, improvement, and above all enrichment. Brit-ish and French surveying practices testify to a common goal of maximizing the economic potential of the islands while avoiding many of the problems that impeded earlier settlements in the Americas. For both crowns, displaying detailed knowledge of the islands also served as a means of demonstrating their capacity to govern territories that had evolved outside the sphere of colo-nial rule until the global reordering of the Seven Years' War.

As the content of these questionnaires suggests, experiences of colonial rule in sugar islands such as Barbados shaped colonization of the eastern Caribbean. By exerting stricter control than their predecessors, authorities hoped to avoid many of the problems that now plagued older colonies, which they deemed to have been settled too quickly and haphazardly. While productivity was desirable, land exhaustion, absenteeism, and the engrossment of large plantations and subsequent emigration of small planters were not. Tacky's Revolt, an enslaved insurgency that paralyzed Jamaica in 1760, served as a warning of what could happen if enslaved people vastly outnumbered free people, and administrators sought to minimize this danger by penalizing absentee planters and encouraging families to settle the islands.[32] Leaving little to chance, the Board of Trade elaborated a plan for how to develop the Ceded Islands quickly, efficiently, and with as little cost to the already indebted crown as possible.

In late 1764, a plan for the settlement of the four islands ceded to Great Britain was put into action.[33] As Max Edelson argues, the minutely detailed instructions provided to the commissioners reflect a conscious desire to improve on earlier settlements while integrating the colonies into an economically and politically centralized empire.[34] The commissioners were instructed to divide the respective islands into parishes of six thousand to ten thousand acres each and to determine the best placement and layout of a town in each parish. In an effort to eradicate the troublesome pirogues long used by Kalinagos and subsequently adopted by settlers throughout the region, roads were to be forged for ease of travel and communication between towns. To encourage planters to put down roots in the islands, surveyors were instructed to reserve sufficient acreage for the construction of a school, a Protestant church, and a glebe for the support of a minister in each parish.[35] Small allotments were also set aside for poor settlers, who could apply for a grant of uncleared land provided that they demonstrated their lack of means to purchase a plot. In a testament to British desire to introduce loyal settlers into the new colonies, Catholics were ineligible to apply for poor settlers' plots.[36]

British plans for the Ceded Islands also betray concerns about human impacts on the environment. While eighteenth-century scientists continued to debate the influence of forest cover on weather conditions, planters and administrators could not deny the devastating ecological and economic effects of near-total deforestation in Barbados. Many contemporaries, including Young, believed that "large tracts of wood . . . contribute to insure rains and fertility, and to produce rivers,"[37] and the fifth instruction to the commissioners accordingly required that they reserve sufficient woodland "for producing those refreshing showers which are so essential to the fertility of the country."[38] Demonstrating their desire not to repeat past mistakes, Young and others harnessed scientific expertise in a deliberate attempt to prevent the drought and soil exhaustion that plagued planters elsewhere in the Caribbean.[39]

In laying claim to both the scientific expertise and the political authority to survey and subdivide the Ceded Islands, the commissioners publicly signaled King George III's newfound right to impose order and rule in spaces that evolved outside the sphere of British rule until the resounding victory of the Seven Years' War. The islands' transformation into British plantation colonies operated at both a practical and an ideological level. As surveyors mapped lands, they also laid claim to them, bestowing familiar English names on an exotic landscape: Ouassigany became Kingstown, St. Vincent, while the French origins of La Baye, Grenada, were subject to a pointed symbolic erasure when the port town was renamed in honor of Prime Minister Grenville.

The map of Grenada below, which shows "the addition of English names, alterations of property, and other improvements" illustrates how British authority was imposed in an island that had been a colony of France for more than a century. Surveyors maintained parish boundaries established when Grenada was under French rule but bestowed new English names on each parish: Basse Terre, "low land," was redubbed St. George, while Sauteurs, the northernmost point of the island from which Grenada's last Kalinago inhabitants were fabled to have jumped—*sauté*—to their deaths, became St. Patrick.[40] The map, which was based on an earlier French survey of Grenada, also illustrated the fruits of British investment in the island by explicitly noting sugar mills driven by water, which significantly outnumbered those driven by cattle. In mapping land, surveyors also participated in symbolically mapping British sovereignty and the progress it promoted.[41]

Even as surveyors, assisted by untold numbers of enslaved people, continued to map the mountainous, often densely forested lands, the commissioners began to sell them—an eagerness that testifies to a desire to raise capital and settle the islands as quickly as possible. In Grenada, many plots of land changed hands privately before the commissioners arrived, as existing planters sold their estates and left the former French colony in the wake of its cession to Great Britain.[42] Such sales were not possible in formerly neutral or Kalinago islands, where existing planters lacked legal title to the lands on which they lived. Instead, at a minimum price of £5 sterling per acre for cleared land and £1 sterling per acre for uncleared land, the commissioners sold lots of up to

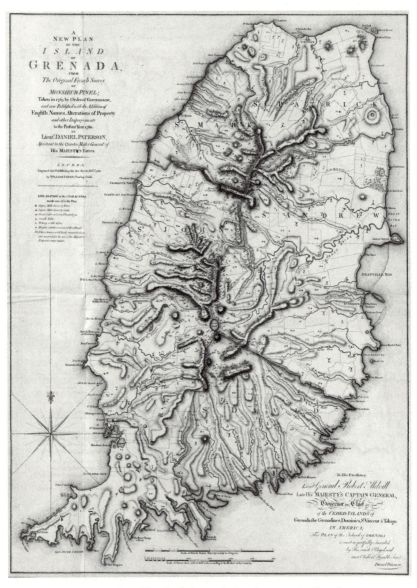

Figure 9. *A new plan of the Island of Grenada.* Based on an earlier French survey, this map of Grenada, published in 1780, was intended to showcase the many "improvements" made under British rule. Courtesy John Carter Brown Library.

five hundred acres at public auction. In order to raise funds, purchasers were required to pay 20 percent of the total purchase price at the time of sale, as well as sixpence per acre to defray the cost of surveying. The remaining balance could be cleared at a rate of 10 percent the following year, then 20 percent per year until the balance was fully paid. The mountainous topography of Dominica persuaded the commissioners that the island lacked the broad, flat expanses of land necessary for the establishment of large sugar plantations; they therefore deemed that lots in the colony should be smaller, between fifty and three hundred acres. To avoid the engrossment of large plantations and subsequent emigration of small planters that occurred in colonies settled earlier, an individual was permitted to buy no more than five hundred acres of land in a single island.[43] This limit did not prevent wealthy and ambitious planters from purchasing the maximum amount of allowable land in several different islands, as Young and many of his fellow commissioners chose to do.

In addition to dictating how land would be divided and used, authorities sought to prescribe who would live on said land. While King George III decreed that "the native Caribbees of St. Vincent are permitted to remain undisturbed in their cottages and Grounds," and a 134-acre plot was also reserved for Kalinagos in Dominica, all other lands in the Ceded Islands were made available to settlers.[44] To encourage planters to develop the lands they bought, administrators imposed strict penalties. Purchasers were required to clear their plots at an annual rate of five acres per hundred, with a fine of £5 sterling per uncleared acre levied on those who failed to do so. These penalties helped offset some of the cost of surveying the new colonies, but they were also intended to ensure that those who purchased lands would transform them into productive estates, taming sparsely populated regions that might provide refuge to Kalinagos or Maroons.

French administrators were equally eager to improve on past practices as they reordered their colonial possessions. In light of the loss of New France, the establishment of a mainland American colony monopolized much of the attention of the Marine, and an estimated 17,000 settlers were recruited to colonize Guiana. Although the expedition proved disastrous—many of those who survived the lengthy voyage to South America perished from disease soon after their arrival, and most survivors abandoned the colony—the undertaking is suggestive of the level of investment the Marine was willing to make in its remaining overseas territories.[45] Although St. Lucia did not attract the same degree of attention, French administrators were aware of the colony's value as a strategic site of maritime defense, a trading entrepot, and a place to settle loyal subjects from elsewhere in France's diminished empire.[46] Attempts to buttress the population of 1,200 Francophone Catholics already resident in the island and to introduce sugar planting reflect Choiseul's desire to protect existing colonies, increase French presence in the Americas, and integrate St. Lucia into existing trade networks.

In October 1763, the Marine dispatched a total of eight *ingénieurs-géographes* to Guadeloupe, Martinique, and St. Lucia and an additional thirteen to the much larger colony of Saint-Domingue. Employees of the Service Hydrographique, a branch of the French navy, the corps of surveyors swelled considerably during the Seven Years' War, and the end of the conflict found forty men with little to occupy their time and expertise.[47] France's crushing defeat in the war convinced Louis XV of the inherent vulnerability of his West Indian possessions, and French surveyors were primarily charged with gaining an accurate account of the islands to ensure the protection of their coasts, allowing the navy to better defend them in future. Three surveyors each were sent to Guadeloupe and Martinique, where by the end of the 1760s they managed to produce maps of the respective islands.[48] The two surveyors dispatched to St. Lucia were not so successful. Landing in the island in November 1763, Nicolas Morancy fell ill soon after his arrival and proved unable to complete the ambitious task of surveying the new colony during his two-and-a-half-year stay.[49] Requests that at least four more surveyors be sent to St. Lucia apparently fell on deaf ears, and a map of the island comparable to those for Guadeloupe and Martinique was not created until the late 1780s.[50] Despite this shortcoming, French surveyors, like their British counterparts, helped signal sovereignty in the reordered archipelago, bestowing the names of political figures such as Choiseul on St. Lucia's burgeoning towns. Although French cartographers sent to the Caribbean after the Treaty of Paris were more focused on generating detailed topographic and coastal surveys than on allocating plantations, they too deployed scientific expertise to assert political authority.[51] This expertise facilitated the growth and centralization of knowledge in both France and Great Britain, as information about the new colonies was sent to newly organized repositories in the respective metropoles.[52]

British and French cartographers who generated detailed maps of their respective crowns' new colonies played a key role in assimilating these spaces into evolving empires after the Seven Years' War. By drawing boundaries, renaming regions, and designating new administrative areas, surveyors publicly signaled that they possessed the expertise and the authority to improve on earlier practices of colonization. From their offices in Europe, agents of

France's Ministry of the Marine and Great Britain's Board of Trade drafted detailed plans to create colonies deliberately engineered to meet postwar imperial goals. French and British officials sent to execute their designs would soon discover just how ambitious these plans were.

Settling Subjects: Promoting White Settlement of the Eastern Caribbean

Aware that their claims to territory might prove tenuous if not anchored with loyal subjects, British and French administrators shared a desire to oversee the settlement of their new colonies. Seeking to create a settler class with strong connections to the imperial state and access to capital, agents of both crowns actively promoted settlement through printed advertisements, the promise of land grants, and ready access to enslaved laborers who would transform the forested lands into productive estates. Both crowns were particularly eager to avoid the problems of planter absenteeism common in Caribbean islands colonized in the seventeenth and early eighteenth centuries, and administrators pursued several means to promote the settlement of white families—not just men—in the region.[53] A comparison of British and French settlement schemes in the period after 1763 testifies to a shared desire to solidify authority in the frequently contested archipelago by populating the new colonies with permanent settlers whose goals were linked to those of the crown under which they lived.

The French Ministry of the Marine initially envisioned the settlement of St. Lucia as a state-directed affair. In the latter half of the eighteenth century, physiocrats experimented with a range of projects to develop agricultural settlements in both France and its colonies.[54] While authorities were particularly eager to entice women and families to populate these settlements, extant lists of passengers who left France for St. Lucia reveal that most were men unaccompanied by family members.[55] The colony's intendant, Marc Antoine Chardon, bemoaned the arrival of single men, explaining that "not being married, they are also of no use for increasing the population." Chardon also deemed settlers from France to be ill suited to the rigors of life in the tropics. "A spirit of laziness and idleness is their lot," he complained, "and of 250 who have arrived thus far, there are no more than thirty who can be of any use to us."[56] The frustrated intendant repeatedly suggested that the Marine abandon the system of sending settlers to the island altogether, condemning the project as "homicide in and of itself."[57]

In keeping with Chardon's wishes, many of the people who settled in St. Lucia in the wake of the Seven Years' War came not from France but from neighboring islands. As hundreds of French Catholic planters abandoned their holdings in Grenada, Dominica, and St. Vincent in the wake of their cession to Great Britain, many families made their way north to St. Lucia, where they contributed to the rapid development of the new French colony.[58] The reported number of settlers in St. Lucia almost doubled in a single year, rising from 1,267 in 1764 to 2,391 in 1765.[59] This initial wave of regional migrants "advanced the colony by 10 years," officials in Martinique reported excitedly after a 1765 visit to St. Lucia.[60] The 1765 census was also the first to note the island's degree of urban development. Separate columns listed the number of houses in each town, as well as the number of plots on which houses would be built during the coming year, testifying to the role of permanent settlement in advancing infrastructure.[61]

While the Board of Trade's designs for the Ceded Islands evidence a similar desire to foster a resident settler population, the British proved less successful than the French. In the wake of Tacky's Revolt, authorities were anxious to populate sugar colonies with loyal subjects who could protect against the dual threats of external attack and internal enslaved insurgency.[62] They therefore passed laws aimed at promoting white settlement: any proprietor who failed to keep one white man or two white women for every thirty enslaved people on his plantation was required to pay a penalty of £40 sterling for every white man and £20 sterling for every white woman deficient from his estate.[63] Similar fines had long been in place in other British West Indian colonies, but the penalties were considerably lower, with planters in the Leeward Islands initially paying a "deficiency tax" of just three shillings per year.[64] Despite not bringing his own large family to the colonies, Young reasoned that the obligation to foster white settlement in the Ceded Islands "can never be seriously complained of . . . when we reflect that the want of [white] people in our West India islands, arises in a great measure from the paucity of [white] women."[65] High deficiency taxes aimed to increase the number of white men who could serve in the militia and of white women who could serve as wives, mothers, and sources of stable family life. Other acts were similarly designed to promote the creation of white families who would permanently reside in the colonies, thereby creating a more stable society less marked by the issues of orphanhood, fragile kinship ties, and disputes over the transmission of property that were believed to mar first-phase colonies.[66] The creation of a capital city in each island, complete with its own customs house, jail, and other institutions of state authority, would ensure that islands administered from the seat of government in Grenada would not become provincial backwaters.[67] Efforts to create institutions of education and religious and family life by reserving land for a Protestant church and a school in each parish testify to a desire to avoid the problems associated with absenteeism by promoting a stable, self-reproducing settler society.[68]

Despite such efforts, the example of planters who made their fortunes in first-phase colonies and subsequently returned to the British Isles proved alluring. Instead of families, most of the people who disembarked in Great Britain's newest Caribbean colonies after 1763 resembled William Young: unaccompanied men, many of whom came from Scotland or from existing West Indian colonies and hoped to return to their place of origin after a profitable sojourn in the Ceded Islands.[69] Owing to the temporary nature of their settlement, these sojourners usually came alone; by 1780, the formerly unsettled island of Tobago was home to just fifty-seven white women, and no white children were reported to live in the colony.[70] In the other Ceded Islands, French Catholics who had carved out small settlements before 1763, many of whom had large families like Marie Catherine La Verge La Feuillée, continued to constitute the majority of free settlers. As Chapter 4 shows, this demographic reality would serve them well as they attempted to negotiate their political status as new British subjects.

While British and French designs for the eastern Caribbean evidence a shared desire to populate the new colonies with resident planters, the reality on the ground was quite different. While French small planters from neighboring islands flocked to St. Lucia, British subjects with the means to purchase lands usually had little intention of permanently relocating to the Ceded Islands, much less bringing their wives and children. Despite British attempts to foster permanent settler populations through legislation, urban planning, and investments in civic and religious institutions, new settlers remained a minority in the Creole society of the eastern Caribbean archipelago.

Absentees Across the Archipelago: Land Sales and the Rise of an Interisland Planter Class

Some British subjects with the means to buy land did not go to the islands at all. Relying on the favorable reports of the commissioners, investors instead purchased large plots sight unseen. The speed and scale at which plantation allotments were sold throughout the Ceded Islands indicates that while many colonists shared the Board of Trade's optimism about the economic promise of the new colonies, they did not share their goal of creating a landed settler population. Instead, examination of land sales throughout the Ceded Islands illustrates how wealthy investors, including Young, capitalized on the islands' integration into the British empire by purchasing large tracts of land in multiple islands, creating a powerful class of absentee planters whose holdings stretched across the archipelago and whose interests competed with those of the many people already resident in the region.

The commissioners held the first public auction of land in the Ceded Islands on May 20, 1765, in Barbados Bay, in one of seven newly created parishes in Tobago. Although the auction was scheduled to take place several days earlier, on arriving in Tobago the commissioners "found there were no persons arrived intending to purchase," and they elected to postpone sales until buyers could make the journey from neighboring islands.[71] Even with this extra time, only eight people, including commissioners Young, Stewart, Wynne, and Hunt, participated in the initial auction; the commissioners noted that although they "expected a considerable number of settlers at Tobago from Barbados especially for the small allotments that are to be given [to poor settlers] . . . we do not find that any have yet gone."[72] The commissioners instead began holding auctions for lands in Tobago in neighboring colonies, allowing investors to purchase plots in the southernmost Ceded Island without actually going there.[73] As a result of this strategy a majority of Tobago planters, including Young, were absentees; even those who traveled to the Ceded Islands generally preferred to establish their main residence in more developed colonies such as Grenada.[74]

Although allowing investors to purchase land from afar promoted absenteeism, it also helped raise capital. By 1770, more than 54,000 acres of land in Tobago had been sold at auctions held throughout the Ceded Islands, for a total price of more than £154,000.[75] As Young explained, "this island, from it's [sic] having been long disputed by different powers, and in consequence deemed neutral, remains wild," but he judged that "it will probably become the most valuable, of any ceded" to Great Britain.[76] A published map of Tobago illustrates how the island's "wild" or unsettled state shaped development. With no existing settlers laying claim to land, plots in Tobago were large and square, with areas reserved for "poor settlers" carved out of marginal lands such as those near the salt lagoon in the island's southwest. The island's flatter topography allowed surveyors to allocate lands even on Tobago's higher ridges, which peak at 1,800 feet. Young's own purchase in Tobago, located in the northeast parish of St. Paul,

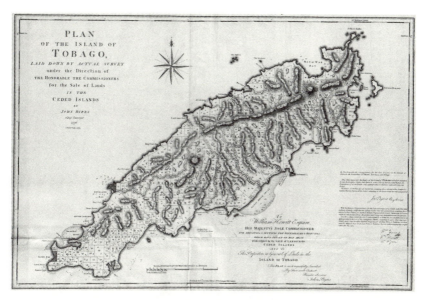

Figure 10. *Plan of the island of Tobago* (London: S. Hooper, 1776). This published map of Tobago was accompanied by an enumerated list indicating the owner of each carefully drawn plot of land. Courtesy John Carter Brown Library.

formed the basis of Betsy's Hope estate, which by the time of Young's death in 1788 had grown to 786 acres worked by 206 enslaved laborers.[77]

This degree of orderliness was not possible in more mountainous islands further north, which were already home to considerable numbers of Kalinagos, enslaved people, and settlers like Marie Catherine. After selling just twelve plantation lots in Tobago, the commissioners sailed to St. Vincent, where they held auctions daily between May 29 and June 1, 1765.[78] Unlike in Tobago, plots in St. Vincent were irregularly shaped, as the commissioners were forced to accommodate both geographic features and competing land claims. Impassable mountains blurred territorial boundaries in St. Vincent's center, where volcanic peaks rising to heights of more than four thousand feet prevented surveyors from completing their work. In accordance with the commissioners' instructions, much of St. Vincent was not subject to survey; all lands on the island's eastern side remained under the control of Kalinagos, and surveyors were prevented from venturing into their territory. Lands abutting the Yambou River, which served as a natural barrier between Kalinago and settler lands, remained unallocated, suggesting that colonists could not be enticed to establish themselves in the contested border region.[79] On St. Vincent's leeward side,

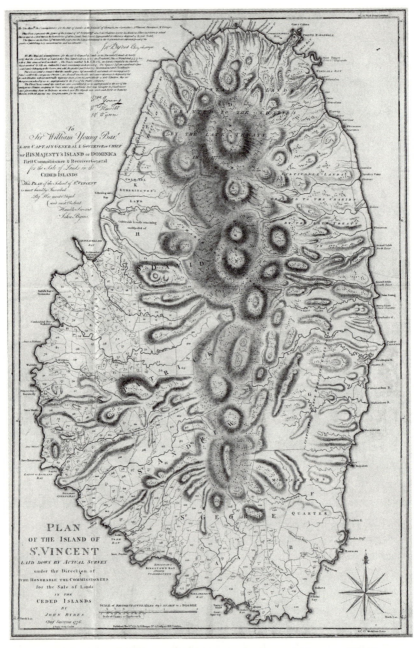

Figure 11. *Plan of the island of St. Vincent* (London: S. Hooper, 1776). This map of St. Vincent, published after the 1772–1773 Carib War, indicates a large swath of land on the island's windward coast that Kalinagos had recently been forced to cede. Courtesy John Carter Brown Library.

larger plots were carved around the many small parcels of land already claimed by planters who had settled in the island before 1763, whose retention of lands as leaseholds is discussed in Chapter 4.

Although approximately half of St. Vincent was not available for settlement, land sales in the colony were quite successful, with cleared plots suitable for planting sugar fetching as much as £59 sterling per acre.[80] "Finding that many of the French inhabitants had quitted their plantations" in the island, the commissioners found eager buyers for already cleared lands, and they managed to sell 7,340 acres over the course of the initial four-day auction in Ouassigany, now called Kingstown.[81] Foreshadowing what would become a common practice among planters throughout the Ceded Islands, several of the commissioners who had already claimed their maximum of 500 acres in Tobago purchased further holdings in St. Vincent. In addition to three town lots in Kingstown, Young acquired a total of 427 cleared and 77 uncleared acres in St. Patrick's parish, slightly exceeding the maximum of 500 acres allowed per purchaser per island.[82] Illustrating Young's belief that "a sugar estate of five hundred acres of good land, properly cleared, and supplied with slaves . . . in an island where lands are new and luxuriant" like St. Vincent "would probably be capable of affording annually, not less than four hundred hogshead of sugar, and a large proportion of rum," he invested almost £10,000 sterling in lands in the island.[83] By the time of his death in 1788, Young's 500-acre Pembroke estate counted 196 enslaved people, while a separate 351-acre estate near Calliaqua, on St. Vincent's southern tip, counted 207 enslaved people.[84]

Young's purchases in St. Vincent allude to some of the changes that accompanied British colonization of the Ceded Islands. In order to establish estates large enough for sugar production, investors like Young consolidated small allotments formerly claimed by several different planters. While these purchases allowed large planters to wield considerable power, they also meant that small planters, whom authorities hoped to retain as resident colonists, abandoned their holdings. Young's acquisition alone was the result of seven proprietors—Mongiraud, Lason, Monguy, Arnaud, Reneterou, Veuve Papin, and Veveigne—quitting their estates on St. Vincent's southwestern coast.[85] As the following chapter explores, many of these small planters relocated to St. Lucia with their families and enslaved laborers, triggering substantial changes in the neighboring French colony.

In late June 1765, the commissioners continued on to Dominica, where they encountered hundreds of existing settlers like Marie Catherine La Verge La Feuillée. Noting that "all the French inhabitants remaining on their estates

[were] very well inclined to continue," the commissioners sought to give them "all possible encouragement to remain" so that Dominica would be better populated by free settlers.[86] More than 240 planters, including Marie Catherine's husband, agreed to lease their existing lands from the commissioners.[87] As a result, areas along Dominica's leeward coast retained the irregularly shaped plots claimed by these early settlers, who prioritized access to water so that enslaved people could ferry the produce of their plantations by pirogue. Surveyors optimistically carved Dominica's unclaimed interior and windward side into large, evenly drawn plots, ignoring the fact that slopes in the island are as steep as 90 degrees.[88] The considerable cost of clearing the tropical forest that covered much of the mountainous island reduced the overall price of land, and on average uncleared lands in Dominica sold for just over £1 sterling per acre, with cleared lands fetching £6 to £7 sterling per acre.[89]

As in St. Vincent, Young's purchases in Dominica signaled his intention to create a large estate in the island, while also securing urban plots on which to establish a residence or commercial venture. In addition to three town lots in Prince Rupert's Bay, the northwesterly settlement designated as Dominica's principal port, Young purchased a total of 334 acres in the island—an amount that slightly exceeded the maximum 300 acres allowed to individual purchasers in "towering and rugged Dominica."[90] Like many investors in the heavily wooded island, however, Young failed to develop these lands, and by 1774 he was forced to advertise them for auction as a means of paying his considerable debts.[91]

Young's initial purchases throughout the new colonies, which amounted to more than 1,300 acres of plantation land and several town plots spread across multiple islands, were not unusual. Fellow commissioner John Hunt also purchased the maximum allowable 500 acres of land in Tobago and multiple town lots in Dominica, while his purchase of 73 cleared and 73 uncleared acres in St. Vincent consolidated the holdings of five former settlers.[92] Scottish planter Alexander Campbell, who in 1763 went to Grenada and "purchased two sugar estates, with upwards of 300 slaves, which cost upwards of £40,000 sterling," went on to buy "fourteen different properties in Grenada, the Grenadines, Saint Vincent, and Tobago" between 1763 and 1791.[93] The substantial investments made by these British subjects indicate that they shared in the orderly vision of colonial settlement conveyed in maps and reports commissioned by the Board of Trade. However, their decision to spread substantial capital investment across multiple islands suggests that they did not share visions of the loyal families British officials had hoped would settle the frontier. Instead, most settlers who came to the Ceded Islands from elsewhere in

Figure 12. *Plan of the island of Dominica* (London: S. Hooper, 1776). This published map of Dominica shows the orderly plots carved out in the center and on the windward side of the island by the Commissioners for the Sale of Lands, as well as the smaller, uneven tracts leased by existing settlers on the leeward coast. Courtesy John Carter Brown Library.

the British empire resembled William Young: ambitious men, unaccompanied by wives or children, who acquired lands in multiple islands.

This pattern of land acquisition had important consequences for the economy, demography, and politics of the new colonies, as well as their place in evolving empires. Although the commissioners sold large quantities of land, it was often to people who spread their holdings throughout the region, meaning that they did not necessarily reside in an island in which they owned land. Instead, these planters wielded economic and political power across the eastern Caribbean archipelago; of the eighteen men initially appointed to the council of the Southern Caribbee Islands, which met in Grenada, more than half owned estates in at least one of the other Ceded Islands.[94] Young, who owned land in Dominica, St. Vincent, and Tobago, was among them; in addition to serving on the council, he was appointed lieutenant governor of Dominica in 1768 and became the colony's first governor in 1770.[95] Like many of his contemporaries, Young retired to England in the 1770s, leaving his estates in the hands of managers.[96] Rather than forming the basis of a permanent settler class whose power was effectively constrained by limits on landholding, as British administrators had hoped, Young and other investors in the Ceded Islands added to the influence of absentees in the metropole.

Attention to the surveying, sale, and settlement of lands in the eastern Caribbean demonstrates that both the British and French crowns consulted and attempted to improve on prior experiences of colonial rule as they reengineered empire in the wake of the Seven Years' War. Yet as the activities of Young and others like him illustrate, those who purchased lands in the new colonies were eager to develop them in ways that mimicked the profitability of earlier colonial ventures. Doing so depended on increasing the transatlantic slave trade, transforming the Creole Archipelago into a center of sugar production.

Slavery and the Economic Transformation of the Ceded Islands

Although slave trafficking came under sustained attack by the end of the eighteenth century, in the wake of the Seven Years' War multiple European powers embraced slavery and slave trading as a means of fulfilling multiple imperial goals. As contemporaneous tracts highlighted, human trafficking provided a captive labor force for American colonies, increased the market for European manufactures in both Africa and the Americas, and gave traders a foothold on the African coast.[97] The colonization of the Ceded Islands was both facilitated by and further stimulated this traffic, linking British and French commerce in Africa to the expansion of their respective colonial frontiers and altering the lives of African people on both sides of the Atlantic.

The end of hurricane season and the drier winter months of November through March typically brought a marked increase in the number of ships arriving in the Caribbean. On December 11, 1766, the *Edgar*, a Liverpool slaving vessel, landed in Grenada. Captains Thomas Chaffers and Edward Williams and their 40-man crew had purchased 377 men and women at Bonny, and they disembarked 364 survivors of the Middle Passage in Grenada's capital, St. George's.[98] The following day, these captives were joined by a further 165 enslaved Africans carried aboard the *Nelly and Nancy*. Also out of Liverpool, the vessel had not fared as well as the *Edgar*: of the 265 captives Captain James Briggs and his 32-man crew brought on board at Calabar, 100 died over the course of the journey.[99] Just one week later, on December 19, 1766, the *Latham*, captained by George Colley and manned by 30 men, sailed into port with 308 captives from Bonny and Calabar aboard. Seventy others had died along the way.[100]

The 837 captives who arrived in this 134-square-mile island in the space of a single week represent only a small fraction of the tens of thousands of individuals trafficked to the Ceded Islands in the wake of the Seven Years' War. The volume of human trafficking from Africa increased markedly after the conflict, as British, French, and Iberian political economists promoted slave trading as a means to increase wealth.[101]

While the increase in transatlantic slave trading testifies to its importance to European crowns after the Seven Years' War, the reorientation of this trade to the eastern Caribbean illustrates the centrality of enslaved labor in developing the new colonies. While French traders disembarked the majority of their captives in Saint-Domingue, in the wake of the Treaty of Paris a significant portion of the British trade was redirected from established colonies such as Barbados to the Ceded Islands.[102] Making use of well-established transatlantic trading routes and practices, British and French slavers carried more than 80,000 people from West Africa to the eastern Caribbean in the decade after the Treaty of Paris. For the period from 1763 to 1773, 387 ships catalogued in the Slave Voyages database list their primary port of disembarkation as Dominica, Grenada, St. Vincent, or Tobago—a group of islands that were collectively visited by just 13 transatlantic slavers in the fifty years prior.[103] Of these 387 voyages, 131 listed their principal place of purchase as the Bight of Biafra, which extends from the Niger Delta in what is now Nigeria south to

Table 5. Number of Enslaved People Trafficked
to Lesser Antillean Islands, 1650-1775

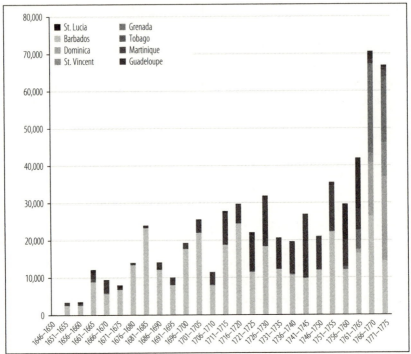

Cape Lopez in present-day Gabon.[104] More than 30,000 captives, or more than one-third of people trafficked to the Ceded Islands in the ten years after they became British colonies, embarked at the Bight of Biafra, most of them at the ports of Bonny and Old Calabar.[105]

The mid-eighteenth century was a period of considerable geopolitical change not only in the Americas and Europe but also in West Africa, as the Bight of Biafra became the primary embarkation zone for English slavers.[106] The respective locations of Bonny and Old Calabar—the former on a small island in the eastern Niger Delta and the latter in the estuary of the Cross River—enabled African merchants, particularly members of the Aro diaspora who traded from Bonny and the Efik who traded from Old Calabar, to control commerce with Europeans.[107] Unable to establish a permanent trading factory or castle, English captains instead relied on African intermediaries to supply them with captives, anchoring off the coast to exchange textiles, firearms, and liquor for ivory, dyewood, yams, and human beings.[108] Experienced canoers, some of them also enslaved, rowed captives from a series of towns located slightly inland to waiting ships.[109] In 1767, English captains allied with Efik families in Duke Town to launch a violent attack on their rivals.[110] The attack resulted in hundreds of captives and allowed Duke Town to emerge as Old Calabar's main trading post, further consolidating human traffic from the region.[111]

The growth of Aro trade diasporas, coupled with the increasing role of private enterprise from the 1740s onward, also changed the scale and nature of slave trading from Bonny.[112] By 1750, the "wholesale market for slaves" at Bonny significantly dwarfed Old Calabar in terms of human commerce, and this persisted throughout the eighteenth century.[113] Between 1763 and 1773, almost twice as many captives embarked at Bonny as at Old Calabar.[114] Although English slavers usually referred to people embarked in the Bight of Biafra as Eboe or Igbo, the region from which captives hailed was characterized by considerable linguistic and cultural diversity.[115] The ways in which captives were acquired further contributed to this diversity. Efik traders traveled by canoe into the interior to attack villages at night, "taking hold of every one [they] could see"; according to an English sailor who accompanied Efik traders on two such raids in 1765, these journeys lasted eight or nine days and yielded approximately forty-five captives.[116] At Bonny, Aro traders sold Igbo- and Ibibio-speaking peoples taken from the northwestern hinterlands as a result of political dissidence or judicial sentences for crimes, debt, or adultery; warfare and kidnapping were less common means of acquiring captives.[117] Owing to these diverse origins, most people embarked at the Bight of Biafra would not have identified fellow captives as members of the same group.[118] Instead, regional identifications may have begun to emerge aboard ship, as captives sought to communicate with one another and respond to the newly imposed reality of their enslavement.[119]

The effects of the postwar growth and reorientation of the transatlantic slave trade could be readily observed in the Ceded Islands. Between 1763 and 1773, Grenada was the first point of disembarkation for more than 41,000 Africans trafficked across the Atlantic. A further 29,000 people first disembarked in Dominica, 10,000 in St. Vincent, and 1,400 in Tobago. In contrast, 5,400 enslaved Africans disembarked in Guadeloupe during the same period, while just 3,600 disembarked in Martinique.[120]

The sheer number of people trafficked to the Ceded Islands in the wake of the Seven Years' War threatens to reduce their experiences to a numerical abstraction, yet each individual was subject to the trauma of capture, commodification, and sale.[121] Ottobah Cugoano, whose 1787 memoir recounts his kidnapping and forced journey from Africa's Cape Coast to Grenada, poignantly

Table 6. African Captives Disembarked in the Lesser Antilles, 1763–1773

| Year | Captives Disembarked in British Ceded Islands | | | | Captives Disembarked in Existing Colonies in the Lesser Antilles | | |
	Dominica	St. Vincent	Grenada	Tobago	Martinique (French)	Guadeloupe (French)	Barbados (British)
1763	0	0	1,034		170	705	3,439
1764	779	167	1,639		885	670	7,969
1765	266	0	2,255		1,188	1,253	4,763
1766	1,090	393	7,090		629	717	4,420
1767	3,045	200	4,172		82	445	5,008
1768	2,681	577	2,657		504	347	4,282
1769	3,929	545	3,725			244	8,573
1770	3,620	794	6,263		52	423	9,119
1771	6,956	2,363	4,739	300	51	130	5,625
1772	4,809	2,544	4,371	770	120	225	4,603
1773	1,701	2,358	2,732	340		209	1,173
TOTAL	28,876	9,941	40,677	1,410	3,681	5,368	58,974
	Total: 80,904				Total: 68,023		

Source: Slave Voyages: Trans-Atlantic Slave Trade Database, https://slavevoyages.org/voyages/qakth28g.

recalled that "when we found ourselves at last taken away, death was more preferable than life."[122] House of Commons testimony confirms Cugoano's vivid account of the "horrible scenes which [captives] saw, and the base treatment which [they] met with in this dreadful captive situation."[123] Aboard ship, captives were separated by sex, and "stowed . . . as close as possible" in cabins below deck.[124] Men, who constituted a majority of people trafficked from Africa to the Ceded Islands in this decade, were typically chained to one another at the neck while vessels were in sight of land to dissuade them from attempting escape.[125] Below deck, they were usually fettered at the ankles in pairs and forced to lie so closely together that "there was not room to put down the point of a stick between one and another."[126] Packed in holds intended for cargo, captives struggled to move or even breathe; as one former Captain testified, "I have often seen in the morning one of the pair dead."[127] Such deaths were all too common; on average, slaving vessels completing the voyage from Africa to the Ceded Islands between 1763 and 1773 lost more than 16 percent of their human cargo.[128] Many people who survived the horrors of this forced journey died not long after arrival; Matthew Terry, who spent four years in Dominica, one in Tobago, and seven in Grenada in the wake of the Treaty of Paris, estimated that "one third of the number imported die within the first year."[129]

For many captives, the long forced journey did not end at the ship's primary point of disembarkation. In Grenada and Dominica, merchants herded people onto smaller boats destined for colonies that were less frequently visited by transatlantic vessels, such as Tobago and St. Vincent.[130] As Gregory O'Malley's work on the intercolonial slave trade shows, the creation of a free port in Dominica in 1767 allowed the island to emerge as an entrepot from which traders reexported Africans to other colonies.[131] O'Malley estimates that at the height of this trade, between 1783 and 1788, fully 57 percent of Africans trafficked to Dominica were subjected to this second Middle Passage.[132] Yet as Dominica's then governor, John Orde, noted, despite this frenzied intercolonial commerce, thousands of Africans remained in the new British colony.[133] Although the intercolonial trade in human beings was important, Dominica was more than an entrepot. In the decade after the Ceded Islands were incorporated into the British Empire and St. Lucia into the French, the eastern Caribbean archipelago became the final destination for tens of thousands of people forced to clear land, plant and harvest crops, and process the commodities that enriched Great Britain and France.

While the increase in transatlantic slave trading to the new colonies is staggering in sheer numbers alone, it would be difficult to overstate its impact on the demography, economy, and infrastructure of the archipelago, not to mention its effect on daily life on the plantations and in the burgeoning towns of the small islands.

Whereas in 1763 no enslaved people were reported in Tobago, by 1773 the 115-square-mile colony counted more than 7,000 enslaved laborers. Grenada's enslaved population doubled in the same decade, rising from approximately 13,000 to more than 26,000 people. A similar trend occurred in Dominica, where the number of enslaved people increased from approximately 5,800 to more than 14,000 between 1763 and 1773. An active regional commerce in human beings meant that the number of enslaved people in French St. Lucia almost tripled in the same period, increasing from slightly more than 5,000 to almost 14,000 individuals. Focusing on the eastern Caribbean illustrates how British and French visions of empire in the period after the Seven Years' War depended on not only the continuation but the expansion of the slave trade. Intent on transforming the Caribbean frontier into a center of sugar production no matter the human cost, both crowns sought to reorient the economy of the islands to benefit the broader empires of which they were now a part.

This reorientation profoundly shaped West African societies, particularly in the Bight of Biafra. To meet the increased demand of European slavers, Efik and Aro merchants expanded the areas in which they traded and raided, driving diverse peoples from the West African hinterland into coastal ports. The Aro incorporated many of these captives into their expanding diaspora, increasing their power in West Africa.[134] For tens of thousands of individuals, however, the lengthy forced journey to the coast was followed by the transformation of "African captives into Atlantic commodities," eligible for sale to transatlantic slavers.[135] As Chapter 5 explores, those who survived the Middle Passage dramatically altered daily life on the Ceded Islands. Yet the personhood of these women and men often disappears in the records of planters and officials, who focused primarily on how enslaved people transformed the colonies' place in transatlantic trade networks.

Ten years after Dominica, Grenada, St. Vincent, and Tobago were incorporated into the British empire, the islands collectively exported almost 300,000 cwt, or more than 33.3 million pounds, of sugar.[136] In the same year Jamaica—an island with a total area more than six times that of the Ceded Islands—exported 1,017,100 cwt of sugar to Great Britain; the Leeward Islands, 248,500 cwt; and Barbados, 110,900 cwt.[137] The fears of pamphleteers who opposed Great Britain's acquisition of the Ceded Islands were forgotten as planters and merchants entered what historian Richard Pares dubbed "the silver age of sugar," a period between 1763 and the American Revolution when the crop fetched on average 50 percent more than it had in the 1730s.[138]

While the majority of sugar exports from the Ceded Islands came from Grenada—the only island where sugar plantations predated the establishment of British rule—sugar production in the other islands increased rapidly. Between 1769 and 1773, the amount of sugar exported from St. Vincent almost tripled, from 21,174 cwt to 58,691 cwt.[139] Exports from French St. Lucia increased at an even faster rate and by 1773 amounted to almost four times what they had been five years earlier.[140] Dominica's exports of sugar during the same period grew an astonishing seventeenfold, from just over 1,500 cwt in 1769 to more than 26,000 cwt by 1773.[141]

These economic transformations reverberated in the lives of enslaved people throughout the region as the kinds of labor they performed, how this labor was organized and policed, and the number, origins, and relationships of the people forced to perform it changed dramatically. Yet investors like William Young

Table 7. Enslaved Populations of the Eastern Caribbean, 1763 and 1773

	St. Lucia		Grenada		Tobago		Dominica	
	1764	*1773*	*1763*	*1773*	*1763*	*1773*	*1763*	*1772*
Enslaved people	5,069	13,782	13,846	26,211	0	7,342	5,872	14,214

Sources: Population figures for 1763 as follows: for St. Lucia, ANOM DPPC G1 506 Recensement 1764; Grenada TNA CO 101/1 N. 5; Dominica TNA CO 101/1 N. 91. For 1773: for St. Lucia ANOM DPPC G1 506 Recensement 1773; for Dominica TNA CO 71/14 N.274; for Tobago TNA CO 101/17 N. 181; for Grenada, TNA CO 101/18 Part II N. 81. Unfortunately, population figures for St. Vincent in this period are not extant.

obscured this reality, choosing instead to use written pamphlets and visual media to present the new colonies as places of order, abundance, and progress. At Young's invitation, in the mid-1760s Italian artist Agostino Brunias traveled to the Ceded Islands. He would ultimately spend more than two decades in the region, serving Young and other wealthy patrons by producing scenes of everyday life that disguised the harsh realities of slavery.[142] Instead, vivid paintings such as *Linen Day, Roseau, Dominica* reflect the predominance of African and Afro-descended people in the new colonies, while ignoring the activities in which they were forced to engage: of the dozens of Brunias pieces that survive, not one depicts plantation production, the violence visited on enslaved people, or the auctions of human beings that regularly occurred throughout the islands.[143]

As depicted by Brunias, the busy market teems with life, as women of color—all clad in impeccably clean dresses or skirts, complemented by colorful kerchiefs and earrings—sell fabrics as well as corn, carrots, plantains, and calabashes. The variety of ships in the painting's background, including simple pirogues on the far right, also nod to the island's bounty and its growing role in wider trade networks, while well-maintained two-story wooden buildings indicate Dominica's urban development. While people from a variety of social classes—from a wealthy white man, to free women of color, to a sailor whose possessions are tucked snugly under his arm—mingle in the crowded marketplace, their respective places in the colonial hierarchy are rendered clear by their dress and the activities in which they engage. Brunias' Dominica is a civilized place, characterized by wealth and harmony, one where slavery flourishes without threatening a social order in which white planters like Young remained a tiny minority.

Brunias's artwork, as well as pamphlets like Young's *Considerations*, obscure how the integration of formerly neutral and Kalinago islands into broader empires irrevocably changed the lives of tens of thousands of Africans

Figure 13. Agostino Brunias, *Linen Day, Roseau, Dominica—A Market Scene*
(c. 1780). Brunias' colorful depiction of life in Dominica disguises the realities
of slavery in the booming British colony. Courtesy Yale Center for British Art.

trafficked to the region, as well as the many people already enslaved in the
islands at the time of their cession. As Chapter 5 shows, in the ensuing years,
enslaved people responded to these changes by deserting plantations and organizing revolts, while Kalinagos engaged in all-out war with British troops. Yet
imperial officials and investors like Young paid little attention to the human
costs of their colonial designs. Vaunting what they saw as the many advantages of developing new territories with the use of enslaved African labor, in
the period after 1763 officials in Great Britain and France, as well as in Spain,
promoted slavery and slave trafficking. Attention to this traffic reveals its centrality to European visions of colonial development, transatlantic commerce,
and the place of West Africa in evolving empires after the Seven Years' War.

* * *

Tracing the surveying, settlement, and economic development of the British
Ceded Islands and of French St. Lucia in the decade after the Seven Years' War

reveals how shared understandings of political economy shaped rival empires. By drawing on and attempting to improve strategies of economic development and colonial rule originally developed in first-phase colonies such as Barbados and Martinique, the British and French crowns succeeded in quickly transforming the eastern Caribbean. As they surveyed and allocated lands, facilitated the free and forced settlement of planters and enslaved people, and encouraged the production of millions of pounds of plantation commodities, particularly sugar, officials and investors like William Young transformed both the islands themselves and their place in broader empires. Just ten short years after Dominica, Grenada, St. Vincent, and Tobago became colonies of Great Britain, they collectively constituted one of the most important sources of wealth in the British empire. This wealth was all the more valuable since older West Indian colonies like Barbados were increasingly suffering the effects of soil exhaustion, resulting in decreased exports of sugar. Although the new French colony of St. Lucia did not produce comparable quantities of sugar, the island fulfilled the complementary goals outlined by the Marine in the wake of the Seven Years' War. In addition to providing a strategic bulwark for France's existing colonies, St. Lucia served as a key node in transatlantic trade, a place to settle French subjects, and a site to grow commodities to enrich the empire.

The rapid economic, demographic, and environmental transformation of the eastern Caribbean came at considerable cost, however. The arrival of colonial officials and new settlers undermined existing agricultural and economic practices as well as structures of authority that free residents of the archipelago like Marie Catherine La Verge La Feuillée proved reluctant to abandon. The ensuing dispute between "natural born" and "new adopted" subjects led the British and French crowns to extend considerable concessions to existing residents of their new colonies, as officials attempted to retain planters and their enslaved laborers in the islands. The conversion of tropical forests to sugarcane fields threatened the dominion Kalinagos had secured through earlier treaties, and they did not hesitate to use force to retain their lands. Faced with harsh new labor regimes, enslaved people engaged in *marronage* and uprisings. Although British and French officials could claim considerable success in the initial implementation of well-researched settlement, agricultural, and economic reforms in their new colonies, they soon discovered that even the best-informed attempts to transform the eastern Caribbean archipelago into a center of plantation production would not be readily accepted by people who had settled in the islands precisely to avoid such transformations. Few people would ever refer to Roseau as Charlottetown, nor would trade be successfully redirected from Dominica's existing port town to the planned capital of Portsmouth. Instead, the imperial reforms and experiments of the post–Seven Years' War era sowed the seeds of contests that would later explode into war.

Chapter 4

Seeking a Place as Colonial Subjects

When Jacques Verger decided to move from the new British colony of St. Vincent to the new French colony of St. Lucia in 1763, he undertook the second interisland and interimperial relocation of his fifty-three years. Born in Les Anses d'Arlet, southwest Martinique, in 1710, Verger married a fellow native of the parish, a woman of color named Victoire Auvray, in 1736.[1] After baptizing their daughter, also named Victoire, in Les Anses d'Arlet later that same year, the family moved to St. Vincent while the island was still a Kalinago domain.[2] Over the course of more than two decades, the Vergers amassed a small estate of thirteen cleared and seven wooded acres on St. Vincent's Leeward coast.[3] But when St. Vincent became a British colony in 1763, Jacques and Victoire elected to leave the island. Along with their mixed-race children—Victoire, Rose, Jacques Jr., Françoise, Pierre, and Marie-Catherine—Jacques and Victoire made the fifty-five-mile journey north from Rothia, St. Vincent, to Anse la Raye, St. Lucia. As they settled on St. Lucia's leeward coast, the Verger family began once again to establish themselves in a new island and under a new political regime.

For the Vergers and the more than one thousand other free residents of the Creole Archipelago who moved to St. Lucia immediately after the 1763 Treaty of Paris, the short ocean journey from one island to another promised new opportunities.[4] Eager to populate the new colony, French officials offered land grants in St. Lucia, and migrants quickly established plantations and forged social and economic relations in the island. For the British crown, however, this same interisland migration posed a threat to broader imperial designs. As William Young, Commissioner for the Sale of Lands in the Ceded Islands, explained, planters who migrated from one island to another—and thus from one empire to another—deprived British colonies of "useful inhabitants." If people like Verger left, Young warned, "their property in negroes to a great amount, together with the produce and revenue arising from their labour, would [be] lost to Great Britain, and acquired by France."[5]

The proximity between competing British and French regimes shaped colonial policies in the eastern Caribbean after the Seven Years' War. As British Secretary of the Treasury Thomas Whately explained, "to insist on the Departure" of people whose "Lands . . . have been cleared by their Labour, and improved with their Substance . . . would be driving them to *St. Lucia,* where great Encouragement is given to Settlers." It was therefore important to convince settlers "of the Advantages arising from the Excellence of the *British* Constitution"; if planters like Verger could not be won over, they could easily decamp to neighboring French colonies. Although Whately was cautious about integrating people he deemed "[s]trangers to our Manners, our Government, and our Religion" into the British empire, he argued that "the Experiment should at least be made." Perhaps these small planters could be transformed into loyal British subjects, "if time be allowed them to familiarize themselves to the Customs and to adopt the Principles" of the crown. After all, Whately reasoned, "they are there; they have Property; they have Wealth; they are People, and People will be very much wanted."[6]

In the wake of the Seven Years' War, the eastern Caribbean became a center of broader contests over the rights and privileges of colonial subjects, as efforts to win the allegiance of existing residents of the Creole Archipelago coincided with wide-ranging debates about the basis and nature of subjecthood. Although the question of whether and how new subjects should be integrated into European empires is often associated with nineteenth- and twentieth-century Africa and Asia, negotiations about the status of colonial subjects also came to the fore in the wake of the 1763 Treaty of Paris.[7] The reorganization of territory in the Americas, India, and the Mediterranean meant that millions of "strangers" now lived in an expanded British empire, and officials had to determine how they should be governed. Drawing parallels between Quebec and Grenada—both former French colonies ceded to Great Britain in 1763—historian Hannah Weiss Muller demonstrates how people termed "new adopted subjects" of King George III used petitions to secure a number of privileges denied to Catholics elsewhere in the empire.[8] Although Muller posits that people in Quebec "were perhaps even more effective" in their quest to "choose and define their subjecthood," the privileges afforded to planters in Grenada actually exceeded those of their fellow former French subjects.[9] In contrast to Quebec, where the decision not to constitute a representative assembly prevented the exercise of electoral privileges, a 1768 Privy Council ruling afforded new subjects in Grenada the right to vote and be elected to Assembly, to be appointed to Colonial Council, and to serve as justices of the peace, all without renouncing their Catholic faith.[10]

While the ruling on new subjects came from the Privy Council, its content was shaped by contests in the Ceded Islands. When Great Britain took control of Grenada in 1763, 646 planters and their families lived alongside more than 13,800 enslaved people in the former French colony.[11] The former Kalinago domain of Dominica counted 1,718 settlers, 5,872 enslaved people, and "from 50 to 60 Caraib familys," while St. Vincent counted 7,414 enslaved and more than 2,100 free residents; only Tobago was reported to be unsettled.[12] British observers who bemoaned that "neither Dominique, nor St. Vincent, had any form of government under the French" missed the many ways in which settlers actively shaped the communities they forged outside the sphere of imperial rule.[13] As heads of households who claimed ownership over lands and people, as members of the Catholic Church, and as defenders of the islands in which they lived, men like Jacques Verger were used to exercising power, albeit not in a formal political capacity. Their determination to maintain this power after 1763 spurred contestation and experimentation throughout the archipelago.

British and French responses to people like Verger illustrate how the very real possibility that resident planters would simply move to another island shaped subjecthood in the eastern Caribbean. Through land grants and leases, the extension of electoral privileges, and the relaxation of legislation that discriminated on the basis of race or religion, in the period after 1763 both crowns sought to convince people like Verger to remain in the islands, where their presence would contribute to broader imperial endeavors. While the crowns' willingness to assimilate people who spoke a different language, practiced a different religion, and in some cases were classified as being of a different race reflects the more expansive understanding of subjecthood that emerged after the Seven Years' War, their policies were also shaped by the actions of new subjects. Conscious of their demographic and economic importance in fledgling sugar colonies, existing planters emphasized the importance of uniting all propertied men against the threat of enslaved insurgency or economic ruin. Through eloquent petitions, French Catholic planters in the Ceded Islands won the right to participate in British colonial politics—provided they were white.

Planters of color who resorted to similar tactics were less successful. Although they also used petitions to argue that they should be granted the same legal and political standing as whites, after the Seven Years' War free people of color throughout the Ceded Islands confronted new laws that diminished their economic and social status and threatened their very freedom. Taking advantage of the region's aqueous geography, many pursued another strategy to maintain the economic and social influence they had built in the decades prior. By migrating to St. Lucia, families like the Vergers continued to exercise the civil rights that served as markers of belonging throughout the French Atlantic, including the right to marry, to create legal contracts, and to own and bequeath property.[14] Examining the various strategies different groups of free people employed to retain rights and influence after 1763 highlights how residents of the Creole Archipelago attempted to maintain key features of the world they had forged outside of empire. In the process, they shaped and challenged evolving understandings of colonial subjecthood in the British and French empires.

The "Yeomanry of the West Indies": New Colonial Subjects in the Eastern Caribbean

British and French officials dispatched to the eastern Caribbean after the Seven Years' War were acutely aware of the benefits of retaining the archipelago's existing settlers, along with the more than 30,000 enslaved people they claimed as their property.[15] With their lands already cleared and worked by an enslaved labor force accustomed to the climate and disease environment of the region, these planters could immediately contribute to the productivity of the new colonies. Better still, rather than living as absentees in Europe, small planters and their families would remain in the islands for generations, serving in the militia and wielding authority over the growing enslaved population. As St. Vincent's British governor explained, this "yeomanry of the West Indies" was "by far the most useful and giving the greatest strength to infant colonies." With "their ideas . . . confined to the spot they have fixed themselves on, their wishes circumscribed to attaining absolute necessaries with a very few comforts for themselves and family," these "yeomen" contributed to the islands' wealth and defense while requiring very little in return.[16] French administrators expressed similar enthusiasm about the role existing planters could play in St. Lucia. "In addition to already being acclimated (which is a great advantage), they are more familiar with the cultivation of the earth and the workings of a plantation," reasoned the colony's intendant.[17] Both crowns were therefore eager to count existing island residents as their subjects, while also securing their allegiance.

It was especially important to do so because planters might just as easily decide to leave. According to Article IV of the 1763 Treaty of Paris, "French inhabitants . . . may retire with all safety and freedom wherever they shall think proper, and may sell their estates, provided it be to the subjects of his Britannick Majesty." Although this article explicitly referred to "inhabitants of Canada," Article IX specified that "the same stipulations in favour of the inhabitants [of Canada]" would apply in Grenada. The treaty further stipulated that former French subjects would have eighteen months to "bring away their effects as well as their persons," meaning planters in Grenada could sell their lands and leave with their enslaved people and the produce of their labor.[18]

These articles did not apply to inhabitants of St. Vincent or Dominica like the Vergers. Unlike French subjects in Grenada, people who settled in Kalinago domains had done so in contravention of earlier treaties. According to British officials, these settlers' "Title to their Estates" were therefore "bad in their Origin, for the king of *France* could not grant where he had not Dominion."[19] Planters in Dominica and St. Vincent were forbidden to sell their lands, and officials were instructed to declare "all such sales . . . null and void."[20]

Despite being prevented from deriving a profit from the lands they claimed, in the wake of the Treaty of Paris dozens of planters like Verger chose to leave Dominica and St. Vincent. Of eighty-three "former French possessors" who relinquished lands in St. Vincent, forty-nine abandoned between ten and fifty acres of cleared land, while a further twenty abandoned between fifty and one hundred acres.[21] The size of their landholdings suggests that these were precisely the sort of small to middling planters that British officials hoped to maintain. Yet in the months after the treaty, Catholic residents of Dominica and St. Vincent, declaring that the prospect of becoming subjects of a Protestant king "revolted them," braved the logistical difficulties of moving family members, enslaved people, livestock, and belongings as much as 130 miles by boat to St. Lucia.[22] Some deliberately destroyed their houses or plantations as they left, depriving the British of their investments.[23]

Eager to avoid this abandonment and destruction, British administrators espoused a "middle way" to retain planters.[24] Rather than having their property confirmed as freehold, as was the case for conquered French subjects in Grenada, existing inhabitants of Dominica and St. Vincent were offered leases of up to forty years, subject to a fine of between £1 and £20 sterling per acre of land.[25] Fines varied depending on the size of landholdings and length of lease and were assessed in addition to an annual quit rent of at least £1 6 d. sterling per acre.[26]

Britain's willingness to allow residents of the Ceded Islands to retain their lands was a direct product of lessons learned in earlier colonial endeavors.[27] When British forces conquered Acadia in 1710, the predominantly French Catholic residents of the new territory were denied title to their lands. People without title to land did not pay taxes to the crown; lacking tax revenue and a representative assembly to allocate the proceeds of that revenue, Acadia languished for decades after its cession to Great Britain. Having failed to reconcile Acadians to British rule, the crown decided instead to expel them, and in 1755 more than ten thousand people were violently removed from the region.[28] This imperial misadventure cast its shadow over British strategies just eight years later, as officials debated how best to rule over people in territories conquered during the Seven Years' War. By treating planters as "new adopted subjects," authorities embraced the possibility that they could be successfully integrated into the body politic.

Reconciling existing settlers to British rule promised to avoid a number of problems that soured attempts like Acadia, and the terms according to which planters in the Ceded Islands were allowed to maintain their lands testify to lessons learned from earlier failures.[29] In order to publicly demonstrate their allegiance to Great Britain, any free settler who wished to continue residing in the islands—regardless of whether they had been a French subject—was required to take oaths of allegiance, supremacy, and abjuration. They were not, however, required to subscribe "the Test," a disavowal of the doctrine of transubstantiation that limited the political participation of Catholics elsewhere in the British empire.[30] Like their fellow new subjects in Quebec, Catholics in Grenada, Dominica, and St. Vincent would be allowed to continue practicing their faith. All that was required in return was that they publicly declare their intention to remain in the colonies and "sincerely promise and swear that I will be faithful and bear true allegiance to His Majesty King George the Third, so help me God."[31]

These terms were enough to convince many planters to remain on their estates. By the middle of 1766, the Commissioners for the Sale of Lands assembled a list of 248 planters in Dominica and 97 in St. Vincent who agreed to retain their lands as leaseholds. While these lists fail to account for the many unpropertied people also in the islands, including planters' wives and children, and urban dwellers such as merchants and artisans, they illuminate the nature of settlements forged outside the sphere of imperial rule. Reflecting

Table 8. Number of Leases in St. Vincent and
Dominica by Cleared Acreage, 1766

Island	10 Acres or Fewer	11 to 50 Acres	51 to 99 Acres	100 Acres or More	Total Leases
St. Vincent	27	47	18	5	97
Dominica	141	92	12	3	248

Sources: TNA CO 106/10 N. 79 and TNA CO 106/10 N. 67, An account of the French inhabitants
. . . whose claims have been allowed by the Commissioners and who paid their fines accordingly,
February 1766.

the importance of maritime routes in the development of the Creole Archipelago, leaseholds tended to hug the islands' calmer leeward coasts. Lands settled
before 1763 were clustered together, testifying to an emphasis on mutual protection against the threat of invasion or enslaved insurgency. The size of plots
suggests the economic activities in which planters engaged: the majority of
lessees claimed fewer than fifty acres of land, enough to cultivate provisions,
coffee, or cacao, but too few to establish a profitable sugar estate. Leaseholds
also reveal the presence of familial networks, suggesting how settlement patterns were shaped by the "micropolitics and microeconomics" of families: of
the forty different lessees in St. Patrick's parish, St. Vincent, four shared the
surname Greaux, four the surname Heude, and four the surname La Roche.[32]
By retaining lands in proximity to one another, lessees maintained personal
and economic relationships forged in the Creole Archipelago.

 These leaseholds demonstrate that many planters who remained in the
islands embodied the yeomen characteristics British officials sought. While a
small number of planters had established large estates in the Kalinago domains,
the overwhelming majority of people who accepted the terms offered by the
British crown had small or middling plantations; in Dominica, more than
half of all leases were for ten acres or fewer of cleared land. Holdings of this
size incurred the minimum required fine of £1 sterling for a forty-year nonre-
newable lease—a considerably smaller financial burden than the cost of relocating to another island. "In compassion to the extreme poverty of a few people,"
the commissioners "suffered a small part of the above account to remain unpaid
until next year," relieving some lessees of even the £1 fine.[33]

 These terms convinced 345 planters who had settled outside of empire to
retain their lands as leases in Dominica and St. Vincent. In Grenada, where former French subjects retained ownership of their lands, the incentive to remain

in the new British colony was even stronger. The 1,225 whites and 455 free people of color resident in Grenada when it was ceded to Great Britain had made considerable investments in the island, creating large sugar estates as well as the smaller coffee and cacao plantations also found in Dominica and St. Vincent.[34] Planters such as Joseph Herbert, whose sugar estate was worked by 169 enslaved adults and 51 enslaved children, risked forfeiting this investment if they chose to leave.[35] Although planters in Grenada, unlike those in Dominica and St. Vincent, were allowed to sell their lands, they were often denied the profits of their estates, as officials did not permit them to include "sugars, coffee, cotton, cacao, or syrops" among the "effects" they took with them if they left.[36]

The prospect of these financial penalties, coupled with the generous terms offered to former French subjects in Grenada, convinced many planters to remain in the new British colony. A 1772 abstract of the state of Grenada counted 334 plantations of at least 10 acres—the minimum acreage required to vote in colonial elections. Of these, 139 were owned by "ancient subjects"— that is, British settlers who came to the island after the Treaty of Paris—and 166 by "new subjects," or former subjects of the French king. Almost a decade after Grenada was ceded to Great Britain, white French planters continued to outnumber their British counterparts. Planters in Grenada laid claim to a total of 26,211 enslaved laborers, who cultivated more than 74,000 acres of land, including more than 32,000 acres of sugar and almost 13,000 acres of coffee. Less than a decade after the Seven Years' War, the vision of plantation production and economic prosperity championed by British officials had been realized. However, the majority of people who contributed to this vision were not natural-born British subjects but Catholic former subjects of the French crown, many of whom were people of color.

A nominative census of Grenada, also taken in 1772, further illuminates the respective positions of French and British planters. The census notes the names of individual planters, as well as the number of enslaved people and number of acres of sugarcane, coffee, cacao, or indigo to which each planter laid claim. Only two people on the nominative list owned fewer than ten acres of land: Madame Ponce, who had seven acres planted in coffee, and Jeanot Paponet, "FM"—free mulatto—in the census, who had nine acres of coffee.[37] Rather than pointing to an absence of small planters in Grenada, this suggests that British census takers did not consider those with small plots of land to be important enough to merit inclusion or that smallholders were able to evade the census. Yet as evidenced by Dominica and St. Vincent, where at least 168 planters leased fewer than ten acres each, it was common for people who grew

Table 9. State of Grenada, 1772

Parish	Old Subjects (British Planters)	New Subjects (French Planters)	Enslaved People	Acres of Sugarcane, Pasture, Provisions	Acres of Coffee, Pasture, Provisions	Acres of Cacao, Pasture, Provisions
St. George	23	39	5,717	6,440	2,061	60
St. John	16	14	2,773	3,139	1,247	335
St. Mark	13	21	2,331	1,716	1,714	92
St. Patrick	27	21	4,765	7,723	1,614	185
St. Andrew	43	44	7,234	8,761	4,160	40
St. David	17	27	3,371	4,232	2,000	0
Total	**139**	**166**	**26,211**	**32,011**	**12,796**	**712**

Source: TNA CO 101/18 Part II, N. 81, Abstract of the State of the Island of Grenada, April 1772.

provisions, coffee, or cacao to do so on small plots. The 1772 abstract therefore failed to count many small French planters who continued to live in Grenada.

The abstract also failed to account for planters of color. While the 1772 list counts 166 "new subjects" and 139 "ancient subjects," the nominative census of the same year names an additional 25 individuals not assigned to either category. Instead, the columns noting whether people like Philibert Fouchier, FM, who had 100 acres planted in coffee, or Agathe, FN ("free negro"), who owned a 32-acre coffee estate, were "ancient" or "new" subjects are left blank, suggesting that British census takers did not consider free people of color to be legitimate colonial subjects. All told, the 25 planters explicitly identified as FM or FN in the nominative census laid claim to 1,198 acres of land and 389 enslaved people. Agathe, whose lack of a surname suggests that she was formerly enslaved, claimed ownership over 20 individuals, while Philibert Fouchier claimed 30.[38] All 25 people of color had French names, indicating that the number of Francophone Catholic planters living under British rule was even greater than the 1772 abstract suggests. While none of these individuals owned sugar estates, they represented an important part of Grenada's class of small to middling French planters. By declining to classify them as new subjects, administrators signaled that the place planters of color had secured for themselves under French rule would not necessarily be recognized by the British.

Declining to count planters of color as new subjects also allowed British authorities to mask the extent to which British settlers remained outnumbered in the new colonies. While the abstract of Grenada noted 39 new and 23 ancient subjects in St. George, eight planters of color, each with more than 10 acres of land, also appeared in the parish's nominative census. This means that French planters outnumbered their British counterparts 47 to 23, or more than two to one, in Grenada's principal parish, with people of color accounting for almost 20 percent of St. George's French planters.[39]

Patterns were similar in St. Patrick and St. John, the two parishes where British planters appeared to enjoy a demographic majority. In St. Patrick, five planters of color raised the total number of French planters with more than 10 acres of land in the parish to 26—just one fewer than their British counterparts. In the parish of St. John, where British officials counted 16 ancient and 14 new subjects, the five planters of color named in the nominative census brought the actual number of French planters to 19; although British authorities declined to afford them the status of new adopted subjects, people identified as being of African descent accounted for more than one-quarter of French planters in the parish.[40]

While French planters in the Ceded Islands, regardless of race, were usually not as wealthy as their British counterparts, they fulfilled the role of resident yeomen vaunted by administrators. Throughout the new colonies, British planters overwhelmingly invested in sugar production, whereas French planters were more likely to retain the coffee or cacao estates they established before 1763. Of 6,440 acres planted in "canes, pastures and provisions" in St. George, 2,365 acres, or just 37 percent of the total, belonged to French planters. French planters also owned just three of the parish's twelve water mills, meaning that while British planters constituted a demographic minority in St. George, they undertook the majority of investment in sugar planting and processing. But British planters invested in sugar at the expense of other commodities: of 2,061 acres planted in coffee in St. George, just 573 belonged to British planters, meaning that French planters—both whites and people of color—controlled more than 70 percent of coffee production in the parish.[41]

The number of enslaved laborers to which French and British planters respectively laid claim further testifies to the kind of production each group pursued. Although French planters in St. George greatly outnumbered their British counterparts, they claimed ownership over 2,548 of the parish's 5,717 enslaved people, or just 44.5 percent of enslaved people; of these, 98 were claimed by the parish's eight planters of color.[42] Similar patterns held true in St. John and St. Patrick, where French planters invested in coffee and cacao rather than sugar and laid claim to far fewer enslaved laborers.[43] Despite being generally less well-off than newly arrived British planters, people who had settled in Grenada before 1763 continued to constitute a demographic majority among the colony's planter class.

The tendency for new subjects in Grenada to continue investing in crops requiring less land and fewer laborers did not mean that there were no wealthy French planters in the colony. By 1772, the heirs of Joseph Herbert increased the number of enslaved people on their plantation from 220 to 280; at 516 acres, theirs was the single largest sugar estate in St. Patrick's parish.[44] In St. Andrew, the most populous of Grenada's six parishes, the biggest sugar estate also belonged to a French planter: Paul Mignot Devoconnu's 576-acre plantation was worked by 170 enslaved people. Elsewhere in the same parish, Pierre Fournillier owned a 372-acre sugar estate worked by 160 enslaved people, while Julien Houe's 388-acre sugar plantation was worked by 150 enslaved people.[45] In addition to fulfilling the role of resident yeoman who could help maintain order in the colonies, some French planters wielded considerable economic power.

By the mid-1770s, the pattern that developed in Grenada also held true in Dominica and St. Vincent. While new British investors laid claim to the majority of land and enslaved people, French-speaking Catholic families, whether white, Black, or mixed race, continued to constitute a majority of the free population in all three islands.[46] French planters in Dominica and St. Vincent were much more likely to lease their lands rather than own them as freeholds, and their plots were generally smaller than those of British planters. Despite this, some laid claim to considerable tracts of land: by 1773, the largest French planter in St. Vincent, Quitell (Questel), leased 177 acres, while in Dominica, Pierre Jolly leased 238 acres.[47] While their tenure was less secure than that of landowners in Grenada, leaseholders in Dominica and St. Vincent were aware that they played essential roles in peopling, defending, and maintaining order in colonies that increasingly depended on the exploitation of an enslaved majority.

Encouraged by the terms offered by the British crown, hundreds of planters who had established themselves in the Creole Archipelago elected to remain in Dominica, Grenada, and St. Vincent when they were ceded to Great Britain in 1763. While most fulfilled the role of resident yeomen sought by British officials, some were among the most prosperous planters in their respective parishes. As heads of household, members of the militia, and the owners of land and enslaved people, these planters—both whites and people of color—contributed to the security and prosperity of the islands, and they expected to continue exercising influence as a result. They soon sought to secure this influence through the official channels offered by British colonial rule, generating debates over subjecthood that reverberated far beyond the archipelago.[48]

Accommodating New Subjects:
Political Participation in the Ceded Islands

The creation of councils and assemblies throughout the Ceded Islands soon provided an opportunity for some existing residents of the Creole Archipelago to translate their economic and demographic influence into formal political power. Despite the vocal protests of many natural-born British subjects, in the decade after 1763 new subjects in the Ceded Islands fought for and secured political privileges that exceeded those of Catholics elsewhere in the British empire. While other scholars have shown how Grenada served as one of several sites where new subjects pushed for a "more flexible and expansive attitude towards subjecthood," less attention has been paid to how planters' experiences shaped their expectations of inclusion.[49] As historian Dominique Rogers argues, in the French Atlantic very few people enjoyed formal political rights such as voting or sitting on a colonial council. Instead, "citizenship was realized in the civil domain," as both whites and free people of color created legal contracts, owned and bequeathed property, and celebrated religious rites.[50] Capitalizing on Great Britain's desire to transform the Ceded Islands into a center of sugar production, existing residents of the archipelago worked to protect those rights, while also securing the privileges of British subjects such as the right to vote, to serve on appointed councils and elected assemblies, and to act as justices of the peace. The decision to allow white French Catholics to participate in British colonial government testifies to their continued influence as the Creole Archipelago was assimilated into existing empires, while simultaneously illustrating how the position of free people of color came under attack following the turn to British colonial rule.

In April 1764, eighteen of the most prominent British subjects in the Ceded Islands, including the respective lieutenant-governors of St. Vincent, Dominica, Grenada, and Tobago, were appointed to a colonial council for the Southern Caribbee Islands.[51] This new administrative entity united the islands into a single government, headquartered in Grenada and placed under the authority of Governor-General Robert Melvill. As was customary elsewhere in the British empire, councilors were all wealthy white Protestant men.

While they were not paid for their services—which included advising Melvill, serving as a court of appeal, and acting as a legislative upper house—they benefited from government patronage, using their position on the council to advance their economic and political agenda.[52]

Soon after the council was established, interested parties requested the creation of a complementary elected assembly, which Melvill granted in February 1766. Although his ordinance was intended to regulate "elections for a general assembly" of all four islands, Melvill noted "the emergencies of Government in Grenada, are so great and pressing, as to make it indispensably necessary" to constitute "an Assembly for Grenada and the Grenadines only"; Dominica, St. Vincent, and Tobago would have to wait until they had "a sufficient number of freeholders to enable them to elect and send representatives."[53] The decision to create an assembly in each colony shaped the nature and extent of political participation in individual islands, as resident planters used their social and economic capital to press for political privileges.

In Grenada, former subjects of the French king immediately asserted what they saw as their right to participate in colonial politics. Arguing that elsewhere in the British West Indies "it has been a long-adopted maxim to permit Roman Catholics and other dissenters from the Church of England, to give their votes in the choice of representatives," in February 1766, thirty-five planters who identified themselves as "His Majesty's Adopted Subjects" petitioned Melvill for voting rights. While the signatories were "conscious of the impropriety of exercising their own persons the functions of representative," they insisted on their right to vote for properly qualified Protestant candidates.[54] The petitioners were drawn from a range of social classes, from small planters such as Olivier, whose thirteen-acre coffee estate barely met the ten-acre minimum required to vote, to Devoconnu, who owned the largest sugar plantation in St. Andrew. None of them were identified as "FM" or "FN," meaning they all benefited from the status of propertied white men.[55]

The petitioners' rhetoric testifies to their political savvy, while their eloquent language strongly suggests that they cultivated ties with Anglophone planters sympathetic to their cause. While acknowledging that planters in Grenada were "gather'd from different quarters," these self-identified "adopted subjects" stressed the importance of uniting all free people against an enslaved majority. "In a colony, whose cultivation, depend[s] on the number, labour and submission of negroes," they argued, it was necessary to have "absolute influence in the hands of every freeholder, in order to maintain [enslaved people] in proper discipline and respect." Asserting that creating inequalities between planters risked "approach[ing] them to the level of their slaves," the petitioners emphasized the importance of policing social boundaries in small islands that relied on slavery. In clear, forceful language, they referenced the "dangerous" and "odious" internal threats Grenada could face if Melvill failed to elevate all planters to the status of voters. It was only right, they argued, that "the rigor of the law concerning the qualifications of electors," that had "been found usefull [sic] to be relaxed" in order to promote the "encouragement of settlers in many of His Majesty's [other] colonies" also be applied in Grenada.[56]

Despite the petitioners' assertion that it was customary for "Roman Catholics and other dissenters from the Church of England to be able to give their votes," elsewhere in the British empire men who professed the Catholic faith were generally excluded from voting.[57] An important exception to this rule was in Montserrat, which was predominantly settled by Catholics from Ireland. Owing to the small number of Protestant men in the island, Catholics were permitted to vote for the Montserrat assembly provided that they swore oaths of allegiance and supremacy to the British crown.[58] Perhaps taking a cue from these practices, Melvill's ordinance stipulated that any of "His Majesty's New-adopted Subjects" age twenty-one or older who owned at least ten acres of land in the island could vote, provided that he produce a certificate showing he had taken the oaths required of all former French subjects who elected to stay in Grenada. Although Catholics could vote, the possibility that they might be elected to Assembly was foreclosed by the stipulation that any candidate be a "*Protestant* Natural Born, or Naturalized Subject" who possessed at least fifty acres of land in the parish where he sought election.[59]

Despite these restrictions, the mere prospect that Catholics—let alone Catholic former subjects of a rival Crown—might have a voice in determining the Grenada assembly alarmed British residents of the colony. Noting "the vast superiority of the French Inhabitants in point of numbers," eighteen British planters presented Melvill with a countermemorial highlighting the dangers of allowing new subjects to vote.[60] The petitioners warned that in addition to the fact that the demographic weight of French planters would allow them to dominate elections, new subjects might attempt to nominate men from their own ranks as candidates. The lead signatories of the tract, Ninian Home and Alexander Campbell, were both Scottish-born planters with estates in St. Andrew. By 1772, six years after they lodged their petition, Home had 160 acres planted in sugar and 100 acres planted in coffee, while Campbell had 233 acres planted in sugar and 190 planted in coffee. Although both estates were considerable, neither rivaled those of French planters such as Devoconnu, who had 576 acres of sugar.[61] Like their fellow signatories, neither Campbell nor Home had been appointed to Council. Serving on the assembly therefore represented their primary opportunity to exercise political influence—an influence they were reluctant to cede.

Not all of Home's and Campbell's fellow subjects shared their fears. In a memorial submitted the same day, twenty-six of "His Majesty's Natural Born Subjects" counseled Melvill against "placing the power of election in too few hands" and urged him to permit Catholic freeholders in Grenada to exercise their "natural right" to vote.[62] Only one of the men who signed the memorial in support of French planters, Frederick Corsar, was a member of Council, and many of the men who supported Catholic voting rights in Grenada were at least as wealthy as their counterparts who were opposed. William Macintosh, who like Home, Campbell, and Devoconnu lived in St. Andrew, had two sugar estates in the parish, of 238 and 218 acres, respectively.[63] While other signatories were less prominent, they nonetheless belonged to Grenada's planter class. Their warning that "the exclusion of so many persons from the natural right they claim of voting for Protestant representatives properly qualified," might occasion "the departure of many wealthy and industrious inhabitants from an island imperfectly settled," was therefore persuasive. Cautioning that failure to allow French planters to vote might "ferment continual jealousies and feuds between the natural and adopted subjects," British petitioners joined with French planters to encourage Melvill not to "alienat[e] the minds of the latter from their attachment to His Majesty's person and government."[64]

While the petitioners could do little to alter Melvill's existing ordinance, their arguments presaged the contentious nature of the assembly that was elected as a result of their competing agendas. Although Melvill allowed freeholders with more than ten acres of land to cast their votes for Protestant representatives, he promptly dissolved the assembly at its inaugural meeting in April 1766, citing the members' desire to obtain privileges "as largely and favourably as possible from those of every British colony of which they had any knowledge."[65] Having publicly demonstrated his power over the assembly, Melvill allowed new elections to be called and regular meetings to resume in October 1766. Of the twenty-one white Protestant men elected to this second Grenada assembly, five had signed the memorial protesting the participation of new subjects, while four others had signed the petition defending French Catholics' right to vote. Home, a lead signatory of the memorial against French participation, became speaker of the assembly, while Macintosh, who publicly defended new subjects, was chairman.[66] Despite the assembly's factious composition, the elected representatives succeeded in passing a number of bills before its scheduled expiration in April 1767.[67]

Encouraged by events in Grenada, leading planters in other Ceded Islands also began agitating for the creation of governing bodies through which they could formally exercise power. In December 1766, British planters in St. Vincent petitioned Melvill for their own assembly. Insisting that St. Vincent's particular "condition and circumstances" necessitated a separate government, the petitioners invoked their familiarity with the colony to secure greater control over day-to-day affairs.[68] Although Melvill was reluctant to abandon the idea of creating a general assembly for all four Ceded Islands, he granted the settlers' request in February 1767.[69] Planters and merchants with interests in Dominica similarly sought to exercise greater control over their affairs, and in December 1767 the Board of Trade ruled that a separate council and assembly be created for the island.[70] As was the case in Grenada, new subjects in St. Vincent and Dominica who had taken the oaths of allegiance, supremacy, and abjuration and who owned more than ten acres of land were permitted to vote for properly qualified Protestant representatives but were not eligible for election.[71] Although most of the people who had settled in the islands before the Seven Years' War failed to meet these property qualifications—by 1773, just eight French planters in St. Vincent and fifty-seven in Dominica had managed to purchase freeholds—the regulations meant that men who had exercised influence in the Creole Archipelago had the opportunity to continue shaping affairs in the new British colonies.[72]

Although propertied new subjects quickly secured voting rights throughout the Ceded Islands, they were forbidden to stand for election. This prohibition was soon tested in Grenada, when in November 1767 Jean Baptiste Dumonchy, a "professed French Roman Catholic, not understanding one syllable of English," presented himself as a candidate for the assembly.[73] A resident of St. Andrew's parish, by 1772 Dumonchy was the joint owner of a 180-acre sugar estate worked by fifty-three enslaved people.[74] While he therefore met the 50-acre minimum freehold required of planters wishing to stand for election, the polling officer refused Dumonchy's candidacy on the basis of his religion. Although Dumonchy was forbidden to run, his fellow new subjects used their voting privileges to elect British planters who would support their cause, resulting in a deeply divided assembly. Lamenting "the excessive terms of difference, and reproach," that characterized relations in Grenada, Melvill complained that no bills would be passed until a less "factious" assembly could be elected. The governor was clear about the consequences of failing to broker peace between planters in Great Britain's most promising new colony:

unless French Catholics could be reconciled to British rule, Melvill warned, the crown stood "a very great risk of losing the colony in the first War."[75]

The fear that planters in Grenada would betray their new sovereign spurred officials in England to take unprecedented measures to win their allegiance. In September 1768, the Court of King's Bench ruled that Catholic subjects of the King of France who were resident in Grenada at the time of the island's cession would be eligible for a number of key positions. Unlike in Quebec, where administrators were forbidden to appoint former French subjects to Council or to serve as superior court judges, in Grenada the governor was empowered to name two new subjects to Council and to appoint a French Catholic justice of the peace in each parish.[76] The ruling further specified that as many as three new subjects could be elected to the Grenada assembly. While French Catholics had to take the oaths of allegiance, supremacy, and abjuration in order to accede to these coveted positions, they were not required to deny transubstantiation. Significantly, these concessions applied only to Catholic former subjects of the king of France; English and Scottish Catholics continued to be barred from Grenada politics unless they publicly subscribed the Test.[77]

The practice of granting concessions to accommodate and appease new British subjects was not unique to the Ceded Islands. In contemporaneous Quebec, former French subjects were permitted to serve as notaries, lawyers, bailiffs, and even judges of the Prerogative Court.[78] Yet the privileges extended to French Catholic planters in Grenada were generous even relative to those granted to their fellow new subjects elsewhere in the British empire. Eager to "restore that Harmony and Tranquillity upon which the peace and welfare of that island so much depend," officials in Great Britain granted unparalleled "indulgence" to people whose support was deemed essential to preventing unrest in the plantation colony.[79] While their decision to do so was intended to win the allegiance of French Catholics, it sowed further discord between natural-born and adopted subjects in Grenada.

Governor Melvill having temporarily returned to England, Ulysses Fitzmaurice, lieutenant-governor of St. Vincent and acting governor of the Southern Caribbee Islands during Melvill's absence, was tasked with implementing the ruling. Careful to select "persons of the most unexceptionable conduct and character as well as of considerable property" in the island, in August 1769 Fitzmaurice appointed Paul Mignot Devoconnu and Charles Nicolas Chanteloupe to Council.[80]

The appointment of Devoconnu and Chanteloupe rather than Dumonchy affirms how local power and influence shaped political inclusion. As of

1772, Devoconnu owned the largest sugar estate in St. Andrew's parish, while Chanteloupe, jointly with Le Quoy, owned a 375-acre estate with 188 acres planted in sugarcane in St. George.[81] As their respective positions suggest, both men were used to exercising influence, and they eagerly accepted Fitzmaurice's nomination. When they presented themselves at Council on August 24, 1769, however, six of the eight councilors present walked out in protest.[82] Justifying their actions on the grounds that as acting governor, Fitzmaurice lacked the power to appoint new members, the councilors drafted a resolution publicly denouncing the appointment of Devoconnu and Chanteloupe.[83] Fitzmaurice, who was supposed to preside over all Council proceedings, found out about the resolution only after it was published in the *Grenada Gazette*. Incensed at their "scandalous" behavior, he suspended the six members who had withdrawn from Council, accusing them of attempting to "throw a contempt upon His Majesty's representative, and to subvert his authority."[84]

With tensions mounting between the acting governor and some of the most prominent planters under his government, the matter was referred to Fitzmaurice's superiors in England. Hoping to "quiet the animosities which have so long disturbed peace" in Grenada, in April 1770 the Court of St. James tried to reconcile natural and adopted subjects to British rule. In addition to reinstating the six suspended councilors, the court ruled that Devoconnu could be sworn in to replace Councilor Gordon, who had previously resigned.[85] Returning to Grenada after his furlough in England, Governor Melvill restored the suspended members and confirmed Devoconnu as councilor on June 22, 1770.[86]

Although British subjects both in the Ceded Islands and in mainland North America continued to protest extending political privileges to Catholics, they were unable to reverse the court's ruling.[87] In February 1771, following the death of Councilor John Harvey, the court also confirmed Chanteloupe's appointment to Council.[88] As Melvill's successor, William Leyborne, reminded members of Grenada's council and assembly in a March 1772 address, "the admission of His Majesty's New Subjects into . . . offices of Trust" was "permanently fixed." "Whatever private wishes or partialitys [sic] may have heretofore prevailed," it was now time for old and new British subjects to "all Unite, and with zeal and alacrity apply ourselves to the dispatch of the publick business."[89]

Eager to retain white planters in what they hoped would be some of their most successful sugar colonies, in the wake of the Seven Years' War British officials significantly enlarged their definition of who could exercise the rights and privileges of colonial subjects. By the 1770s, propertied French Catholics throughout the Ceded Islands had translated their demographic weight into voting rights, and in Grenada former subjects of the French king were also eligible for election to the assembly and appointment as councilors and justices of the peace. Yet even this broader definition of colonial subjecthood had limits. While white French Catholics succeeded in obtaining unparalleled accommodations from the British crown, free people of color who had settled in the Creole Archipelago soon discovered that the extension of British colonial rule threatened the rights they had long exercised, and even their very freedom.

"Without any discriminating regard to complexion": Planters of Color and the Limits of British Colonial Subjecthood

The period after the Seven Years' War was marked by a proliferation of legislation limiting the economic and social standing of free people of African descent throughout the Atlantic World, as officials sought to link Blackness with debasement.[90] While laws that restrained the property rights of free people of color, diminished their legal personhood, and subjected them to the direct surveillance of whites had been in place in other British colonies for decades, efforts to extend this legislation to the Ceded Islands met with resistance.[91] Planters of color who had established themselves in the Creole Archipelago before 1763 drew on a variety of strategies to counter attempts to limit the economic and social status they had built. Like their white counterparts, some free people of color in the Ceded Islands turned to petitions to safeguard their rights, publicly asserting that their race should not prevent them from participating in plantation society. Others capitalized on the proximity of a competing colonial regime, migrating to French St. Lucia to maintain property and influence. While planters of color did not always succeed in defending their status as equal members of plantation society, their efforts to do so highlight a lengthy contest between colonial law and local understandings of legitimate authority first developed outside the sphere of imperial rule. Rather than emphasizing their connections with whites, as wealthy people of color did in contemporaneous Jamaica, in the Ceded Islands people of African descent insisted that their ancestry should not prevent them from continuing to enjoy the rights they had exercised for generations.

In eighteenth-century Jamaica, a small number of mixed-race elites used privilege bills to obtain rights otherwise reserved for white men.[92] Yet these bills depended on an individual successfully "invoking . . . their blood ties to the white community," and the privileges they afforded became increasingly rare as administrators sought to police the growing population of people of color.[93] In 1761, the Jamaica assembly forbid "mulattoes"—broadly defined to include anyone less than four generations removed from an African ancestor—to inherit property worth more than £2,000.[94] Like the 1726 law barring people of color from receiving bequests from whites in Martinique, such decrees relegated people of African descent to a degraded position in colonial society by attacking their right to control and transmit property.[95]

Laws introduced in the Ceded Islands after 1763 similarly sought to prevent free people of African descent from exercising the same rights as whites. In 1767, a law "for the better government of slaves and free negroes" forbid people of color from owning more than eight acres of land. In addition to restraining their economic prospects, this cap ensured that men of color would not amass the minimum ten acres of land required to exercise voting rights. Unpropertied people of color such as urban artisans were in an even more tenuous position, as the same law required them to "choose some master or mistress . . . with whom they shall live and take their abode, to the intent that their lives and conversations may be known and observed."[96] Other acts threatened their very freedom; any "Negroe or Mulattoe" who failed to furnish proof of free status would be "advertized [sic] . . . in the most Publick Places of Resort in the Islands," and thereafter sold "at Publick Outcry, as a Slave."[97] The humiliating nature of these acts provides a chilling glimpse of the new regime of racial violence that accompanied the introduction of British rule. Even if such laws were rarely enforced, the fact that they were passed illustrates how people who had amassed property and influence in the Creole Archipelago faced new threats under colonial regimes.

In addition to the twenty-five planters listed as FN or FM in Grenada, who each owned between ten and one hundred acres of land—far more than the maximum eight acres now allowed by law—planters explicitly identified as people of color were among those who retained their lands as leaseholds elsewhere in the Ceded Islands. In Dominica, Paul Dubois, "free negroe," paid the minimum fine of £1 to lease ten acres, while Henry St. Onge, "mullato," paid a total of £68 to lease two plots of sixteen acres each.[98] While people of color like Roy Le Train, who owned seventy-four acres worked by forty enslaved people in Grenada, risked losing their status as middling planters as a result of laws limiting land ownership, many other free people of color now faced increased surveillance, suspicion, and harassment, and even possible enslavement.[99]

Objecting to "exceedingly oppressive" laws that "abstracted, particularized, and distinguished them from the rest of their fellow subjects with an inequality totally unmerited," in 1777 more than 110 self-identified "free negros, mulatto's and mustees" in Dominica petitioned King George III for the abolition of a 1774 act pertaining to free people of color.[100] The act included clauses that allowed justices of the peace to order summary punishments for free people of color, including whipping, at their discretion; that prevented any free person of color from giving evidence against any white person in capital cases; and that explicitly disqualified free people of color from voting for the election of representatives to the island's colonial assembly—all of which, the petitioners argued, violated the principles by which "their most Gracious and Religious Sovereign . . . governs his people indiscriminately."[101]

The organized and vehement opposition to this legislation indicates that people of color who had settled outside of empire, like their white counterparts, expected to continue exercising influence in the islands in which they lived. The more than 110 individuals who signed their names or made their marks on the petition stated that they "humbly expect[ed] to partake (in common with the rest of their fellows subjects and without any discriminating regard had to complexion) of the common constitutional blessings which they, as Your Majesty's dutiful loyal subjects most humbly apprehend themselves to be justly intitled."[102] Like the memorial of former French subjects who asserted their right to participate in British government in Grenada eleven years earlier, the petition supporting the rights of free people of color in Dominica evidences considerable political savvy and a strong grasp of the English language. The names of some petitioners, such as Abigail Oats and Samuel Buckley, hint at origins in the English Atlantic, suggesting their role in crafting the call for inclusion. But the majority of those who lent their names to the petition indicated their support with a simple cross, suggesting that although as individuals they lacked the literacy to mount such an eloquent protest against discriminatory legislation, as a community they affirmed the importance and influence of free people of color in the eastern Caribbean.

Some of the signatories were not previously identified as people of color, illustrating how African ancestry became a more salient marker after the introduction of colonial rule. When they agreed to lease their existing lands in Dominica in 1766, men like Jean Baptiste Scipion, who paid £28 for nine cleared and ten wooded acres, and Louis Martin, who paid £32 for thirteen cleared and thirteen wooded acres, did not have a racial descriptor attached to their names.[103] Instead, their claims to land, and to enslaved people to work that land, afforded them membership in Dominica's small planter class. Yet by 1777, both men chose to identify themselves among the "free negroes, mulatto's and mustees" who publicly objected to their treatment under British rule. As legislation increasingly limited the status of people of African descent throughout the Atlantic World, these small planters, who may have been "mustees," or people three generations removed from an African ancestor, aligned themselves not with white planters but with people of color.[104]

The specific clauses to which the petitioners objected reveal the status they were accustomed to enjoying. Among the clauses they found most injurious were those that vested justices of the peace with "a discretionary power of whipping" free people of color, that "disqualified [them] from voting for persons to represent them in [Dominica's] House of Assembly," and that prohibited them from giving testimony against whites. The preamble to the 1773 act specified that "whereas free Negroes Mulattos and Mustees *have been admitted to give evidence* in the courts of Justice of this Island in Capital Cases against White people," their testimony would no longer be allowed.[105] That free people of color in Dominica were permitted to testify against whites suggests the extent to which they continued to benefit from rights and privileges denied to their counterparts in colonies such as Barbados, where free people of color were prohibited from giving evidence in court trials as of 1721.[106] By defending their right to participate in the judicial system—even when it involved testifying against people the colonial state considered to be of inherently higher status—free people of color in Dominica asserted the continued legitimacy of their claims to property, status, and respect.[107]

The petitioners' objection to not being allowed to vote for the assembly is even more intriguing. Might free people of color in the Ceded Islands have participated in colonial elections in the 1760s and 1770s—a participation long denied to their counterparts in other British colonies?[108] The clause respecting voting rights in the 1773 act has no preamble, and surviving voter returns for the colonies indicate only how many votes by old and new subjects were cast for each candidate; because the names of individual voters are not given, their race cannot be ascertained.[109] Nonetheless, the fact that people who identified as and were recognized by others to be "Negro, Mulatto, or Mustee" felt justified in petitioning for electoral privileges illustrates how ideas of respectability, authority, and inclusion developed outside the sphere of imperial rule continued to compete with those introduced by colonial officials. Rather than seeking the privileges of whites on an individual basis, as in Jamaica, in the

Ceded Islands people of African descent joined together to insist that their roles as the owners of property in land and people, heads of household, and defenders against an enslaved majority entitled them to the same rights as their fellow subjects.

Once again, officials in England saw fit to intervene in disputes in the Ceded Islands. In June 1778, the Board of Trade ruled that while the clause pertaining to the inadmissibility of evidence given by free people of color was justified, "the discretionary power of punishment . . . appears to us reprehensible." Instead, the board amended the act so that "free negroes, mulattoes, and mustees will be distinguished from those in actual slavery, and at the same time be put upon such a different footing from His Majesty's white subjects . . . as true policy requires, and indeed renders, in our opinion, absolutely necessary."[110] Although free people of African descent highlighted their contributions to colonial society as planters, heads of household, and "dutiful loyal subjects," in the wake of the Seven Years' War they failed to secure the same rights as their white counterparts. The introduction of British rule placed new limits on free people of color by formally diminishing their economic and legal standing, explicitly differentiating them from whites, and consigning them to a middle status between planters and their human chattel. Unable to exercise the rights they had established in the Creole Archipelago, in the period after 1763 some free people of color began to seek spaces where they could continue to participate in plantation society, "without any discriminating regard had to complexion."

Interisland Migration and Attempts to Retain Rights

The proximity of a competing colonial regime offered planters of color in the eastern Caribbean opportunities increasingly unavailable to them elsewhere in the colonial Americas. Like their British counterparts, French colonial officials sought to bolster the permanent population of their new colony, St. Lucia, and they therefore offered migrants a number of incentives. Unlike in British Dominica and St. Vincent, where existing planters saw their landholdings converted into leases, in St. Lucia planters and migrants received land grants "according to the number and strength of each family."[111] By abolishing the *droit d'aubaine*, which confiscated the property of foreigners who died within the French realm, officials sought to encourage the subjects of other crowns to settle in the nascent colony.[112] Perhaps even more important to mixed-race migrants, in St. Lucia laws that limited the economic and legal status of free people of color were frequently disregarded or loosely enforced.

When Jacques Verger, his wife Victoire Auvray, and their six mixed-race children made the difficult decision to leave their home in St. Vincent to journey to St. Lucia, they may have been buoyed by thoughts of the economic, legal, and social benefits their interisland migration could offer. By moving to the French colony, Verger obtained title to land that he could sell or bequeath to his children, whose status as *gens de couleur,* or free people of color, would not restrict them to owning just eight acres of land as it would in neighboring British colonies. Instead of limits, St. Lucia offered opportunities for this large Creole family: while Verger abandoned thirteen cleared and seven wooded acres of land in St. Vincent, by 1771 he owned 40 quarrés, or 128 acres, in Anse la Raye, just south of St. Lucia's new capital, Castries.[113]

In addition to improving their status as landholders, moving from St. Vincent to St. Lucia allowed the Vergers to preserve familial and social connections first forged outside of empire. Surviving Catholic records for Anse la Raye show that in the late 1760s and early 1770s, six Verger children celebrated marriages in the parish. On July 14, 1767, Françoise Verger married Jean Baptiste Fournier, a fellow former resident of St. Vincent.[114] Like the Vergers, the Fourniers were a mixed-race family who improved their economic position by moving from St. Vincent to St. Lucia. Jean Baptiste's father, Jean Fournier, abandoned forty-one cleared acres, a house, and a storehouse in Ouassigany, which British planter Harry Alexander purchased from the Commissioners for the Sale of Lands for £17 sterling per acre—a price that suggests the land was well developed.[115] By 1771, Jean Fournier had accumulated 63 quarrés, or more than 200 acres, in Anse la Raye. His son Jean Baptiste, Françoise Verger's husband, had 20 quarrés, or approximately 64 acres, in the same parish, considerably more than he would have stood to inherit from his father in St. Vincent—had he, as a person of color, had the right to inherit land at all.[116]

Like his sister Françoise, Pierre Verger married a fellow native of St. Vincent in Anse la Raye, St. Lucia, suggesting that relationships forged in one island persisted and even deepened in diaspora.[117] Pierre's eighteen-year-old bride, a mulatresse named Marianne Caumond, was orphaned by the time of their 1772 marriage, but her father, Baptiste Caumond, had also made the journey from St. Vincent to St. Lucia after the Seven Years' War. Like the Fournier family, the twenty-one cleared and thirteen wooded acres of land that Baptiste Caumond abandoned in Ouassigany were purchased by Harry Alexander: the Verger siblings' new spouses had been neighbors in St. Vincent.

Marianne's uncle, Pierre Caumond, who acted as her guardian, had also moved from St. Vincent to St. Lucia, abandoning twelve cleared and eight wooded acres in Ouassigany.[118]

As the maintenance of familial and personal ties across islands and empires suggests, some of the factors that motivated individuals and families to remove themselves beyond the reach of British rule were less tangible—but no less important—than those of finances or title to land. For the Verger, Fournier, and Caumond families, these factors likely included the opportunity to evade attempts to police people of color. As in the British West Indies, the period following the Seven Years' War as marked by the introduction of increasingly restrictive legislation against people of African descent in the French Atlantic. In Saint-Domingue, an influx of migrants from the metropole heightened distinctions between whites and free people of color, as colonial authorities sought to undermine Creole power and instead "orient colonial 'patriotism' toward France."[119] In addition to being required to furnish proof of their free status, beginning in 1764 free people of color were banned from certain professions, including medicine; nine years later they were formally forbidden to employ the same surnames as whites; and as of 1781 officials were prohibited from affording people of African ancestry respectful titles such as Monsieur or Madame in religious and legal documents.[120] Yet surviving parish and notary records indicate that such legislation was only loosely enforced in St. Lucia, suggesting that free people of color continued to enjoy greater opportunities in this peripheral region of the French Atlantic.

At the time of his marriage to Françoise Verger in 1768, Jean Baptiste Fournier was afforded the title of Sieur, an honorific customarily reserved for white men in France's Caribbean colonies. Yet Jean Baptiste, like his wife, had both European and African ancestry: in a 1772 burial record for their infant daughter, Marie Françoise, Jean Baptiste is described as *mestif* and his wife as *carteronne*.[121] When the couple welcomed their son, Baptiste, on June 3, 1768, the baby was also described in his baptismal record as "carteron."[122] Françoise's thirty-three-year-old brother, Jacques Verger, received the same racial ascription when he married Brigitte Bernege, a St. Lucia native described as a "free mulatresse" in Anse la Raye in June 1772.[123] Françoise and Jacques Verger's mother, Victoire Auvray, to whose name no racial designator was attached in the record of Françoise's marriage in 1767 or the 1769 and 1771 marriage records of Françoise's sisters, Marie Catherine, Rose, and Victoire Verger, was by the time of Jacques Jr.'s 1772 marriage described as a "free mestive."[124] Just four months later, when her son Pierre Verger married eighteen-year-old mulatresse Marianne Caumond, Victoire Auvray morphed from a mestive into a mulatresse.[125]

As the complicated and inconsistent nature of these racial assignations suggests, their use in colonial documents varied considerably. The decision of whether to describe an individual as mulatto, mestif/ve, or carteron[ne]—or to refrain from attaching any racial descriptor to a person's name, thereby indicating that the individual was free from what contemporaries perceived as the taint of African ancestry—depended to a large extent on the official drafting the document and the context in which it was created.[126] Victoire Auvray's changing racial status provides a vivid illustration of how this context evolved as colonial rule was extended throughout the Creole Archipelago. In the 1760s and 1770s, the racial status Victoire was assigned varied from one unmarked by racial descriptors, suggesting that she was white, to one suggesting a small degree of African ancestry, to that of "mulatto"—the offspring of one black and one white parent. When Victoire Auvray's daughter, Victoire Verger, married Sieur Claude Hiacinthe Lalouette, a "bourgeois" from Paris, in January 1771, both mother and daughter received the respectful title of Demoiselle.[127] The same was true one month later, when Demoiselle Rose Verger married Sieur Louis Thomas Pilet, a fellow native of St. Vincent.[128] Yet when Victoire Auvray's son Pierre married a woman described as mulatresse one year later, in 1772, Victoire was also described as mulatresse. In all three cases, the assignations were likely intended to indicate that the Verger children had selected marital partners of similar—and therefore appropriate—racial status.[129] Just four months earlier, when the same priest officiated at the marriage of Victoire Auvray's son Jacques to a woman of color who was the widow of a white man, Victoire had received the more courteous designation "mestive."[130] As an amorphous term, mestive did not directly correspond to a specific degree of African ancestry but was instead used by colonial officials in the Lesser Antilles to somewhat politely indicate that an individual was not of uniquely European descent.[131]

Similar inconsistencies in the application of racial descriptors to members of the extended Verger family testify to the persistence of racial fluidity in St. Lucia and suggest how this could allow people of color to continue exercising economic, social, and informal political influence in the peripheral French colony. In the 1768 baptismal record for Françoise Verger and Jean Baptiste Fournier's son Baptiste, who was described as carteron, as well as in subsequent baptismal records for children later born to the couple, the title of Sieur was dropped from Jean Baptiste's name. The denial of an honorific afforded to white men in France's Caribbean colonies signaled Jean Baptiste's partial

African ancestry in a way that would not have been lost on his contemporaries.[132] As French legislation increasingly elevated white subjects above all others, such distinctions became less subtle. In a 1784 survey of St. Lucia, both the Fournier and Verger families were explicitly categorized as gens de couleur and listed separately from their white neighbors.[133] Yet when Jean Baptiste Fournier sold a sixth of his share in his late father's plantation to his brothers in 1787, none of the men had a racial descriptor attached to his name, suggesting that Royal Notary Boze either did not know or did not care to note that they were of mixed race. The family's economic position likely influenced Boze's decision: Jean Baptiste sold his share for the considerable sum of 26,175 livres, indicating that the Fourniers were a family of some prominence in Anse la Raye.[134] Nor did Boze use racial descriptors when Jean Baptiste purchased Bibianne, an enslaved Creole woman who had made the journey from St. Vincent to St. Lucia with the man who claimed ownership over her, Louis Tiffaigne.[135] While Fournier and Tiffaigne were both men of color, they transacted business as members of St. Lucia's planter class, and it was their status as property owners—not their race—that mattered most to the notary creating a record of their dealings.

Several additional factors confirm that the discriminatory measures increasingly applied to people of African descent in the latter half of the eighteenth century were not enforced as strictly in peripheral areas of the French Atlantic, further suggesting why the Fourniers and the Vergers might choose to go there. Free people of color were among those who received land grants in St. Lucia after the Treaty of Paris, indicating that French colonial officials did not discriminate when it came to enticing experienced planters to settle the colony.[136] In defiance of the 1782 law prohibiting free people of color from using the same surnames as whites, the Fournier and Verger families continued to employ the surnames of their French ancestors in parish and notary records, such as the 1787 bill of sale for Bibianne. The reluctance of locally based militia captains who conducted St. Lucia's censuses to distinguish between white and free-colored women and children—officials in the colony did not consistently enumerate women and children according to race until 1773—suggests that people in positions of authority considered interracial families to be socially legitimate, or at least not an appropriate subject of commentary. This sense of legitimacy was further bolstered by the connections such families repeatedly and publicly affirmed: rather than choosing powerful patrons to serve as godparents to their son Baptiste, a practice common among free people of color in other slave societies, Françoise and Jean Baptiste Fournier appointed Françoise's mother, Victoire Auvray, to the important role.[137]

The decision to repeatedly and publicly draw on extended networks of mixed-race family and friends as marital partners, business associates, and spiritual kin suggests the many means by which residents of the Creole Archipelago continued exercising influence after the transition to formal colonial rule. While French colonial subjects, regardless of race, did not participate in elected assemblies like their British counterparts, free people of color publicly performed their belonging to colonial society by continuing to exercise civil rights such as creating contracts, buying and bequeathing property, and celebrating religious rites. By migrating to a region of the French Atlantic where they could continue to exercise these rights, the Fourniers, the Vergers, and hundreds of others actively endeavored to preserve and perpetuate the Creole society they and their families had built before the Seven Years' War. It was an endeavor that would become more difficult as the eighteenth century progressed.

*   *   *

As British and French administrators worked to reconcile residents of the eastern Caribbean to direct colonial rule in order to retain their knowledge and their productive and reproductive capacities, officials repeatedly found themselves forced to modify or abandon established features of colonial rule in plantation societies. In the quotidian contest between imperial designs and existing practices, new colonial subjects were well aware that they were, in the words of Thomas Whately, "very much wanted," and they capitalized on this want to extract accommodations. Emphasizing their value to the broader imperial project of transforming the Ceded Islands into centers of sugar production, residents of Great Britain's newest plantation colonies used diplomatic means to retain the rights they had exercised outside of empire, while also obtaining new privileges under British rule. While white planters enjoyed considerable success, gaining electoral and legal privileges that surpassed those of their counterparts elsewhere in the British empire, for free people of color the extension of British rule heralded harassment, humiliation, and the threat of enslavement. Rather than accept these assaults on the rights they formerly exercised, many free people of color took advantage of their proximity to a competing colonial regime by making the journey to St. Lucia. By settling in a peripheral colony where the social relations established by Creoles continued to prevail, planters of color retained the rights that served as hallmarks of belonging in French colonial society.

People like Jacques Verger and Victoire Auvray could not predict the many changes that would accompany the end of the Seven Years' War, but they could use their location at the interstices of competing empires to continue to seek opportunities for themselves and their families. As people who had helped forge the Creole Archipelago, these were opportunities to which they felt "justly intitled."[138] As the following chapter shows, the many residents of the eastern Caribbean who did not benefit from this interisland mobility, including Kalinagos and enslaved people, did not have the same chance to use diplomacy to extract concessions. Instead, in the 1760s and 1770s some island residents responded to the extension of colonial rule with violence, further complicating imperial attempts to transform the Creole Archipelago into an orderly center of sugar production.

Chapter 5

Surviving the Turn to Sugar

As the *Tobago Packet* made the 350-mile journey south from Antigua to Grenada, many of the people on board felt a growing sense of apprehension. When the 15-ton schooner arrived in Grenada's capital, St. George's, on April 11, 1765, Captain James Allison and his seven-man crew disembarked two "new negroes" and twenty-two "seasoned negroes" in the new British colony.[1] While extant records reveal little about these captives—we do not know whether they were men or women, how old they were, or how they experienced this second Middle Passage—the designations of "new" and "seasoned" hint at their experiences.[2] In contrast to "new negroes" who were recently trafficked from West Africa, the schooner's "seasoned" captives would have been accustomed to the climate and disease environment of the Caribbean. They also likely possessed skills, such as carpentry, distilling, or household management, that made them especially sought after by planters planning to establish new estates in the island. The captives' forced journey from one British colony to another heralded a dramatic transformation in their daily lives, as they found themselves separated from friends or family, surrounded by enslaved people from different cultural and linguistic groups, and forced to labor in an unfamiliar island. In the weeks and months that followed, most would adapt to their changed circumstances, continuing to survive as they cleared lands, planted cane, and instructed other enslaved people in the workings of a sugar estate.[3] Others would run away, joining Maroon communities in the islands' mountainous interiors. Still others would turn to violence, launching uprisings that threatened the stability and prosperity of colonies already marred by deep divisions within the plantocracy.

The *Tobago Packet*'s journey illustrates one of the many consequences of the turn to sugar production in the Ceded Islands. As eager investors extended the plantation complex to new lands, they altered many of the elements that characterized the Creole Archipelago in the decades prior. The transition from small, mixed-agriculture plantations to sprawling sugar estates changed the region's demography, as enslaved people from West Africa and from existing colonies began to outnumber free people to an extent commonly seen in larger sugar islands such as Jamaica and Saint-Domingue. Regardless of their place of origin, enslaved people in the eastern Caribbean experienced changes in their labor, social relations, and the legal regime under which they lived. Many of the changes they experienced, as well as how they responded to them, echo what happened in colonies that transitioned to sugar production in the seventeenth and early eighteenth centuries, suggesting that attention to transformations in slavery in the Ceded Islands could offer insights on less-documented eras.

The turn to sugar planting also affected Kalinagos, as planters sought to establish estates in spaces formerly recognized as Indigenous domains. In addition to challenging Kalinago rights to land, after 1763 colonists increasingly undermined their claims to indigeneity. Eager to create plantations on St. Vincent's windward side, planters and officials seized on the notion that Kalinagos were not native to the Caribbean but were the descendants of shipwrecked or fugitive enslaved Africans. Casting Kalinagos as "Black Caribs" transformed a practical and ideological dilemma rarely encountered elsewhere in the colonial Caribbean—the question of Indigenous dominion—into a problem common across slave societies: how to deal with Maroons.

Unlike adopted subjects who used diplomacy to obtain concessions, or free people who took advantage of the geography of the eastern Caribbean to migrate to other islands, in the period after 1763 Kalinagos and enslaved people faced new limitations on the strategies they formerly used to carve out lives in the Creole Archipelago. The small size of the islands meant that both groups struggled to find spaces not claimed by planters, while new demographic realities increasingly relegated them to the lowest rung in the rigid hierarchy of plantation society. Despite these limitations, Kalinagos and enslaved people began complicating imperial attempts to transform the Creole Archipelago into a center of sugar production almost as soon as the islands were incorporated into existing empires. Although unrest increased considerably during the intra- and interimperial wars of the 1770s and 1790s, it was not confined to those eras. Instead, in the midst of heated contests over land and voting rights that divided the plantocracy, enslaved and Indigenous people pursued a variety of means to maintain some of the key features of daily life forged beyond the reach of colonial rule. Attention to their actions and experiences sheds light on how enslaved and Indigenous people were affected by the turn to sugar planting and on some of the strategies they used to try to stall its advance.

Changes in Slavery in the Ceded Islands

The unnamed captives aboard the *Tobago Packet* were among more than two thousand enslaved people forced to travel from an established Caribbean colony to the Ceded Islands in the decade after 1763.[4] While this interisland trade pales in comparison to the scale of human traffic from Africa in the same period, it was key in shaping the new colonies. As merchants transported tens of thousands of West Africans to the eastern Caribbean, planters relied on the experience and expertise of enslaved people from existing colonies to extend sugar production to new lands. The evolving demography and labor regimes of the islands changed the dynamics of daily life on plantations, while also altering how planters and authorities viewed and treated all enslaved people.

Similar forced transfers of people and the knowledge they carried shaped the demography, economy, and culture of other parts of the circum-Caribbean, but rarely are these changes as well documented as in the eighteenth-century Ceded Islands.[5] In addition to customs and plantation records and colonial correspondence, detailed testimonies contained in the six-volume *House of Commons Sessional Papers Report on the Slave Trade* offer insight on how slavery evolved with the turn to sugar. Although this inquiry was conducted in 1789–1791, hundreds of pages that pertain specifically to the Ceded Islands offer detailed reflections on the changes that accompanied the extension of British rule and the rise of sugar planting after 1763.[6] Records in the transatlantic and intra-American slave trade databases, which are more complete for the eighteenth century than for earlier periods, also yield important clues about the circulation of enslaved people and knowledge. Schooners like the *Tobago Packet* often plied the same route numerous times, linking established sugar islands such as Antigua and Barbados to new colonies farther south. On April 30, 1765, Captain Allison used the *Tobago Packet* to retrace his journey from Antigua to Grenada, transporting a single "Negro wench" between the two colonies.[7] Captain Thomas Farmer repeatedly ferried people from Montserrat to St. Vincent, carrying three captives between the islands in June 1764 and fifteen in December of the same year, while Elisha Hunt forcibly relocated a total of thirty-two captives during two voyages from Barbados to Tobago in October and November 1766.[8] A small number of vessels, such as Jean Baptiste Chevilly's sloop *Neptune*, traveled between Grenada and St. Lucia, carrying people from the recently surrendered French possession to France's newest colony 130 miles north.[9]

While the intra-American slave trade database records ninety-one voyages that ferried approximately two thousand individuals from established Caribbean colonies to the Ceded Islands between 1763 and 1773, records not yet reflected in the database suggest that this trade was even more significant. In the first year after the Treaty of Paris, the Customs House of Fort Royal, Grenada— soon to be renamed St. George's—recorded thirteen vessels that disembarked enslaved people from other Caribbean islands.[10] Slaving vessels arriving from other colonies tended to be much smaller than those from West Africa, with human cargoes ranging from as few as one to a maximum of forty enslaved people.[11] Despite the vessels' small size, in the years after 1763 they were used to forcibly relocate hundreds of "seasoned slaves from their estates in the other islands to make new settlements" in the Ceded Islands. "Negroe tradesmen" with special skills, "being master worksmen," were especially sought after.[12]

While customs records fail to specify the roles of individual captives, the cargo that accompanied enslaved people hints at the purpose of their forced voyages. In September 1763 the *Royal Charlotte* arrived in Grenada from Antigua. In addition to sixteen enslaved people, the sloop carried "lumber and plantation utensils," suggesting that its owners, Jeremiah Nibbs and Patrick Maxwell, intended to task those aboard with constructing the dwellings, storehouses, and mills associated with sugar estates.[13] After being "engaged to come from the neighbouring islands to erect works and other buildings," skilled laborers such as these anonymous captives were "frequently returned" to the island from which they came, testifying to a feverish interisland commerce not only in enslaved people but also in the expertise and experience they offered.[14] Shipping returns also suggest that planters relied on interisland trafficking to forcibly relocate people with experience managing and serving their households. In September 1763 Joseph Tomlinson transported fourteen people from Guadeloupe—an island occupied by the British during the Seven Years' War—to Grenada. The captives traveled with "2 puncheons [of] rum and sundry household furniture," suggesting that Tomlinson planned to reconstitute his household, complete with its enslaved staff, in the Ceded Islands.[15]

Victims of this interisland trade were powerless to prevent their forcible relocation. While commissioner and planter William Young advocated

transporting "a few able and sensible tradesmen and negroes, who are con-
tented from a love of novelty, or other causes and encouragements," from
existing colonies to the Ceded Islands, he cautioned that "none should on
any account be compelled to this against their inclinations."[16] Despite Young's
apparent concern, contemporaries noted that "some of the first English settlers . . . brought negros who had only been in the capacity of domestics" and
forced them to labor in more physically demanding roles. As Thomas Atwood,
a planter and judge in Dominica, later noted, "the consequences of [this] . . .
rather imprudent conduct . . . soon after appeared," as many enslaved people
died or ran away in response to the altered conditions of their bondage.[17]

The increase in both interisland and transatlantic human trafficking
profoundly altered the demography of the eastern Caribbean, which in turn
shaped the place of enslaved people in plantation society. In St. Lucia, the
enslaved population grew by almost nine thousand individuals in the decade
after the Seven Years' War, from 5,069 people in 1764 to 13,982 people by 1773.[18]
According to the Slave Voyages databases, a single ship, the *Sisters,* trafficked
248 captives from Benin to Grenada and on to St. Lucia during this period,
while a total of three hundred captives arrived in St. Lucia aboard ten small
vessels sailing from neighboring islands such as St. Vincent and Grenada.[19]
The origins, experiences, and forced journeys of the vast majority of people
forced into slavery in St. Lucia in the decade after the Seven Years' War—some
8,300 women, men, and children—remain undocumented.

This absence of documentation inadvertently sheds light on the nature of
the captives' involuntary voyages. Rather than being trafficked as human commodities, whose sale in other ports was recorded in shipping manifests and
merchants' logs, thousands of enslaved people were forcibly relocated as part of
households. Individuals and families who moved between islands, like the Vergers, compelled countless enslaved people to accompany them on their interimperial voyages, separating them from friends and kin in Grenada, St. Vincent,
Dominica, or Martinique and thrusting them into unfamiliar lands.

Although this little-studied regional trade caused St. Lucia's enslaved
population to more than double in the space of a decade, the simultaneous
increase of more than 2,000 free settlers caused by regional migrations to the
new colony meant that the growth of the enslaved population did not outstrip
that of the free population to the same extent as in the British Ceded Islands.
By 1773, enslaved people in St. Lucia outnumbered free people by a ratio
of 4.4:1—a higher ratio than in mainland North America or Barbados, but
lower than elsewhere in the Caribbean.[20] In Dominica, the ratio of enslaved

Table 10. Ratio of Enslaved to Free People in the Eastern Caribbean, 1763 and 1773

	St. Lucia		Grenada		Tobago		Dominica	
	1764	*1773*	*1763*	*1773*	*1763*	*1773*	*1763*	*1772*
Free people	1,267	3,159	1,680	2,076	0	416	1,718	1,633
Enslaved people	5,069	13,782	13,846	26,211	0	7,342	5,872	14,214
Ratio of enslaved to free people	4:1	4.4:1	8.2:1	12.6:1	0	17.6:1	3.4:1	8.7

Sources: Population figures for St. Lucia are from ANOM DPPC G1 506, 1764 and 1773; for Dominica, TNA CO 101/1 N. 91 and TNA CO N. 274; for Tobago, TNA CO 101/17 N. 181; and for Grenada, TNA CO 101/28 N. 123, TNA CO 101/1 N. 5, and TNA CO 101/18 Part II, N. 81. Population figures for St. Vincent are not extant.

to free people grew from 3.4:1 to almost 9:1 in the space of a decade, creating a demographic profile comparable to that of Jamaica. The rapid expansion of sugar cultivation in Grenada increased the ratio of enslaved to free people in the island to more than 12.5:1, higher than all established British West Indian colonies except Antigua.[21] But the most dramatic transformation occurred in Tobago, where by 1773, 7,300 enslaved people outnumbered the island's 416 settlers almost 18:1—a ratio greater than in Saint-Domingue on the eve of the Haitian Revolution.[22]

Planters and officials who sought to capitalize on the availability of enslaved laborers were acutely aware of the dangers inherent in the resultant demographic imbalance. As Robert Melvill, governor-general of the Ceded Islands, explained in 1765, reports of unrest in the new colonies were "naturally to be expected after such a change of properties, and from such a jarring mixture of slaves."[23] Melvill's comment suggests how the extension of the transatlantic slave trade and the turn to sugar production disrupted the institution of slavery as it had formerly operated in the Creole Archipelago. Before 1763, many enslaved people, like the people who held them in bondage, were born and brought up in the region.[24] Most lived in proximity to those who claimed ownership over them—a proximity that left enslaved people particularly vulnerable to violence on an intimate scale.[25] Yet this proximity also meant that members of this "charter generation" were versed in the language, cultural, and religious practices of those who claimed to own them, allowing some enslaved people to draw on shared cultural practices to secure a degree of autonomy.[26] The smaller number of enslaved people, and planters' resultant desire to promote a self-reproducing enslaved population, meant that sexual violence pervaded the lives of enslaved women.[27] But it also meant that before 1763, enslaved people in the eastern Caribbean could form and maintain families to a greater extent than was common in colonies where labor was more readily bought and sold. The arrival of "a jarring mixture of" people, foreign to the language and practices of the islands and deprived of familial or social bonds, threatened both the security of planters and—less obviously but no less importantly—the distinctive society that enslaved people managed to create and maintain in the Creole Archipelago.

Regardless of their place of birth, after 1763 enslaved people throughout the archipelago experienced changes to the labor they were forced to perform. Large swaths of land in the volcanic islands of the eastern Caribbean remained forested, and planters seeking to establish new estates tasked their enslaved workforce with cutting down trees, removing stumps, and burning branches and underbrush before planting crops.[28] The work was grueling, and even supporters of slavery were forced to admit that many people died as a result of this forced labor.[29] Planters soon determined that "none other but full-grown strong Negroes [were] equal to the arduous business of clearing the lands."[30] They therefore sought to hire experienced laborers to prepare lands for planting, leading to the creation of work gangs that moved between estates and between islands.[31]

Enslaved people with experience cultivating and processing sugarcane were also expected to train others in the workings of a sugar estate, further highlighting planters' reliance on enslaved expertise to replicate the plantation system.[32] James Bailie, a defender of the slave trade who purchased an estate in Grenada in 1765 and remained in the island until 1771, explained that newly arrived Africans were "always committed to the care of the old and experienced Slaves," who were expected to introduce them to the language, customs, and labor routine of the plantation.[33] Another planter confirmed this practice, testifying that "every purchaser endeavoured to get a few seasoned Negroes in order to instruct and take care of full-grown new Negroes."[34] Only after "two or three years," when West Africans were "acquainted with the language and manners" of the islands, were they considered "seasoned Negro[es]" who no longer required the supervision of other enslaved people.[35]

Accounts of relations between already enslaved people and West Africans vary. Although some plantations were "furnished . . . entirely with Negroes from the Coast of Africa," other estates became sites in which smaller numbers of enslaved Creoles met with an influx of African captives.[36] Alexander Campbell, a proponent of the slave trade who purchased fourteen estates in various

Ceded Islands, claimed that "Nothing makes the [existing] Slaves more happy than to see new Negroes come on the estate, as it eases their labour, and is the means of their getting wives."[37] As Campbell explained, "when new Negroes are purchased, they are . . . distributed in the houses of the principal Negroes of the estate," suggesting that Africans were thrust into established dwellings or even family units.[38] Echoing Campbell, Grenada planter Gordon Turnbull wrote that "the principal and best disposed negroes . . . adopt[ed] one or two of these new subjects into each family, to assist them in all their little domestic offices of cookery, carrying water, wood, &c."[39] William Young confirmed that existing members of the enslaved population sought to gain from the new arrivals, as those who took them into their homes had "a right to the benefit of [their] work."[40] Campbell further testified that "seasoned slaves . . . in general wished to be thought not African Negroes, and it is a common expression among them, when they quarrel 'You are a Salt Water Negro,' which is as much as to say, You are a savage."[41] Such comments, while brief, suggest the emergence of a hierarchy in which existing members of the enslaved population— particularly those recognized as "principals," or people in positions of skill or authority such as drivers—wielded a degree of power over recent survivors of the Middle Passage. Rather than engaging in open resistance, some enslaved people survived the turn to sugar by seeking to improve their position and the benefits they derived within the world of the plantation.[42]

In addition to shaping how enslaved people related to one another, the increased availability of African captives changed how enslavers viewed and treated all laborers. For many planters, the extension of the transatlantic slave trade and the turn to sugar production meant that it now seemed more expedient to work enslaved people to death and replace them with West Africans than to invest in keeping people alive.[43] As Ashton Warner Byam, attorney general of Grenada and owner of lands in Dominica and St. Vincent, explained, it was common "for the slaves to be at their work in the field by break of day" and to labor until "the close of day," after which time all enslaved people, including children, were required to locate enough fodder to feed livestock on the estate.[44] Labor demands were even greater at harvest time, and Byam admitted that "on some plantations the manufacture is carried on night and day without intermission."[45] Nor did sugar planters favor the creation of enslaved families, as some small planters in the Creole Archipelago did before 1763. Gilbert Francklyn, who owned two thousand acres of land in Tobago and traveled throughout the Ceded Islands, testified that many planters "consider a child born on the estate to cost as much or more than a new Negro before they come to be useful on an estate, [and therefore] treat pregnant women with any want of tenderness."[46] In addition to altering the nature of their forced labor, the extension of sugar production to the Creole Archipelago meant that fewer enslaved people could form or maintain families.

The creation of large estates also changed the nature of surveillance to which enslaved people were subjected.[47] While the larger number of people on individual estates fostered the growth of villages where people could socialize at a remove from those who claimed ownership over them, newly appointed authorities also sought to regulate all aspects of life in bondage. Slave codes promulgated throughout the Ceded Islands in the 1760s and 1770s stipulated that "all . . . negroe houses . . . be searched every 14 days at the least for run-away negroes, clubs, wooden swords and other mischievous weapons and also for stolen goods."[48] In addition to hinting at planters' anxieties about the actions of an enslaved majority that now lived at a remove from their households, these new laws illustrate how the daily lives of enslaved people changed with the transition to formal colonial rule. Forbidden to "beat any drums . . . or to blow horns," to purchase or barter for rum or other spirits, to assemble with people from other plantations or be "off their owner's plantation without a permission in writing," enslaved people found that many activities in which they formerly engaged—including things as simple as visiting friends or family on neighboring estates—were now outlawed.[49] The turn to sugar production and the extension of the transatlantic slave trade to the Creole Archipelago changed both the daily lives and labors of enslaved people and the way they were viewed and treated by those who claimed ownership over them.

Responding to Changes in Slavery

Like enslaved people in islands that transitioned to sugar planting earlier in the colonial era, in the eastern Caribbean people responded to the changes in demography, work regimes, and law that accompanied the expansion of plantation production in a variety of ways.[50] While the overwhelming majority of enslaved people throughout the colonial Americas found means to survive the conditions of their bondage, others took advantage of less-accessible areas such as forests, mountains, and swamps to run away, forming Maroon camps.[51] A few organized uprisings that led to the deaths of small numbers of white people and the torture, banishment, and execution of much larger numbers of enslaved people, as authorities responded to threats to the plantation regime with acts of state terror designed to strike fear in anyone who might similarly contemplate revolt.[52] While enslaved insurgency was relatively uncommon in the colonial Americas, historians speculate that it was more likely to occur when the plantocracy was experiencing discord within its ranks.[53] Conflicts between new and existing planters, along with the political, demographic, and economic changes that marked the eastern Caribbean in the wake of the Seven Years' War, helped fuel a number of uprisings throughout the archipelago.

Enslaved people already living in the islands at the time of their cession began responding to changes to their labor and living conditions as quickly as they were introduced. As French philosopher the Abbé Raynal reported, as planters "attempted to alter the mode of living among their slaves," enslaved Creoles, "who . . . are more attached to their customs than other men . . . revolted."[54] Jean Baptiste Leblond, who chronicled his stay in the Lesser Antilles in the 1760s and 1770s, also attributed uprisings in Grenada to the new labor system introduced by English planters, explaining that as "the regime of the French slaves was changed and became harder . . . they revolted."[55] Writing in 1791, Thomas Atwood made a similar observation about how enslaved people on a Jesuit estate in Dominica that was disbanded and sold after the Treaty of Paris responded. "Either from their attachment to [the Jesuits] or dislike of their new masters," they "soon after betook themselves to the woods with their wives and children, where they were joined, from time to time, by others from different estates."[56] In islands settled earlier in the colonial era, such as Martinique, planters complained about a rise in marronage in the wake of the turn to sugar.[57] In the eastern Caribbean, enslaved people similarly responded to the introduction of a new work regime associated with sugar production by abandoning estates.

The threat that large bands of fugitives could pose to plantation production was all too familiar to British authorities, who had brokered peace with Maroons in Jamaica just twenty-five years earlier, in 1739, and faced further coordinated uprisings throughout Jamaica in 1760–1761.[58] As Governor Melvill reported, "runaway slaves" in Grenada, "of whom there has always been 2 or 3 hundred sheltered in the woody mountains . . . became, soon after the establishment of Civil Government, more than ordinarily audacious." After first offering amnesty to fugitives who surrendered, beginning in April 1765 Melvill ordered troops against Maroons.[59] By October 1766, he reported that most had been killed or "suffered exemplary punishments, in consequence of which many of the less guilty have returned to their Masters." Despite Melvill's assurances that Maroons who "are still in the Woods are become few in numbers, and for the present little formidable," subsequent acts passed in Grenada suggest the persistence of marronage.[60] In December 1766, Melvill approved an act "for the more speedy and effectual suppression of runaway slaves," and the following month Grenada's council and assembly passed a bill ordering "Free Mulattoes and Free Negroes" to join detachments to pursue fugitives and penalizing those who refused to serve with a fine of up to £10 or three weeks in jail.[61]

These acts also hint at how the changes that accompanied the turn to sugar production affected enslaved people. The act for the suppression of runaways noted that "one great Cause of many Negroes absenting themselves . . . is the scarcity of Ground-Provisions in the respective Plantations."[62] The admission that enslaved people lacked adequate food echoes complaints in Barbados and Martinique earlier in the colonial era, indicating that enslaved people went hungry as more land was devoted to sugar.[63] Although acts passed after the Seven Years' War decreed that plantations be inspected twice yearly to ensure they had adequate provisions, subsequent testimony from planters in the Ceded Islands suggests that problems of food scarcity persisted. As Henry Hew Dalrymple recollected of his experiences in Grenada in 1773, enslaved people did not "receive a sufficient quantity of food." Instead, "on Sunday they labour to supply themselves with food for the rest of the week, and on this day, instead of amusing themselves, they do more work than on any other day of the week," as "without working hard on this day they could not have subsistence."[64] Running away could serve as a protest against these conditions, or it could allow fugitives to ensure their survival in the face of a harsh new regime, as they fished or found food in the islands' forested interiors.

As in islands that turned to sugar production earlier in the colonial era, however, the widespread land clearing that accompanied sugar planting soon diminished the possibility of marronage.[65] With estates becoming larger and more widespread throughout the eastern Caribbean, the mountainous, forested regions that once sheltered both Kalinagos and enslaved people shrank, and authorities began to worry instead about the possibility of organized revolt. Elsewhere in the Caribbean, the intensification of sugar production coincided with the discovery of conspiracies in which large numbers of enslaved Creoles were implicated, as officials sought to identify and violently punish would-be insurgents in Barbados in 1692, Martinique in 1710, and Antigua in 1736.[66] As historian Jason Sharples argues, the discovery and prosecution of such conspiracies may reveal more about the fears of enslavers than the intentions of the enslaved; finding themselves vastly outnumbered by people they were willing to work to death, planters began "to speculate about violence that might occur."[67]

In the intervisible islands of the eastern Caribbean archipelago, planters were particularly worried about the possibility of insurgency stretching across the region. Authorities soon sought to limit the circulation of enslaved people between islands, suggesting that regional slave trafficking, which was supposed to allow planters to dispatch "able and sensible tradesmen and negroes" to new plantations, also had more dangerous consequences.[68] In 1769, officials in Dominica prohibited the importation of any enslaved person guilty of capital offenses, citing "many evils [that] have already happened and still continue to happen . . . by gangs of runaway negroes, headed and encouraged by other slaves imported from neighbouring colonies."[69] The legislation suggests that some planters used the interisland trade as a means to rid themselves of people they deemed unruly or disruptive. The forcible movement of enslaved people— and any information or ideologies they brought with them—threatened to sow unrest throughout the region.

Despite officials' stated fears about the actions of "slaves imported from neighbouring colonies," attention to insurgencies in the Ceded Islands demonstrates that West Africans also responded to enslavement with violence. In November 1770, an enslaved man known as Sandy, "the most daring and dangerous villain," led an uprising in Tobago.[70] Although Tobago's lieutenant governor, Robert Stewart, later reported that "it does not appear there were ever more than between 30 and 40 [insurrectionists], and of those about 8 or 10 dangerous," Sandy's actions shaped the response of planters throughout the archipelago.[71] They identified Sandy and his followers as Coromantee, an ethnonym for Akan-speaking people that derived from the slave-trading post of Cormantin, on Africa's Gold Coast.[72] People termed Coromantee had already earned a reputation as dangerous among planters, having been implicated in conspiracies in Barbados in 1675, New York in 1712 and 1741, Antigua in 1736, and most recently in Tacky's Revolt in Jamaica.[73] The revolt, which paralyzed Britain's largest sugar colony between April and October 1760, reverberated in smaller rebellions on various Jamaican estates in 1765, 1766, and 1767.[74] In the wake of Sandy's uprising in 1770, Tobago planters began to enumerate Coromantees separately on censuses, suggesting that they, like their counterparts in Jamaica, were wary of people they erroneously identified as belonging to a cohesive ethnic group.[75]

The considerable "publick expences . . . as well as . . . losses to individuals in negroes, and . . . interruption of labour" occasioned by Sandy's rebellion also put planters and officials in other islands on high alert, testifying to how the actions of enslaved people—as well as the danger they were seen to pose—rippled across the region.[76] These fears seemed confirmed just two weeks later, when Maroons in Grenada grew increasingly emboldened. In a deposition hurriedly taken at eleven o'clock on the night of December 3, 1770, a planter who had been menaced by a band of fugitives reported that they declared themselves "ready to meet and fight the detachment in the King's high roads." The frightened planter further stated that the Maroons vowed "they would not do it in a dark clandestine manner but with day light with drums beating and shells blowing"; in no time, they allegedly threatened, "Grenada would be overturned."[77]

The planter's reference to drums and shells—instruments that were expressly banned in slave codes in the Ceded Islands—as well as his contention that Maroons were bold enough to rise up during the day testifies to the climate of fear that gripped planters in the wake of the turn to sugar. Worried that the actions of the Maroons would incite "no less than a general insurrection if very speedy methods are not taken to suppress it," planters in Grenada, like their fellow colonists in Tobago, requested that military forces be dispatched to quell the uprising.[78] The "great disproportion of white people to slaves" heightened their sense of danger, and they sought to ensure that the island's population of free people of color would not make common cause with any restive enslaved people or Maroons.[79] As Leblond later reported, approximately one hundred members of the free-colored militia, divided into five companies, were ordered to launch a campaign against the Grenada Maroons. Over the course of their initial three-day expedition, the militia killed more than one hundred Maroons and brought in thirty-nine heads as proof—numbers that hint at how many fugitives fled to Grenada's mountainous interior within the first decade of British rule.[80]

Although there is nothing to suggest that the uprisings that took place in Tobago and Grenada in late 1770 constituted a coordinated attempt at revolt, residents of neighboring colonies worried that insurgency would spread to their shores. In December 1770, the St. Vincent assembly expressed concern that "the negroe and mulatto slaves in two of our neighbouring islands have committed many outrages . . . [and] slaves within this island may be spirited up to the like rebellion and insurrection." Fearful that the approaching Christmas season would provide enslaved people with the opportunity to revolt, the assembly ordered extra guards and patrols throughout the island.[81] While no such uprising materialized, the assembly's worries reveal their awareness of the dangers inherent in transforming largely uncultivated islands into centers of sugar production. In the more settled island of Barbados, the features associated with a developed sugar economy—including the availability of food, the enslaved's ability to form and maintain families, and more lax control on the part of planters—meant that authorities did not report any conspiracies or rebellions among enslaved people throughout the eighteenth century.[82] Yet real or rumored uprisings persisted as more land was devoted to sugar production in Jamaica and the Ceded Islands.[83] Marronage was particularly widespread in densely forested Dominica, resulting in conflicts dubbed the Maroon Wars in the mid-1780s and again in the 1810s.[84]

The punishments visited on enslaved people further testify to planters' fears, as they used exemplary violence to quell even the smallest expressions of rebellion. As Ottobah Cugoano, who experienced slavery in Grenada in the 1760s, later remembered, "for eating a piece of sugar-cane, some . . . had their teeth pulled out, to deter others, and to prevent them from eating any cane in future."[85] People called to testify before the House of Commons confirmed that "for very trivial offences" planters would "cut off the ears and legs, and otherways . . . mutilate" the bodies of enslaved people, with no "attempts made to bring them to legal punishment."[86] Punishments mandated by law were also severe. Slave codes in the Ceded Islands stipulated that an enslaved person who absented him or herself "from his or her Master, Owner, or Renter's Service" for three months or longer would be sentenced to death, while enslaved people found guilty of helping runaways would be "whipped upon the Bare-Back, with any Number of Stripes." In order to discourage people from running away together, the same codes specified that if ten or more enslaved people absented themselves from the same plantation for ten days or more, "one of the said Slaves . . . shall suffer Death."[87] In addition to marronage, the threat of destruction remained at the forefront of planters' minds. Enslaved people who attempted to set fire to crops were subject to execution, while those found carrying a torch through a cane field would "receive any number of lashes not exceeding thirty-nine."[88]

The most violent punishments were reserved for people who organized uprisings, as planters deployed public torture and execution to deter others who might contemplate revolt.[89] In 1774, people enslaved on a Tobago estate owned by William Young killed three white people before fleeing to the woods, where they eluded capture for more than a week.[90] In this instance, authorities' attempt to use human suffering to strike fear in observers may have backfired. As Ninian Jefferys testified, the "right arms" of seven of the fugitives "were chopped off; they were then dragged to seven stakes, and a fire, consisting of trash and dry wood was lighted about them." Jeffreys' testimony provides a chilling glimpse of the measures that some West Africans were willing to take to escape their bondage. As Jeffreys related, in "a strong instance of human fortitude," he did not hear any of those sentenced "murmur, complain, cry, or do any thing that indicated fear" as they endured the executioner's torture. Turning to Jeffreys, one of the men condemned to die declared, "'Buchra, you see me now, but to-morrow I shall be like that,' kicking up the dust with his foot," perhaps as an expression of his belief that death would afford him the freedom to move about as he wished.[91] In the face of the planters' legally sanctioned brutality, this remarkable display of stoicism undermined the attempt to use terror as a means of demonstrating authority.

Given the horrors that awaited enslaved people who chose to rebel, the fact that even a small number did so suggests the severity of conditions associated with the turn to sugar production. As evidenced by the fact that the Ceded Islands quickly became some of the most productive plantation colonies in the British Empire, most enslaved people responded to the transformations that accompanied the rise of sugar by surviving them. While the ways in which individuals made sense of these changes remain largely invisible to historians, available documents can be used to understand not only how the shift to sugar production altered demography and work routines but also how these changes affected the community dynamics of enslaved people throughout the archipelago. They also demonstrate that enslaved people—both those born in the islands and those trafficked from Africa—did not need external provocation to begin contesting their bondage. While desertion and destruction of plantations would intensify during the revolutionary era, these responses began to manifest almost as soon as sugar planting was extended to the Creole Archipelago, echoing many of the patterns seen in islands where sugar production was adopted earlier in the colonial era.

The Expansion of the Plantation Complex and the Birth of "Black Caribs"

The shift to sugar also affected Kalinagos, altering not only their daily lives and their claims to dominion but also how they were characterized and treated by colonists and officials. As the British crown extended its rule over a diversity of Native American peoples in the wake of the Seven Years' War, policy makers debated whether and how to assimilate them into the empire.[92] The small space of the Ceded Islands made this issue somewhat different in St. Vincent than in mainland North America, but British authorities were initially optimistic about the possibility of sharing the 150-square-mile island with people they described as "quiet and well disposed." As William Young claimed in a 1764 pamphlet designed to promote the settlement of the Ceded Islands, "when [Kalinagos] are duly apprized of the humanity and generosity of our gracious Sovereign, and assured of the enjoyment of their lands, freedom, favor and protection, they may be gained over to our cause, and even rendered useful."[93] Yet the arrival of settlers who prized St. Vincent's windward coast as "the most extensive and finest part of the island" soon diminished the possibility of a peaceful sharing of space between Kalinagos and colonists.[94] Although Kalinagos initially sought to relocate elsewhere, the spread of the plantation complex throughout the eastern Caribbean meant that they could no longer rely on interisland mobility to secure spaces of dominion. Instead, in the decade after 1763 Kalinagos engaged in increasingly heated confrontations with settlers and surveyors, culminating in a 1772–1773 conflict known as the Carib War. As Kalinagos turned from diplomacy to force to halt the advance of sugar planting, colonists and officials increasingly depicted them not as "quiet and well disposed" but as the descendants of fugitives from slavery, a rhetorical alienation that allowed settlers to advance their own claims to the lands on which Kalinagos lived.[95] Although politicians and commenters in Great Britain continued to depict Kalinagos as Indigenous victims of rapacious planters, they could do little to protect them. Just ten years after St. Vincent's cession to Great Britain, the descendants of people who in 1660 had secured dominion over the entire island found their territory reduced to its northernmost reaches. Worse still, they were now frequently depicted not as people with a primordial right to this land but as violent Maroons whose continued presence in St. Vincent threatened the colony from within.

Experience had taught Kalinagos that the growth of the plantation complex would diminish the territory available to them, and they therefore sought to secure lands elsewhere in the eastern Caribbean. In August 1763, just six months after the Treaty of Paris was signed, a group of Kalinagos canoed across the channel separating St. Vincent from St. Lucia. There, they sought permission to relocate to the new French colony from St. Lucia's recently appointed governor, the Comte de Jumilhac.[96] Although de Jumilhac reassured the Kalinago emissaries that he would do everything in his power to help them, he declined their request. With so many French planters streaming into St. Lucia from the new British colonies of Grenada, Dominica, and St. Vincent, de

Jumilhac explained, it would be impossible for Kalinagos—whom he estimated to number five thousand individuals—to find suitable lands on which to establish themselves.[97]

Denied assistance from the French, Kalinagos next attempted to negotiate with British authorities. In April 1766, less than a year after eager colonists began purchasing plots of up to five hundred acres in St. Vincent, a number of Kalinagos met with the Commissioners for the Sale of Lands. The Commissioners reported that Kalinagos were "solicitous of having their cleared land confirmed to them, and of being secured in possession of such pieces of woodland as may be sufficient." The Kalinagos further stated that they were "willing to take the oaths and become faithfull subjects" of King George III.[98]

Kalinago willingness to "become faithfull subjects" highlights the confusion surrounding their political status in the wake of the Treaty of Paris. As Commissioner William Young explained, "[t]he French King, till the late cession of [St. Vincent] to the Crown of Great Britain, always affected to acknowledge it as the property of the Charibbs, and the latter have accordingly imagined they had the best right to it."[99] Although the proposed oaths were similar to those administered to former French subjects who wished to remain in Grenada after its cession to Great Britain, the Treaty of 1660 meant that Kalinagos were not, in fact, subjects of a European sovereign conquered in a just war. Nor were they squatters with no legal title to the land on which they lived, like the small planters who had settled in Dominica and on St. Vincent's leeward side in the decades prior. A third possibility, that Kalinagos were akin to Maroons, was for Kalinagos a frightening and all-too-plausible prospect. Tales of a slave ship that allegedly wrecked off St. Vincent's coast emerged as early as 1661, and by the beginning of the eighteenth century, French chroniclers reported that the number of African people on the island's windward side "greatly surpasses that of" Indigenous people.[100] While colonists acknowledged that the two groups "intermixed," they increasingly used Kalinagos' partially African ancestry as a means of negating their claims to indigeneity.[101] The many elements of Kalinago culture rooted in Indigenous practices, including their diet, dress, and agricultural and maritime technologies, did not erase their dark skin or curly hair in the minds of settlers.[102] Asserting that Black Caribs were more Black than Carib allowed colonists to simultaneously challenge Kalinago claims to land and assign them a degraded position in the strict racial hierarchy on which American slave societies rested.[103]

As slave ships disembarked thousands of captives in St. Vincent in the years after 1763, the increasingly important role of African slavery in the eastern

Caribbean raised Kalinagos' concern that they, too, might be enslaved.[104] Kalinagos were already in the habit of "flattening the foreheads of their infants in order that their race may be kept distinct," a practice that Young attributed to their desire to differentiate themselves from Africans.[105] While the Caribbean's Indigenous inhabitants practiced forehead flattening long before the rise of chattel slavery in the region, Young's comment suggests that it was increasingly necessary for Kalinagos to take measures to distinguish themselves from the growing number of enslaved people in the islands.[106] In a society that increasingly required nonwhite people to prove their free status, securing documents that identified them as "faithfull subjects" could serve as one such proof.[107] "Apprehensive that there was a design not only of depriving them of their grounds, but also of reducing them into slavery," Kalinagos approached the commissioners to protect their title to land and the security of their persons.[108]

Representatives of the British Crown were eager to win the allegiance of people who "said they were independent of either the King of Great Britain or of France, but at the same time . . . confessed a great partiality to the French."[109] Although French officials had declined to offer formal assistance to Kalinagos, British officials were acutely aware that the geography of the eastern Caribbean archipelago facilitated "short and easy . . . intercourse in open canoes between them and the French Inhabitants of St. Lucia," and they sought to diminish the possibility of Kalinago alliance with the rival crown.[110] Nonetheless, the commissioners were reluctant to forfeit any lands suitable for sugar production. Rather than recognizing Kalinago dominion over St. Vincent's windward coast, Young proposed relocating Kalinagos to plots fit for subsistence agriculture, but ill suited to sugar, elsewhere in the island. Kalinagos would be afforded a grace period of up to five years in which to establish dwellings and plant crops on their newly conceded lands before being required to permanently quit their existing homes. Once settled on their new allotments, Kalinagos would be legally prohibited from alienating land "to any white person." As further compensation for having to abandon their homes, Young proposed that Kalinagos be awarded 13 pounds 4 shillings per acre of cleared land. Wooded land, which accounted for the overwhelming majority of Kalinago holdings, would not be subject to compensation.[111] Given that lands suitable for planting sugar in St. Vincent had recently fetched as much as 59 pounds sterling per acre at auction, the proposed terms were far from generous.[112] Yet in May 1768, King George III approved Young's proposal.[113]

Correctly anticipating that Kalinagos would be reluctant to accept Young's terms, the commissioners decided to send "some Indians, Mulatto's and Free Negroes, well acquainted with the Charibees" to explain their proposal. Those tasked with this communication also included French priest the Abbé Valladares and several "French Gentlemen," who were dispatched to different Kalinago settlements on St. Vincent's windward side.[114] Envoys who returned to Kingstown one week later reported that "the Indians of Ravaca, and some of Grand Sable, would not venture to pass through Coubimarou and Ouarroarrou, on account of some difference they had with the tribes there." Despite these divisions within Kalinago society, the emissaries signaled that the Kalinagos with whom they managed to speak "seemed much pleased" with their proposal.[115]

In a spirited defense of his father's plan published more than twenty years later, Sir William Young, Jr., who served as agent for St. Vincent from 1795 until 1802 and subsequently became governor of Tobago, offered a different version of events. According to Young Jr., on reaching the main Kalinago settlement at Grand Sable, Valladares was confronted by a group of Kalinagos headed by a chief named Joseph Chatoyer. The Kalinago leader listened as the Catholic priest, acting as an emissary of the British Crown, informed him in French of King George III's plans for the Ceded Islands. In a gesture intended to "communicate the gracious disposition of His Majesty towards them," the abbé assured Chatoyer that once resettled, Kalinagos would not be expected to pay rents or other fines to the king who since 1763 had held sovereignty over St. Vincent.[116] As Valladares later reported, Chatoyer had only one question: "Quel roi?" Chatoyer and his followers, the abbé testified, "would listen to the governor of Martinique, and no other."[117]

Although Young Jr. likely intended for this striking anecdote to serve as an illustration of the Kalinagos' inherently bellicose nature—to deny allegiance to the king was treason—the exchange between Chatoyer and Valladares also offers insight on the chief's understanding of sovereignty and diplomacy. Aware of earlier treaties guaranteeing Kalinago dominion over St. Vincent, Chatoyer refused to recognize the legitimacy of King George III's claim to the lands on which he and his people had lived for generations. Instead, Chatoyer looked to a representative of Great Britain's enemy in the recent war, France, to protect Kalinago sovereignty and honor the treaty broached a century earlier. Rather than the savage warrior depicted throughout Young Jr.'s account, this passage provides a glimpse of Chatoyer the diplomat, determined to engage in negotiations as a legitimate representative of his people.

In the wake of the Seven Years' War, the view of Kalinagos as "a defenceless, innocent, and inoffensive people" prevailed in Great Britain, restraining planters' ability to extend sugar planting onto Kalinago lands. In addition to vocal critiques of "avaricious merchants, land holders and venal commissioners" in the press, land-hungry settlers were denounced in Parliament.[118] Bemoaning the prospect that "the last remains of the Aborigines from South America are to be totally extirpated," members of the House of Commons argued that "before we pretend to extirpate those poor people, we should examine our right." "By the terms of the last peace," one member reminded his fellow representatives, "we are to live with them." Condemning the "planters [who] have taken a fancy to their part of the island" and attributing their desire for lands with "that rage for making a fortune," members of Parliament advised that "some step should be taken to limit the dangerous ambition, and uncommon avarice" of St. Vincent's planters.[119] Amid ongoing crises over British rule in India, efforts to depict the empire as a civilizing and humane institution would soon be undermined by events in St. Vincent.[120] Although politicians and observers in England continued to defend the interests of people they characterized as aboriginal to the eastern Caribbean, the shift to sugar production throughout the Ceded Islands increasingly threatened Kalinago claims to sovereignty and even to indigeneity.

From Diplomacy to War

Following Chatoyer's refusal to acknowledge King George III, any semblance of diplomacy in the dispute over Kalinago lands was abandoned. Instead, less than a decade after the Treaty of Paris, the conflict between planters and Kalinagos turned to all-out war. While the 1772–1773 Carib War provoked heated debates in the House of Commons, distant politicians proved powerless to stop the advance of British troops in St. Vincent. Although Chatoyer and twenty-eight other Kalinago leaders agreed to a treaty with British forces in 1773, planters in St. Vincent harnessed the bloody conflict to advance their depiction of Kalinagos as savages who had more in common with fugitives from slavery than with Indigenous Americans.

With Young Sr.'s plan to expropriate Kalinagos lands officially approved, in 1768 administrators ordered that a road be forged through St. Vincent's previously inaccessible windward side. As a tool of the colonial state, the road was explicitly intended not only to facilitate future surveys but to enable military forces to more easily march on Kalinago territory should the need arise. Under the direction of Robert Wynne, the only Commissioner for the Sale of Lands present in St. Vincent at the time, the construction of a road running north-east from the capital of Kingstown toward the windward coast was undertaken at the beginning of the dry season in autumn 1768. Workers got as far as the Yambou River, long recognized as a natural boundary between Kalinago and settler lands, before being stopped in their tracks by Chatoyer and his followers. Electing not to proceed further without military assistance, they abandoned their road building until the following spring.[121] Returning in April 1769 with a military escort of forty men, the surveyors were again rebuffed by approximately two hundred Kalinagos. Finding themselves "sixteen miles advanced in the Heart of the Charibb Country . . . cut off from every supply of water and provisions [and] surrounded by a numerous Body of vile Savages," the party had no choice but to retreat.[122] The Kalinagos then set fire to the surveyors' tools and burned their cabins to the ground, destroying both the instruments and the symbols of British colonization. "For God's sake endeavour to get the regiment up here as soon as possible," surveyor John Byres implored his superiors, explaining that he had been forced to abandon his maps in some bushes while beating a hasty retreat. "I fancy if the Inhabitants don't put themselves in Arms, [Kalinagos will] overrun the Island."[123] Although a militia composed of planters and enslaved people returned to confront Kalinagos the following day, the president of St. Vincent's colonial council, Harry Alexander, decided it would be prudent to honor "His Majesty's boundless Humanity and tender Disposition . . . and for a time, I hope it will be short, quit that fine cream part of this island with a regret I cannot express."[124]

As Alexander's comment suggests, by the end of the 1760s settlers in St. Vincent were eager to extend sugar planting to an area they prized as one of the finest in the archipelago. Despite their decision not to engage in open confrontation without further military reinforcements, Alexander and his fellow councilors were therefore unwilling to abandon their goal of obtaining Kalinago lands. At a May 10, 1769, meeting of St. Vincent's council, the assembled members declared it "their duty most humbly to represent to His Majesty, how much his lenity to so worthless a set of savages will hurt his faithful, loyal and obedient subjects," explicitly counterposing the fate of British settlers with that of "savage" Kalinagos. The councilors also addressed the elected assembly, urging them to draft a militia bill and to consider under what circumstances martial law might be implemented so as to "guard against any future insult or attack from these wretches."[125]

The assembly's response illustrates how a desire to expand the plantation complex shaped depictions of and relations with those who stood in the way of sugar planting. Agreeing that military force would likely be necessary, the assembly proposed to procure all available arms, ammunition, and troops from neighboring islands to protect St. Vincent "from the late rebellions & Conduct of the *fugitive Negroes distinguished by the name of black Charribbs*."[126] By characterizing Kalinagos as "fugitive negroes" rather than Native Americans, the assembly simultaneously delegitimized Indigenous claims to land and cast Kalinagos not as a sovereign people but as a group of outlaws whose very existence threatened the foundation of plantation society. Like the Maroons who would strike fear in planters across the archipelago the following year, Kalinagos undermined colonial attempts to transform the Creole Archipelago into an orderly center of sugar production.

Despite the planters' rhetorical assault on Kalinagos, they agreed to postpone surveying St. Vincent's windward side "until the King's further pleasure shall be known."[127] Denied permission to take Kalinago lands by force, enterprising colonists instead endeavored to obtain plots by purchase. Kalinagos who declined to part with their lands were aware that this put them in a precarious position, and in late 1769 and early 1770 "about 50" Kalinagos "in three different boats" journeyed to Grenada. Alleging that any complaints against them were created "by their enemies, who want to sell or buy their lands," Kalinago representatives entreated Governor Melvill to protect them.[128] Upon the advice of King's Counsel in St. Vincent, Charles Payne Sharpe, Melvill put a stop to the sale of lands. This measure was not, however, intended to protect Kalinagos. Instead, Sharpe ruled that because King George III had "never Relinquished any part of that Right in the wood or other Lands to the Charibs," they could "make no Legal sale and Conveyance . . . of any such Lands in any part of the Island to any person whatever." According to Sharpe, the four Johannes per acre of cleared land offered to Kalinagos in the commissioners' instructions did not constitute an attempt to purchase plots to which they had legal title but was merely a "compensation or allowance for their labour." As a result, any settler who "purchased lands from the Charibs or . . . treated for the same or . . . used any means to persuade [Kalinagos] that they have a right to dispose of any lands in St. Vincent" would be guilty of a misdemeanor. In order to further discourage these sales, Sharpe ordered that in future any settlers found north of the Yambou River be punished for trespassing on crown—not Kalinago—lands.[129] Sharpe's ruling temporarily put a stop to the sale of Kalinago lands, but it simultaneously struck a further blow to Indigenous sovereignty by denying that Kalinagos had any right to said lands.

After learning that their purchases were legally void, members of St. Vincent's planter elite renewed their rhetorical assault on Kalinagos. Claiming that the acquisition of land was "only a secondary, and very inferior object," resident planters insisted that the "more important and natural consideration [was] the security of our property, and the safety of our persons" against the "most dangerous and insolent rebels." In a collective address to King George III, members of St. Vincent's council and assembly again invoked the prospect of a Kalinago alliance with French colonists in nearby Martinique or St. Lucia. Citing the formers' "strong attachment . . . to that nation with whose subjects and language they have been so long conversant, and whose interests they are at any time ready to espouse to the Prejudice of those of your Majesty and to the sacrifice of our lives and fortunes," they beseeched the king to protect his loyal subjects. Even if the French refused to ally with Kalinagos, they argued, "suffering such a separate empire as these Indians claim within your Majesty's dominion is not only incompatible with the safety of your subjects, but highly derogatory from the Honor and Dignity of the British Crown."[130] The planters' address was clear: the "separate empire" that Kalinagos had maintained for generations—one guaranteed to them by the Treaty of 1660—had no place in the expanding plantation society of the eastern Caribbean.

As the notion that Kalinagos were not a sovereign people or potential British subjects but rather internal enemies gained traction in St. Vincent, the prospect that they might be accommodated within the island began to seem increasingly implausible.[131] Insisting once again that Kalinagos were not native to St. Vincent but were instead descended from the survivors of a shipwrecked slaving vessel, members of the island's court suggested that Kalinagos be "removed to the part of the world from whence their ancestors came." Equating Kalinagos with the descendants of Africans, the court suggested that "any unoccupied tract of 10,000 acres of woodland upon any part of the coast of Africa having one or more rivers running through it would afford them all the necessaries of life which they have been accustomed to."[132]

Yielding to colonists' increasingly desperate entreaties, in April 1772 Lord Hillsborough, Secretary of State for the Colonies, ordered that two regiments from North America be dispatched to St. Vincent to "take effectual measures for the reduction of [Kalinagos] as the only means of giving security to the settlements of His Majesty's Subjects in that island."[133] Diplomacy appearing to have failed, Hillsborough resolved to secure the safety of the colony and its resident planters by force. Illustrating the threat that Kalinagos were perceived to pose, the regiments' commanding officer, Lieutenant Colonel Dalrymple, was explicitly instructed not to make the troops' destination known "least the Charibs . . . receiving notice from some of the French Islands of a force going against them, should rise and massacre the White Inhabitants before you arrive to protect them."[134]

In a vivid illustration of the Kalinagos' transformation into "Black Caribs," plans for how to deal with people who impeded the spread of sugar production were informed not by experiences with Indigenous people in North America but with Maroons in Jamaica.[135] Equating Kalinagos with fugitives from slavery, Hillsborough enclosed in a "separate and secret" communiqué to St. Vincent's new governor, William Leyborne, a copy of the 1739 treaty reached with Jamaica Maroons. Hillsborough expressed his hope that the treaty might "possibly furnish [Leyborne] with some useful hints" on how to reconcile Kalinagos to British rule.[136] In keeping with the 1739 treaty, which stipulated that Maroons would "all live together . . . in a perfect state of Freedom and Liberty" on a 1,500-acre settlement in Jamaica, Hillsborough expressed a preference for resettling Kalinagos elsewhere in St. Vincent. Recognizing that such a solution might not be acceptable to colonists in the 150-square-mile island, he took the additional precaution of ordering that ships be obtained that could transport Kalinagos "to some unfrequented part of the coast of Africa or to some desert island adjacent thereto." In a nod to the potential challenges of such a journey, Hillsborough specified that Kalinagos should "be treated upon the voyage with every degree of humanity their situation will admit of."[137]

Hillsborough's instructions illustrate how the rhetoric of resident planters influenced the policy of a distant crown. Equating Kalinagos with fugitives from slavery, the secretary of state for the colonies implied that they were simply too dangerous to be tolerated within the small borders of a colony increasingly dependent on enslaved labor. Although members of Parliament continued to debate proper policy toward Kalinagos, their deliberations came too late to affect the conduct of troops more than four thousand miles away: as of February 10, 1773, the last communication the House had received from regiments in St. Vincent was dated November 14, 1772.[138] Instead, "interested men on the spot" helped determine the subsequent course of events.[139] As British military forces dispatched from North America and the West Indies gathered in St. Vincent, Governor Leyborne made a final heavy-handed attempt at diplomacy, issuing a proclamation on September 7, 1772, "that all such Charaibbes as shall within the space of 14 days from the date hereof, peaceably and without arms, come into the town of Kingstown and there in my presence submit themselves implicitly to His Majesty's pleasure, may be assured of a perfect security as to their persons, the enjoyment of their freedom and a reasonable portion of land . . . but on the other hand, such Charibbes as shall not come in and submit themselves . . . will be treated as enemies and . . . experience the utmost rigour of His [Majesty's] displeasure."[140] Chatoyer and his followers declined to accept Leyborne's offer, and in the ensuing months, British Marines and eight ground regiments from the Caribbean and North America—amounting to more than 2,200 men—mounted a military campaign against the people their sovereign had until recently hoped to transform into loyal subjects.[141] Kalinagos proved elusive enemies; as a British general reported, "the woods are so thick, that they knock our men down . . . as it is impossible we can see them," and no decisive battles were fought during the Carib War.[142] Even as Parliament continued to debate the wisdom of ordering troops to St. Vincent, between September 1772 and February 1773, seventy-two members of the British military were killed in the process of driving Kalinagos from their settlements and cutting them off from the island's windward coast. A further 83 British soldiers were wounded, 110 died of illness, and 4 deserted.[143] The number of Kalinagos who lost their lives in the conflict is unknown, but casualties were high enough to persuade their leaders to approach General Dalrymple to negotiate terms of surrender. On February 17, 1773—just two days after Parliament resolved to issue a formal address to ask King George III "by whose advice the measure was undertaken, of attacking the Caribbs"—Chatoyer and twenty-eight other Kalinago Chiefs signed "a treaty of peace and friendship" with Dalrymple.[144]

In accordance with Hillsborough's earlier suggestion, the terms of peace mirrored those reached with Jamaica Maroons more than thirty years earlier. In exchange for laying down their arms, swearing fidelity to King George III, and allowing roads to be forged through their territory, Kalinagos were permitted to retain a portion of their lands, were granted entire liberty of fishing, and were promised assistance if they decided to leave the island. Although Kalinagos would not be relocated elsewhere in St. Vincent, the treaty specified that the southern boundary of their territory be moved north from the Yambou River to the Byera River, netting British settlers some four thousand acres of land on which to cultivate sugar. The agreement also required that "runaway slaves in the possession of the Charibbs, are to be delivered up" and specified that in future any Kalinago who harbored fugitives from slavery or carried them off the island would be guilty of a capital crime.[145] The treaty starkly illustrates how the shift to sugar limited Indigenous autonomy in the Caribbean: standing in the way of slavery was now a crime punishable by death.

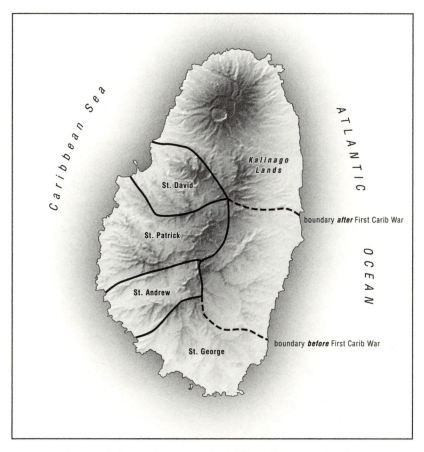

Figure 14. Following the 1772–1773 Carib War, Kalinagos were forced to cede more than four thousand acres of land on the windward coast to British settlers. Edited map based on original in John Carter Brown Library.

After years of conflict and the loss of many lives, the Kalinago and the British managed to reach an agreement that ultimately proved satisfactory to neither side; although peace had been reached on paper, both parties remained tense. Chatoyer and the twenty-eight other Kalinago representatives who made peace on behalf of their people appear to have lacked the authority to do so: several months after the treaty, a flustered Governor Leyborne reported that "the inferior Charibbs seem very much incensed at their Chiefs for making peace, declaring that they have been sold."[146] Surveyors sent to forge a road through recently acquired Kalinago lands corroborated Dalrymple's sense that many Kalinagos remained disaffected, and the commissioners requested that "a sufficient Force to overaw the Charibbs" be provided so that they might complete their work.[147] Once surveyed, the contested and vulnerable tract proved difficult to sell, with one General ultimately parting with his grant for £6 per acre, or about one-tenth the price of prime sugar lands elsewhere in the island.[148]

Following the 1772–1773 war, the Kalinagos' reputation as bellicose neighbors gained traction both in St. Vincent and in Great Britain. Artwork

Figure 15. Agostino Brunias, *Chatoyer The Chief of the Black Charaibes in St. Vincent with his five Wives* (1796). In Brunias' depiction, Kalinago leader Joseph Chatoyer is at home in the rugged landscape of St. Vincent's windward side. Courtesy John Carter Brown Library.

by Agostino Brunias, the classically trained Italian painter who went to the Ceded Islands at William Young's invitation, served to reinforce the plantocracy's depiction of "Black Caribs" as a savage and alien people.[149] In the 1773 painting *Chatoyer the Chief of the Black Charaibes in St. Vincent with his Five Wives*, Brunias depicts the Kalinago leader as "the tyrannical overseer of an army of ill-treated wives."[150] Clad only in loincloths, their black hair cropped close to their heads, the women struggle to bear the weight of children and supplies as Chatoyer stands idly by, smoking a pipe as he watches them work.

Any parallel between Chatoyer's imperious demeanor and that of planters who grew rich from the labor of others was apparently lost on settlers like Young, who increasingly highlighted Kalinagos' polygynous unions as evidence that they were brutes undeserving of the crown's protection. Another Brunias piece, *Treaty between the British and the Black Caribs*, which commemorated the signing of the 1773 accord, also served to equate Kalinagos with fugitives from slavery: the 1801 edition of Bryan Edwards' influential history of the West Indies reproduced the work but erroneously titled it *Pacification of the Maroon Negroes*, implying that it depicted self-emancipated residents of Jamaica rather than Indigenous inhabitants of St. Vincent.[151] For Edwards and other planters, there was little difference, whether physical or ideological, between Maroons in Jamaica and Black Caribs in St. Vincent. Both groups posed a threat to the advance of the plantation complex and the safety and prosperity of British subjects. After the shift to sugar production in the Ceded Islands, these threats increasingly met with violent repression.

*   *   *

Despite imperial attempts to implement well-researched plans for the development of some of the last Caribbean islands to be colonized by Europeans, and officials' willingness to revise these plans to fit local circumstances, a variety of people began challenging attempts to transform the Creole Archipelago into a center of sugar production almost as soon as the process began. As the following chapters show, contests between enslaved people and planters, Kalinagos and surveyors, and new colonists and existing settlers intensified as the conflicts that shook the Atlantic World during the Age of Revolutions reached the region. Yet the seeds of these contests were sown years earlier, in the decade after the Treaty of Paris. The rapid shift to sugar production in the Ceded Islands prompted clear demographic, economic, and legal changes, as well as alterations to the daily lives and labor of enslaved and Indigenous people that are less easy to measure but no less significant. While most people weathered these changes by finding ways to survive their new realities, others responded by running away, engaging in armed conflict, or trying to broker peace with those who sought to displace them. Their actions challenged colonial designs for the Ceded Islands, leading planters and officials to deploy real and rhetorical violence against people who threatened the advance of plantation production. In addition to responding to enslaved and Indigenous insurgency with dramatic displays of state power, colonial authorities played a key role in transforming Kalinagos into "Black Caribs"—a transformation that would ultimately facilitate Kalinago exile from the eastern Caribbean. Close attention to how a variety of people experienced and responded to the turn to sugar in the Creole Archipelago suggests parallels with similar shifts during less well-documented eras and provides further evidence of the link between Indigenous dispossession and the expansion of the plantation complex in the colonial Americas.[152]

Chapter 6

An Empire Disordered

Chatoyer was eager to put his plan into action. "Besides daily bringing over arms and ammunition from the French" in Martinique, in December 1778 the chief and his fellow Kalinagos welcomed two Frenchmen "of some consequence" to their recently reduced territory north of the Byera River, on St. Vincent's rugged windward coast. The island's British governor, Valentine Morris, had placed St. Vincent under martial law following the 1778 declaration of war between Great Britain and France, but this measure did little to stop the longstanding "intercourse of [Kalinagos] in their canoes and pettiaugers with the French" in neighboring islands.[1] As Chatoyer and his followers continued to use maritime routes to communicate and court an alliance with Great Britain's avowed enemy, Morris grew increasingly agitated. "I have from Martinique, Dominica and St. Lucia received several informations that some French, chiefly of the mulattoe, free negroe and mongrel tribe had slipped in and were with the Caraibs concealed in their woods, to direct their operations when a further landing of the French should take place," he informed his superiors.[2] "Until some step is taken to totally remove" Kalinagos, Morris warned, St. Vincent "can never enjoy internal security."[3]

The British governor's anxiety about the facility with which Kalinagos in St. Vincent could trade arms and information with people in neighboring French colonies provides a new vantage point on the American War of Independence. While the rebellion of thirteen of Great Britain's twenty-six American colonies prompted many colonial subjects in the West Indies to strengthen their ties to the crown, others saw imperial rupture as an opportunity. The 1776 outbreak of civil war in the British empire came just fourteen years after Chatoyer and thousands of other residents of the Creole Archipelago were brought under British rule. They therefore failed to resist—and in fact often welcomed—the privateering, conquest, and occupation that characterized the American Revolutionary era in the eastern Caribbean.

British officials dispatched to the Ceded Islands after the Seven Years' War repeatedly warned their superiors that the region's existing inhabitants—whether Indigenous, enslaved, or free—were "incapable of any sincere attachment" to the distant crown.[4] Yet nothing could more clearly demonstrate the limits of this attachment than the response of King George III's new subjects to French invasion and occupation of the islands in the late 1770s and early 1780s. Capitalizing on events on the North American main, beginning in 1778 French forces wrested control of the Ceded Islands from Great Britain. By June 1781, Grenada, Dominica, St. Vincent, and Tobago were under French rule, while the French colony of St. Lucia was a strategic site for the British Navy. These conquests were facilitated in part by people like Chatoyer, who ferried arms, ammunition, and information between islands and between empires.

Analyzing the American War of Independence as an episode of civil and interimperial war highlights how the small planters, free people of color, and enslaved and Indigenous people who constituted the overwhelming majority of the Caribbean population responded to the outbreak of yet another conflict between Great Britain and France.[5] Existing studies of how the war affected the Caribbean tend to focus on elites, contrasting the loyalty of planters in places like Jamaica with the rebellious conduct of their fellow British subjects on the North American main.[6] A variety of demographic, economic, cultural, and military differences help explain why Britain's twenty-six American colonies were divided in their response to the imperial reforms of the post–Seven Years' War era. In colonies where enslaved people constituted an overwhelming majority of the population, the free minority relied on military support from Great Britain to protect against both internal and external threats.[7] This demographic reality also meant that unlike in mainland North America, Caribbean colonies lacked a free population that could provide mass support for the initiatives of the colonial elite.[8] Planter absenteeism, the resultant lack of family life, and colonists' regular travel between the West Indies and Great Britain further reinforced social and cultural ties with the metropole, preventing the consolidation of distinctly creole or "American" institutions and identities comparable to those that developed in mainland colonies.[9] West Indians were also more dependent on imperial trade, particularly the transatlantic slave trade.[10] The economic protections of mercantilism further ensured planters' loyalty, as they lobbied for and secured privileged access to British markets.[11]

Yet Grenada, Dominica, and St. Vincent differed from older British West Indian colonies in significant ways, and this in turn shaped how free, enslaved, and Indigenous residents of the islands responded to the war. Many planters were born and spent their lives in the region, giving rise to a creolized community with deep familial, economic, and social connections to neighboring French colonies. While British planters began purchasing lands throughout the archipelago in the 1760s, many were absentees; as a result, French-speaking Catholic subjects still outnumbered their English-speaking Protestant counterparts, with officials in Dominica estimating that "French adopted subjects [constituted] about 2/3 of the white people actually residing in the colony."[12] Free people of color, who resented recently introduced legislation that degraded their social and economic status, were also well represented among existing residents of the archipelago, and St. Vincent was home to thousands of Kalinagos like Chatoyer, who lost substantial territory to British forces in the 1772–1773 Carib War. As was the case throughout the West Indies, all of these groups were vastly outnumbered by enslaved people, many of whom embraced the opportunity to disrupt the plantation regime. The prospect of French conquest and occupation therefore appealed to many residents of the eastern Caribbean, who declined to resist and sometimes even aided invading troops.

Rather than pursuing independence, during French occupation various residents of the islands sought to reassert features that characterized life in the Creole Archipelago before British rule. Planters regained control of their lands by converting leaseholds to freeholds, while Kalinagos moved back onto territory they had lost just a few years earlier. Professing their loyalty to France, French Catholics claimed positions of authority formerly occupied by British planters, while enslaved people engaged in marronage and attacks. After just a decade and a half of British rule, many residents of the eastern Caribbean welcomed renewed warfare as an opportunity to reestablish economic and social practices and structures of authority they had created before the islands were incorporated into the British empire.

At the 1783 Peace of Paris, Dominica, Grenada, and St. Vincent were restored to Great Britain and St. Lucia was restored to France; only Tobago remained in the hands of the conquering crown. Yet the resumption of peace did not mean a return to the status quo ante bellum, as the actions of island residents during the conflict influenced subsequent British and French strategies of colonial rule. Responding to what they perceived as treasonous conduct on the part of adopted subjects, British officials abandoned earlier attempts to assimilate French Catholics, opting instead to attract Loyalist settlers on whom they could depend. The economic consequences of conquest and occupation confirmed the importance of these small islands in the broader economies of the respective French and British empires, prompting the further acceleration of transatlantic slave trading and sugar planting. Attention to the eastern Caribbean during and immediately after the American War of Independence provides new insight on the conflict elsewhere in the Americas and highlights its impact on the many West Indians who were not members of the planter elite. For diverse residents of lesser-known British American colonies like Chief Chatoyer, the resumption of war with France after little more than a decade of peace presented welcome opportunities to reassert power, gain title to land, and improve their daily lives under a different political regime.

"The Turbulent Example of North America": Initial Responses to Civil War in the British Empire, 1774–1778

In the late 1760s and early 1770s, British subjects in the West Indies trained a close eye on contests over parliamentary prerogatives. Like their counterparts in other Caribbean colonies, planters in the Ceded Islands were eager to avoid any disruption to commercial relations. In a June 1775 address to King George III, the Grenada council and assembly "deplore[d] the horror of a civil war already manifested in the effusion of the blood of our countrymen *and friends on both sides.*"[13] Planters expressed two paramount concerns about the possible consequences of this "civil war": first, that the trade system on which they depended both for supplies and for markets for their produce would be disrupted or destroyed, and second, that the circulation of revolutionary ideas would incite enslaved and Indigenous people. Both concerns proved well founded. As American privateers swarmed Caribbean waters, cutting off trade and capturing ships, "the turbulent example of North America seemed so much to pervade every part of the colonys."[14] Maritime emissaries who carried information about the American patriots found a receptive audience in the eastern Caribbean, as Kalinagos once again sought to forge alliances with common enemies of Great Britain, and enslaved people capitalized on the disruptions of the rising conflict to liberate themselves.

Of course, not all residents of the Ceded Islands were disaffected. Like their counterparts in Barbados and Jamaica, the islands' British planters, all of whom had established themselves in the new colonies after 1763, had deep personal and financial connections to the metropole. Planters in the Ceded

Islands also benefited from a tax exemption that other West Indians did not. Successfully invoking the concept of "no taxation without representation," in 1774 they became the only British Caribbean planters legally exempt from the payment of a customary 4.5 percent duty on exports.

The exemption resulted from planter Alexander Campbell's lawsuit against William Hall, a collector of customs in Grenada. Born in Scotland, Campbell invested heavily in the Ceded Islands, purchasing his first plantation in Grenada on March 3, 1763.[15] By 1772, Campbell had amassed a considerable estate in the colony, with 233 acres planted in sugar and 190 acres planted in coffee.[16] Eager to maximize the return on his investments, Campbell sought to recover the 4.5 percent duty on exports he had been required to pay for the previous decade. In his suit against Hall, Campbell alleged that customs officers lacked the authority to impose the duty on exports, which was customarily collected throughout the British West Indies and first introduced in the Ceded Islands in July 1764, because the tax had been levied without the explicit consent of the islands' representative assembly. In finding for Campbell, Justice Lord Mansfield ruled that King George III "had *immediately and irrevocably granted* . . . that the subordinate Legislation over the Island should be exercised by the Assembly, with the Consent of the Governor and Council."[17] In short, any act introduced subsequent to the king's 1763 instructions to constitute a colonial council and assembly required the assent of both bodies to enter into force. Because the council and assembly were not consulted about the initial imposition of the 4.5 percent tax on exports, the duty could not be collected.

While historians acknowledge that the Mansfield decision "was a milestone in British legal history," little attention has been paid to a ruling that applied in only four of Great Britain's twenty-six American colonies.[18] Yet freedom from additional taxation was immensely important for planters like Campbell, who now had additional capital to devote to developing their estates and investing in technologies such as mills. Although colonial officials repeatedly attempted to introduce the tax, the respective island assemblies refused their assent. As British subjects in North America increasingly challenged Parliament's right to levy taxes, planters in the Ceded Islands could take comfort in the knowledge that they benefited from exemptions that even their counterparts elsewhere in the West Indies did not enjoy.[19]

Yet even this concession proved insufficient to placate many colonial subjects. Planters relied on North American provisions such as salt fish to feed their enslaved laborers, and these items all but disappeared following the Continental Congress's resolution to end exports to England, Ireland, and the West Indies in 1775.[20] The disruption of trade threatened not only the prosperity but also the very survival of some island residents, and planters complained that the crown did not do enough to provision them. Food shortages were most acute in the small, densely populated Leeward Islands, where hundreds of enslaved people died of starvation or malnutrition.[21] While the situation was not as dire in Jamaica or the Ceded Islands, where enslaved people had better access to provision grounds, by the latter half of the 1770s administrators regularly complained of a scarcity of necessities and a lack of specie with which to buy what few provisions were available.[22] A longstanding trade with neighboring French colonies "carried out in small French vessels, Petit Augres, and canoes" was blamed for the lack of currency, as planters traded coin for French "wine, oil, soap, silks, stockings, millinery and other articles of dress."[23]

The 1775 outbreak of war between Great Britain and thirteen of its colonies initially promised to provide some relief to the Caribbean, as British ships intercepted American vessels laden with provisions destined for French colonies.[24] Yet the "robberies and depredations" of American privateers soon disrupted trade between Britain and its remaining colonies as well as between different islands.[25] In a region where waterways, not roads, continued to serve as the main routes for commerce and travel, privateers inhibited even the most basic activities. Protesting what they claimed was inadequate protection from the British Navy, planters in Tobago complained that privateers prevented them from conveying the produce of their estates to their usual ports by boat, as ships were vulnerable even when "passing from one Bay of the Island to another." Highlighting the continued importance of cabotage, they explained that "not only all intercourse with the neighbouring islands but even with the different parts of the island itself is cut off." The disruption in intra- and interisland trade also "prevented [planters] from attending to the cultivation of their estates," as all free men in the island—who numbered just 417 individuals—needed to remain on alert.[26]

In addition to disrupting commerce, American privateers threatened to upset the balance of power on which the plantation regime rested. In one instance, privateers on the coast of Grenada "stripped quite naked all the white Inhabitants who fell into their hands," in a display that visibly undermined the authority of the colony's white minority.[27] Planters feared that this loss of control could mean the end of their profits or even their lives and were particularly worried about how the presence of American privateers affected the "language and conduct" of enslaved people and Kalinagos. By March 1777, Governor

Morris reported that the number of fugitives from slavery in St. Vincent had grown to an estimated 1,100 individuals, or almost 10 percent of the colony's enslaved population. The "more than uncommonly insolent talk" of enslaved people was reportedly spurred by their interactions with American privateers, who landed and "stayed several hours on shore in conference with" them. These conversations doubtlessly contributed to enslaved people's belief that an imminent war with France would "be the time for them to emancipate themselves."[28] Seeking refuge among St. Vincent's Kalinagos, growing numbers of enslaved people armed themselves with help from privateers and from French allies in Martinique. Morris demanded that Martinique's governor put a stop to this interisland arms smuggling, warning that if it persisted, he would send "two or three little schooners" to attack Kalinago canoes engaged "in this type of commerce." "Each one would sink fifteen or more of their pirogues," Morris threatened, and "two or three hundred of their best men would drown" as a result.[29]

Although Morris failed to follow through on his dramatic warning, his missive illustrates how the outbreak of civil war in the British empire made existing realities in the eastern Caribbean seem newly dangerous. As American privateers made their way into Caribbean waters, they posed a financial, military, and ideological threat to British rule, offering enslaved and Indigenous people hope that the recently instituted colonial regime would not be permanent. Despite persistent concerns about the information that privateers could relay to restive Kalinagos, enslaved people, and disaffected subjects, colonial officials were unable to restrain "the turbulent example of North America." The problems this example posed would only increase as France entered the conflict in 1778, turning civil war in the British empire into another Franco-British contest—one in which the Caribbean would again serve as a key theater of war.

Naval Conquests of the Eastern Caribbean, 1778–1781

As conflict mounted between Great Britain and thirteen of its American colonies, the Caribbean assumed an increasingly important strategic role. On July 3, 1776—just one day before issuing the declaration of independence—the Continental Congress dispatched twenty-four-year-old Philadelphia native William Bingham to Martinique. Although Bingham was instructed to act as a private agent, he was tasked with generating support for the American cause, determining which products were most in demand in the French colonies, and obtaining arms. Joining Bingham in Martinique was a French squadron sent to secure the newly sanctioned and already flourishing trade between the French West Indies and the new United States. In addition to opening its ports to prizes seized by American vessels and providing a place to fit out privateers, Martinique soon became a key site for funneling French munitions to mainland North America.[30] By the time that Great Britain declared war on the Americans' ally in March 1778, France's principal Lesser Antillean colony was already serving as a source of arms and information for disaffected subjects in neighboring British colonies. Capitalizing on the geography of the eastern Caribbean, Kalinagos, enslaved people, and adopted British subjects clandestinely mobilized in support of French conquest, as "a Banditti of all Nations, chiefly French," continued to carry information, goods, and people across the narrow channels separating British and French colonies.[31] Little more than a year after entering the war, French forces had taken Dominica, St. Vincent, and Grenada with very little bloodshed. While Tobago proved more difficult to conquer, the island also fell to French forces in 1781. Attention to contests over the eastern Caribbean enlarges the geopolitical dimensions of the American War of Independence and highlights how the region's aqueous geography shaped the nature of warfare.

Located directly between the colonies of Guadeloupe and Martinique, Dominica was a logical first target for French forces. Some 1,800 soldiers and volunteers from Martinique landed in Dominica at dawn on September 7, 1778, and French forces took control of the island by five o'clock the same evening.[32] While neither side suffered many casualties, a surviving firsthand account of the attack, published more than a decade later by British planter and assistant judge of the Dominica supreme court Thomas Atwood, bemoaned "the most poignant distress" of the island's inhabitants. Atwood particularly lamented "the situation of the white women and their children" who fled "shrieking and crying through the streets . . . to wade through rapid rivers, exposed to the inclemency of the weather"; to Atwood, the attack on the island was an attack on the civility and order that characterized British rule.[33] The account of Dominica's British governor, William Stuart, is decidedly less dramatic: aware that the island's 46 regular troops and 150 militiamen stood little chance against the invading force, Stuart signed a treaty he deemed "honourable to His Majesty and beneficial to his subjects."[34]

In addition to their superior military forces, the French conquered Dominica with the help of island residents. Dominica's location just twenty-four miles north of Martinique had long facilitated travel and communication between the islands, and according to Atwood, a group of "His Majesty's new adopted subjects," informed of the impending French attack, visited the island's main fort on the evening of September 6, 1778. There, they "contrived to make the few soldiers on duty intoxicated with liquor, and afterwards filled up the touch-holes of the cannon with sand," thereby ruining the soldiers' ability to fire on French troops the following day.[35] British officials noted that during the invasion many adopted subjects in Dominica "were actually in arms leading the different attacks of the enemy against us. . . . And now are embodying in militia for their new masters."[36] Despite the concessions extended to them after Dominica became a British colony in 1763, the men and women who continued to be identified as French inhabitants preferred to collaborate with invading forces who spoke their language and practiced their religion.

The terms of capitulation for Dominica, which subsequently served as a model elsewhere in the region, aimed to buttress the island as a site of communication and defense while also encouraging commercial relations that would benefit the French crown. In his speech to Dominica Council, which convened as usual the following Monday, French commander the Marquis Duchilleau assured the six British councilors present that his occupation government would "always endeavour . . . to merit the approbation of the two nations that inhabit" the island and would strive "to lighten the trouble which you feel by a change of Government."[37] Provided they paid the duties levied in other French colonies, merchants in Dominica were permitted to trade with any nation except Great Britain. The occupying government also promised to preserve the English civil government and laws then in place and allow both Catholics and Protestants to practice their religion. Colonists who occupied administrative or judicial roles at the time of surrender, such as councilors, were permitted to continue exercising office. Residents of Dominica were not required to take up arms in support of French troops, although they could do so if they wished. Most generous was article 5 of the capitulation, which stipulated that should Dominica be ceded to France after the war, "inhabitants shall have their choice either to keep their own Political Government, or accept that which is established at Martinico and the other French Islands."[38] These terms helped reconcile both British and French planters to military occupation, promoting the continued productivity of plantations by diminishing unrest.

British forces responded to the conquest of Dominica by seeking another stronghold from which they could easily reach and defend their remaining

Ceded Islands. Noting that St. Lucia "from its proximity to Martinique . . . in a manner looks into" the French colony, British commanders determined that the island would best enable them to counter any further French action in the region.[39] Sailing from Sandy Hook, New Jersey, in November 1778, the British fleet first made for Barbados, where they were joined by additional reinforcements. They then spent almost two days battling winds as they sailed the one hundred miles west from Barbados to St. Lucia—a voyage that confirmed the importance of establishing a foothold in the Windward Island chain. French commanders in Martinique quickly dispatched nine thousand troops across the twenty-one-mile channel south to St. Lucia, but in the ensuing weeks, French forces suffered an estimated five hundred casualties. On the morning of December 29, 1778, French troops left St. Lucia, and the island's inhabitants agreed to capitulate the following day.[40]

The time it took British vessels to sail from Barbados to St. Lucia confirmed the importance of maintaining a base in the eastern Caribbean archipelago. Given that troops from Martinique could reach the island in "a few hours," it was imperative that "a considerable force [be] kept in garrison" in St. Lucia.[41] Conquering St. Lucia also helped staunch communication with St. Vincent, "where the landing from that island in even canoes, and in the night is very easy, and the distance scarce three hours voyage."[42] With Dominica serving as an example of the consequences of allowing people to ferry information and arms between colonies, the British sought to control St. Lucia, "which is so well situated to watch the motions" of people in Martinique and St. Vincent.[43]

The terms of capitulation for St. Lucia largely mirrored those for Dominica. Although residents of St. Lucia were now deemed British subjects, they were allowed to exercise their Catholic religion and "be governed by the established laws of the colony." People in positions of authority, such as judges, would retain their posts, and planters would not be disturbed in possession of their estates; as in French-occupied Dominica, the goal was to maintain peace and profitability.[44] These generous terms had the desired effect of minimizing resistance to the conquest of other islands; regardless of their linguistic, religious, or political allegiance, planters were eager to preserve their property in land and people. In St. Vincent, Governor Morris reported that planters openly admitted their reluctance to "make a vigorous, if any defence," and several expressed their opinion "that such would be to no other purpose, than to prevent this Island receiving such good terms as were granted to Dominica."[45] In June 1779, French and Kalinago forces secured the surrender of British St. Vincent without a single casualty.[46]

From the perspective of planters and colonial officials, St. Vincent's peaceful surrender had the additional benefit of denying the island's Kalinago inhabitants the opportunity to attack from within. Still reeling from the 1772–1773 Carib War, officials in St. Vincent trained a close eye on Kalinagos, who "flew over in great numbers to Martinique and St. Lucia to buy arms and ammunition for themselves and friends"—fugitives from slavery who increasingly sought refuge among them.[47] After receiving word of the outbreak of war between France and Great Britain in the summer of 1778, Kalinagos wasted no time in offering their support to Martinique's governor, who "treats them always, lets them breakfast and dine in his presence; gives them money which they directly lay out in arms and ammunition."[48]

French conquest of Dominica provided Kalinagos with another opportunity to reiterate their support for the French cause. In September 1778, "between 5 and 600 stout, able bodied different Charibs" traveled to St. Lucia by pirogue to offer their services in the war. Displaying their allegiance by sporting French colors, Kalinagos demonstrated their knowledge of European imperial rivalries and their desire to align themselves with a crown that they judged more likely to support their claims to territory.[49] Although Governor Morris proposed "to stave to pieces all their pettiaugers or large canoes" to prevent Kalinagos from circulating between islands, he failed to receive permission for his proposed destruction.[50] Eager to preserve their lives and possessions, as well as their claims to land, Vincentian planters readily surrendered to French forces in part to prevent Kalinagos—of whom a reported 1,100 assisted in French conquest—from destroying their settlements.[51]

Following the June 1779 conquest of St. Vincent, a French fleet consisting of twelve frigates and twenty-five battleships proceeded to Grenada, where Governor Macartney succeeded in mobilizing just 125 regular troops and fewer than 400 militiamen against an estimated 6,500 French soldiers.[52] A state of Grenada's militia taken in May 1778 indicated 1,360 men "able to carry arms" in the colony: 790 natural-born British subjects, 324 adopted subjects, and 256 "free mulattoes and mestifs, mostly French."[53] The political sympathies of the latter groups alarmed the British; as Macartney reported in January 1779, "the French of every denomination and color are totally disaffected."[54] It therefore came as little surprise when the island's meager defenses were further diminished by "the desertion of almost all the colored people and the greatest part of the new subjects," and Grenada surrendered to French forces on July 4, 1779.[55] Among those who suffered during the French invasion was Councilor George Staunton, who was subsequently sent to France as a hostage. In a request for redress lodged in 1780, Staunton alleged that invading soldiers "pillaged his house, stole all the furnishings, livestock, and other transportable effects, [and] damaged the buildings."[56]

Despite the destruction that Staunton experienced, French conquest of Dominica, St. Vincent, and Grenada proceeded with relatively little violence.[57] This was due in no small part to British settlers' awareness that they constituted a minority in all three islands. Perceiving threats from both external and internal enemies, British authorities capitulated to avoid the destruction of some of their most profitable Caribbean colonies. Only in Tobago, where all 417 white men and 57 white women who composed the island's free population were identified as natural-born British subjects, did settlers mount sustained resistance to French invasion. Located southeast of the Windward archipelago, Tobago was the last Ceded Island to be conquered during the war. Appearing off the coast on May 22, 1781, with 3,000 troops, French forces spent several days in pursuit of Tobago's small militia, which retreated to the leeward side of the island along with an estimated 400 British soldiers.[58] Although there were no adopted subjects or Kalinagos to support French invasion, Tobago lacked adequate naval protection. A British squadron belatedly dispatched to the island was captured by the French fleet, and on June 5, 1781, Lieutenant Governor Ferguson agreed to terms of surrender that the island's principal planters judged to be "upon the whole better than the Dominica articles."[59]

Conquests in the eastern Caribbean reveal how the region's populace and geography continued to distinguish it from other parts of the West Indies. Kalinagos, enslaved people, and adopted British subjects accustomed to traveling and trading across the archipelago's narrow channels now ferried arms and information that facilitated French invasion. The presence of these internal enemies minimized British resistance to conquest; already outnumbered by enslaved and Indigenous people and French planters, recently arrived British settlers now found themselves under the rule of a rival crown.

Life Under Occupation, 1778–1783

Despite the considerable disruptions wrought by civil and interimperial war, during occupation many elements of daily life in the eastern Caribbean remained much the same as they had been in the years prior. As suggested by the terms of capitulation, British and French officials sought above all to ensure the colonies' security and continued productivity, and the multilingual, multireligious nature of these communities persisted as a result. Throughout the war, the islands continued to produce millions of pounds of sugar, coffee, and cacao. In French-occupied islands, legal documents such as deeds and leases, acts of manumission, and wills were registered in either French or English according to the preference of the people drafting the document, and monetary values were given in British pounds sterling or the corresponding amount of French livres.[60] Government proclamations were issued in both English and French, and surviving newspapers from the period contain advertisements and official announcements printed in both languages. In British-occupied St. Lucia, the overwhelmingly Catholic population continued to marry, baptize their children, and bury their dead under the care of the same priests who tended to the parishes when the island was under French rule. Despite exchanging one distant crown for another, free residents of the islands retained many features of religious life, political culture, agricultural and economic practices that characterized their creolized communities.

Yet the period of occupation also allowed various groups to seek opportunities that a decade and a half of British rule had made more difficult to secure. French planters capitalized on the presence of occupying troops to settle personal and legal grievances, convert leaseholds to freeholds, and seek positions of authority. Kalinagos used relationships with French officials to gain assurances of their autonomy and to move back onto lands relinquished in the Carib War, while enslaved people benefited from the period of disruption to strengthen Maroon communities and launch attacks. These changes prompted many British planters to leave the islands, further reducing their demographic and socioeconomic influence. Events during occupation suggest the limits of assimilationist policies introduced after the Seven Years' War, as residents of the Creole Archipelago quickly reestablished many features of daily life before British rule.

The presence of occupying troops quickly alienated many island residents. Colonists were required to furnish troops with cattle, which exacerbated the existing scarcity of provisions while also threatening the productivity of plantations. As British planter Charles Winstone lamented, "[e]very sugar estate . . . [is] in want of cattle to make dung to manure the land. . . . Where this evil will end God knows."[61] The conduct of occupying troops further stoked planter resentment. As Thomas Atwood later alleged, the behavior of French soldiers drove many British settlers to leave. The embittered planter cited the soldiers' regular insults to Englishmen, their practice of "throwing showers of stones on their houses in the night-time," and of "saluting the

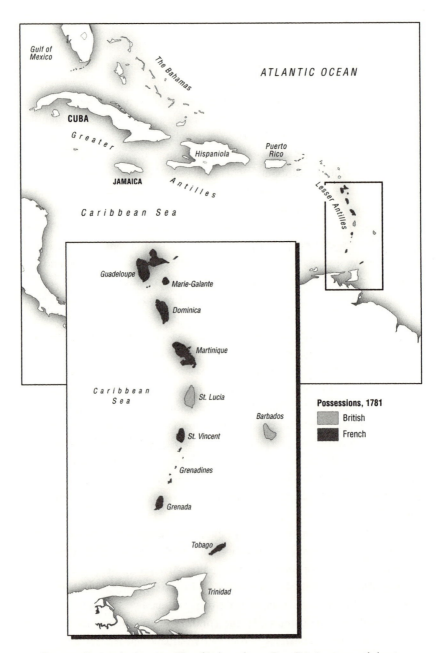

Figure 16. During the American War of Independence, Great Britain temporarily lost its dominance in the eastern Caribbean, as French forces conquered the Ceded Islands.

English white women with indecent expressions as they passed by" as evidence of their abuses.[62]

Although Atwood's account is clouded by resentment, there is little doubt that the presence of French occupying forces provided both soldiers and civilians with a chance to exercise power, as individuals seized the opportunity to settle both personal scores and perceived administrative injustices. Judging the behavior of French planters to be just as reprehensible as that of French occupying troops, Atwood singled out two individuals whose conduct he found particularly offensive: one "insolently drew his sword on a respectable English merchant in a public tavern," while the other, "a Frenchman of colour, of the name Blanchdelablong . . . had the audacity to strike the English Chief Justice."[63] Emboldened by the presence of occupying troops who spoke their language and practised their religion, individuals who might otherwise have avoided confrontation began to openly—and sometimes violently—challenge men who had been elevated to positions of authority under British rule.

French planters also used the occupation to accede to positions denied to them under the British regime. As existing British Protestant members of Dominica Council died or left the island, occupying officials appointed French Catholics to replace them. In February 1779, just five months after Dominica capitulated to France, Nicolas Crocquet de Belligny—who, along with his late wife, Marie Catherine La Verge La Feuillée, had lived in Dominica for decades—was appointed to the council.[64] Four months later, François Alexandre Colas Dauchamps was appointed to replace the late John Weir, while in July 1781, Jean Louis Fournier Desravinieres was appointed in the place of William Garnier, who had been absent from Dominica since 1777.[65] Both Belligny and Desravinieres were considerable planters: by 1773, the former had one hundred acres of land on lease, while the latter held eighty-two acres on lease and a further eighty-one acres as freehold. But Dauchamps owned just twenty-three acres of land, suggesting that he occupied a socioeconomic position far below that of the wealthy British planters with whom he served on the council.[66] His appointment owed not to his wealth but to his loyalty to the French cause. As commander of Dominica's militia during the occupation, Dauchamps convinced "the better part of the inhabitants" to take up arms for the French, despite the fact that such service was optional.[67] Marginalized under British rule, planters like Dauchamps used French occupation to reassert authority.

In St. Vincent, where Governor Morris had dissolved the council and the assembly several months before French invasion, planters did not have the same opportunity to formally exercise power.[68] They were, however, able to use French occupation to convert their leases to freeholds, thereby gaining permanent title to lands.[69] "The intention of his Majesty [Louis XVI] being to treat favorably the inhabitants" of St. Vincent, French officials decreed that planters who wished to be "free of all Quit-Rents and Duties" could do so by making a one-time payment of 8 livres per acre of land in their possession, thereby assuring "them the full and entire property of Lands they are possessed of."[70] By offering all planters in St. Vincent the opportunity to establish permanent title to land, French authorities sought to reconcile them to their rule, promote the continued productivity of plantations, and ensure that French planters would have legal cause to remain in the island regardless of the crown to which it belonged.

The greatest changes occurred in the former French colony of Grenada, where the nature of occupation differed in several ways from that in Dominica, St. Vincent, and Tobago. Whereas existing British laws and personnel were allowed to remain in place in the other islands, in Grenada all laws introduced during British rule were abolished.[71] Instead, conquering forces in Grenada decreed that the island would be governed by the same laws as those then in force in the French colonies of Guadeloupe and Martinique. A comparison of the terms of capitulation for Grenada versus those for the other conquered islands suggests that French administrators conceived of their presence in Grenada not as a temporary military occupation but as a reassertion of sovereignty. From the perspective of the French, the conquest of 1779 was merely a continuation of an earlier conflict that had not been resolved to their satisfaction; French invasion aimed to end British occupation of what was rightfully a French colony. King Louis XVI's proclamation on the matter was unambiguous: "From and after the 4th of July, 1779, being the Day on which the Island of Grenada *returned under the Sovereignty of his Majesty*, the Persons and Estates of all the Inhabitants of the said Island . . . shall be ruled and governed by the Laws, Customs, and Usages, observed in the French Windward American Islands."[72]

The restoration of French laws was accompanied by significant changes in personnel. Unlike in Dominica, where the terms of capitulation stipulated that active councilors, assemblymen, and judges could continue to sit, in Grenada existing colonial bodies were dissolved in favor of a newly constituted Conseil Superieur.[73] In contrast to the situation under British rule, in which both British Protestants and a limited number of French Catholics were eligible for seats on the Grenada council and assembly, only Roman Catholic men could be appointed to the Conseil.[74] While several members were administrators recently arrived from France, resident planters such as Etienne Molenier, who owned a sugar estate in St. George's and acted as commander of the parish after French conquest, also acceded to positions of power under French rule.[75] Stripped of their positions, British former members of the council and the assembly seethed as their French Catholic neighbors exercised new influence.

British planters were further marginalized as the restoration of French rule drew residents of neighboring colonies to Grenada. When French officials resumed assessing the customary capitation tax, in 1779, Grenada counted 1,757 free people, of whom 895 were identified as "European," or white, and 862 as people of color.[76] By 1783, the colony's free population had grown considerably, to 1,447 whites and 1,237 people of color. Significantly, the bulk of this population was identified as French: Grenada counted 594 "white English people of all ages and sex" compared to 853 French people of the same description, along with 190 English and 1,072 French free people of color.[77] The increase of 552 whites and 375 people of color in just four years suggests that French subjects elsewhere in the empire also believed French rule in Grenada would be permanent and migrated to the conquered colony in response. Their regional resettlement meant that the language and religion of the French crown continued to flourish, despite Britain's decade-and-a-half-long attempt to anglicize Grenada.

In addition to planters, other island residents used French invasion and occupation to their advantage. With their 1773 defeat by British forces still fresh in their minds, Chatoyer and his fellow Kalinagos in St. Vincent were eager to join with French troops against what was now a common enemy.[78] Displaying their allegiance by wearing French colors, in the wake of French conquest of Dominica groups of Kalinagos traveled by pirogue from St. Vincent to St. Lucia, where they "were introduced to the Governor or Commandant . . . [and] always received . . . muskets, powder, balls, and cartouche boxes" from their allies.[79] "Constantly armed" and on "regular guard," Kalinagos "kept themselves in readiness to receive and join" invading forces.[80] When presented with the opportunity to do so in June 1779, a reported 1,100 Kalinagos participated in the conquest of St. Vincent—"by far the largest component of the invasion force."[81] As a result of their crucial role in French conquest of St. Vincent, Chatoyer, "one or two of his brothers," and another Kalinago representative attended negotiations regarding the terms of capitulation. As Governor Morris later reported, Chatoyer took the opportunity to "set forth exactly his complaints against the English, for infractions of the [1773] treaty with them."[82] Emphasizing that Kalinagos were equal partners in the conquest of St. Vincent, Chatoyer sought to ensure that the renewal of interimperial war would also serve the interests of his people.

Kalinago actions during occupation illustrate how these interests sometimes diverged from those of the French. Reporting on a failed British attempt to retake the island in December 1780, French officials noted that Kalinagos "conducted themselves very well" and also "destroyed some estates of the English inhabitants."[83] While Kalinagos assisted French troops, they did so in part to retaliate against people who had begun encroaching on their lands in the previous decade, weakening the plantation system that the occupying crown hoped to protect. Kalinagos continued to take revenge on British settlers throughout French occupation, "some of whom they have murther'd, and others they have driven off their plantations and burn'd their houses."[84]

Kalinagos also capitalized on French rule to move back onto territory lost during the 1772–1773 Carib War. While British authorities asserted that "by treaty all his Majesty's subjects have a right to due intercourse in and through their country," in the late 1770s Kalinagos began policing boundaries between settler and Indigenous lands.[85] They also enlarged the boundaries of this territory, moving back onto recently ceded lands south of the Byera River. During negotiations over the terms of capitulation, Chatoyer used a map of St. Vincent to pinpoint what he asserted was the lawful border between Indigenous and settler lands—a border that significantly diminished the territory recently ceded to settlers.[86] French authorities supported Kalinago claims to lands relinquished by the 1773 treaty by offering Kalinagos legal channels denied to them under British rule. If any difficulties arose between Kalinagos and planters who encroached on their territory, the French promised to "name commissioners to hear the complaints and resolve grievances."[87] While Kalinagos could not oust settlers, they used French occupation to secure a division of St. Vincent that more closely mirrored the form it had taken before 1763, reasserting dominion over the island's windward side.

The presence of a rival sovereign further allowed Kalinagos to gain formal assurances that they would not be removed from St. Vincent. Representing themselves as "faithful subjects" of the French Crown, in 1781 a group of Kalinagos, headed by Chatoyer, directly petitioned the governor of Martinique. Reminding him that they had shed blood in defense of St. Vincent—"something they had never done while the English were masters of the island"—they condemned a rumored plan to "deprive them of their wives and children and expose them to the fury of the Waquérys" by removing them to Trinidad.[88] Forming an alliance with the French allowed Kalinagos to reverse some of the territorial losses sustained under British rule, while gaining assurances that proposed plans to exile them would not be executed.

Enslaved people also used the disruptions of war and occupation to their advantage. The best-known instance of coordinated rebellion during this period—a foiled conspiracy in Hanover, Jamaica, allegedly involving insurgents on forty-three estates in July 1776—suggests that enslaved people recognized this moment of upheaval as an opportune time to revolt.[89] Yet as Jason Sharples notes, the growing imperial crisis also made planters more vigilant about the possibility of insurrection, leading them to seek out and violently suppress any suspected sedition.[90] Rather than organizing uprisings, during the American war increasing numbers of enslaved people in the eastern Caribbean engaged in marronage, drawing on a well-established tactic to weather yet another era of war.

With "many fresh negroes of the estates resorting" to existing Maroon encampments, by the late 1770s the number of fugitives from slavery in St. Vincent grew to an estimated 1,100 people, or approximately 10 percent of the colony's enslaved population. Aware of the danger to settlers if "the negroes' quarrel [became] a common one with all the Caraibs," Governor Morris deliberately sought to sow divisions between the two groups.[91] Yet attempts to arm Kalinagos so that they could pursue runaways backfired, as Kalinagos instead used the opportunity to "defraud" the British "of much provision and ammunition from the King's stores."[92] Assisted by a Kalinago chief named Bigo, Maroons in St. Vincent refused to surrender until British troops destroyed the "amazing quantity of provisions . . . to the extent of some miles behind" their camp, using the threat of starvation to drive fugitives from their mountain stronghold. Even then, Maroons who surrendered did so on condition that they were "never to be returned to their former masters." By insisting instead that they should "belong to his Majesty," Maroons hinted that their flight from slavery was in direct response to the conditions they experienced as St. Vincent's plantations transitioned to sugar production under British rule.[93]

In Dominica, Maroons also emerged "in great numbers [and] in a most audacious manner" during the war.[94] "To the great terror and danger of the inhabitants," they grew particularly emboldened during French occupation and began "parading the high roads in the vicinity of the town armed with cutlasses [and] pistols." In addition to robbing people traveling on the road, Maroons began to "attack planters in their dwelling houses on their plantations," going so far as to shoot and kill English planter Robert Graham.[95]

Rather than carrying out their activities under cover of night, Maroons "often came ... with conk shells blowing and French colours flying, close to the town of Roseau in the day-time."[96] The display of French colors illustrates that enslaved people, like Kalinagos, were aware of the enmity between the British and French and consciously courted the support of the latter. Atwood claimed that Commander Duchilleau encouraged this alliance by "engag[ing] with them for defending the island," providing Maroons with "the muskets and bayonets which he took from the English inhabitants."[97] While members of Dominica Council did not go so far as to accuse Duchilleau of arming Maroons, they noted that during the French occupation fugitives had little "fear of being apprehended and being brought to justice." "An example so dangerous," they warned, "must have the obvious consequence of occasioning the remaining slaves to join the runaways."[98]

As Maroons increased in number during foreign occupation, some began to exact revenge on the people who had held them in bondage. Members of Dominica Council complained that Maroons "have sent and are daily sending to the *English* planters, menaces against their lives, and their property." With "many of the English white inhabitants as well as the English people of color having quitted the island," and "the French people of color being embodied as a military corps," the councilors alleged that "the force of the civil power is become insufficient to subdue these formidable bands"; in short, those who engaged in attacks were unlikely to be apprehended while the French were in charge.[99] Only after Maroons killed another white resident of Dominica in 1782 were planters permitted to raise a detachment against runaways—one supported by planters' own funds.[100] Following an engagement in which Maroons "suffered considerably, both in killed and wounded," they ended their attacks on planters.[101] Nonetheless, the actions Maroons took during the war were enough to reduce some settlers "to the necessity of abandoning their estates and quitting the Island after having been plundered."[102] As in Grenada, French occupation affected Dominica's population, increasing the size and influence of the French planter class vis-à-vis the British.[103]

The problem of enslaved insurgency during the American War was not confined to islands occupied by the French. In British-occupied St. Lucia, French planters complained that they earned respite from Maroons only after engaging in "highly deadly hunts which necessarily diminished the number of [enslaved] workers."[104] War between France and Great Britain provided enslaved people in the Ceded Islands with new opportunities to gain freedom and to exact vengeance on those who had held them in bondage. Throughout the archipelago, thousands of people took to the islands' mountainous interiors, where they continued to be "exceedingly troublesome" both during and immediately after the conflict.[105]

Concerns about the desertion or insurgency of enslaved people were all the more pressing because renewed warfare between Great Britain and France once again interrupted the transatlantic slave trade.[106] Following French conquest of Dominica, Grenada, and St. Vincent in 1778 and 1779, the trade ceased almost entirely: just one ship, the *Spy*, disembarked captives in Dominica during this period, after being captured by the French in 1781.[107] While British conquest of St. Lucia in December 1778 redirected some traffic toward the former French colony, increased naval activity in the Caribbean in the early 1780s meant that the transatlantic slave trade to the Ceded Islands amounted to only a tiny fraction of what it had been before the war.[108]

Although enslaved laborers in the eastern Caribbean continued to produce millions of pounds of sugar, coffee, and cacao throughout the war, exports were significantly reduced by French occupation, as well as by hurricanes that "destroyed all the provisions . . . the canes and coffee," in 1779 and 1780.[109] Between 1779 and 1780—the first year after French forces captured Dominica, St. Vincent, and Grenada—the amount of coffee shipped from the West Indies to Great Britain declined by 1,873,000 pounds. From a prewar high of 1,525,833 cwt in 1779, exports of sugar from the West Indies to Great Britain declined to 1,080,848 cwt in 1781—a decrease of almost fifty million pounds.[110] While these decreases were due in part to disruptions in transatlantic shipping that affected merchants throughout the Caribbean, French occupation also diverted exports from the Ceded Islands to the neighboring free port of St. Eustatius.

These disruptions in trade, production, and internal security provided clear proof of where the loyalties of Great Britain's new subjects lay. By capitalizing on the second interimperial war in fifteen years to ally with French forces, reassert title to land, and assume positions of authority, French planters frustrated several elements of Britain's attempt to transform the islands in the decade and a half prior. Welcoming French occupation further allowed the islands' enslaved majorities, as well as Kalinagos, to disrupt economic activity, assert autonomy, and seek freedom. Events in the Ceded Islands during the American War of Independence would shape subsequent imperial policies, as the actions of people the British Crown had recently sought to assimilate contributed to authorities' convictions that "the temper of these people is too well known, to depend upon their faith."[111]

The Eastern Caribbean After
American Independence, 1784–1789

The 1783 Peace of Paris largely reaffirmed the terms of the 1763 Treaty of Paris as they pertained to the Ceded Islands. Although Great Britain lost its thirteen rebellious colonies, as well as the short-lived colonies of East and West Florida, the redirection of naval resources to the Caribbean after the 1781 Battle of Yorktown allowed George III to enter negotiations with France from a position of strength.[112] Following British victory at the 1782 Battle of the Saintes, France was forced to restore Dominica, Grenada, and St. Vincent to Britain, while St. Lucia was restored to France. Only Tobago was retained by the conquering crown; the island would remain a French colony until it was retaken by British forces in 1793, during yet another interimperial war.[113] Despite this return to the status quo, events in the eastern Caribbean during the American War of Independence served as vivid proof that imperial policies adopted in the wake of the Seven Years' War were insufficient to win the loyalty of new colonial subjects and eradicate the threat that enslaved and Indigenous peoples were seen to pose. The loss of Tobago and the mainland colonies made the resumption of economic profitability in Britain's remaining West Indian possessions all the more pressing. In the wake of U.S. independence, British administrators therefore pursued a variety of measures designed to ensure the profitability of their remaining colonies and the loyalty of the subjects who resided there.[114] Despite claims that "the same policy of toleration returned" after the Ceded Islands were restored to Great Britain, the 1780s witnessed the revocation of many of the political and economic gains that island residents successfully fought to secure between the 1763 Treaty of Paris and the outbreak of the American Revolution.[115] Prominent British planters who had unsuccessfully opposed the admission of French planters to the council and assembly in the 1760s were adamant that the "gross misconduct" of adopted subjects during the war warranted the immediate "abolition of the indiscreet and improper privilege which had been formerly granted to them."[116] In addition to refusing to allow new subjects to accede to positions they had enjoyed in the 1760s and 1770s, in the 1780s British officials imposed stricter controls on free people of color and sought to entice Loyalists to bolster the population of British subjects resident in the colonies. The era of experimentation came to an end as the British crown grew more assertive in its efforts to create profitable plantation colonies—colonies with little room for Indigenous dominion or Black freedom.[117]

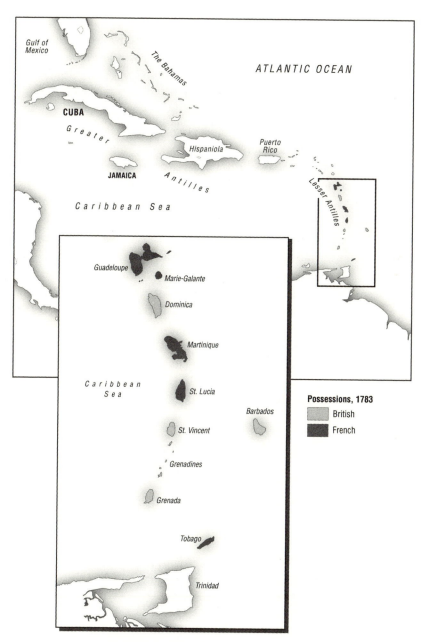

Figure 17. Following the American War of Independence, France retained control of Tobago. All other islands conquered during the conflict were restored to the crowns that claimed them before the war.

British authorities who resumed control of Dominica, Grenada, and
St. Vincent in January 1784 confronted colonies mired by debt, destruction,
and disorder. Eager to reestablish estates damaged by war, hurricanes, and the
death or desertion of enslaved laborers, planters and officials welcomed the
Ceded Islands' return to their former role as a key node in the transatlantic
slave trade; as a trader in St. Vincent remarked in 1784, people were sold "at
higher prices than ever was known to be given for slaves in this island."[118] In
the first six years of peace, more than 77,200 West African captives disembarked in the Ceded Islands, as British slavers redoubled their participation in
human trafficking. As was the case before the American Revolution, many of
these captives were subsequently trafficked to other parts of the Americas. The
St. Vincent Customs House recorded 3,926 enslaved people carried out of the
island between January 1784 and July 1789, but British officials estimated that
the actual number was closer to 8,000, as traders often bypassed the customs
house to avoid paying duties.[119] Much of this commerce was regional; as the
St. Vincent trader remarked, "the demand for slaves here is likely to continue
for some time, as the Islands of Tobago and St. Lucia will be entirely supplied
from here, and it lies very convenient for supplying Martinique."[120]

In addition to renewing their participation in human trafficking, colonial officials sought to increase profitability by diminishing the possibility of
future disruptions to island politics. Justifiably concerned about the loyalties
of people who had welcomed or even facilitated foreign occupation, the new

Table 11. Number of Enslaved Africans Disembarked
in the Ceded Islands, 1784–1789

Year	Dominica	St. Lucia	St. Vincent	Grenada	Tobago	Annual Total
1784	5,521	660	2,145	1,714	328	10,368
1785	7,152	277	1,297	3,266	195	12,634
1786	7,053		1,934	1,910	526	11,423
1787	6,137		2,988	4,130	656	13,912
1788	6,411		3,155	7,773	358	17,697
1789	3,294		903	6,491	500	11,188
Totals	35,568	937	12,422	25,284	2,563	76,774

Source: Slave Voyages: Trans-Atlantic Slave Trade Database, https://slavevoyages.org/voyages/T2uys3C9.
This table does not indicate the number of people subsequently trafficked out of the respective islands.

British governors of Dominica, Grenada, and St. Vincent sought to confirm the allegiance of adopted subjects by requiring all free males over the age of fourteen and all women who held property in the Ceded Islands to publicly take oaths of allegiance, supremacy, and abjuration within thirty days of the islands' restoration to Great Britain.[121] While these conditions mirrored those applied in the wake of the 1763 Treaty of Paris, after American independence the benefits that planters derived from making the required oaths were significantly reduced.

Although Grenada's governor, Edward Mathew, received explicit instructions to reinstate the favorable terms under which former subjects of the French crown were permitted to stand for election, be appointed to the council, and act as justices of the peace, the island's British planters declined to afford French Catholics the privileges they enjoyed before the war.[122] As Mathew explained, "the appointment of a French Counsellor, or the election of a French Representative, would occasion a total interruption to public business," as Grenada's governing bodies, which were now entirely composed of natural-born British subjects, resisted any attempt to allow adopted subjects to rejoin their ranks. "The general sense is so much against the French pretensions, that I think but a revocation of that part of the instructions can confirm the tranquility of this government," Mathew advised his superiors.[123] When a French candidate "was returned, as having a majority of votes," for election in St. George's parish, "the House of Assembly [simply] set aside the return" and installed his English Protestant opponent instead.[124] Grenada's Protestant-controlled council and assembly further sought to limit the threat adopted subjects might pose by issuing a new elections bill. In addition to stipulating that all candidates for office be Protestants—not Catholics—possessed of at least fifty acres of land in the island, the bill required that anyone wishing to vote publicly declare "that I am not now a subject of, or bear or owe any allegiance" to the French crown.[125]

French Catholic planters vehemently protested the denial of privileges formerly afforded to them, but they lacked the power to enforce the crown's instructions. Along with repeatedly appealing to both local administrators and officials in London, French planters declared that they would oppose any candidate who did not pledge to "restore to the new subjects, the priviledges of citizens of which they have been unjustly deprived."[126] Despite these pleas, British planters and officials in the Ceded Islands maintained their conviction that "principles of Liberality towards the New Subjects . . . proved to be destructive of the Constitution."[127] In response to their increasing marginalization under British rule, some French planters began to quit the islands, migrating to Spanish Trinidad, where their Catholic religion enabled them to obtain grants of land.[128] Eschewing accommodationist policies that characterized British rule in the Ceded Islands before American independence, planters and officials trained a watchful eye on Great Britain's remaining colonial subjects.

They also focused greater attention on free people of color. While British administrators reported no free people of color in Tobago before the American Revolution, by 1783 the newly French colony counted 118 free people of color and 405 whites.[129] The increase in the number of French free people of color in Grenada gave administrators particular cause for concern. British officials who resumed control of Grenada in 1784 reported 996 white inhabitants, of whom 440 were British and 556 were former French subjects, along with 185 free people of color counted as English and 940 as French.[130] These figures were slightly lower than those given by French officials the year before, suggesting that some residents of Grenada left the island when it was restored to Great Britain.[131] Despite this emigration, by the mid-1780s French people of color constituted the single largest group of free people in Grenada, and adopted subjects of all races outnumbered natural-born subjects 1,496 to 625. Although the 520 free people of color in Dominica were outnumbered by 1,400 whites, colonial officials were careful to note that among those capable of bearing arms were 200 free men of color, 260 British, and 340 adopted subjects.[132] If free men of color and adopted subjects were to unite, both Grenada and Dominica could again be lost to internal enemies. With "the desertion of almost all the colored people and the greatest part of the new subjects" during the war still fresh in

Table 12. Free and Enslaved Populations of the Eastern Caribbean, c. 1783

	Dominica (British)	Grenada (British)	St. Lucia (French)	St. Vincent (British)	Tobago (French)
White people	1,400	996	2,114	1,276	405
Free people of color	520	1,125	1,024	214	118
Enslaved people	13,265	24,620	15,163	12,380	10,530
Kalinagos	—	—	—	4,000	—
Total population	15,185	26,741	18,301	17,870	11,053

Sources: Dominica: TNA CO 71/8 N. 190. Grenada: TNA CO 101/28 N. 123, State of Grenada. St. Lucia: ANOM DPPC G1 506, Recensement Sainte-Lucie, 1784. St. Vincent: ANOM FM C10D 2, Recensement general, 1782. Tobago: ANOM FM C10E 7, Recensement general, 1783.

the minds of administrators, verifying both the loyalty and the legal status of the colonies' growing population of free people of color became a priority.[133]

Acutely aware of the precarious position they occupied in societies dominated by chattel slavery, in the wake of the war people of African descent took particular care to have their free status registered with relevant British authorities. In Dominica, free people of color produced certificates of manumission, wills, and baptismal records dating back as far as the 1740s, testifying to their residence in the island decades before it became a British colony.[134] In Grenada, those who lacked documentation were required to find fellow subjects who would swear before justices of the peace that they were "reputed and regarded to be, to all Intents and Purposes whatsoever, Free from Slavery," and that they "did behave and demean . . . themselves decently, and as becoming Free Persons of . . . their complexion." In addition to subjecting people of color to public scrutiny of their behavior and demeanor, this law threatened their very freedom: anyone who failed to produce "two credible freeholders" to confirm their free status could be imprisoned or sold "at public Outcry, as a Slave."[135] As Great Britain tightened its hold on its remaining colonial subjects, many of the individuals who had established themselves in the eastern Caribbean in the decades prior found their claims to residence, respectability, and even freedom under threat.

Longtime island residents were also marginalized by the arrival of British subjects from elsewhere in the empire. When the short-lived British colony of East Florida was returned to Spain in 1783, planters from Georgia and South Carolina who had taken refuge in the British stronghold found themselves once again without a home. Motivated by the proclamation of East Florida's British governor, Patrick Tonyn, that his fellow governors in the British West Indies would provide Loyalists with tracts of land and twelve months' provisions, in the years after 1783 approximately 3,400 white and more than 6,500 enslaved people left East Florida.[136] Although many of these refugees sailed for the Bahamas and a smaller number for Jamaica, as many as 450 Loyalist planters took approximately 2,000 enslaved people and attempted to establish themselves in Dominica.[137]

Both resident planters and the Committee of Dominica Proprietors in London explicitly sought to increase the "strength of the colony as well as its prosperity," and the presence of slaveholding Loyalists promised to do both.[138] To encourage Loyalist settlement, the Dominica Assembly voted to exempt any Loyalist who arrived in the colony before April 20, 1786, from all public taxes for a period of fifteen years. To provide particular encouragement to settlers bringing enslaved laborers, the act further exempted Loyalists from the customary head tax on enslaved people for the same fifteen-year period. All that was asked in return was that Loyalists swear before a magistrate that they intended to permanently settle in Dominica.[139]

The proposed measures soon confronted the realities of scarcity caused by the recent war. In June 1785, 150 refugees from East Florida joined the estimated 110 Loyalists who had arrived in Dominica the previous year, and the new arrivals reported that another 400 to 500 people were already en route. With rainy season fast approaching, Governor Orde despaired of finding a place to lodge the growing Loyalist population.[140] In addition to the immediate challenges of sheltering and provisioning Loyalists, there was the problem of where to settle them long-term. The thousands of unclaimed acres that the Committee of Dominica Proprietors highlighted in their proposal to attract Loyalists were unsettled for a reason: located in swampy mangroves, on the sides of steep volcanic peaks, or deep in the island's densely forested interior, the proposed plots were ill suited to plantations.

Despite the problems attendant in settling Loyalists in Dominica, the island's British planters persevered in the task. In the years after U.S. independence, the governor, the council, and the assembly repeatedly attempted to satisfy Loyalist petitions for further aid.[141] The measures taken to accommodate Loyalists in Dominica contrast with the situation in Jamaica, where Loyalists were initially welcomed but soon aroused the ire of established planters who resented any relief afforded to their would-be competitors.[142] With a landed elite already long established in Jamaica, Loyalists were seen not as a means to bolster the population faithful to Great Britain but as a challenge to the interests of existing planters. News that Jamaican planters had extended only a lackluster welcome to earlier waves of Loyalists from Savannah and Charleston influenced the actions of the East Florida refugees; despite Jamaica's much larger size, more Loyalists left East Florida for Dominica than for Jamaica.[143]

The migration of British Loyalists to Dominica illustrates evolving understandings of colonial subjecthood in the eastern Caribbean. Given that Dominica's free population in 1784 numbered approximately 1,400 whites and 520 people of color—most them adopted subjects—the arrival of several hundred Loyalists was significant. Settling Loyalists in Dominica promised to provide both a political and a military buffer against the internal threat of a population that had repeatedly shown itself hostile to British rule, and to increase the number of British subjects capable of bearing arms. The governor of St. Vincent openly expressed his regret that a similar settlement was not undertaken in the island, where the presence of Loyalists might guard against Kalinagos, "an enemy hostile to us, and blindly attached to the French."[144] Loyalists who received encouragement to settle in the eastern Caribbean embodied the British crown's desire to ensure order and profitability in an empire intent on preserving its plantation colonies.

With the free population of the new French colony of Tobago composed primarily of Scottish planters, the island's governor, Arthur Dillon, similarly sought to encourage the settlement of subjects who would be loyal to France. Noting that as many as four thousand French free people of color had recently been enticed to Trinidad by the Spanish crown's offer of land grants for Catholic subjects of any crown, Dillon suggested that settlers of color might be persuaded to relocate to Tobago if they were offered greater privileges than those enjoyed by their counterparts in other colonies.[145] Although Dillon's plan was not realized, his proposal reflects prevailing imperial attitudes about the utility of relocating settlers in order to people the colonies with subjects who could be relied on in the event of future wars. Abandoning earlier attempts to assimilate existing residents of the Creole Archipelago, in the wake of the American war both British and French officials sought to entice loyal subjects to settle in the islands, thereby diminishing the threat of potential internal enemies.

In the wake of U.S. independence, Great Britain renewed its commitment to creating profitable plantation colonies on the Caribbean frontier. Abandoning earlier attempts to assimilate existing residents of the Ceded Islands, administrators instead sought to entice loyal subjects to the colonies. Citing the threat of adopted subjects, free people of color, Kalinagos, and enslaved majorities who had repeatedly demonstrated their hostility to British rule, in the 1780s the islands' British planter minority increasingly asserted its power against longtime residents of the archipelago like Chatoyer and Nicolas Crocquet de Belligny.

*   *   *

Despite their attempts to draw on experiences of colonial rule to devise idealized plans for the settlement and development of the Ceded Islands, British authorities had good reason to heed commissioner William Young's warning that in times of crisis "the whole chain of American islands . . . would . . . accompany that continent, of which it seems to have once constituted a part."[146] During the civil and interimperial war that engulfed both mainland and island North America in the late 1770s and early 1780s, free, enslaved, and Indigenous people in the eastern Caribbean took measures to reassert many features of daily life in the Creole Archipelago. By facilitating French occupation, reasserting title to land, and seeking freedom, authority, and autonomy, existing residents of the islands manifested a desire to return to a state of economic, social, and informal political affairs more closely resembling that which they had created and maintained in the region before the assertion of British colonial rule—a return they had first sought through diplomatic means in the period preceding the American Revolution.

The increasingly authoritarian strategies British officials adopted in the 1780s therefore represented a response not just to the loss of most of the mainland colonies and the emergence of a new American republic but to the "gross misconduct" of planters, Kalinagos, and enslaved people in the Ceded Islands.[147] Civil and interimperial war dramatically exposed some of the geographic and demographic realities that threatened British control of the archipelago. By restricting the rights of adopted subjects, limiting Indigenous dominion, and increasing their policing of enslaved and free people of color in the wake of the war, authorities grew more assertive in their efforts to create productive plantation colonies.

Although the 1783 Treaty of Paris brought peace between European powers, for many residents of the eastern Caribbean the promise of revolution remained unfulfilled. The events of the war suggested that the state of affairs during the brief period of peace from 1763 to 1775 was not necessarily permanent and that various groups could benefit from an alliance with French forces located just across the islands' narrow channels. As Chatoyer and thirty-five other Kalinago signatories expressed in a letter to the French general Marquis de Bouillé, "we are waiting with impatience for a revolution that will return us under the laws of a sovereign that we have learned from the beginning to love and respect."[148] The opportunity for this return would come just six years later, with the outbreak of the French Revolution.

Chapter 7

Revolutions and the
End of Accommodation

With sixty experienced rowers propelling the 45-foot pirogue, the 140-mile voyage from St. Vincent south to Trinidad took just ten hours. After navigating along the "basalt pathway" of the Grenadines and passing Grenada's "high cliffs," the vessel raised sail, and soon the "lands were only visible in the distance." As they neared Trinidad, the Kalinago seafarers used "all their skill, strength, and experience" to paddle against the churning waters of the Dragon's Mouth, a series of rough straits created as the Gulf of Paria, which separates Trinidad from Venezuela, meets the Caribbean Sea. Since their "vessel could go anywhere," they steered the nimble pirogue into the main dock in Port of Spain, "like the canoes of the savages from . . . Guyana and Venezuela . . . do every day." With the support of a French Republican soldier, Alexandre Moreau de Jonnès, the Kalinago seafarers negotiated the purchase of provisions to replenish their people on St. Vincent. Although they worried about "incurring the displeasure of the English" by engaging in this interimperial trade, Kalinagos were in dire need. By the time of their voyage, in August 1795, they had been at war with British forces in St. Vincent for more than five months.[1]

Jonnès' journey with Kalinago combatants illustrates how the contests that emerged after the Seven Years' War and intensified during the American War of Independence persisted in the era of the French Revolution. In the 1790s, as the eastern Caribbean became embroiled in yet another civil and interimperial war, various residents of the Ceded Islands seized the opportunity to violently contest the restrictions they had fought by a variety of means in the decades prior. Capitalizing on the disturbances rippling out from the

French and Haitian revolutions, Kalinagos, free people of color, Catholics, and enslaved people once again joined with French forces to attack British colonies from within. Their efforts would inadvertently help bring about the demise of the Creole Archipelago, as the British crown executed or exiled thousands of Indigenous, white, enslaved, and free insurrectionists of color.

In the wake of the Seven Years' War, British authorities had experimented with two strategies for incorporating existing residents of the Creole Archipelago: the extension of political, religious, and legal accommodations to planters they hoped to assimilate, and the toleration of Indigenous dominion for Kalinagos. Yet events in the 1770s and 1780s, including the Carib War and French occupation of Dominica, Grenada, St. Vincent, and Tobago during the American War of Independence, dramatically illustrated that these measures were not enough to reconcile new subjects to British rule. After reestablishing control over all but Tobago in 1783, British authorities therefore abandoned earlier policies of assimilation and accommodation in favor of force. Beginning in the mid-1780s, they subjected Catholics to the same handicaps that limited their political participation elsewhere in the empire, while also restricting their freedom of worship; required free people of color to prove their legal status; and ordered Kalinagos to remain behind a boundary line established in 1773. Repressive measures intensified following the outbreak of revolution in neighboring French colonies.[2] In the 1790s, British officials heightened their surveillance of free and enslaved residents of the Ceded Islands; forbade all foreigners, particularly people of color, from setting foot in the colonies; and extracted promises of fidelity from Kalinagos.

These repressive actions further alienated new subjects, and as unrest rippled through the late-eighteenth-century Atlantic World, insurgents in Grenada and St. Vincent launched particularly violent attacks against British rule.[3] Between March 1795 and June 1796, broad coalitions of Kalinagos, French Catholics, and enslaved and free people of color successfully gained control over all but the capital cities of the respective colonies. During more than a year of armed conflict, over 10,000 British troops deployed to two islands whose combined area amounts to approximately 275 square miles.[4] Reported damages totaled over £3,000,000 sterling, and officials in Grenada estimated that half of the colony's 25,000 enslaved people were lost to combat, desertion, or execution.[5]

While the insurgencies that came to be known as Fedon's Rebellion and the Second Carib War had important transatlantic dimensions, they were also a response to the denial of rights and privileges previously afforded to diverse residents of the Creole Archipelago.[6] In Grenada, attempts to limit the religious freedoms and the economic and political influence of French Catholics and free people of color sparked a violent uprising that united participants across economic and racial lines, while in St. Vincent, continued threats to Kalinago dominion precipitated the second war between British and Kalinago forces in as many decades. Examining the deep local and regional roots of these insurgencies expands current understandings of the origins and extent of late-eighteenth-century Atlantic revolutions. Insurgency was not confined to the French and later the Iberian Atlantic; armed rebellion in some of Great Britain's most promising plantation colonies also threatened the economic and naval strength of the British empire. While free and enslaved people in the eastern Caribbean were influenced by revolutionary ideologies and events emanating from France and its colonies, their struggle against British rule was not a product of these currents alone, nor was it confined to the 1790s. Subsequent narratives that depicted the insurgencies as composed of and driven by disaffected nonwhites deliberately sought to minimize the broader stakes of these conflicts, ignoring the cross-racial, cross-class responses to long-simmering tensions brought about by attempts to transform the eastern Caribbean into a center of plantation production. Just as they had during the Carib War and the American War of Independence, in 1795–1796 residents of the region would once against violently test the limits of imperial experiments. Their attempts to regain many of the customary rights they had secured outside the sphere of colonial rule would ultimately lead to their expulsion beyond the boundaries of the eastern Caribbean.

The French Revolution in the Eastern Caribbean

The short period of peace following the 1783 Treaty of Paris came to a violent end in 1789, with the outbreak of armed contests between revolutionaries and people who remained loyal to the monarchy in the French colonies of Martinique, Guadeloupe, and St. Lucia. In the early 1790s, British authorities took steps to prevent these contests from reaching neighboring islands by declaring martial law, forbidding French subjects from entering their colonies, and obtaining formal assurances of fidelity from colonial subjects. While these measures were intended to enforce order, they further alienated a range of people. When civil war in the French Atlantic transformed into yet another interimperial conflict following the declaration of war between Great Britain and France in February 1793, French forces once again found receptive allies in Britain's newest Caribbean colonies.

Although news of the July 14 storming of the Bastille did not reach the eastern Caribbean until September 1789, the actions of people in the islands suggest that they were closely following developments in the metropole.[7] On August 30, 1789, several hundred enslaved people massed near Saint-Pierre, Martinique, to demand the full and immediate emancipation they claimed King Louis XVI had granted.[8] Although the insurgents' methods were relatively traditional—they appealed to God and to the monarchy to deliver them from slavery—the language they employed was decidedly revolutionary.[9] Identifying themselves as an "entire nation of black slaves united together . . . with one unanimous voice," the insurgents proclaimed that "suffering has enlightened [them] and has determined [them] to spill [their] last drop of blood rather than support the yoke of slavery, a horrible yoke attacked by the laws, by humanity, and by all of nature."[10]

As historian Laurent Dubois has shown, the events of August 1789 are particularly significant because they illustrate how enslaved people lent new meaning to French revolutionary contests—a meaning that French authorities were reluctant to entertain.[11] Attributing the insurgents' demands to the "seditious insinuations" of a Capuchin priest and to antislavery rhetoric emanating from France, Martinique's interim governor wasted no time in suppressing the attempted insurrection, publicly executing the principal conspirators on September 3, 1789.[12] Yet officials both in Martinique and in nearby islands remained on edge, and the first news of the French Revolution—which arrived in the form of tricolor *cocardes* worn by several ship passengers who disembarked in Saint-Pierre in September 1789—did little to calm their fears.[13] The subsequent contest between Royalist and revolutionary factions in Martinique plunged the island into civil war, and in the ensuing years officials in neighboring colonies were quick to blame any attempted uprisings not on the influence of France or Saint-Domingue but on the "dangerous, execrable example" of Martinique.[14]

Armed conflict between supporters of the French Revolution and self-styled aristocratic planters who remained loyal to the crown in Martinique had important consequences throughout the eastern Caribbean.[15] Emissaries who arrived in December 1792 to announce the founding of the French Republic discovered that Royalists controlled Martinique and Guadeloupe; only St. Lucia welcomed the revolutionaries. Using St. Lucia as a base, French Republican forces took control of Martinique and Guadeloupe in January 1793, leading hundreds of Royalists to seek refuge in neighboring British colonies.[16]

Although Martinique and Guadeloupe fell to invading British forces little more than a year later, troops under Victor Hugues managed to reconquer Guadeloupe in June 1794, and the island subsequently served as the primary base for French Republican forces in the Lesser Antilles.[17] Hugues' enactment of the February 1794 French National Assembly decree abolishing slavery ensured that his troops found willing allies among "citizens of all colors" in Guadeloupe and in neighboring islands, while also putting British planters on high alert.[18]

Alarmed by events occurring just across the channels from their colonies, British authorities in the Ceded Islands took steps to keep the conflict from reaching their shores. In January 1793, the respective governors of Dominica, St. Vincent, and Grenada issued proclamations forbidding entry to "all foreigners" and ordering those who had recently arrived to leave.[19] The measures they took betray particular concern about foreigners of color. White foreigners who wished to remain in Grenada could obtain permission to do so from Lieutenant-Governor Ninian Home, but after January 1793 "no free people of colour [could] resort to . . . Grenada . . . or be suffered to take up their abode therein under any pretence whatsoever."[20] "French mulattoes and free negroes" were also specifically targeted in Dominica, where the council agreed that Royalist planters from Guadeloupe and Martinique could remain but deemed that "the danger to be apprehended from the lower classes of white Frenchmen as well as free people of color" made it necessary to order members of both groups to depart.[21] In light of the French Republic's 1792 extension of citizenship to all free men, regardless of color, the mere presence of "French mulattoes and free negroes" threatened a British colonial regime predicated on the debasement of Black people.[22]

Eager to allay fears that Kalinagos, free people of color, and French-speaking Catholics might organize insurgencies from within British colonies, in the early 1790s authorities also obtained promises of allegiance from these adopted subjects. While some of these promises were unsolicited, such as a written pledge by self-identified free people of color in Grenada who declared themselves "fully sensible of the peculiar advantages [they] enjoy under the most Excellent Constitution of England," others required prompting.[23] Following the 1793 declaration of war between France and Great Britain, St. Vincent's council requested that Kalinago representatives attend their meeting. After explicitly reiterating the terms of the 1773 Treaty that ended the Carib War, the council extracted the representatives' promise that all Kalinagos would remain neutral and would "not suffer any French person or persons to stay amongst them."[24] As was the case in 1773, however, the representatives who attended Council did not necessarily speak for all Kalinagos. Just four days after representatives made their pledge, a chief identified as Dirand informed the council that two of his fellow chiefs, Durocher and Palankie, were making the short ocean journey to Martinique to seek French support.[25] Nor did free people of color who pledged loyalty to the British crown in Grenada represent all of King George III's adopted subjects. Instead, in the 1790s various residents of the eastern Caribbean once again capitalized on intra- and interimperial conflicts to find allies who would support their claims to land, freedom, and political inclusion.

The extension of the French Revolution to France's Windward Islands had important consequences both in the colonies and beyond their shores. Throughout the archipelago, residents watched closely as enslaved people deployed revolutionary rhetoric, the free minority cleaved in their responses to metropolitan declarations, and French fleets descended on St. Lucia, Martinique, and Guadeloupe. Just as they had during the American War of Independence only a decade before, in the early 1790s Indigenous, enslaved, and free people recognized that conflict in the eastern Caribbean provided fresh opportunities to engage in a longstanding contest over political, religious, and economic participation in Great Britain's newest American colonies. It was an opportunity they proved eager to seize.

Prelude to Rebellion

During the first years of the French Revolution, as Victor Hugues' Republican regime oversaw the abolition of slavery and the extension of citizenship to men of color in Guadeloupe, many residents of neighboring islands instead experienced a drastic reduction in the rights and privileges they formerly exercised. In Grenada, British officials revoked many of the political, economic, and religious accommodations that had been extended to French Catholics and free people of color after the Seven Years' War. When residents of the Ceded Islands accepted the support offered by Hugues and his Republican forces, many therefore sought not a revolution but a restoration of the political and economic influence, as well as the religious freedoms, denied to them in the 1780s.[26] For people like mixed-race planter Julien Fedon, the revolutionary war provided an opportunity to exact revenge on the very people who had restricted the rights of French Catholics and free people of color in the island and had perhaps even defrauded him personally.

Julien Fedon was in many ways emblematic of residents of the Creole Archipelago. His father, a white man named Pierre Fedon, was born in Saintonge, on France's Atlantic coast, near the end of the seventeenth century. The son of a laborer, Pierre moved to Grenada while the island was still a French colony. Establishing himself in Grand Pauvre, on Grenada's northwest coast, he began fathering children by an enslaved woman named Brigitte, who was claimed as the property of Raymond Ronzier, a native of Clermont, France.[27] By 1758, sixty-year-old Pierre and Brigitte, who was presumably much younger, had six children: twelve-year-old Marie, Jean, Scolastique, Étienne, Julien, and baby Marie Louise, who was just fourteen months old. But Brigitte was still considered Ronzier's human property, and according to French law, any children born to her were also enslaved. Explicitly invoking the 1685 Code Noir, which stated that if a free man married an enslaved woman she and her children would be freed, in 1758 Pierre and Brigitte went before Royal Notary Aubin to ensure the freedom of Brigitte and their children. In a document drafted on Ronzier's estate, "Pierre Fedon and Brigitte negresse . . . promise[d] to take each other as man and wife as is permitted by the King's edict of 1685 . . . and to celebrate the sacrament [of marriage] in the Roman Catholic Church on the first day [possible]." Ronzier and several other planters and merchants indicated their support for the union by signing as witnesses, as both Pierre and Brigitte "declared that they did not know how to write nor sign" their names. Curiously, the document only specifically legitimated "the mulatresses Marie and Marie Louise"; the legal status of the other four children "born to" Pierre and Brigitte went unmentioned.[28]

Regardless of his status at the time of his parents' 1758 marriage, by 1779 Julien Fedon had succeeded in joining Grenada's growing class of planters of color. He lived in Gouyave, which the British had unsuccessfully attempted to rename Charlotte Town, with his wife, Marie Rose Cavelan, a free woman of color he had probably known for much of his life. Like the Fedons, the Cavelans settled in Grand Pauvre before the Seven Years' War; on a list of former French subjects who signed the oath of allegiance required of anyone who wished to remain in Grenada after its 1763 cession to Great Britain, the name of Marie Rose's father, Michel Cavelan, appears a few lines below an entry listing "Fedon her mark"—Julien's mother, Brigitte.[29]

The Fedons and Cavelans resembled many other families who settled in Grand Pauvre before the Seven Years' War.[30] Like their neighbors, both families owned small plantations that produced coffee rather than sugar and that were worked by small numbers of enslaved people. As of 1763, the majority of planters in Grand Pauvre—thirty-seven of sixty-one planters—laid claim to ten or fewer enslaved people; of these, eleven claimed ownership of a single enslaved adult. Pierre Fedon laid claim to three enslaved people, and like most of his neighbors, including the Cavelans, he was too poor to afford livestock: just twenty-two planters in Grand Pauvre owned a horse or ox.[31] As poor to middling members of Grenada's planter class, the Fedons and Cavelans also made collective decisions designed to maximize family resources. Eager to avoid the division of land that resulted from French practices of partible inheritance, three of the Fedon brothers—Julien, Jean, and Étienne—married three of the Cavelan sisters, a pattern of "family networking" also employed by planters of color in Saint-Domingue.[32] As Catholics, the families also publicly affirmed their connections through spiritual kinship. Surviving Catholic baptismal records reveal that Julien's mother, Brigitte, acted as godmother to a daughter born to her son Étienne Fedon and Marie Rose's sister, Elizabeth Cavelan, while Julien's older sister, Marie, was godmother to Julien and Marie Rose's daughter.[33] The connections forged by these religious rites would have important consequences in the years to come, as Julien Fedon's siblings, in-laws, friends, and neighbors became active participants in the struggle against British rule in Grenada.

Although the Fedon and Cavelan families managed to maintain many of their existing religious, social, and economic practices under British rule, the interimperial conflicts of the late eighteenth century also affected their daily lives and provided practical and ideological motivations for rebellion. As new laws limited the economic and political possibilities of people of color, the mixed-race origins of both families grew more salient. Despite laying claim to twenty-five acres of land and fifteen enslaved people, in a 1772 census of Grenada a Cavelan, whose first name was not noted, was explicitly listed as "FM," or free mulatto, and excluded from the tally of new subjects in the island.[34] Although he was a member of Grenada's small planter class, after the Seven Years' War Cavelan's race foreclosed the possibility that he would participate in British colonial society to the same extent as his white neighbors.

In addition to being increasingly marginalized because of their race, Catholic families like the Fedons and Cavelans experienced religious prejudice under British rule. When Julien and Marie Rose baptized their daughter, also named Marie Rose, on December 25, 1779, the baby was considered illegitimate; the record notes that her parents had wed "according to the English custom," without observing Catholic marriage rites. Only after French conquest of Grenada during the American War of Independence were Julien and Marie Rose able to marry in a Catholic ceremony. On February 7, 1780, the couple "revalidated their marriage according to the rites of the Roman Catholic Church," thereby legitimating baby Marie Rose.[35] Although the record is silent on the couple's reason for first marrying "according to the English custom," it is possible that a Catholic marriage, or a priest to perform the ceremony, was unavailable to Julien and Marie Rose while they were living under British rule.[36] Tellingly, despite a 1777 law requiring French religious authorities to record the color of their parishioners, the 1780 record does not explicitly note the couple's race.[37] Although the Dominican priest who performed the baptism did not afford Julien and Marie Rose the respectful titles of "Sieur" and "Madame"—honorifics increasingly reserved for white people in the French Atlantic—he declined to attach a racial descriptor to these legitimately married, propertied members of his congregation. French occupation of Grenada provided the Fedons, along with other residents of the eastern Caribbean, with a welcome respite from the restrictions and degradations they faced as British subjects, and reminded them of the religious, juridical, and civil opportunities they might enjoy under a different regime.[38]

The restoration of British rule in January 1784 brought fresh challenges for people like the Fedons. Despite petitioning for the restoration of "priviledges of citizens of which they have been unjustly deprived," after the American War of Independence new subjects in the Ceded Islands were no longer eligible for election to colonial assembly or appointment to colonial council.[39] Arguing that "Roman Catholics of Grenada are not intitled either by Treaty, or on any other Ground to expect more than a Toleration of their Worship when performed with that decency and privacy which our Statute Laws require," in the 1780s Grenada's council and assembly also sought to limit the public nature and extent of Catholic worship in the colony.[40] Authorities ordered that existing Catholic Churches also be made available for Protestant services and that Catholic rites such as baptism and marriage also be registered with Protestant clergy. As new subjects complained, this attack on Catholicism meant that people who had long used religious ceremonies as a means of publicly solidifying familial and personal ties now found themselves forced to worship in private homes.[41] Catholics further alleged that "images, and other ornaments of the Roman Catholic worship, [were] thrown out, and trampled under feet in the streets," suggesting that contests over the place of new subjects increasingly took the form of deeply personal affronts by one sector of Grenada's small planter class against another.[42]

Free people of color were even more affected by changes introduced after the war. Wary of the allegiance of people who were widely reputed to have welcomed French occupation of Dominica, Grenada, and St. Vincent, in the 1780s British officials enforced a 1767 law that required people of African descent to furnish documents attesting to their free status. Claiming that "many Persons have for a number of years past pretended to be free," in the wake of U.S. independence British authorities took steps to "ascertain . . . the number, as well as the quality, of Free persons residing in" the islands.[43] Those who lacked adequate documentation were required to find witnesses who would formally attest that they were free; anyone who failed to do so faced dire consequences.[44] In 1787, Marie Rose Cavelan was among those forced to find "two credible freeholders" who would corroborate her status as a free woman or face being sold "at Publick Outcry, as a slave."[45] Despite being legitimately married, accumulating property in land and people, and forging familial, social, and business ties, in the 1780s people like the Fedons were repeatedly and publicly reminded that the position they occupied under British rule was a precarious one.

As a Grenada planter outlined in an impassioned 1785 letter, after two decades of British rule, adopted subjects like the Fedons found themselves deprived of their churches, excluded from politics, and even forbidden to serve as officers in the militia. In addition to limiting the rights of new subjects, regulations introduced after 1783 embarrassed them—leaving them "reduced to serving as simple soldiers . . . under their own overseers," forced to worship in private, and subject to harassment over their legal status.[46] In the wake of the American War of Independence, newly enforced British laws undermined many features of the lives that residents of the Creole Archipelago had created for themselves and their families across generations. As people in neighboring French colonies embraced Republican rule, Fedon and many others could not help but contemplate whether yet another regime change might restore the "priviledges of citizens of which they have been unjustly deprived."[47]

Fedon's Rebellion

Surviving accounts of Fedon's Rebellion are deeply biased. Condemned as traitors, Fedon and his followers were denied the benefit of a trial at which they could articulate the precise factors that prompted them to launch the island-wide uprising that began in March 1795 and ended in June 1796. Instead, a number of white, Protestant planters published accounts of the insurrection. Despite their bias, these accounts provide key details about the insurgency and shed light on the composition and motivations of participants. Two self-proclaimed eyewitnesses, one a planter named Gordon Turnbull and the other "a sincere wellwisher to the colony" later identified as Grenada lawyer Thomas Turner Wise, published their narratives while the conflict was still underway, while Henry Thornhill's account of events "to the conclusion" appeared in 1798.[48] The recollections of Dr. John Hay and of Reverend Francis McMahon, two of only three men to survive captivity under Fedon, both appeared in 1823, as works that explicitly sought to defend the interests of planters, while D. G. Garraway, a descendant of one of the British militiamen who battled the insurgents, synthesized the earlier accounts in a book published in 1877.[49]

Although observers and authorities repeatedly referred to "a general insurrection of the French free colored people," closer examination of the estimated 7,200 insurgents reveals alliances that crossed racial, juridical, and class lines.[50] Enslaved people constituted the overwhelming majority of participants, but contemporaries mentioned them only in passing, choosing instead to focus on the rebellion's leaders.[51] As historian Caitlin Anderson notes, by failing to explore what motivated enslaved insurgents, chroniclers and officials ensured that "their political personhood and independent agency was suppressed."[52] Yet even as observers silenced the role of enslaved people by alleging that they were either "forced to it, or seduced . . . by the flattering and fallacious promises of liberty," the insurgents' actions betray their motivations.[53] Widespread destruction of estates during the insurgency indicates that a majority of participants in Fedon's Rebellion, like their counterparts in Saint-Domingue, were enslaved people with little interest in preserving the plantation regime.

White men, some of whom reportedly had "a numerous progeny of coloured children," were also well represented among the insurgents.[54] At the outbreak of rebellion, British officials took the time to explicitly identify "white insurgents of landed property who have joined in the rebellion," while Turnbull published the names of more than 50 white participants.[55] By listing these insurgents separately, authorities betrayed deep concern about white subjects' involvement in what they repeatedly characterized as a "free colored" rebellion. The economic positions of insurgents further highlight alliances that crossed class lines. Just 3 of the 160 individuals whose property was declared forfeit because of their participation in the rebellion—all three of them white men—laid claim to more than 100 enslaved people each. A further 9 participants, including Julien Fedon, each forfeited more than 50 enslaved people, indicating that they were larger planters. But the majority of insurgents—119 of the 160 individuals identified—forfeited enslaved people "unattached to estates," meaning that they did not live on plantations but lived in one of Grenada's towns. Of these urban insurgents, almost three-quarters—88 of 119 owners—claimed 5 or fewer enslaved people. Thirty-two laid claim to a single enslaved person.[56] This simple list testifies to considerable dissonance between the composition of insurgents and the way that British planters and officials later characterized them. Belying the notion of an uprising of disaffected people of color, the list shows that insurgents came from a range of geographic, economic, and social milieus. Their decision to participate in Fedon's Rebellion testifies to complex and widely shared anti-British sentiments that had been developing for decades.

Colonial correspondence and published accounts of Fedon's Rebellion largely agree on the course of events.[57] Called to combat elsewhere in the revolutionary Caribbean, British forces lacked the means to police the colony; when insurrection broke out in March 1795, there were fewer than 300 regular troops in Grenada.[58] Just after midnight on the night of March 2 to 3, 1795, a group of insurgents under Fedon's command stormed the homes of English residents of Grenville, a port town on Grenada's east coast. In his narrative of the attack, Wise writes that the insurgents "not only murdered in cold Blood every Man they could find, but cut and mangled their unhappy Victims with all the wanton Cruelty, which Savage Ferocity could devise"; accounts agree that only four British men in Grenville escaped the massacre.[59] A simultaneous attack on Gouyave, Julien Fedon's home parish on Grenada's west coast, was considerably less violent. The insurgents, led by planters of color Étienne Ventour and Joachim Philip, took Gouyave's British planters hostage. Among the hostages were Dr. John Hay and Reverend Francis McMahon, who later authored accounts of their experiences.

As Hay relates, the number of captives swelled later on March 3, when a group of insurgents led by Julien's brother, Jean Fedon, captured a sloop attempting to make its way to Grenada's fortified capital, St. George's. Among those captured were Lieutenant-Governor Ninian Home and Alexander Campbell, both wealthy planters who had vocally opposed the extension of political rights to new subjects since the 1760s.[60] The hostages, now numbering forty-three, were marched to Belvidere, Fedon's estate in Grenada's mountainous interior. Although the hostages "all considered [their] lives in imminent danger," Hay was permitted to return under guard to Gouyave to collect supplies, and he and his fellow hostages "were twice served with boiled beef and plantains" on their first day of captivity.[61]

How Belvidere came to be the insurgents' stronghold is a mystery that further hints at possible motivations for Fedon's Rebellion. Deeds retained in the Grenada Registry Office indicate that in April 1786, Michael Scott sold the 220-square-acre estate, along with two other Grenada plantations, for a total price of £24,813, to Ninian Home and his associates James Stewart and Thomas Alexander Vanderdussen. Included in the sale of Belvidere were 133 enslaved people, which suggests that the estate was well developed.[62] Just five years later, in 1791, Belvidere was again sold, this time to Julien Fedon. The estate, now worked by 80 enslaved people, sold for £15,000, to be paid by Fedon in installments.[63]

It is unclear where Fedon, the son of a formerly enslaved woman and a Frenchman who laid claim to just three enslaved laborers, would obtain the money to make such a large purchase. The price Fedon paid, which amounts to more than half the sum that Home and his associates paid for three estates and more than four hundred enslaved people just five years earlier, suggests that he was overcharged. In the wake of the rebellion, authorities noted that Belvidere, which under Fedon was reportedly worked by ninety-six enslaved people producing five thousand pounds of coffee and twenty thousand pounds of cacao, "is at present in possession of a mortgagee who . . . never received any part of the purchase money *which was much more than the real value of the estate*."[64] Fedon's purchase of Belvidere may have represented one more insult he endured under British rule: with opportunities for French free people of color to join Grenada's planter elite few and far between, he may have been forced to accept less-than-ideal terms of sale. Regardless of how Fedon came to own Belvidere, the estate served him well; located in Grenada's mountainous interior, the plantation furnished Fedon and his followers with provisions while also providing natural protection against attack.

With Lieutenant-Governor Home held captive at the Belvidere camp, control of Grenada transferred to Kenneth Francis Mackenzie, then president of the island's council. On the morning of March 4, two emissaries of color, Joachim Philip and Charles Nogues—the former a member of a prosperous planter family and the latter Fedon's brother-in-law—presented the council with two declarations.[65] The first, signed by Fedon and by Stanislaus Besson, who identified themselves as officers of the French Republic, ordered "all individuals to . . . surrender within two hours to the forces of the [French] Republic under our orders."[66] Those who surrendered within the time allotted would be assured the safety of their persons and property; anyone who failed to do so would experience "all the scourges of a disastrous war."[67] Nogues and Philip also furnished a copy of Victor Hugues' February 1795 Declaration, which informed British commanders that the "assassination of each and every individual Republican (of whatever colour he is, and in whatever Island it may happen) shall be expiated by the death of two English officers our prisoners" and that "any Frenchman [who] shall not join against our common enemy is outlawed, and his property forfeited to the Republic."[68]

These declarations, which identify Fedon as "General of the Republican forces," confirm that Fedon and his emissaries communicated with representatives of the French Republic in Guadeloupe.[69] But with many battles being waged simultaneously throughout the French Atlantic, Republican authorities were ultimately able to offer little support to insurgents in Grenada; as a political opponent of Hugues later alleged, the Commissioner "abandoned this attempt to its own devices for the space of eight months without doing anything to support it."[70] While Republican commissions likely afforded the emissaries additional legitimacy in the eyes of Grenada's council, it was Fedon and his followers, not Hugues, who determined the course of events in the colony.

Despite the ultimatums issued to the council, as well as a further entreaty sent by Ninian Home on March 6, Mackenzie and his fellow councilors declined to negotiate. Asserting that "we are all equally willing to spill the last drop of our blood rather than disgrace eternally ourselves and our country by a concession to men capable of such a proposition," the council decided instead to order troops against Fedon's camp.[71] Yet weeks of poor weather, coupled with the desertion of "upwards of one Half of the Militia," who left Gouyave to take refuge in St. George's, prevented British forces from coordinating an attack on Belvidere during the month of March.[72] Although insurgents frequently plundered British estates throughout the island, they did not attempt to enter Grenada's fortified capital during the month-long stalemate. Reinforcements from Barbados who reached Grenada on March 29 were also of little help. Reporting that the regiments "are composed of men unaccustomed to service and unseasoned to the climate," Mackenzie expressed concern that the delayed attack had simply "given to the insurgents strength, numbers and confidence."[73]

The attack that eventually took place did little to buoy British spirits. Attempting to storm Belvidere on the morning of April 8, 1795, regular troops and militia found that "the heavy rains which had fallen made it scarce possible for [them] to keep their feet in climbing the hill, and making their way through the fallen trees and underwood their arms were of no service to them." Although British forces succeeded in killing a number of insurgents, including Julien's brother Jean Fedon, the troops soon found themselves "exposed to a very heavy and galling fire from the enemy" and were forced to retreat.[74] Keeping his earlier promise to execute his captives if the British attempted to attack, a bereaved Fedon ordered that all but three of the fifty-one prisoners be shot. Only Dr. Hay, along with Reverend Francis McMahon and William Kerr, were spared.[75]

Accounts of the executions dramatically juxtapose the merciless conduct of the executioners—whom McMahon listed by name and identified as either "mulatto, black, [or] cafre"—with the dignity and grace of their white victims.[76] In his report of the executions, which he did not witness, Wise wrote that the captives "received every Mark of Insult, which could be shewn them," as they "were pushed along with brutal Violence to the Spot fixed upon for their Butchery." After being "deliberately put to Death by the infernal Monsters," they were buried in "Pits . . . so superficially dug, That the Hogs about the Place rooted them up," desecrating their bodies.[77] Wise's vivid account, published while Fedon's Rebellion was still underway, was no doubt intended to rouse readers' indignation. Turnbull's decidedly less dramatic narrative of events similarly sought to contrast the dignity of the victims with the barbarity of their executioners. Noting that "the manner of their being put to death has been variously related," Turnbull wrote simply that the captives "met their fate, for which they were prepared by uncommon sufferings, with fortitude, with calm and pious resignation."[78]

The respective accounts of Wise and Turnbull end here. In mid-May 1795, with British forces and insurgents locked in a stalemate that would last more than a year, both writers defended the leadership of acting Governor Mackenzie, condemned the insurgents, and expressed their hope that the conflict would soon be over.[79] Although both narratives sought to rally British subjects to Grenada's defense, the ensuing months failed to bring any relief. Both British and French troops were preoccupied with conflicts elsewhere in the region—including a failed French invasion of Dominica in June 1795 and British conquest of Republican St. Lucia in March 1796—and were unable to spare sufficient troops to either defeat or support Fedon.[80] Transported to Guadeloupe as prisoners of war, the three surviving hostages received little news of subsequent events in Grenada; as Hay later reported, "the murder of the prisoners was . . . an action held in such horror and detestation by Hugues, that he had abandoned the insurgents to their fate, and determined to send them no relief, lest he be considered an accomplice to their crimes."[81] Fedon's hold on Grenada was to last a total of sixteen months, as thousands of British troops struggled to regain control over restive colonial subjects throughout the eastern Caribbean.[82]

While surviving accounts of Fedon's Rebellion largely agree on the general course of events, less attention has been paid to the roots of the insurgency.

In the decades preceding the French Revolution, many residents of Grenada, both whites and free people of color, were stripped of the rights and privileges they and their ancestors had enjoyed for generations. French Catholic planters chafed under the religious and political handicaps imposed on them in the 1780s, while free people of color were additionally resentful of the humiliations and threats they faced under British rule. For enslaved people, these rifts among the planter class offered multiple avenues to freedom: while thousands participated in the insurgency, others joined the Corps of Loyal Black Rangers that British authorities created to quell the rebellion.[83] Across many segments of Grenada society, the outbreak of yet another war in the Atlantic World provided opportunities to assert greater control over their lives and futures.

The Second Carib War

Although relations in St. Vincent, like those in Grenada, remained relatively calm during the first years of the French Revolution, news of the uprising in Grenada spurred Kalinago and French Catholic residents of the colony to also seize the moment to rebel. The leadership and actions of this cross-racial alliance testify to its roots in earlier contests. Just as they had done during the American War of Independence some twenty years earlier, Chief Joseph Chatoyer and his fellow Kalinagos capitalized on their proximity to French strongholds in St. Lucia and Guadeloupe to arm themselves and ally with French forces, while new subjects in St. Vincent welcomed the possibility of a French regime. The fact that this regime was now Republican rather than Royalist mattered less than the fact that the outbreak of war gave Kalinagos another opportunity to overthrow British rule in St. Vincent.[84] In the ensuing months, Kalinagos once again turned to force to reassert the dominion that had been eroding for decades, while new subjects joined with them in an attempt to oust British authorities.

Kalinagos' initial actions made their motivations clear. After hearing of the outbreak of Fedon's Rebellion, they immediately began to attack "all the cane fields and dwelling houses" north of their former boundary at the Yambou River, demonstrating their anger at the establishment of sugar plantations on St. Vincent's windward coast. Subsequent assaults on leeward estates, led by Chatoyer, succeeded in rallying disaffected new subjects to the Kalinagos' side, and by March 10—one week after the first coordinated attacks in Grenada—"all the French inhabitants in that neighbourhood . . . [also] embarked in the cause with the utmost eagerness and zeal." The insurgents, who now numbered "about one hundred and fifty whites and coloured people, and from two hundred to three hundred Caribs," made their way toward St. Vincent's capital.[85] On March 12, 1795, they conquered the British fort at Dorsetshire Hill, just outside Kingstown, and replaced the British flag with the tricolor flag of the French Republic.[86] The same day—a day that Chatoyer declared "the first day of our liberty"— St. Vincent's French planters received a strongly worded ultimatum written in French and bearing the chief's distinctive mark. Echoing the revolutionary rhetoric of *La Marseillaise*, the missive asked, "[w]hat Frenchman would not join with his brothers at a time when liberty cries out in our hearts?" "If some men are still . . . restrained by fear," it warned, "we say to them in the name of the Law, that those who do not join with us today, will be regarded as Traitors to the Nation, and treated as Enemies." The declaration vowed that "the Iron and the Fire will be used against" anyone who failed to join the cause, as revolutionaries would "burn their goods and slit the throats of their wives and their children to wipe out their race."[87]

The vivid terms of Chatoyer's declaration suggest that it was shaped by allies with a strong grasp both of the French language and of the rhetoric that would incite settlers in St. Vincent. The threat to slit the throats of women and children no doubt succeeded in striking fear in the hearts of readers who thought of Kalinagos as a people for whom "it was a principle of their religion to wage inexpiable war."[88] While colonial correspondence and subsequent narratives of what came to be called the Second Carib War blamed the insurgency squarely on the people for whom the conflict was named, the missive suggests that Kalinagos consciously appealed to, and sought to collaborate with, free people of color and white French Catholics in St. Vincent and with French Republican troops.[89]

Collaboration should not be mistaken for instigation. Although Hugues is credited with "pushing the Caribs" by capitalizing on their "hatred of the English," Chatoyer and his fellow Kalinagos needed no such pushing when they launched their first war against British settlers in 1772, or when they sought an alliance with the French during the American War of Independence.[90] Owing in part to the shorter distance separating them from French Republican forces in St. Lucia and Guadeloupe, combatants in St. Vincent received greater reinforcements from Hugues than did their fellow insurgents in Grenada, but in neither island were such reinforcements indispensable in provoking or pursuing insurgency. In fact, Kalinagos did not receive formal support from Hugues until after they launched their attack, suggesting that

French Republicans sought to harness an existing conflict rather than initiating it themselves. In a public address to Chatoyer as "chief of a free nation" on March 13, 1795, Hugues averred that "the French nation, in fighting despotism, has allied itself with all free peoples." Proudly proclaiming that France "has always supported its brothers the Caribs," Hugues urged Chatoyer and his followers to "attack [and] exterminate . . . all that is English, but give the French the means to support you." Hugues further informed Chatoyer that he had named two Frenchmen, Citizen Toraille and Citizen Michel Mathieu, to the respective roles of captain and lieutenant.[91] Hugues' attempted alliance with Chatoyer was short-lived: on March 14, 1795, less than a week after the outbreak of insurgency, British forces killed the Kalinago leader in combat.[92]

Aware of the state of civil war into which Grenada had just plunged, St. Vincent's governor, James Seton, wasted no time in countering the internal threat his government faced. After apprehending and executing "about twenty" new subjects who had participated in the initial insurgency, Seton sought to broker peace with resident French planters.[93] Declaring himself "ready and anxious to make allowances for those who have been seduced from their Duty, or who may have been reluctantly compelled to join a desperate and cruel Enemy," on March 20, 1795, Seton issued a proclamation promising mercy for insurgents who surrendered within five days.[94] His offer failed to sway the combatants, and over the course of the ensuing months, troops dispatched from Barbados and from British-occupied Martinique battled Kalinagos and their French allies throughout St. Vincent. In his account of a second battle over Dorsetshire Hill on May 7, Seton attributed the Kalinagos' initial success to the efforts of approximately 150 French troops, "dressed in new uniforms," who had recently arrived from Guadeloupe. As Seton reported, a force of approximately 300 French and Kalinago combatants, armed with 100 pikes, 100 muskets, and 10 barrels of gunpowder, overpowered the 115 British soldiers and militiamen sent to defend the hill. Determined to keep control of Dorsetshire Hill, Seton deployed a further 200 troops and succeeded in routing the insurgents the following morning.[95]

With his overtures to new subjects in St. Vincent roundly rejected, Seton determined that "all the French Inhabitants within this Government were more or less concerned in fomenting and supporting the Insurrection of the Charaibs." Following British victory in the battle over Dorsetshire Hill, Seton accordingly ordered that "the greatest part" of the island's French residents be detained on ships in Kingstown harbor to await examination by "some of the most respectable English inhabitants." Of those detained, seventy-four deemed "most inimical to the safety of the colony" were sent to British-occupied Martinique to await transfer to England; the others were "ordered to quit this colony without delay."[96] As in Grenada, existing planters that British officials had once hoped to assimilate were now seen as an inherent threat to St. Vincent.

Seton's anxieties about new subjects in St. Vincent was surpassed only by his fear that insurgents would receive reinforcements from French Republicans. In order to stanch communications with neighboring islands, over the course of the conflict British forces burned at least two hundred Kalinago pirogues, many of which "were so large as to be stiled 'their Men of War.'"[97] Both sides also razed crops and buildings that might furnish cover or aid to their enemy; by July 1795, Seton reported that the island's leeward side "is the only part . . . that remains undestroyed." The governor worried that although Kalinagos were suffering from a lack of provisions, "should they possess themselves of this tract [of land] they will be plentifully supplied." The need to protect the coast was especially great because it offered "several excellent Bays nearly opposite to St. Lucia," from which insurgents could receive both information and reinforcements.[98] Despite Seton's efforts, in the ensuing months French soldiers from St. Lucia, many of them people of color, as well as "disaffected Negroes and Mulattoes of" St. Vincent made their way to the Kalinagos' side.[99] While the insurgents "dismantled plantations" and engaged in battles with British forces, British troops "continued to destroy the provisions of the Caribs"; by October 1795, several enslaved insurgents who deserted to the British reported that "they were driven to subsist on the mules they had with them, which were nearly expended."[100]

It was under these circumstances that Kalinagos journeyed with Republican soldier Alexandre Moreau de Jonnès to obtain supplies from Spanish Trinidad. Jonnès, who was just eighteen years old when he left France to participate in Hugues' Republican campaign, was hardly an impartial observer. In his account of events, which was not published until decades later, Jonnès characterizes St. Vincent's Kalinago territory as an "Eden" and makes no effort to hide the romantic feelings he developed for Eliama, the young daughter of a Kalinago chief. Despite Jonnès' nostalgia for a time when his "days were woven of silk and gold," his writing provides valuable insight on Kalinago culture and politics, as well as Kalinago actions during the French Revolutionary era.[101]

Unlike British commentators, Jonnès does not focus on Chatoyer or his successor, Duvallé, as the principal leaders of the insurgency. Instead, Jonnès primarily cooperated with Eliama's father, a chief named Pakiri. The young soldier's identification of Pakiri as the "Grand Chief" hints at the diverse and sometimes competing motivations of insurgents often collapsed into the monolithic category of "the Caribs." While Europeans, including Hugues, assumed or sought to create a unified Kalinago leadership by affording titles or offering gifts to leaders they sought to win to their side, the more than four thousand people identified as "Carib" did not necessarily share a single agenda.[102] Jonnès' account indicates that rather than coordinating with Chatoyer and Duvallé, Pakiri and his followers organized independently.[103] They also had little communication with Hugues; alleging that the French Republican commissioner "used the Caribs' national hatred of the English to his benefit," a bitter Jonnès complained that Hugues was slow to provide Kalinagos with troops or ammunition.[104] The corsairs who arrived in time to aid Kalinagos were in Jonnès' opinion nothing more than "rejects." Few of the French combatants, Jonnès judged, were worthy of supporting the Kalinagos, whom he deemed to be "the most civilized men in the army . . . [with] the least penchant for pillage, arson, and devastation."[105] The uncoordinated or competing efforts of French Republicans, white, enslaved and free combatants of color from St. Vincent, and the Kalinagos who sought their support had important consequences in the ensuing conflict, as different groups attacked, negotiated with, and capitulated to British forces at different moments.

Despite Hugues' inability to provide adequate material support for insurgencies in Grenada or St. Vincent, British forces remained locked in a stalemate with Kalinago, enslaved, white, and free combatants of color in both islands throughout 1795 and into 1796.[106] More than a year after the initial attacks in St. Vincent, insurgents "still occup[ied] nearly the same ground"; while British troops retained control of the capital, Seton warned that Kalinagos were "within a few miles of Kingstown, and in considerable force."[107] The lengthy stalemate only began to unravel in mid-1796, after British conquest of St. Lucia following the arrival of 17,000 British troops dispatched to the Windward Islands under Sir Ralph Abercromby.[108] On June 10, 1796, an attack by Abercromby and 4,000 of his men on St. Vincent produced the immediate surrender of French combatants—both Republican soldiers and free and enslaved island residents who had joined the insurgency—who numbered approximately 460 people. According to the terms of capitulation, all enslaved combatants "are to return to their respective proprietors," while "the Commandant of the French troops shall cause to be given up . . . all the posts which the French troops are in possession of."[109] Although Hugues would continue to govern Guadeloupe for more than a year, his attempt to extend the French Republic to St. Vincent was at an end.[110]

In a testament to the divergent nature of French Republican and Kalinago goals in St. Vincent, Kalinagos refused to surrender.[111] Although Hugues complained of the Kalinagos' "weakness," they proved strong enough to continue their fight unaided.[112] French Republicans promised to send arms, ammunition, and reinforcements to St. Vincent, but a successful British blockade of the island ensured that the aid never arrived.[113] In the ensuing weeks, continued assaults by almost four thousand British soldiers slowly began to undermine Kalinago resolves.[114] On July 18, 1796—more than a month after French troops capitulated in St. Vincent—the first group of Kalinagos surrendered to British forces. Kalinago capitulation was far from unanimous: the day after the initial surrender, on July 19, a group of Kalinagos confronted British troops at Chatoyer's former stronghold of Grand Sable and declared "they never would submit to the English, and they did not revolt so much from the prospect of death, as from the idea of submission."[115] But in the coming months, the first group of combatants would be joined by many more, until almost five thousand Kalinagos admitted defeat at the hands of British forces.

Jonnès provides a vivid account of the consequences of Abercromby's campaign. On hearing that British forces were planning to attack St. Vincent, he immediately sailed from Hugues' camp in Guadeloupe back to the island. Arriving too late to warn his Kalinago allies of the attack, Jonnès made his way toward the village of which he had such fond memories, taking time to examine "all of the bodies that lay strewn on the ground." On his arrival, Jonnès was dismayed to discover that "nothing remained of the carbet but ashes."[116] Despite Jonnès' faith that "if ever Providence protected the weak against iniquity, it must assuredly give victory to . . . the last aboriginal people of this vast archipelago," British assaults in the summer of 1796 largely brought an end to the Kalinagos' centuries-long battle against the advance of colonial rule in the eastern Caribbean.[117]

British victory in Grenada was more decisive. Reinforced by almost five thousand of Abercromby's troops, British forces captured Fedon's Belvidere stronghold on June 19, 1796, effectively ending the conflict. Although many insurgents were killed in the attack, Fedon disappeared, his alleged escape by canoe only adding to his allure.[118] By early July, Grenada's governor was pleased to report that approximately eighty white men found in the camp, along with roughly the same number of free men of color, had surrendered or been captured alive.[119] Although British rule was restored, much of the island lay in ruins. Reporting from Grenville, the site of Fedon's initial attack, officials lamented that "all the houses in this town were burnt in the beginning of the insurrection, and the sea has since that time encroached upon the land." From St. Patrick came reports that "the town will never be rebuilt."[120]

Thus ended almost one and a half years of combat between British troops and new British subjects in what had long promised to be two of Great Britain's most prosperous colonies. Although large numbers of enslaved, Indigenous, white, and free combatants of color joined forces to overthrow British rule, their attempts ultimately foundered in the face of "the 'great push' in the West Indies." Great Britain's determination to retain possession of the Ceded Islands was so strong that initial war plans called for 15,000 troops to deploy to the Lesser Antilles and 12,000 "to conquer the whole island of St. Domingo, French and Spanish"—an island of almost 30,000 square miles.[121]

The actions of insurgents in Grenada and St. Vincent—including welcoming the participation of enslaved people, destroying plantations, and forcing British planters and authorities to retreat to the islands' respective capitals—provoked anger and mistrust among British subjects who survived the rebellions. As Grenada's new governor reported, "The excessive cruelties committed by the enemy, their devastations for 16 months past, and the consequent ruin of the inhabitants have naturally raised a strong spirit of resentment against the whole body of the insurgents."[122] While revolution continued to rage throughout the Atlantic World, British authorities in the Ceded Islands pursued harsh punishments to ensure that new colonial subjects, Kalinagos, and enslaved people would not have another opportunity to rebel.

Retribution and the End of Accommodation

Available records provide frustratingly little insight into what motivated thousands of people of European, African, and Indigenous descent to join the insurgencies that gripped Grenada and St. Vincent for more than a year. For colonial authorities, ascertaining the motivations for rebellion was far less important than ensuring that such uprisings would not happen again. In the waning months of 1796 and into 1797, authorities therefore publicly executed dozens of insurgents and exiled thousands more. These acts of state terror worked to dissuade other enslaved and free people from joining revolutionary movements while also allowing British planters to consolidate power across the islands. In the final years of the eighteenth century, the forcible removal of many Kalinagos, free people of color, and small planters from the Ceded Islands provided an opportunity for the expansion of the plantation complex that British officials first envisioned decades before.

In Grenada, participants in Fedon's Rebellion were subject to an act of attainder.[123] British authorities used this "antiquated and morally dubious" legal proceeding on only one subsequent occasion, after a 1798 uprising against colonial rule in Ireland.[124] Individuals named in an act of attainder are declared guilty without the benefit of trial, leaving them with only two options: a person either can argue that they are not, in fact, one of the individuals named in the act or can confirm their identity, thereby acknowledging guilt and accepting the sentence of the court. Such was the case when more than 460 participants in Fedon's Rebellion came before a special court of oyer and terminer established in St. George's in the summer of 1796. Gordon Turnbull, who had already condemned the "barbarous insurgents" in print, was among the jurors, while lawyer Thomas Turner Wise, whose narrative cast the accused as "Monsters in human shape," acted as their only counsel.[125] By July 30, just eleven days after the insurgents surrendered, the court had already judged fifty-nine of those named in the act; of those, thirty-eight had been sentenced to death. Justifying the court's actions on the grounds that it was necessary to use "the severest examples" in order "to check, if possible, the restless and vindictive spirit of this worthless class of people, who began the war here with murder and devastation," Grenada's governor, Alexander Houston, agreed that the rest should be "respited until His Majesty's pleasure shall be known." Insurgents who escaped execution spent the humid summer months of 1796 confined on boats in St. George's harbor, "their numbers not admitting of their being confined in the common gaol." Houston was adamant that those who escaped execution "ought not to be suffered to remain in the colony," proposing instead that they "should be sent to England, there to undergo transportation or banishment according to their different degrees of guilt."[126] Like the prominent British colonists who composed Grenada's court of oyer and terminer, Houston was determined to eradicate the threat of internal enemies in the sugar colony.

Despite the fact that 6,000 or more of the estimated 7,200 participants in Fedon's Rebellion were enslaved, those who appeared before the court were all white or free men of color. This does not mean that enslaved participants escaped punishment. Instead, in the wake of the rebellion, enslaved people found within Fedon's camp were summarily sentenced—to corporal punishment, sale, or execution—by largely untrained justices of the peace.[127] British

authorities declined to bring enslaved people before the court for both ideological and financial reasons. Because enslaved people were considered property rather than subjects of the crown, they were legally incapable of bearing
allegiance to a monarch and could therefore not be judged guilty of treason.[128]
The death or desertion of an estimated 50 percent of Grenada's enslaved population served as a powerful incentive to retain the labor of those who could
be returned to the plantations or "be made useful to the nation by serving in
the navy without pay."[129] Enslaved people formerly claimed as the property of
insurgents—including nine people once claimed by the late Jean Fedon—were
also sold for the benefit of the colony, thereby raising funds to help compensate for the estimated £2.5 million sterling in losses.[130] Finally, contemporary
portrayals of Fedon's Rebellion as the work of free people of color deliberately
sought to avoid laying blame on enslaved insurgents. Turnbull stressed that "the
African negroes who had not been long in the island . . . were the last to join the
insurgents"; in his account, enslaved Creoles posed the greatest threat, in part
because of their connections with free people of color.[131] By deflecting attention
away from the enslaved people who constituted the overwhelming majority
of insurgents, planters and officials implied that it was Black freedom—not
slavery—that threatened to destroy Britain's plantation colonies from within.

Ultimately, almost 100 of the more than 460 men named in the act of
attainder received death sentences. In a decision calculated to inspire fear in
colonial subjects, eight insurgents—three white men and five free men of
color—were publicly executed in St. George's on July 25, 1796.[132] Further public executions were held on September 26 and 27 and on October 12.[133] Arguing that new subjects had definitively proven that they could not be trusted,
members of the court made several additional recommendations intended "to
prevent a return of those evils under which we have so long and so severely
suffered." First, they reiterated that no foreigner would be allowed to land in
Grenada for the duration of the ongoing Franco-British war. They further
recommended "the removal, from all public trust and confidence of every
Foreigner of whatever description whether capitulant or naturalized." Most
significantly, the court advised that "every Female white, black, or coloured,
who by any ties of blood or marriage are or have been attached in any manner
to any person who has been concerned in the late dreadful insurrection" be
immediately removed from Grenada.[134]

The recommendation that every foreigner "whether capitulant or naturalized," as well as all women with any connection to Fedon's Rebellion,
be expelled from Grenada hints at the broader stakes of the contest between

British colonial officials and the subjects they once sought to assimilate. Although the court did not name any women as participants in Fedon's Rebellion, surviving accounts suggest that women's support for the insurgency did not pass unnoticed. Hay remembered the kindness of women who gave the prisoners water and even "a large jug of warm toddy" but claimed that women of color also looked on as "unfeeling spectators of . . . the bloody massacre" of prisoners.[135] Noting that "there were in St. Georges, many women living with Englishmen, whose fathers and brothers" were among the insurgents, McMahon speculated that "the rebels got certain and constant information" from them.[136] Despite forming intimate relationships with British subjects, French women, like French men, had shown they could not be trusted.

Regardless of whether new subjects took up arms in support of the insurgencies, by the end of the eighteenth century their very presence was seen as an inherent threat to British colonial rule. The court's judgments reveal the extent to which revolutionary-era conflicts in the eastern Caribbean were both produced by and experienced through the lens of deep-rooted local and regional contests. If British colonial officials were reluctant to pardon the conduct of new subjects during the American War of Independence, they were adamant about not forgiving their trespasses during the 1790s. All foreigners, "whether capitulant or naturalized," had proven that they were unworthy of inclusion in the British body politic. As members of extended Catholic families that included both whites and free people of color, knit together by religious, economic, and social ties, longtime residents of the Creole Archipelago could no longer be tolerated within the borders of some of the most promising plantation colonies in the British empire.

Imperial strategies of forcible relocation adopted in the revolutionary era were not limited to Grenada. In the last years of the eighteenth century, British authorities also orchestrated the forcible relocation of French insurgents in St. Vincent and of hundreds of people who supported a failed French invasion of Dominica.[137] But by far the largest exile was reserved for the thousands of people whose ancestral claims to land competed with those of aspiring sugar planters. Immediately after the first surrender of Kalinago combatants in July 1796, British troops began transporting insurgents and their families off St. Vincent. British plans for Kalinago removal first proposed as early as 1763 were finally enacted in the 1790s, as officials decided that Indigenous dominion was incompatible with their plans for the expansion of plantation production.[138]

The first ship made landfall on the only strip of flat land in the Grenadine island of Baliceaux on July 21, 1796, discharging 276 Kalinagos on to the rocky beach.[139] Over the course of the following six months, these 65 men, 89 women, and 122 children were joined by thousands of fellow Kalinagos, as successive groups of insurgents surrendered to British forces and were exiled from St. Vincent.[140] By February 1797, British troops had transported 4,776 Kalinagos to an island one and a quarter miles long and half a mile wide.[141] Although Baliceaux is just ten miles from the southern tip of St. Vincent, the now uninhabited 320-acre rock is a world apart from the densely forested territory Kalinagos called home. Baliceaux lacks any source of fresh water, so all provisions for the transportees had to be imported at the expense of St. Vincent's colonial government.[142] With the only beach suitable for landing watercraft located in the center of the hilly island, Kalinagos were unable to rely on their usual canáoa for fishing or for transportation around and between islands. Exhausted from more than sixteen months of combat against thousands of British troops, kept crowded together in close quarters, and exposed to typhus, yellow fever, and other illnesses, the exiles began to succumb to "a malignant, pestilential disease."[143] By March 1797, when a convoy of ten ships arrived to carry the surviving Kalinagos to the Spanish island of Roatán, in the Bay of Honduras, only half of those originally transported from St. Vincent—just 2,248 individuals—remained alive.[144] Less than thirty-five years after formal colonial rule was extended to St. Vincent, the last people to assert that they were Indigenous to the eastern Caribbean were exiled more than 1,800 miles beyond the region's borders.[145]

The forcible removal of thousands of residents of the Creole Archipelago made large swaths of land available for plantation production for the first time. Eager to capitalize on these new lands, between the end of the insurgencies in 1796 and the passage of the Slave Trade Act of 1807, British slavers trafficked more than 39,000 Africans to the Ceded Islands, including more than 16,000 to St. Vincent.[146] While many captives subsequently endured a second Middle Passage, other survivors of the transatlantic slave trade were forced to participate in Indigenous dispossession. As they labored to clear dense woods and forge roads on St. Vincent's windward side, enslaved men and women were enlisted against their will in the colonial project of ensuring that any remaining Kalinagos "will be driven from the impenetrable holds" over which they formerly held dominion.[147] Expansive sugar estates, each worked by hundreds of enslaved people, soon replaced the small mixed-agriculture plantations established in the islands in the middle decades of the eighteenth century. When the Slavery Abolition Act was passed in 1833, the single largest estate at Grand Sable, St. Vincent—the site where thirty-seven years earlier,

Kalinago combatants declared that "they did not revolt so much from the prospect of death, as from the idea of submission"—counted almost seven hundred enslaved people.[148]

The retributive justice pursued by British planters and authorities in the Ceded Islands thus had both practical and ideological impacts. Public executions dissuaded free and enslaved people from contemplating further revolt, while the forcible removal of thousands of people—particularly Indigenous people with competing claims to land—allowed sugar planters to expand their holdings and strengthen their power, further enriching themselves as a tiny landed elite. During the tumultuous era of the French Revolution, after decades of negotiation, contestation, and experimentation with diverse residents of the Creole Archipelago, British authorities finally succeeded in consolidating their hold over the Ceded Islands.

*   *   *

The insurgencies known as Fedon's Rebellion and the Second Carib War provide two striking examples of how the appeal of French Revolutionary ideology stretched beyond the borders of the French Atlantic, as broad coalitions of enslaved, Indigenous, and free people embraced the promises of liberty and equality. But they are also part of a much longer history of opposition—both diplomatic and military—to British colonial reforms and experiments. In the decades after the Seven Years' War, as the British crown sought to transform the Ceded Islands into key sites of sugar production, existing residents of the region pursued a variety of means to retain the property, autonomy, and privileges they had enjoyed for generations. While residents initially enjoyed some success through diplomatic means, their concessions began to erode after the American War of Independence. When presented with the opportunity to ally with a regime that seemed more likely to honor or even extend the legal, territorial, and economic claims that they formerly exercised, enslaved and Indigenous people, French Catholics, and free people of color did not hesitate to do so.

In the eyes of British authorities, the events of the late 1770s through the 1790s provided a vivid illustration of the limits of imperial experiments and reforms. Despite residing in British colonies for decades and being allowed to retain territory and property, practice their religion, and in some cases exercise political rights, Kalinagos, French Catholics, and free people of color repeatedly and violently rejected the crown that attempted to assimilate them. British colonists and officials who had long regarded new subjects with suspicion

saw their fears violently confirmed in the 1790s, as people who had "incorporated themselves as members of this society under the most solemn promises
of duty and allegiance to his Majesty's government . . . attempt[ed] to subvert
the government."[149] It was a treason they would not ignore. No longer willing to tolerate a demonstrated threat to the prosperity of what they hoped
would be among their most productive Caribbean colonies, at the turn of the
nineteenth century, British officials instead took steps to physically remove
all traces of the Creole Archipelago beyond the borders of the British empire.

Conclusion

Echoes of the Creole Archipelago

During their 1837 mission to report on the progress of gradual emancipation in the British West Indies, Quaker abolitionists Joseph Sturge and Thomas Harvey traveled through the eastern Caribbean by canoe.[1] Since "the principal ports of these islands are situated . . . to the leeward, which renders the navigation . . . in sailing vessels, very tedious and uncertain," it was much more practical to adopt the local custom of traveling "in a canoe manned by free blacks, which shot through the water at the rate of six or seven miles an hour."[2] "The negroes are expert rowers," Sturge and Harvey remarked, and since the islands' few roads were "impassable except on mules or horses," these "long narrow boats, cut out of a single tree," were an ideal way to navigate "the ocean . . . high-way" between and around the islands.[3] As Sturge and Harvey traveled to the British colonies of Barbados, Antigua, Montserrat, Dominica, Jamaica, and St. Lucia—the latter of which had been conquered during the Napoleonic Wars and ceded to Great Britain at the 1814 Treaty of Paris—they drew frequent comparisons between them. "The character of the two islands" of Dominica and St. Lucia "is very similar," they observed; "both possess a feature of singular beauty, in their large and perfectly level savannas, enclosed by precipitous hills," and "the cane is of more luxuriant growth than in Antigua or Barbados."[4] Even Jamaica, "though often grand and beautiful, has not the freshness which characterises Dominica and St. Lucia."[5]

As Sturge and Harvey repeatedly noted, Dominica and St. Lucia are geographically distinct from other British Caribbean colonies, and this in turn shaped the economy, demography, and culture of the islands. In contrast to Barbados, which had "rather a sterile aspect," in the 1830s Dominica and St. Lucia still appeared to be "an unoccupied wilderness."[6] Whereas colonies like Jamaica and Antigua boasted large Moravian, Baptist, and other

Protestant congregations, Sturge and Harvey noted that in both Dominica and St. Lucia, "nearly the whole population are Roman Catholic."[7] Free and apprenticed (recently emancipated) residents of both islands were also predominantly French speaking, and in the recently acquired colony of St. Lucia, Sturge and Harvey attended a court session where "the proceedings were entirely in French."[8] Given that "the distance from land to land," between the French colony of Martinique and "Dominica on the one side, and St. Lucia on the other, is only twenty miles," this French influence came as little surprise to Sturge and Harvey. During the time of their visit, people from Martinique frequently crossed the channels "in mere rafts," frustrating attempts to police the maritime border between British and French colonial spheres.[9]

In addition to showcasing the clear imprint left by centuries of sociocultural, legal, economic, and population exchanges across islands and across empires, Sturge and Harvey's observations powerfully illustrate how regional connections shaped the everyday lives and imagined futures of people throughout the Caribbean. In the mid-nineteenth century, islands such as Dominica and St. Lucia once again became sites of refuge for people in bondage in neighboring French colonies, where slavery persisted until 1848.[10] For the more than three thousand individuals who seized "the hope of freedom . . . [to] make their escape," the proximity of a competing colonial regime was more than a geopolitical abstraction.[11] Instead, these fugitives, like generations of Indigenous, enslaved, and free people before them, capitalized on the interconnected geography of the eastern Caribbean to access other shores and other possibilities.[12]

The interisland and intercolonial mobility that helped give rise to the Creole Archipelago was not unique to the Windward Islands of the eastern Caribbean. Similar geographic realities shaped the Leeward Islands, where the channel separating the English colony of St. Kitts from the Dutch port of St. Eustatius is less than nine miles wide.[13] In the Greater Antilles, Great Britain's wealthiest Caribbean colony, Jamaica, took shape less than one hundred miles south of Spanish Cuba, whose easternmost point was in turn barely fifty miles from French Saint-Domingue—a colony that shared the island of Hispaniola with Spanish Santo Domingo. While residents of these much larger islands could not generally see the other colonies from their shores, the lack of interisland visibility did not prevent free and enslaved people from forging routes and relationships that bypassed official circuits.[14] As a wealth of recent scholarship reveals, focusing on these maritime connections, rather than on colonial borders, offers new perspectives on the Caribbean and its connections to early America and the Atlantic World.[15]

By analyzing the early modern Caribbean in a way that would have made sense to those who lived there, *The Creole Archipelago* reorients understandings of the region's entangled past, revealing parallels and connections that remain obscured when individual islands are examined as discrete entities or as part of administrative and political units such as the British West Indies or the French Antilles. To gain a clear picture of the societies that emerged at the interstices of competing Indigenous, European, and Creole regimes, it is instead necessary to draw on correspondence, firsthand accounts, and cartographic and religious records in multiple languages, retained in repositories scattered throughout the Caribbean, Europe, and the United States. While such an approach is familiar to historians of borderlands, *The Creole Archipelago* demonstrates that much can be gained by applying similar methodologies to the greater Caribbean.

Focusing attention on the diversity of people who lived and labored in this maritime borderland reminds us that European settlers remained a small—albeit powerful—minority in the Caribbean, just as they were in most parts of the early Americas. Although Europeans authored most of the documents on which historians now rely, the ways that we interpret and use such documents does not have to hew to the logic of the archives that they created. As historian Jessica Marie Johnson notes, some historical actors "seem extraordinary because they appear in an archive structured to erase them."[16] While Kalinago diplomats, enslaved experts who traversed islands, and people of color who claimed ownership over other people of color may seem striking in histories typically populated by wealthy British planters, situating them in the Creole Archipelago shows that they were quite ordinary members of the world of which they were a part.

Combining archaeological, cartographic, and ethnographic evidence with written accounts calls attention to the many ways that Indigenous people, technologies, and practices affected the colonial Caribbean, ensuring that Indigenous people remain central to understandings of a region and an era from which they are too often excluded. Failure to recognize the political, intellectual, cultural, and technological influence of Kalinagos does not owe to their absence, but to their erasure.[17] By centering Kalinagos as political and military actors, *The Creole Archipelago* insists that the Caribbean, like the mainland Americas, was indelibly shaped by Indigenous peoples.

For generations after Columbus, the overwhelming majority of people thrust into Indigenous lands throughout the Americas came not from Europe but from Africa. Reconstructing their forced journeys, as well as the evolving realities of their daily lives, enlarges current understandings of the emergence and features of slave societies in the Americas. In regions that were subject to multiple legal and labor regimes, enslaved people were forced to navigate many different forms of power, from the intimate violence that characterized small-scale slaveholding to the hierarchies that emerged as survivors of the Middle Passage flooded onto existing estates. For these women and men, bondage was both a legal condition and, much more saliently, a shifting set of challenges that they were forced to navigate each day.

Throughout the Atlantic World, the free descendants of these forced migrants repeatedly rejected attempts to link Blackness with debasement. By tracing how individuals and families of African descent forged freedom and fought to defend religious and civil rights, *The Creole Archipelago* shows how regimes of racial exclusion were challenged even as they were being erected. As they engaged in seemingly simple acts such as serving as godparents, making strategic marriage decisions, amassing and bequeathing property, and settling new lands, free people of color constructed communities that acted as an alternative and an inherent challenge to the legal and racial regimes on which slave societies rested. The fact that they often did so as part of extended networks of real and fictive kin calls attention to families and households as central sites in which the broader Atlantic World was configured.[18]

In the eastern Caribbean, as in many other American borderlands, the post–Seven Years' War era heralded the start of new attacks on these families and communities. The arrival of agents of empire such as the Commissioners for the Sale of Lands ushered in contests over property rights, agricultural and economic practices, and social, political, and racial belonging that would explode during the Age of Revolutions. Integrating the region into analyses of postwar reforms and their consequences provides an important counterpoint to histories that trace the birth of new republics such as the United States and Haiti.[19] Viewed from the eastern Caribbean, diplomatic and violent calls for Indigenous dominion, political inclusion for free people of color and Catholics, and the amelioration or end of the forced labor system associated with sugar production seem less like revolutions and more like attempts to preserve longstanding realities increasingly at risk of being erased by encroaching colonial regimes. For people who formerly lived beyond the effective reach of colonial rule in diverse regions of the Americas, however, the Age of Revolutions resulted in the retrenchment rather than the rejection of state power.[20]

In addition to collapsing many of the distinctions commonly drawn between island and mainland early American history, a focus on the Creole

Archipelago reveals links between eras and regions often treated as distinct. The demographic, environmental, and economic changes wrought by the adoption of sugar planting in the Ceded Islands had been seen before, as the plantation complex took hold in colonies such as Barbados, Jamaica, and Saint-Domingue. But some elements of the turn to sugar in the eastern Caribbean—particularly the mass trafficking of enslaved people to new zones of production, the rationalization of landholding for the purposes of production, and the attempt to harness technological and management innovations to maximize labor efficiency—bore features more commonly associated with the "second slavery" of the nineteenth century.[21] The fact that these features emerged in the early 1760s supports Elena Schneider's observation that the expansion and reorganization of slavery in some parts of the Americas was not necessarily a response to its abolition elsewhere, while also demonstrating that the eastern Caribbean served as an important, if little studied, site of experimentation in both the British and French Atlantic.[22]

Experiments in colonial subjecthood also point to the eastern Caribbean's place as a little-examined node in evolving eighteenth- and nineteenth-century British imperial practices and ideologies, particularly as they pertained to race. While P. J. Marshall and Hannah Weiss Muller have convincingly shown that British authorities grappled with the question of how to govern non-Anglophone, non-Protestant subjects in Asia and the Americas simultaneously, scholarly explorations of debates over the standing of the empire's nonwhite subjects continue to concentrate primarily on India.[23] By focusing on new British subjects who insisted on their right to participate in colonial politics "without any discriminating regard had to complexion," *The Creole Archipelago* shows that British authorities also encountered competing understandings of racial belonging in the Americas.[24] Their decision to reject these competing understandings in favor of asserting a more authoritarian style of rule, both in the Caribbean and in India, suggests that much could be gained by studying interactions, circulations, and exchanges that linked regions often thought of as part of the "First" and "Second" British empires.[25]

Attention to the Creole Archipelago further demonstrates that demographic and political features often analyzed as unique to the nineteenth-century southern Caribbean also characterized the eastern Caribbean decades earlier.[26] British authorities tasked with transforming former Spanish and Dutch outposts such as Trinidad and Demerara, Essequibo, and Berbice (now Guyana) into sugar colonies engaged in significant experimentation as they attempted to govern what historian James Epstein characterizes as "an

extraordinarily cosmopolitan population."[27] While nineteenth-century officials were considerably more authoritarian in their administration of these
populations, they shared their predecessors' strategy of marshaling the latest
understandings of political economy to assimilate and transform Caribbean
borderlands.

Many residents of these porous, polyglot southern Caribbean colonies—
both free and enslaved—had in fact arrived there from the eastern Caribbean,
as they followed the shifting boundaries of the sugar frontier further south.[28]
As of 1813, the enslaved sugar boiler at Union Hall, an estate in Trinidad
owned by Mrs. Henrietta Hall, was forty-nine-year-old Claude Black, a "Creole of St. Vincent." Like Claude, Union Hall's enslaved cook, Andrew Chap-
pell, had survived a second Middle Passage to Trinidad, having been born in
Martinique forty-eight years earlier. Fifty-year-old Marie Anne Baptiste, the
estate's "sick nurse," was also listed as a "Creole of Martinique."[29] In Berbice,
thirty-year-old "mulatto carpenter" John, who was claimed as the property
of David Barry, was listed as a Creole of Grenada. Also in Barry's household,
forty-year old "mulatta seamstress" Franckey, who was "reputed free but not
manumitted"—a curious, though not uncommon formulation that hints at
the everyday negotiations of bondage—had been born in St. Kitts.[30] By forcing people with specific skills to relocate to these new colonies, people like
Hall and Barry continued to exploit enslaved expertise to help establish or
reconstitute their estates and households, just as planters in the Ceded Islands
had done in the 1760s. In order to better grasp the transimperial world of
the nineteenth-century southern Caribbean and the free and enslaved people
who populated it, then, historians should be particularly attentive to its many
antecedents in the Ceded Islands.

*   *   *

Just as important as the political, economic, and demographic forces that
shaped the eastern Caribbean in the long eighteenth century were the ways
that individuals and families experienced and responded to these forces. By
assembling an array of records to reconstruct the geographic and personal
trajectories of ordinary people, *The Creole Archipelago* foregrounds how they
navigated and made sense of broader Atlantic transformations. On their visit
to Dominica, Sturge and Harvey traveled by canoe from Roseau "about eight
miles [to] the southwest extremity of the island," closest to Martinique.[31]
There, they visited the estate of Jean Louis Bellot, the grandfather of one of

the men accompanying them around Dominica. At eighty-five years old, Bellot was reputed to be the oldest white resident of the island. "He is very infirm but retains his mental powers, and much of his French vivacity," the visitors remarked, noting that the elderly planter's "reminiscences extended over nearly three quarters of a century."[32] Born in the early 1750s, Bellot witnessed countless changes over the course of his life in Dominica. From the "parapet wall" of his estate "situated immediately above the sea," he may have watched as successive naval conquests of the island shifted its political status from Kalinago territory to British colony to French-occupied zone and back to British colony—all in the space of just twenty years. His location above Soufriere Bay, on Dominica's southwest coast, would have afforded him a bird's-eye view of some of the 423 slaving vessels that trafficked more than 100,000 Africans to the 290-square-mile island during his lifetime, and of the countless small sloops and schooners that carried many of these captives on to other colonies.[33] As the number of enslaved people in the island grew precipitously following the reorientation of the transatlantic slave trade in the post–Seven Years' War era, Bellot may have noticed the "small diamond shaped fields" of coffee being replaced by large sugar estates.[34] Certainly, he would not have failed to note the increase in marronage and the subsequent armed contests with fugitives from slavery that rocked Dominica following the introduction of sugar planting, or the anxiety that gripped planters as insurgencies and revolution rocked neighboring colonies in the 1790s.

Like the man who held them in bondage, many of the people enslaved on Bellot's estate experienced momentous changes as Dominica underwent a lengthy and contested transition from Kalinago domain to British colony. In the 1817 register of enslaved people in Dominica, the oldest person on the estate, George, had a "reputed age" of eighty—considerably older than sixty-year-old Tom, a driver identified as being from the Mina nation, or forty-eight-year-old Nicholas, a "mongrel" described as "a Creole of this isle."[35] George was identified as a "Creole of Martinique," and like the man who claimed him as his human property, he likely made the journey from the neighboring French colony by pirogue years before Dominica became part of the British empire. Born around 1737, George was still a child when small French planters began to cross the narrow channel separating Martinique and Dominica in order to establish themselves in the Kalinago territory. As a young man, he may have been among the people forced to clear the land, plant the coffee, and help construct the wall and buildings on Bellot's estate. As George entered his thirties, the number of other enslaved people in Dominica swelled considerably, and he found himself surrounded by men and women identified as "Ibo," "Congo," "Moco," and "Fullah."[36] Even as the language, culture, and labor regime of the plantation on which he lived changed, George managed to use his experience to retain a position of respect and authority; in the 1817 register, his "ordinary employment" on the estate was listed as "doctor."[37] While George did not live to see emancipation, over the course of his eighty years he survived numerous changes in his location, the regime under which he labored, and the laws under which he lived. Reconstructing his experiences vividly illustrates how seemingly abstract imperial transitions reverberated in the lives of countless enslaved people, reminding us that slave societies throughout the Atlantic World were constructed, maintained, and expanded by denying freedom to individuals like George every day of their lives.

Like other early American borderlands, the Creole Archipelago was not a utopia. Far more of its residents lived and died in slavery than found freedom in the islands, and warfare punctuated the region throughout the long eighteenth century. The maritime technology that Kalinagos developed to forge an interconnected world was ultimately used to dispossess them of their lands, as settlers appropriated canóa to establish themselves on new shores. While pirogues allowed a variety of people to traverse the colonial Caribbean, the vessels were also little-explored sites of human suffering. "Nothing could be more wretched in appearance" than the many men, "some of them quite naked, and all nearly so," who were daily put to the "painful and laborious employment" of rowing "vessels of considerable burthen . . . for the shipment of produce immediately from the estates to the coast," or for ferrying people like Sturge and Harvey along "the inlets and outlets of the shore."[38] The ubiquity of slavery in the early Americas meant that much of the labor that enslaved people were forced to perform, much less how these women, men, and children made sense of their world, passed without mention.[39] The abolitionists' description serves as a forceful reminder that virtually every colonial artifact—from shipping records, diaries, and travelogues to buildings, pottery, and foodways—bears witness to the presence and experiences of enslaved people all too often silenced in the correspondence of colonial officials.

In contrast to the "wretched" scenes on the coast, Sturge and Harvey depicted Bellot's small Dominica estate as a haven, where "this benevolent old gentleman seemed to live in patriarchal style in the midst of his people," playing and eating meals with "the young [Black] children [who] almost lived in his house."[40] Given their role as observers of the apprenticeship system then in place in the British West Indies, Sturge and Harvey likely intended for this anecdote to illustrate the benefits of treating formerly enslaved people well.[41] But the abolitionists' sentimental portrait of domestic life also suggests that both tangible and intangible features of the Creole society forged outside the sphere of imperial rule persisted long after the British crown supposedly established hegemony in the eastern Caribbean. In his language, religion, and customs, the elderly French Catholic planter resembled many of the thousands of individuals who forged and maintained the Creole Archipelago throughout the long eighteenth century. Nor was his family so different from those of the Nouets, Dorivals, Vergers, or Fedons, who in their business dealings, religious rituals, and migrations through the eastern Caribbean sought to reaffirm bonds of family and community in the face of increasingly restrictive colonial regimes. Bellot's wife, whom Sturge and Harvey judged to be "still older than himself," was "slightly coloured."[42]

Using the stories of people like George and Bellot, *The Creole Archipelago* traces the evolution of a little-studied region of the colonial Caribbean. Doing so significantly broadens and diversifies current understandings of Caribbean, early American, and Atlantic history, but it also serves as an invitation to reexamine the ways that such histories often take shape. Rather than charting how the many projects of competing colonial regimes were visited on the archipelago, this book looks outward from the eastern Caribbean chain. Adopting this perspective demonstrates that these small islands served as microcosms of many broader historical processes central to our understanding of early American and Atlantic history, including European usurpation of Indigenous lands; the rise of slavery and plantation production; and the creation and codification of racial difference. By looking beyond the archives of a single empire, *The Creole Archipelago* foregrounds how free, enslaved, and Indigenous island residents experienced and grappled with these processes in their own lifetimes and across generations. Their stories serve as a reminder that imperial endeavors, no matter how well formulated, were repeatedly reshaped by the individuals and families they meant to colonize.

Abbreviations

Archives and Databases

Archives Départementales de la Martinique, Fort-de-France, Martinique	ADM
Conseil Souverain	CS
Archives Nationales, Paris, France	AN
Archives Nationales d'Outre-Mer, Aix-en-Provence, France	ANOM
Archives Privées	AP
Dépôt des Papiers Publics des Colonies	DPPC
Fonds Ministériels	FM
Serie E, Personnel Colonial Ancien	E
Notariat	NOT
Bibliothèque Nationale, Paris, France	BNF
British Library, London, United Kingdom	BL
The Church of Jesus Christ of Latter-day Saints Microfilms	LDS
Clements Library, University of Michigan	CL
David Library of the American Revolution	DLAR
Dominica National Archives	DNA
Minutes of the Privy Council	PC
Endangered Archives Project	EAP
Grenada Registry Office	GRO
Hamilton College Library, Clinton, New York	HCL
National Archives of the United Kingdom, Kew	TNA
House of Commons Sessional Papers	HCSP
Probate Records	PR
Records of the Colonial Office	CO
Records of the Treasury	T
Records of the Privy Council	PC
War Office	WO

University of London Library   ULL
University College London Legacies of British Slave
        Ownership Database   UCL
Voyages: The Trans-Atlantic and Intra-American Slave
        Trade Databases   Voyages

Journals

Bulletin de la Société d'Histoire de la Guadeloupe	*BSHG*
Early American Studies	*EAS*
French Historical Studies	*FHS*
Journal of American History	*JAH*
Journal of Caribbean History	*JCH*
Journal of Early American History	*JEAH*
Revue française d'histoire d'outre-mer	*RFHOM*
American Historical Review	*AHR*
English Historical Review	*EHR*
Hispanic American Historical Review	*HAHR*
William and Mary Quarterly	*WMQ*

Notes

INTRODUCTION

1. For the Kalinago word *canóa,* Raymond Breton, *Dictionnaire Caraïbe-François* (Auxerre: Gilles Bouquet, 1665), 108, and Raymond Breton, *Dictionnaire François-Caraïbe* (Leipzig: B. G. Teubner, 1900), 58. My use of Kalinago terms is intended to illustrate continued Indigenous influences on the Caribbean, particularly with respect to technologies such as canoes.

2. For *Ioüànalao* and *Ioüánacaéra,* Breton, *Dictionnaire François-Caraïbe,* 352, 239.

3. On Kalinagos using conch shells to announce their intent to disembark, Raymond Breton, *Dictionnaire Caraïbe-François,* 467–468; for huéitinocou, 241.

4. On the use of the term Kalinago as opposed to Carib see Tessa Murphy, "Kalinago Colonizers: Indigenous People and the Settlement of the Lesser Antilles, 1635–1700" in L. H. Roper, ed., *The Torrid Zone: Colonization and Cultural Interaction in the Seventeenth-Century Caribbean* (Columbia: University of South Carolina Press, 2018), 17–30.

5. For the names of individual islands see Breton, *Dictionnaire Caraïbe-François,* 410–416.

6. On the establishment of a "'commuter' economy dependent on widely scattered natural resources" in the pre-contact Lesser Antilles see Philip Boucher, *Cannibal Encounters: Europeans and Island Caribs, 1492–1763* (Baltimore: Johns Hopkins University Press, 1992), 36.

7. On pirogues in the colonial era, Daniel Marc Antoine Chardon, *Essai sur la colonie de Sainte-Lucie, par un Ancien Intendant de cette Isle* (Neufchatel: L'Imprimerie de la Société Typographique, 1779), 30. On watercraft in maritime Bermuda, Michael J. Jarvis, *In the Eye of All Trade: Bermuda, Bermudians, and the Maritime Atlantic World, 1680–1783* (Chapel Hill: University of North Carolina Press for the Omohundro Institute of Early American History and Culture, 2010), especially 120–130; on canoe culture in the African diaspora, Kevin Dawson, *Undercurrents of Power: Aquatic Culture in the African Diaspora* (Philadelphia: University of Pennsylvania Press, 2018), Part II.

8. An important exception is John Angus Martin, *Island Caribs and French Settlers in Grenada, 1498–1763* (St. George's, Grenada: Grenada National Museum Press, 2013). Two books each devote a detailed chapter to the islands after their cession to Great Britain: S. Max Edelson, *The New Map of Empire: How Britain Imagined America Before Independence* (Cambridge, MA: Harvard University Press, 2017), and Hannah Weiss Muller, *Subjects and Sovereign: Bonds of Belonging in the Eighteenth-Century British Empire* (New York: Oxford University Press, 2017).

9. Michel-Rolph Trouillot, *Silencing the Past: Power and the Production of History* (Boston: Beacon Press, 1995), 48.

10. Matthew Bahar, *Storm of the Sea: Indians and Empires in the Atlantic's Age of Sail* (New York: Oxford University Press, 2018); Ernesto Bassi, *An Aqueous Territory: Sailor Geographies and New Granada's Transimperial Greater Caribbean World* (Durham: Duke University Press, 2016);

Jarvis, *In the Eye of All Trade*; Andrew Lipman, *Saltwater Frontier: Indians and the Contest for the American Coast* (New Haven: Yale University Press, 2015); Joshua L. Reid, *The Sea is my Country: The Maritime World of the Makahs, an Indigenous Borderlands People* (New Haven: Yale University Press, 2015); Daviken Studnicki-Gizbert, *A Nation upon the Ocean Sea: Portugal's Atlantic Diaspora and the Crisis of the Spanish Empire, 1492–1640* (New York: Oxford University Press, 2007).

11. Dawson, *Undercurrents of Power*, 1.

12. The idea of islands as "naturally bounded spaces that could be thoroughly discovered and surveyed" inadvertently "rendered their rule a matter of legal complexity." Lauren Benton, *A Search for Sovereignty: Law and Geography in European Empires, 1400–1900* (New York: Cambridge University Press, 2010), 164.

13. While Jarvis evocatively asks readers to consider "what did early America look like from the deck of a ship," the maritime world created by the Bermudians on whom he focuses nonetheless remains an Anglo-American one, largely informed by archives of the British colonial state. Jarvis, *In the Eye of all Trade*, 1.

14. Marisa Fuentes, *Dispossessed Lives: Enslaved Women, Violence, and the Archive* (Philadelphia: University of Pennsylvania Press, 2016), 1.

15. For debates over an "entangled empires" approach to early American history, see *AHR* 112, N. 3 (June 2007).

16. The term "archipelago" has been applied to decidedly terrestrial formations, perhaps most famously in Aleksandr Solzhenitsyn, *The Gulag Archipelago 1918–1956* (New York: Harper & Row, 1973). Scholarly literature on creolization is vast; on the etymology and evolving understandings of what constitutes a creole person, Ralph Bauer and José Antonio Mazzotti, eds., *Creole Subjects in the Colonial Americas: Empires, Texts, Identities* (Chapel Hill: University of North Carolina Press, 2009), 1–59; for foundational work on cultural creolization in the Caribbean, Kamau Brathwaite, *The Development of Creole Society in Jamaica* (New York: Oxford University Press, 1971); on the creolization of language, Robert Chaudenson, *La créolisation: théorie, applications, implications* (Paris: L'Harmattan, 2003). For a scholarly overview of Caribbean creolization, Verene Shepherd and Glen L. Richards, eds., *Questioning Creole: Creolisation Discourses in Caribbean Culture* (Kingston: Ian Randle Publishers, 2002).

17. The approach is indebted to historian Fernand Braudel, whose exploration of the Mediterranean was guided by the question of whether this sea "did not possess, beyond the long-distance and irregular actions of Spain, a history and a destiny of its own." Fernand Braudel, *The Mediterranean and the Mediterranean World in the Age of Philip II Vol. I.* Translated by Sian Reynolds (Berkeley: University of California Press, 1995 [1949]), 19–20.

18. Charles Stewart, ed. *Creolization: History Ethnography Theory* (Walnut Creek: Left Coast Press, 2007), 7.

19. Cécile Vidal, *Caribbean New Orleans: Empire, Race, and the Making of a Slave Society* (Chapel Hill: University of North Carolina Press for the Omohundro Institute of Early American History and Culture, 2019), 455.

20. For an exception see Lucy Eldersveld Murphy, *Great Lakes Creoles: A French-Indian Community on the Northern Borderlands, Prairie du Chien, 1750–1860* (New York: Cambridge University Press, 2014).

21. For an example of how an emphasis on "racial integrity" led to "reservation loss, detribalization, and ethnic reclassification" in Virginia, see Arica L. Coleman, *That the Blood Stay Pure: African Americans, Native Americans, and the Predicament of Race and Identity in Virginia* (Bloomington: Indiana University Press, 2013), 9.

22. Patrick Wolfe, "Settler Colonialism and the Elimination of the Native," *Journal of Genocide Research* 8, N. 4 (December 2006: 387–409), 388.

23. Melanie J. Newton, "Returns to a Native Land? Indigeneity and Decolonization in the Anglophone Caribbean," *small axe* 41, N. 2 (July 2013: 108–122), 121.

24. Nancie Solien Gonzalez, *Sojourners of the Caribbean: Ethnogenesis and Ethnohistory of the Garifuna* (Urbana: University of Illinois Press, 1988), 4.

25. For an overview of this process, Solien Gonzalez, *Sojourners*, 3–74.

26. "Elles composent une chaine en demi-cercle dont les deux bouts sont terminés par la Grenade et la Guadeloupe." ANOM FM C10C 1 Dossier 3 N. 33.

27. David Brading, *The First America: The Spanish Monarchy, Creole Patriotism and the Liberal State 1492–1867* (New York: Cambridge University Press, 1991).

28. James C. Scott, *The Art of Not Being Governed: An Anarchist History of Upland Southeast Asia* (New Haven: Yale University Press, 2009), 20–27.

29. On people of European-Indigenous ancestry and their roles in the colonial Caribbean, Gérard Lafleur, *Les Caraïbes des Petites Antilles* (Paris: Éditions Karthala, 1992), 33–56; on relations between African and Indigenous peoples in the colonial Americas, Matthew Restall, *Beyond Black and Red: African-Native Relations in Colonial Latin America* (Albuquerque: University of New Mexico Press, 2005); on people of mixed race as cultural brokers, Alida Metcalf, *Go-Betweens and the Colonization of Brazil, 1500–1600* (Austin: University of Texas Press, 2005).

30. On the importance of free people of color in other regions of the Caribbean where sugar planting did not predominate, John Garrigus, *Before Haiti: Race and Citizenship in French Saint-Domingue* (New York: Palgrave Macmillan, 2006); Michel-Rolph Trouillot, "Motion in the System: Coffee, Color, and Slavery in Eighteenth-Century Saint-Domingue," *Review (Fernand Braudel Center)* 5, N. 3 (Winter 1982): 331–388; Molly Warsh, *American Baroque: Pearls and the Nature of Empire, 1492–1700* (Chapel Hill: University of North Carolina Press for the Omohundro Institute of Early American History and Culture, 2018); David Wheat, *Atlantic Africa and the Spanish Caribbean, 1570–1640* (Chapel Hill: University of North Carolina Press for the Omohundro Institute of Early American History and Culture, 2016).

31. Eric Hinderaker and Peter C. Mancall, *At the Edges of Empire: The Backcountry in British North America* (Baltimore: John Hopkins University Press, 2003).

32. As scholars of nineteenth- and twentieth-century imperialism argue, "Turning to this particularly shifting ground of empire, to an exploration of how colonized peoples maneuvered within and between empires, suggests a new set of questions. How did ordinary people conjugate the dislocative tense of empire . . . . What imprint did successive empires leave on a population?" Ann Laura Stoler, Carole McGranahan, and Peter C. Perdue, eds., *Imperial Formations* (Santa Fe: School for Advanced Research Press, 2007), 19.

33. On the importance of interisland and interimperial connections in colonial development, Kristen Block, *Ordinary Lives in the Early Caribbean: Religion, Colonial Competition, and the Politics of Profit* (Athens: University of Georgia Press, 2012); Christian Koot, *Empire at the Periphery: British Colonists, Anglo-Dutch Trade, and the Development of the British Atlantic, 1621–1713* (New York: New York University Press, 2011); Linda Rupert, *Creolization and Contraband: Curacao in the Early Modern Atlantic World* (Athens: University of Georgia Press, 2012).

34. David Watts, *The West Indies: Patterns of Development, Culture and Environmental Change Since 1492* (New York: Cambridge University Press, 1987), 4–40.

35. Boucher, *Cannibal Encounters*, 36.

36. Watts, *The West Indies*, 4.

37. Corinne L. Hofman, Alistair J. Bright, Arie Boomert, and Sebastiaan Knippenberg, "Island Rhythms: The Web of Social Relationships and Interaction Networks in the Lesser Antillean Archipelago Between 400 B.C. and A.D. 1492," *Latin American Antiquity* 18, N. 3 (September 2007: 243–268).

38. Carleton Mitchell, *Islands to Windward: Cruising the Caribbees* (Toronto: D. Van Nostrand, 1948), 34.

39. Scott M. Fitzpatrick, "The Pre-Columbian Caribbean: Colonization, Population Dispersal, and Island Adaptations," *PaleoAmerica* 1, N. 4 (November 2015: 301–331), 310.

40. Jesuit missionary Père Lavalette, who lived in Saint-Pierre, Martinique but supervised a plantation in southern Dominica, journeyed to the neighboring island every Sunday after giving mass. "Combien de fois ai-je passé le canal de la Dominique en pirogue!" he remarked. Quoted in Camille de Rochmonteix, *Le Père Antoine Lavalette à la Martinique: D'après beaucoup de documents inédits* (Paris: Librairie Alphonse Picard et Fils, 1907), 77. A five-hour journey from Dominica to Martinique is given in Jean Baptiste Labat, *Nouveau Voyage aux Isles de l'Amérique* Tome II, Part IV (Paris: J. B. Delespine, 1724), 100.

41. Jean Baptiste Labat, *The Memoirs of Père Labat, 1693–1705*, translated by John Eaden (London: Frank Cass, 1970 [1722]), 140, 142.

42. On individuals forging their own routes elsewhere in the circum-Caribbean see, among others, Bassi, *An Aqueous Territory*; Jarvis, *In the Eye of all Trade*; Rupert, *Creolization and Contraband*; Casey Schmitt, "Virtue in Corruption: Privateers, Smugglers, and the Shape of Empire in the Eighteenth-Century Caribbean," *Early American Studies* 13, N. 1 (Winter 2015: 80–110).

43. "Où les mers sont bien plus rudes & les rivières bien plus rapides, neantmoins quand ils voyent dans ces vagues les uns la teste en bas les pieds en haut, & les autres les pieds en bas, & le corps quasi debout, c'est à rire, ou nous frissonnerions de peur." Breton, *Dictionnaire Caraïbe-François* (1665), 314–315.

44. On marronage see Sylviane Diouf, *Slavery's Exiles: The Story of the American Maroons* (New York: New York University Press, 2014).

45. James Rice, *Nature and History in the Potomac Country: From Hunter-Gatherers to the Age of Jefferson* (Baltimore: Johns Hopkins University Press, 2009), Chapter 6; Timothy Silver, *A New Face on the Countryside: Indians, Colonists, and Slaves in South Atlantic Forests, 1500–1800* (New York: Cambridge University Press, 1990).

46. On interisland marronage, Linda Rupert, "Seeking the Water of Baptism: Fugitive Slaves and Imperial Jurisdiction in the Early Modern Caribbean," in Lauren Benton and Richard J. Ross, eds., *Legal Pluralism and Empires, 1500–1850* (New York: New York University Press, 2013), 199–231.

47. On Barbadians in South Carolina see Richard Dunn, "The English Sugar Islands and the Founding of South Carolina," *South Carolina Historical Magazine* 72, N. 2 (April 1971), 81–93; for the Leeward Islands, Natalie Zacek, *Settler Society in the English Leeward Islands, 1670–1776* (New York: Cambridge University Press, 2010); for Surinam, Justin Roberts, "Surrendering Surinam: The Barbadian Diaspora and the Expansion of the English Sugar Frontier, 1650–75," *WMQ* 73, N. 2 (April 2016: 225–256). While Jamaica was a less frequent site of diaspora, at least nine hundred Barbadians accompanied former Barbados governor Modyford to the island in 1664. Carla Gardina Pestana, *The English Conquest of Jamaica: Oliver Cromwell's Bid for Empire* (Cambridge, MA: Harvard Belknap, 2017), 238.

48. On Hispaniola, Richard Lee Turits, *Foundations of Despotism: Peasants, the Trujillo Regime, and Modernity in Dominican History* (Stanford: Stanford University Press, 2003), Chapter 1; Trouillot, "Motion in the System"; on Cuba, Manuel Barcia, *Seeds of Insurrection: Domination and Resistance on Western Cuban Plantations, 1808–1848* (Baton Rouge: Louisiana State University Press, 2008), 49–70.

49. Foundational examples include Liliane Chauleau, *Dans les iles du vent: La Martinique XVIIe-XIXe siècles* (Paris: Éditions Harmattan, 1993), and Richard Dunn, *Sugar and Slaves: The Rise of the Planter Class in the English West Indies, 1624–1713* (Chapel Hill: University of North Carolina Press, 1972).

50. Andrew Jackson O'Shaughnessy, *An Empire Divided: The American Revolution and the British Caribbean* (Philadelphia: University of Pennsylvania Press, 2000).

51. The idea of a Creole Archipelago is indebted to Richard White's "Middle Ground." Yet as White later reflected, the term referred not only to a process of negotiation and mutual accommodation but also to "a quite particular historical space that was the outcome of this larger process." Richard White, *The Middle Ground: Indians, Empires, and Republics in the Great Lakes Region, 1650–1815* (New York: Cambridge University Press, 2011 [1991]), xii.

52. Pekka Hämäläinen and Samuel Truett, "On Borderlands," *JAH* 98, N. 2 (September 2011: 338–361), 343; Kathleen DuVal, *The Native Ground: Indians and Colonists in the Heart of the Continent* (Philadelphia: University of Pennsylvania Press, 2006).

53. Tanis C. Thorne, *The Many Hands of My Relations: French and Indians on the Lower Missouri* (Columbia: University of Missouri Press, 1996).

54. Ned Blackhawk, *Violence Over the Land: Indians and Empires in the Early American West* (Cambridge, MA.: Harvard University Press, 2006).

55. Jeremy Adelman and Stephen Aron, "From Borderlands to Borders: Empires, Nation-States, and the Peoples in Between in North American History," *AHR* 104 (June 1999: 814–841).

56. DuVal, *The Native Ground*.

57. Hämäläinen and Truett, "On Borderlands," 351–354.

58. On Indigenous erasure see Melanie J. Newton, "The Race Leapt at Sauteurs: Genocide, Narrative, and Indigenous Exile from the Caribbean Archipelago," *Caribbean Quarterly* 60, N. 2 (2014: 5–28).

59. On silencing, Trouillot, *Silencing the Past*, especially 26–30. On the archives produced by insurrections, Jason Sharples, *The World That Fear Made: Slave Revolts and Conspiracy Scares in Early America* (Philadelphia: University of Pennsylvania Press, 2020).

60. Fuentes, *Dispossessed Lives*, 7. Emphasis in original.

61. Verene Shephard, *Slavery Without Sugar: Diversity in Caribbean Economy and Society Since the 17th Century* (Gainesville: University of Florida Press, 2002); Warsh, *American Baroque*.

62. Alison Games, "Atlantic History: Definitions, Challenges, and Opportunities," *AHR* 111, N. 3 (June 2006: 741–757), 750.

63. Nancy Van Deusen, *Global Indios: The Indigenous Struggle for Justice in Sixteenth-Century Spain* (Durham: Duke University Press, 2015), 3.

64. On commons, see Jarvis, *In the Eye of all Trade*, Chapter 4; on marronage from Barbados, William Young, Jr., *An account of the black Charaibs in the island of St. Vincent's: With the Charaib Treaty of 1773, and other original documents* (London: J. Sewell, 1795), 6–8.

65. For examples, see ANOM FM C8A 54 F. 10, M. de Champigny, January 16, 1742.

66. Eliga H. Gould, "Entangled Histories, Entangled Worlds: The English-Speaking Atlantic as a Spanish Periphery," *AHR* 112, N. 3 (June 2007: 764–786), 766.

67. Shannon Dawdy, *Building the Devil's Empire: French Colonial New Orleans* (Chicago: University of Chicago Press, 2008), 4–5.

68. Gordon K. Lewis, *Main Currents in Caribbean Thought: The Historical Evolution of Caribbean Society in its Ideological Aspects, 1492–1900* (Omaha: University of Nebraska Press, 1983), 17.

69. On the erasure of Indigenous people as political actors elsewhere in the early Americas see Jean O'Brien, *Firsting and Lasting: Writing Indians out of Existence in New England* (Minneapolis: University of Minnesota Press, 2010); on Indigenous erasure in the Caribbean see Newton, "The Race Leapt at Sauteurs," and Newton, "Returns to a Native Land?"

70. Martin, *Island Caribs and French Settlers*, 392–394.

71. On the colonization of the Lesser Antilles see Paul Butel, *Histoire de Antilles françaises, XVIIe–XXe siècles* (Paris: Éditions Perrin, 2002) ; Chauleau, *Dans les iles du vent;* Gabriel Debien, *Les Engagés pour les Antilles (1634–1715)* (Paris: Société de l'Histoire des Colonies Françaises, 1952); Dunn, *Sugar and Slaves*; J. H. Parry and William Sherlock, *A Short History of the West Indies* (New York: St. Martin's Press, 1987).

72. Eric Schnakenbourg, "Neutres et neutralité dans le monde antillais du XVIIIe siècle," *Bulletin de la société d'histoire de la Guadeloupe* 174 (May–August 2016: 5–19).

73. Although British officials who assumed control of Tobago in 1763 reported that the new colony was uninhabited, a visitor to the island in 1757 noted that "there are about three hundred families of Indians . . . [who] seem to live in great union with the French, who are settled on Tobago to the number of not above eight or nine families." Quoted in Jean-Claude Nardin, *La mise en valeur de l'ile de Tobago (1763–1783)* (Paris: Mouton & Co., 1969), 291. A 1760 census of St. Lucia indicates a population of approximately 4,000 enslaved people, 800 white people, and 200 free people of color; although Kalinagos regularly appear in the island's baptismal records throughout the eighteenth century, the census failed to count them. ANOM DPPC G1/506, Recensement Sainte Lucie 1760. The population of Dominica in the wake of the 1763 Treaty was reported to be 1,718 free and 5,872 enslaved people, and "from 50 to 60 Caraib familys" TNA CO 101/1 N. 91; the population of St. Vincent was estimated at 7,414 enslaved and at least 2,104 free people. TNA CO 101/1 N. 1. French officials in St. Vincent in 1763 also counted 1,138 "Caribs." TNA CO 101/1 N. 9, État présent de l'ile St. Vincent. Grenada's population as of 1763 was reported to be 1,680 free and 13,000 enslaved people. TNA CO 101/28 N. 123 and TNA CO 101/1 N. 5.

74. On the British Ceded Islands as laboratories, Edelson, *The New Map*, 198. For French attempts to create a mainland American colony in the same period, Marion Godfroy, *Kourou 1763, le dernier rêve de l'Amérique française* (Paris: Editions Vendemiaire, 2012); on French visions of empire in the latter half of the eighteenth century, Pernille Røge, *Economistes and the Reinvention of Empire: France in the Americas and Africa, c. 1750–1802* (New York: Cambridge University Press, 2019). For more on experiments in political economy in the region, Tessa Murphy "A Reassertion of Rights: Fedon's Rebellion, Grenada, 1795–96," *La Révolution française* 14 (June 2018); on Enlightenment-era approaches to plantation management, Justin Roberts, *Slavery and the Enlightenment in the British Atlantic, 1750–1807* (New York: Cambridge University Press, 2013).

75. On evolving notions of British subjecthood after the Seven Years' War, Muller, *Subjects and Sovereign*.

76. On the Caribbean during the American War of Independence see Jarvis, *In the Eye of All Trade,* Chapter 7; O'Shaughnessy, *An Empire Divided;* Trevor Burnard, *Jamaica in the Age of Revolution* (Philadelphia: University of Pennsylvania Press, 2020).

CHAPTER 1

1. Breton describes canáoa as "the galleons of the savages, they are sixty feet long . . . manned by fifty to sixty men or more, eight or ten feet wide in the middle . . . they go two [or] three hundred leagues in them by sea." Breton, *Dictionnaire Caraïbe-François*, 108.

2. The use of sails in the pre-contact Caribbean is subject to debate; however, recent scholarship states that "there is no historical, linguistic, or archaeological evidence to suggest that Caribbean Amerindians ever developed th[is] technolog[y]." Scott M. Fitzpatrick, "Seafaring Capabilities in the Pre-Columbian Caribbean," *Journal of Maritime Archaeology* 8 (June 2013: 101–138), 117.

3. Terms sourced from Breton, *Dictionnaire Caraïbe-François*; for mannatoüi, pages 349–350; for Oüàitoucoubouli, 414. This origin story is sourced from Jean Baptiste Du Tertre, *Histoire générale des isles de S. Christophe, de la Guadeloupe, de la Martinique* [1654], Vol. 1: 401–402. "Leur premier père nommé *Kalinago,* ennuyé de vivre parmy sa nation, & desireux de conquester de nouvelles terres, fit embarquer toute sa famille, & apres avoir vogué assez long-temps, qu'ils s'establit à la Dominique." Sieur de la Borde, who assisted the Jesuit mission in St. Vincent, also reported that Kalinagos told him they descended from Galibis in South America; see La Borde, *Relation de l'origine, moeurs, coustumes, religion, guerres et voyages des Caraïbes Sauvages des isles Antilles de l'Amérique* (Paris: Imprimerie des Roziers, 1684), 4.

4. On early human settlement of the Lesser Antilles, see Scott M. Fitzpatrick, "The Pre-Columbian Caribbean: Colonization, Population Dispersal, and Island Adaptations," *Paleoamerica* 1, N. 4 (2015: 305–331); William F. Keegan and Corinne L. Hofman, *The Caribbean Before Columbus* (New York: Oxford University Press, 2017), 197–238. For pioneering work in Caribbean archaeology, Louis Allaire, "On the Historicity of Carib Migrations in the Lesser Antilles," *American Antiquity* 45, N. 2 (April 1980: 238–245); Irving Rouse, *Migrations in Prehistory: Inferring Population Movement from Cultural Remains* (New Haven: Yale University Press, 1986), 106–156.

5. All names given in Breton, *Dictionnaire Caraïbe-François*, 410–416.

6. On carbets see Jean Baptiste Labat, *Nouveau Voyage aux Isles de l'Amérique* Tome II (Paris: J. B. Delespine, 1724), 148–149.

7. Other references to Indigenous peoples leaving one island to seek refuge in another can be found in Jacques Bouton, *Relation de l'établissement des François depuis l'an 1635 en l'isle de la Martinique, l'une des Antilles de l'Amérique* (Paris: Sébastien Cramoisy, 1640), 105; Pierre Pelleprat, *Relation des missions des PP. de la Compagnie de Jesus dans les Isles, et dans la terre ferme de l'Amérique Méridionale* (Paris: Sébastien Cramoisy & Gabriel Cramoisy, 1655), 67. On the free and forced movement of Indigenous peoples between islands following European contact see Karen Anderson-Córdova, *Surviving Spanish Conquest: Indian Fight, Flight, and Cultural Transformation in Hispaniola and Puerto Rico* (Tuscaloosa: University of Alabama Press, 2017).

8. "La Dominique n'est habitée que de sauvages ramassés, lesquels, ayant été chassés par les chrétiens, tant de la terre ferme que des iles voisines qu'on leur a ôtées, s'y trouvent environ au nombre de trois mille," P. Pacifique de Provins, *Le Voyage de Perse et Brève Relation du Voyage des Iles de l'Amérique*. P. Godefroy de Paris and P. Hilaire de Wingene, eds. (Assisi: Collegio S. Lorenzo da Brindisi Dei Minori Cappuccini, 1939 [1646]), 38–39.

9. "Nos Sauvages ne sont . . . que le reste des innombrables barbares, que les Chrestiens Espagnols ont exterminé, & dont une partie des plus vieux d'entr'eux ont esté témoins oculaires des extrémes cruautez, que les Chrestiens ont exercé sur eux & sur leurs pères." Du Tertre, *Histoire générale des isles*, 460.

10. First published in 1558, Las Casas' vivid account of Indigenous death and enslavement at the hands of conquistadors helped create the Black Legend of Spanish rule in the Americas. Bartolomé de Las Casas, *A Short Account of the Destruction of the Indies* (New York: Penguin Classics, 1992 [1542]). On the diffusion of the legend in Europe and America, see Benjamin Keen, "The Black Legend Revisited: Assumptions and Realities," *HAHR* 49, N. 4 (Nov. 1969: 703–719).

11. On aqueous geography, Bassi, *An Aqueous Territory.* Recent research on mainland North America similarly attests to how waterways allowed Indigenous peoples to confront European expansion; see Bahar, *Storm of the Sea*; Lipman, *Saltwater Frontier*; Reid, *The Sea is my Country.*

12. Massimo Livi-Bassi, "Return to Hispaniola: Reassessing a Demographic Catastrophe," *HAHR* 83, N. 1 (Feb. 2003: 3–51). On extinction narratives see Newton, "The Race Leapt at Sauteurs."

13. Samuel M. Wilson, "Surviving European Conquest in the Caribbean," *Revista de Arqueología Americana* 12 (Jan.–June 1997: 141–160). For a detailed discussion of the effects of European colonization on the peoples of the Lesser Antilles, Gérard Lafleur, *Les Caraïbes des Petites Antilles* (Paris: Éditions Karthala, 1992), especially pages 11–32 and 155–170. For an archaeological perspective on Kalinago adaptations to Europeans, Corinne Hofman, Angus Mol, Menno Hoogland, and Roberto Valcárcel Rojas, "Stages of Encounters: Migration, Mobility, and Interaction in the Pre-colonial and Early Colonial Caribbean," *World Archaeology* 46, N. 4 (2014: 590–604), especially 599–602.

14. Lennox Honychurch, "Crossroads in the Caribbean: A Site of Encounter and Exchange on Dominica," *World Archaeology* 28, N. 3 (Feb. 1997: 291–304).

15. On Indigenous refugees from the Greater Antilles, Jalil Sued-Badillo, "The Island Caribs, New Approaches to the Question of Ethnicity in the Early Colonial Caribbean," in Neil Whitehead, ed., *Wolves from the Sea: Readings in the Anthropology of the Native Caribbean* (Leiden: KITLV Press, 1995), 61–90. On the evolution of Indigenous alliance networks in response to Europeans, Ann Cody Holdren, "Raiders and Traders: Caraïbe Social and Political Networks at the Time of European Contact and Colonization in the Eastern Caribbean" (PhD dissertation, University of California, Los Angeles, 1998).

16. On sixteenth-century Spanish slave-raiding expeditions to the Lesser Antilles see Carl Sauer, *The Early Spanish Main* (Berkeley: University of California Press, 1966), 192–194, and Moreau, ed., *Les Petites Antilles*, 33–38. On Spanish slave raiding throughout the sixteenth-century Caribbean, Erin Woodruff Stone, "Indian Harvest: The Rise of the Indigenous Slave Trade and Diaspora from Espanola to the Circum-Caribbean, 1492–1542" (PhD dissertation, Vanderbilt University, 2014).

17. The 1797 exile is discussed in Chapter 7. On the creation of a reservation in Dominica, see Peter Hulme and Neil Whitehead, *Wild Majesty: Encounters with Caribs from Columbus to the Present Day: An Anthology* (Oxford: Clarendon Press, 1992), 258–265.

18. On the phenomenon of "disappearing Indians" elsewhere in the colonial Americas, O'Brien, *Firsting and Lasting.*

19. Indigenous peoples similarly succeeded in preventing large-scale European colonization of many parts of the mainland Americas during the same period. For examples, see White, *The Middle Ground*; DuVal, *The Native Ground*; Pekka Hämäläinen, *Comanche Empire* (New Haven: Yale University Press, 2008).

20. On historical silencing, see Trouillot, *Silencing the Past.* In one example of how the notion of Indigenous extinction has been extended throughout the Caribbean, James Pritchard states, "The French met few natives in the West Indies. . . . By 1670, few Caribs remained." James Pritchard,

In Search of Empire: The French in the Americas, 1670–1730 (New York: Cambridge University Press, 2004), 3–4. While Philip Boucher notes that Indigenous inhabitants of the Greater Antilles were "far more susceptible to epidemiological disasters" than those of the Lesser Antilles, he adds that "growing contacts with Europeans and their African captives after 1635 likely took an increasing toll" in the smaller islands. Boucher, *France and the American Tropics to 1700: Tropics of Discontent?* (Baltimore: Johns Hopkins University Press, 2008), 71. Important exceptions to the tendency to ignore or downplay the importance of Kalinagos include Hilary McD. Beckles, "Kalinago (Carib) Resistance to European Colonisation of the Caribbean," *Caribbean Quarterly* 38, N. 2–3 (June 1992): 1–17; Moreau, *Les Petites Antilles*; Martin, *Island Caribs and French Settlers in Grenada.*

21. On the plantation complex in the seventeenth-century Caribbean, see Philip D. Curtin, *The Rise and Fall of the Plantation Complex: Essays in Atlantic History* (New York: Cambridge University Press, 1990), 73–110. Curtin attributes the rapid rise of sugar planting on Barbados to "the clean slate of a new territory" and states that the turn to sugar in the English Leeward Islands "progressed much more slowly, partly because of insecurity during the long series of Anglo-French wars"; the role of Indigenous peoples in attacking European settlements is not mentioned. Curtin, *The Rise and Fall*, 83–84.

22. Boucher inventively describes this interisland organization as a "commuter economy"; Boucher, *Cannibal Encounters*, 36. On the Indigenous circum-Caribbean as an interconnected area, see Corrine Hofman, Alistair Bright, and Reniel Rodríguez Ramos, "Crossing the Caribbean Sea: Towards a Holistic View of Pre-colonial Mobility and Exchange," *Journal of Caribbean Archaeology*, Special Publication 3 (2010: 1–18). On Kalinago swimming, see Breton, *Dictionnaire François-Caraïbe*, 256; on surfing, Breton, *Dictionnaire Caraïbe-François*, 314–315. For non-European attitudes to the sea, Dawson, *Undercurrents of Power.*

23. The word *Taino*, which roughly translates to "good," or "noble," was first suggested as a name for the Indigenous inhabitants of the Greater Antilles in the mid-nineteenth century and gained popularity among scholars and Indigenous activists in the 1980s. See Keegan and Hofman, *The Caribbean before Columbus*, 246. On the European invention of "Arawak" and "Carib" see Peter Hulme, *Colonial Encounters: Europe and the Native Caribbean, 1492–1797* (London: Methuen, 1986), 46.

24. Samuel M. Wilson, "The Cultural Mosaic of the Indigenous Caribbean," in Warwick Bray, ed., *The Meeting of Two Worlds: Europe and the Americas, 1492–1650* (New York: Oxford University Press, 1993): 37–66. On the heterogeneity of the pre-contact and early colonial Caribbean, see also Stephan Lenik, "Carib as a Colonial Category: Comparing Ethnohistoric and Archaeological Evidence from Dominica, West Indies," *Ethnohistory* 59, N. 1 (Winter 2012: 79–107).

25. Dave Davis and Christopher Goodwin, "Island Carib Origins: Evidence and Nonevidence," *American Antiquity* 55, N. 1 (January 1990: 37–48). For more on the Iberian creation of this dichotomy see Woodruff-Stone, "Indian Harvest," 65–72.

26. Corinne L. Hofman and Anne van Duijevenbode, eds., *Communities in Contact: Essays in Archaeology, Ethnohistory & Ethnography of the Amerindian Circum-Caribbean* (Leiden: Sidestone Press, 2011), 31. On the "inter-related, politically autonomous ethnic groups" that populated the pre-contact eastern Caribbean and began to unite in response to European incursion, see Holdren, "Raiders and Traders," xxi.

27. "J'ay enfin appris des Capitaines de l'isle de la Dominique, que les mots de Galibi & Caraibe estoient des noms que les Européens leur avoient donnez, & que leur véritable nom estoit Callinago, qu'ils ne se distinguoient que par ses mots Oubaóbanum, Balouébonum, c'est-à-dire, des Isles, ou de terre ferme." Breton, *Dictionnaire Caraïbe-François,* 229.

28. At the request of Kalinago people presently residing in Dominica, in 2010 the island's government replaced the term Carib with Kalinago. Lenik, "Carib as a Colonial Category," 82. Other scholars elect to retain the term Carib, arguing that it has specific historical connotations that should not be elided and that Kalinago people likely came into being as a result of European actions in the Caribbean. See, for example, Hulme and Whitehead, *Wild Majesty,* 3.

29. For example, archaeological evidence suggests that environmental factors led Indigenous people to abandon Barbados before European arrival in the Caribbean. Peter L. Drewett and José R. Oliver, "Prehistoric Settlements in the Caribbean," *Archaeology International* 1 (1997: 43–46).

30. Anderson-Córdova, *Surviving Spanish Conquest,* 125–128.

31. On Kalinago preference for the less-accessible coasts of the islands, see Abbé Joseph Rennard, *Les Caraïbes la Guadeloupe 1635–1656: Histoires des vingt premières années de la Colonisation de la Guadeloupe d'après les Relations du R. P. Breton* (Paris: Librairie générale et internationale G. Ficker, 1929), 69.

32. ANOM DPPC G1 498 N. 54, Table contenant le nombre des habitans et des bestiaux des Isles, 1671.

33. For 1683, ANOM FM C8B 17 N. 9, Recensement des iles d'Amérique, 1683; for 1685, ANOM DPPC G1 498, Recensement général de toutes les Isles 1685. On a visit to the colony in 1705, Labat encountered several Kalinagos and noted that "lots of others" ("beaucoup d'autres") lived on the Cabesterre, or Atlantic, side of the island. See Labat, *Nouveau Voyage* II: 146. On Indigenous slavery in the Caribbean, Carolyn Arena, "Indian Slaves from Caribana: Trade and Labor in the Seventeenth-Century Caribbean" (PhD dissertation, Columbia University, 2017); Stone, "Indian Harvest"; Linford Fisher, "'Dangerous Designes': The 1676 Barbados Act to Prohibit New England Slave Importation," *WMQ* 71, N. 1 (January 2014: 99–124); Rushforth, *Bonds of Alliance,* 110–122.

34. Many early censuses lack a category for "sauvages" or Indigenous people, suggesting that French authorities did not bother to count them. In some instances, Kalinagos reemerge in the censuses of islands where they were previously absent; for example, in 1718 officials in Grenada reported 124 "sauvages libres" in the island, whereas in 1696 no category for "sauvage" appeared on the census. ANOM DPPC G1 498, Recensement de l'Isle de la Grenade de l'année 1696 & ANOM DPPC G1 498 N. 41, La Grenade Recensement année 1718.

35. The status of "sauvages" living in the households of French colonists in the Caribbean was often unclear; it is likely that as in other regions of early America, they were expected to work in those households for life. A nominative muster roll from Grenada, created in 1683, is instructive. The roll provides the names and ages of individuals residing in each "caze," with separate headings for "neigres," "neigresses," and "sauvagesses"—no "sauvages," or Indigenous men, are listed. One woman, Francois, is explicitly listed as the "sauvagesse *de*," that is, *of,* Jean Thomasson, suggesting a relationship of ownership. ANOM DPPC G1 498 N. 29, Rolles de la Colonie, 1683. Emphasis added.

36. On Kalinago success against the Spanish in Dominica, Joseph Boromé, "Spain and Dominica, 1493–1697," *Caribbean Quarterly* 12 N. 4 (December 1966: 30–46). On the failed English attempt to establish a colony in Grenada in 1609, see Martin, *Island Caribs,* 31–53.

37. The October 31, 1626, establishment of France's *Compagnie de l'isle de Saint-Christophe* is noted in Du Tertre, *Histoire générale des isles,* 7. On English colonization of St. Christopher, Sarah Barber, "Indigeneity and Authority in the Lesser Antilles: The Warners Revisited," in Roper, ed., *The Torrid Zone,* 46–57.

38. This definition is offered by Bryan Edwards, *The History, Civil and Commercial, of the British Colonies in the West Indies* (London: John Stockdale, 1793), 1:454. Breton translates St. Christophle [sic] as "liamáiga." Breton, *Dictionnaire François-Caraïbe,* 352.

39. "Le Diable leur persuada . . . que ces Nations Estrangeres n'estoient abordées dans l'Isle que pour les y massacrer cruellement, commes elles avoient tué leurs ancestres dans toutes les terres qu'elles occupét." Du Tertre, *Histoire générale des isles,* 6.

40. On the conflict over St. Christopher, Boucher, *Cannibal Encounters,* 39–41; Barber in Roper, *The Torrid Zone,* 46–57; James F. Dator, "Search for a New Land: Imperial Power and Afro-Creole Resistance in the British Leeward Islands, 1624–1745" (PhD dissertation, University of Michigan, 2011), 35.

41. As Dator points out, "the episode of racial violence suggests the extent to which the English and French men on the island viewed themselves as more similar to each other and collectively different from the island's 'savages.'" Dator, "Search for a New Land," 35.

42. In response to continued Kalinago attacks elsewhere in the region, the terms by which St. Christopher was first shared were reasserted in 1657. See Du Tertre, *Histoire générale des Antilles,* 1: 476–479.

43. Richard Dunn notes that English settlement "was only feasible in sites removed as far as possible from contact with the Spanish and Indian population centers" and that the English purposely refrained from settling Guadeloupe and Martinique "because these places were so heavily populated by Caribs," though he does not elaborate on the presence or influence of Indigenous people elsewhere in his text. Dunn, *Sugar and Slaves,* 17–19.

44. On attacks against English settlers elsewhere in the Leewards, see Anonymous, *Antigua and the Antiguans: A Full Account of the Colony and its Inhabitants* (New York: Cambridge University Press, 2010 [1844]), Chapter 2..

45. "Les Sauvages commencèrent à lascher le pied, & à quitter leurs habitations les plus voisines des Francois, mettant le feu à toutes les cases, & arranchant tous les vivres qui estoient dessus." Du Tertre, *Histoire générale des isles,* 72.

46. "Ils sont tellement séparez par des mornes inaccessibles, que nous les voyons rarement." Bouton, IX, 106.

47. "Qui ont leur quartier a part." Provins, 17.

48. François Regourd, "Coloniser les blancs de la carte. Quelques réflexions sur le vide cartographique dans le contexte colonial français de l'Ancien Régime (Guyanes et Antilles françaises, XVIIe–XVIIIe siècle)," in Isabelle Laboulais-Lesage, ed., *Combler les Blancs de la Carte: Modalités et enjeux de la construction des savoirs géographiques* (XVIe–XXe siècle) (Strasbourg: Presses Universitaires de Strasbourg, 2004), 223.

49. On the practical and ideological role of maps, see John Brian Harley, *The New Nature of Maps: Essays in the History of Cartography* (Baltimore: Johns Hopkins University Press, 2001).

50. "Les Sauvages pourtant ne se croyans pas assez forts, crurent que pour chasser entièrement les Francois de l'Isle, il falloit avoir recours à leurs voisins. Pour ce sujet ils appelèrent à leurs secours, ceux de la Dominique, de Saint Vincent, & de la Guadeloupe; & ayant composé un corps de quinze cens hommes, ils se présentèrent sous le Fort . . . ils coururent avec une vitesse incroyable, vers leurs pirogues & regagnèrent la Mer." Du Tertre, *Histoire Générale des Antilles,* 1: 102. Du Tertre also describes the Indigenous inhabitants of Guadeloupe making alliances with those of St. Vincent and Dominica in order to launch attacks on the new French colony; ibid., 1: 89.

51. On Indigenous alliances in response to European settlement, see Holdren, "Raiders and Traders."

52. Details of these battles can be found in Rennard, *Les Caraïbes la Guadeloupe,* especially Part III.

53. On nonverbal communication in the early Atlantic World, Céline Carayon, *Eloquence Embodied: Nonverbal Communication among French and Indigenous People in the Americas* (Chapel Hill: University of North Carolina Press for the Omohundro Institute of Early American History and Culture, 2019).

54. "Après beaucoup d'entretiens, tels qu'on les put avoir avec des gens qui s'expriment plus par signes que par paroles, & qui n'ont guère plus de raisons que des brutes; La paix fut conclue, promesses furent réciproquement faites de part & d'autre, de ne se faire jamais aucun tort, & de se traiter d'oresnavant comme bons amys." Du Tertre, *Histoire générale des Antilles,* 1: 196.

55. "Le bruit de cette paix s'estendit par toutes les Isles circonvoisines, & mesme jusques en France, ce qui attira beaucoup de monde à la Guadeloupe pour y prendre des places." Du Tertre, *Histoire générale des Antilles* 1: 197.

56. "Ils abandonnèrent l'Isle de la Guadeloupe, & se retirèrent dans celle de la Dominique. . .se contentant d'y laisser les plus industrieux d'entre eux, pour épier les François, observer leur conduite, & reconnoistre leur foible." Du Tertre, *Histoire Générale des Antilles,* 1: 89.

57. "On ne scauroit dire au vray leur nombre, pource qu'ils sont en de continuelles visites actives & passives avec ceux de la Dominique & autres isles." Bouton, IX, 105.

58. "Allumèrent les esprits des autres qui estoient déjà disposez à la guerre." Breton, *Dictionnaire Caraïbe-François,* 415.

59. On the importance of Kalinagos in preventing colonization of Grenada, see Martin, *Island Caribs,* especially 54–77; Newton, "The Race Leapt," 11–14. Other historians place less emphasis on Kalinagos in Grenada; Boucher states that "most were massacred, but some . . . committed mass suicide. Remaining Caribs were reduced to conducting guerilla actions." Boucher, *Cannibal Encounters,* 48. Pritchard writes that "early colonizing attempts [in Grenada] failed in the face of successful Carib attacks, internal divisions among the settlers, and the brutal tyranny of the island's owner." Pritchard, *In Search of Empire,* 59.

60. Accounts of how the French initially acquired the island vary. Labat claims that du Parquet negotiated the purchase of the island from Kalinagos, who later sought to negate the terms of sale. Labat, *Nouveau Voyage,* II: 141. Du Tertre claims that "Kaierouane, captain of all the savages of the island," agreed to allow Du Parquet to "have their island" in exchange for trade goods including knives and *eau de vie.* Du Tertre, *Histoire Générale des Antilles* 1: 428; the story of Du Parquet's purchase of Grenada from Kaierouane is also given in Boucher, *Cannibal Encounters,* 48, and Boucher, *France and the American Tropics,* 91. Martin claims that Du Parquet took possession of Grenada "in the name of the French King" and that while the French and Kalinago did exchange gifts, no sale of land that Kalinagos understood as such took place. Martin, *Island Caribs,* 59–63. When Du Parquet sold Grenada to the Comte de Cerillac in 1656, the deed of sale specified only that Du Parquet acquired the island from the Compagnie des Indes on September 27, 1650; no prior sale on the part of Kalinago representatives is mentioned. ANOM FM C10A 1 Dossier 1, Contrat d'acquisition de l'isle de la Grenade et Grenadins faite le 30 8bre 1656 par M. le Comte de Cerillac [et] de M. Du Parquet. This evolving justification is itself significant, as the Europeans' need to prove their claims with respect to Kalinagos diminished over time.

61. The account was published by Jacques Petitjean Roget, *L'histoire de l'Isle de Grenade en Amérique 1649–1659* (Montréal: Les Presses de l'Université de Montréal, 1975). "Les Sauvages s'en estant apperceut le vinrent trouver et luy demanderent pourqouy il avoit ainsy pris pied sur leur terre; en y commençant sans leur permission une demeure." Petitjean Roget, *L'histoire,* 48.

62. "Les Sauvages dirent qu'on devoit donc se contenter du lieu qu'ils avoient disposé, sans se loger ailleurs" Petitjean Roget, *L'Histoire*, 56.

63. For accounts of this warfare see Du Tertre, *Histoire générale des Antilles*, 1: 429–433, 465–504; Martin, *Island Caribs*, 54–87; Petitjean Roget, *Histoire*, 58–78, 98–148.

64. "S'en allèrent en Terre Ferme pour en tirer du secours soit des Galiouage soit d'autres." Petitjean Roget, *Histoire*, 78.

65. "Retranchées dans leur fort, sans oser en sortir." Petitjean Roget, *Histoire*, 66.

66. Petitjean Roget, *Histoire*, 108.

67. The Indigenous strategy of joining forces in interisland groups as a response to European incursion in Grenada is discussed in Holdren, "Raiders and Traders." For accounts of Kalinago military engagement against the French in the early 1650s see Petitjean Roget, *Histoire*, 71–78, 98–108, 113–142, and Martin, *Island Caribs*, 64–77.

68. "Les navires du Roy ne sont pas propres non plus pour cette Expedition. . . ces grands Batiments ne prendroient pas en dix ans une pirogue." ANOM C8A 23 N. 544, M. de Baas, June 25 1674. On European recognition of the utility of Indigenous watercraft, see Lipman, *The Saltwater Frontier*, 70–73.

69. ANOM DPPC G1 498 N. 28, Desnombrement des hommes, femmes, enfans, blancs, negres . . . à Grenade, 1669.

70. On null values see Johnson, *Wicked Flesh: Black Women, Freedom, and Intimacy in the Atlantic World* (Philadelphia: University of Pennsylvania Press, 2020) 134–143.

71. "Nous apportant le rameau d'une paix généralle avec trois belles tortues, un riche caret, et de lezards pour présents et marques de l'acceptation et ratification de tous autre *Caraïbes* et Galibis des toutes les isles adjacentes . . . on les régala comme on pust, et on leurs donna pour présens et pour gages et asseurance de paix des haches, des serpes et des cousteaux." Petitjean Roget, *L'histoire*, 150.

72. "Ils sont tous vestus de la mesme sorte, portent les mesme couleurs, avec le mesme langage portent les mesme armes, ont les mesme intérests, vivent tous ensemble et sont de mesme intelligence. Ce qui faict q'une paix ne seauroit estre bonne si elle n'est qu'avec quelques particuliers." Petitjean Roget, *L'histoire*, 149.

73. On English and French attempts to settle St. Lucia, Marie-Galante, Tobago, St. Vincent, and Dominica in the mid-seventeenth century, Boucher, *Cannibal Encounters*, 45–50.

74. For detailed analysis of this treaty see Murphy, "Kalinago Colonizers," in Roper, ed., *The Torrid Zone*, 17–30.

75. Sugar exports surpassed tobacco exports for the first time in 1664, but this trend developed over time. Pritchard, *In Search of Empire*, 163. On the development of the sugar economy in France's Windward Islands, Boucher, *France and the American Tropics*, 229–248; Watts, *The West Indies*, 296–300; Jean-Pierre Sainton, *Histoire et Civilisation de la Caraïbe*, Tome I (Paris: Karthala, 2015), 309–319.

76. The earliest extant census of Martinique records 969 "serviteurs blancs" (white servants) and 6,582 enslaved people. ANOM DPPC G 1/498, Estat Abregé des hommes . . . dans les isles francaises de l'Amérique, 1671.

77. "Les Sauvages se servirent quelque-temps après de ces Negres pour recommencer leurs irruptions . . . les Francois voyant bien qu'ils n'en pourroient jamais conserver tandis que les Sauvages leur donneroient retraite, ou leurs preteroient leurs pirogues pour s'en aller ailleurs." Du Tertre, *Histoire générale des Antilles*, 1: 503.

78. "S'embarquèrent avec les autres dans leurs Pirogues, & se retirèrent les uns à Saint Vincent, les autres à la Dominique, & la paisible possession de toute l'Isle de la Martinique

demeura aux Francois vers la fin de l'année mil six cens cinquante-huit." Du Tertre, *Histoire générale des Antilles,* 1: 543–546.

79. "Assassiné plusieurs notables habitans . . . soustrait jusques a cinq cens Negres qu'ils ont transportez ou bon leur a semblé." Du Tertre, *Histoire générale des Antilles* I: 574.

80. "Quinze des plus nottables et recommandés entre les Caraybes des d. isles de St. Vincent, la Dominique et ceux qui ont cy devant habités l'isle Martinique." ANOM FM C8B 1 f. 4, Traité conclu entre Charles Hoüel, gouverneur de la Guadeloupe et le Caraibes, March 31, 1660. For an account of the peace see also Du Tertre, *Histoire générale des Antilles,* 1: 572–580.

81. "Parland et entendant la langue des sauvages . . . demander aux dits Caraybes, sils avoient pouvoir de traiter pour eux et au nom de tous les autres des d. isles St. Vincent, la Dominique auroient faits reponce qu'ils se faisoient forts pour tous ayant parlé à la plus grande partie des dits sauvages qui y consentoient." ANOM FM C8B 1 f. 4, Traité.

82. "La ditte isle Martinique estoit engagé dans la guerre avec les sauvages il y a plus de six ans qui a cauzé de très grands malheurs par les meurtres incendies et enlèvements de negres faits par les dits sauvages . . . les dites nations françoises et angloises habitants des isles Monsarat, Antigoa, et Nieves et les d. Caraybes des d. isles St. Vincent la Dominique et qui ont cy devant demeurez en la d. isle Martinique demeureront en paix toutes actions d'hostilitez cessantes." ANOM FM C8B 1 f. 4.

83. "A le dit Baba demandé qu'en considération de ses peines et soins il luy soit rendus par les habitans de la Martinique ses neveux qui ont esté pris par le nommé Billaudel de la d. isle sur quoy a esté représenté par les d. Peres Missionnaires qu'il este non seulement juste mais nécessaires de faire la d. restitution qui sera un moyen de confirmer et entretenir la paix et dacleminer la conversion des d. sauvages." ANOM FM C8B 1 f. 4.

84. "On a fait demander aux d. Caraïbes s'ils ne désiraient pas apprendre a prier dieu à notre imitation et souffrir que les d. pères missionnaires les aillent instruire." ANOM FM C8B 1 f. 4.

85. "L'une ou l'autre nation d'habituer les deux isles de St. Vincent et la Dominique quy seullent leur reste pour retraitte." ANOM FM C8B 1 f. 4.

86. Labat, *Nouveau Voyage,* I : 28–30.

87. Labat, *Nouveau Voyage,* I: 32–33.

88. Labat, *Nouveau Voyage,* II: 103.

89. "Tous les vieux Caraïbes que je vis, scavoient encore faire le signe de la Croix, & les Prières chrétiennes en leur langue, & quelques uns meme en François." Labat, *Nouveau Voyage,* II: 102.

90. Labat, *Nouveau Voyage,* II: 103.

91. Boucher argues that "By 1660, all fighting had ceased, and the islands could thus share the fruits of peace with the mother country," Boucher, *France and the American Tropics,* 93. In his general history of the French Caribbean, Paul Butel writes that the 1660 treaty created "une paix générale." Paul Butel, *Histoire de Antilles françaises, XVIIe–XXe siècles* (Paris: Éditions Perrin, 2002), 34. On subsequent attacks on the Leeward Islands see Laurent Dubois and Richard Turits, *Freedom Roots: Histories from the Caribbean* (Chapel Hill: University of North Carolina Press, 2019).

92. On coordinated Kalinago attacks on Grenada in the 1670s see Martin, *Island Caribs,* 125–126.

93. "Avec des gens sans foy, et sans Religion et qui sont plus bestes qu'ils ne sont hommes, il n'y a nul fondement a faire." ANOM FM C8A1 f.294, Jean-Charles de Baas Castelmore, June 1674.

94. "Ne pourront pas aller habiter à l'isle de Grenade." ANOM FM C8A 2 f. 41, Comte de Blénac, February 13, 1678.

95. For censuses, see ANOM DPPC G 1 498 N. 54, État abrégé des. . . isles françaises de l'Amérique, 1671, and ANOM DPPC G 1 498 N. 62, Recensement général des isles, 1700. As a further point of comparison, as of 1684 the white population of the 166-square-mile island of Barbados totaled more than 19,500 individuals—a decline from a high of almost 22,000 in 1676—while the number of enslaved people reached 46,600. Dunn, *Sugar and Slaves*, 87.

96. By 1669, two-thirds of arable land in Martinique was planted in sugar cane. Boucher, *France and the American Tropics*, 242.

97. Pritchard, *In Search of Empire*, 171.

98. ANOM DPPC G1 498, Recensement générale des isles d'Amérique, 1686.

99. Pritchard confirms that "sugar production during the [seventeenth] century probably peaked that year." Pritchard, *In Search of Empire*, 170.

100. For examples of Kalinago attacks against Grenada in the 1690s, ANOM FM C10A 1 Dossier 2.

101. ANOM DPPC G1 498 N. 62, Recensement générale des isles d'Amérique, 1700.

102. "Qu'une tradition perpétuelle, de père en fils, rendront toujour très dangereux dans les esprits . . . qu'il fallait les mener le baton sur l'oreille, pour en être les maitres." ANOM FM C10A 1 dossier 3 n. 105, M. de Bouloc, 13 7bre 1706.

103. On the sugar boom in Barbados, Dunn, *Sugar and Slaves*; on sugar in France's Lesser Antillean colonies, Pritchard, *In Search of Empire*, 162–188. On *engagés*, Gabriel Debien, *Les Engagés pour les Antilles (1634–1715)* (Paris: Société de l'Histoire des Colonies Françaises, 1952).

104. On Barbadians in Carolina, Richard Dunn, "The English Sugar Islands and the Founding of South Carolina," *South Carolina Historical Magazine* 72, N. 2 (April 1971): 81–93.

105. On the secondary economy that flourished in Martinique see Brett Rushforth, "The *Gaoulet* Uprising of 1710: Maroons, Rebels, and the Informal Exchange Economy of a Caribbean Sugar Islands," *WMQ* 76, N. 1 (Jan. 2019: 75–110).

106. TNA CO 71/2 N. 18, Extract of a letter from Stede to Shrewsbury, May 30, 1689.

107. On the role of the "marine underground" in facilitating marronage from small islands see Neville A. T. Hall, "Maritime Maroons: *Grand Marronage* from the Danish West Indies," *WMQ* 62, N. 4 (October 1985: 476–498). On interimperial marronage, Linda Rupert, "Contraband Trade and the Shaping of Colonial Societies in Curacao and Tierra Firme," *Itinerario* 30, N. 3 (November 2006: 35–54); Simon P. Newman, "Rethinking Runaways in the British Atlantic World: Britain, the Caribbean, West Africa and North America," *Slavery & Abolition* 38, N. 1 (2017: 49–75).

108. "C'est-là le centre de la République Caraïbe . . . Je ne scai par quelle raison . . . les a portez à les recevoir parmi eux . . . le nombre des Negres s'est tellement accru . . . qu'il surpasse de beaucoup celui des Caraïbes . . . les obligeront peut-être un jour d'aller chercher une autre Isle." Labat, *Nouveau Voyage* II: 148.

109. "Il est arrivé il y a desja bien longtems qu'un vaisseau chargé de negres alla eschouer et se perdre a la Capesterre de la dite isle St. Vincent, beaucoup de negres et negresses . . . furent receus humainement par les Caraïbes . . . divers de ces negres ont épousé des filles de Caraïbes, de la vient qu'ils ont augmenté en nombre." ANOM C8A 12 f. 100, M. Robert, February 12, 1700.

110. "Les Caraïbes de la dite isle voudroient que les negres qui y son etablis en fussent dehors . . . il y a bien de ces negres allies avec des Caraïbes et qui vivent ensemble en bonne intelligence." ANOM C8A 12 f. 100, M. Robert, February 12, 1700.

111. This rhetorical transformation and its consequences are discussed in greater detail in Chapter 5. Neil Whitehead traces the gradual process by which Black Caribs came to be seen as

a group separate from—and often in opposition to—the supposedly peaceable "red" or "yellow" Caribs; see Neil L. Whitehead, "Black Read as Red: Ethnic Transgression and Hybridity in Northeastern South America and the Caribbean," in Restall, ed., *Beyond Black and Red,* 223–243.

112. "Ils ayment mieux veoir deux mil negres establis dans leur isle, que d'y veoir desbarquer seulement 50 francois armez. " ANOM C8A 12 f. 100, M. Robert, February 12, 1700.

113. The Custom of Paris, which dictated partible inheritance rather than primogeniture, was adopted in the French Antilles and appears to have also extended into neighboring islands. On the Custom of Paris in France's colonies, see Pritchard, *In Search of Empire,* 251–254. On its extension into Dominica before 1763, see TNA 101/1 N. 91.

114. ANOM FM C8A 33 F. 57, Feuquières and Blondel, August 2, 1724. The petition is especially interesting in that it makes the case that existing residents of the Antilles—not subjects from France—would be best suited to settle new colonies, an idea that would be echoed by colonists and officials alike in the decades to come.

115. In 1710, Martinique produced about 10,000 tons of sugar, more than islands such as Barbados and Jamaica. Rushforth, "The *Gaulet,*" 78. For the number of people trafficked, https://slavevoyages.org/voyages/pXdikbdg.

116. De la Borde noted that Maroons "have multiplied so much that they are now as powerful as" Kalinagos. "Il y a quantité de Negres qui vivent comme eux, particulièrement à St. Vincent où est leur fort. Ils ont tellement multiplié qu'ils sont à présent aussi puissans qu'eux." De la Borde, *Relation de l'origine,* 27.

117. Jacques Petitjean Roget, *Le Gaoulé: La révolte de la Martinique en 1717* (Fort de France: Société d'histoire de la Martinique, 1966).

118. "Quantités de mauvais sujets et gens sans aveu, qui ne s'habituent dans les dites isles . . . que dans la veue du libertinage de l'indépendance." ANOM C8A 28 F. 153, M. de Pas de Feuquières, November 15, 1721.

119. "Aussy prejudiciable a la sureté du commerce de ces isles et aux interets du Roy et des habitans . . . une guerre dure sans relache." ANOM FM C8A 28 F.157 Ordonnance prescrivant à tous les Français qui se sont établis sans permission dans les iles de Dominique, Ste. Lucie, St. Vincent de rentrer au plus tôt dans les iles Français, November 18, 1721.

120. On the ease of traveling distances of up to twenty-five miles in small watercraft, Arthur Stinchcombe, *Sugar Island Slavery in the Age of Enlightenment: The Political Economy of the Caribbean World* (Princeton: Princeton University Press, 1995), 47. Autonomous movement between Bermuda and surrounding islands is discussed in Jarvis, *In the Eye of All Trade.*

121. ANOM FM C10A 1 dossier 5, September, 20 1721.

122. "Si nécessaires dans une isle pour la pêche, pour le transport des denrées, celuis des personnes d'un quartier à un autre, et de leurs habitations à la paroisse." ANOM FM C10A 2 F. 2.

123. "En qui réside toute l'autorité et représentant le corps de la nation . . . que nous serons maintenant par la suitte dans la possession des habitations, sur lesquelles nous sommes établis . . . sans qu'il soit permis a aucun francois . . . de nous en faire déguerpir . . . nous assister contre les negres nos ennemis." For the full text of the nine-article treaty see FM A25 N. 18, 3xbre 1719, Traité avec les Sauvages de St. Vincent.

124. "Seront exempt les ecclésiastiques réguliers et séculiers . . . les femmes et filles blanches de quell pays qu'elles soient . . . les masles et femelles Creols natifs de l'Isle . . . les negres au dessous de quatorze ans; les blancs et negres au dessus de 60 ans." ANOM FM A24 N. 824, Règlement de M. de Baas du 12 février 1671 pour les droits de capitation et exemptions des dits droits.

125. "Le chatiment que les francois infligent à leurs negres esclaves lors qu'ils mettont la main sur les blancs sera executée lorsqu'ils maltraiteront quelqu'un d'entre nous." ANOM FM A25 N. 18, 3xbre 1719, Traité avec les Sauvages de St. Vincent.

126. For quote, see notation on Figure 4, *L'isle de la Martinique* (Paris: Pierre Mariette, c. 1652)

127. According to the map, northwest Martinique counted one windmill, thirteen water mills, and forty-five cattle mills, while the southwest counted one windmill, twenty-one water mills, and eighty-four cattle mills. My thanks to Miriam Rothenberg for sharing these counts.

CHAPTER 2

1. For Etienne's baptism see ADM 2Mi 309/2E2/1, June 29, 1733.

2. On enslaved canoers see Dawson, *Undercurrents of Power*, Part II.

3. A 1727 census of Martinique counts 340 white people, 211 free people of color, and 1,747 enslaved people in Les Anses d'Arlet. ANOM FM C8A 37 F. 14, Recensement général de l'isle Martinique fait à la fin de l'année mil sept cent vingt six, 21–22.

4. For their marriage record, ADM 2Mi 309/2E2/1, October 30, 1730. The record specifies that Marianne was born in Diamant, Martinique, while Etienne was born in Bordeaux. In this respect, they resembled many couples in eighteenth-century Martinique: by 1730, 94.9 percent of women who married in the island were born in the Americas, compared with 59.6 percent of men. Jacques Houdaille, "Le métissage dans les anciennes colonies françaises," *Population* 36, N. 2 (March 1981: 267–286), 271.

5. On settlers' adoption of Indigenous watercraft elsewhere in the Americas see Lipman, *Saltwater Frontier*, 70–75.

6. For contests over St. Lucia and Tobago see Henry H. Breen, *St. Lucia: Historical, Statistical, and Descriptive* (London: Longman, Brown, and Green, 1844), 45–54; Henry Iles Woodcock, *A History of Tobago* (London: Frank Cass & Co., 1971 [1867]), 23–37.

7. For an early study of this phenomenon see Frederick Jackson Turner, "The Significance of the Frontier in American History," *Proceedings of the State Historical Society of Wisconsin*, 1893; more recently see Hinderaker and Mancall, *At the Edge of Empire*.

8. On islands as naturally bounded spaces, Philip Steinberg, "Insularity, Sovereignty and Statehood: The Representation of Islands on Portolan Charts and the Construction of the Territorial State," *Geografiska Annaler* 87, N. 4 (2005: 253–265).

9. On Catholic rites as "both a public and private matter" in early modern France, see Guillaume Aubert, "The Blood of France: Race and Purity of Blood in the French Atlantic World," *WMQ* 61, N. 3 (July 2004: 439–478), 446–448; on the development of the "family-state compact" see Sarah Hanley, "Engendering the State: Family Formation and State Building in Early Modern France," *FHS* 16, N. 1 (Spring 1989: 4–27).

10. A further 1,680 free and 13,000 enslaved people lived in the French colony of Grenada. TNA CO 101/28 N. 123 and TNA CO 101/1 N. 5. St. Lucia counted approximately 4,000 enslaved people, 800 white people, and 200 free people of color; Kalinagos were not counted. ANOM DPPC G1/506, Recensement Sainte Lucie 1760. The French census measures the number of pieds planted in a specific crop rather than the yield of said crop; for this reason, production amounts for St. Lucia are not included in the above estimate. However, it is worth noting that 1,419,000 pieds, or approximately 1.5 million English feet, were planted in coffee, while 248,600 pieds, or approximately 265,000 feet, were planted in cacao.

Dominica's population in 1763 was reported to be 1,718 free settlers, 5,872 enslaved people, and "from 50 to 60 Caraib familys"; I have estimated five people per family for a total of 250 Kalinagos in Dominica. The island was reported to produce 1,690,360 "pounds weight" of coffee, 271,650 of cacao, and 17,400 of cotton annually. TNA CO 101/1 N. 91.

By March 1764, British officials reported St. Vincent's population as 7,414 enslaved and at least 2,104 free people producing 1,249,012 pounds of coffee, 644,077 pounds of cacao, and 164,766 pounds of tobacco. TNA CO 101/1 N.150. An undated French census archived by British officials counted 1,138 "Caribs"; given that more than four times as many were deported from the island in 1797, actual numbers were probably much higher. TNA CO 101/1 N. 9. État présent de l'ile St. Vincent.

11. Mary Draper, "Timbering and Turtling: The Maritime Hinterlands of Early Modern British Caribbean Cities," *EAS* 15, N. 4 (Fall 2017: 769–800), 778.

12. On attempted English settlement of St. Lucia, Draper, "Timbering," especially 777–785; as Draper notes, "Barbadians never successfully defended their claims to St. Lucia," 773.

13. Nathaniel Uring, *A Relation of the Late Intended Settlement of St. Lucia and St. Vincent in America* (London: J. Peele, 1725), 18.

14. For the first order to evacuate, Uring, *A Relation,* 8; on the landing of French troops, 71.

15. For the treaty see Uring, *A Relation,* 81–86.

16. The evacuation of one or more of the islands was ordered in 1660, 1721, 1723, 1735, and 1748, yet settlers remained. Richard Pares, *War and Trade in the West Indies* (Oxford: Clarendon Press, 1936), 179–256.

17. On "rogue colonialism" in French New Orleans, see Dawdy, *Building the Devil's Empire,* quotation page 11.

18. "La plupart de ces hommes sont sortis du quartier du Diamant de la Martinique, qui par la mauvaise qualité des terres de ce quartier et la sècheresse qui y règne, on pris le party d'aller faire des établissements à Sainte Lucie, d'où ils vont vendre leur denrées au quartier du Diamant, pour en rapporter ce qui leur est nécessaire. Ces habitants font, pour la plupart, des vivres et élèvent des volailles, quelques'un ont planté des cotons; il y a quelques ateliers pour la fabrique des bois à batir." ANOM FM C10A 2 dossier 1 N. 18, Marquis de Champigny, February 29, 1732.

19. On the *Exclusif* see Jean Tarrade, *Le commerce colonial de la France à la fin de l'Ancien Régime: l'évolution du régime de l'Exclusif de 1763–1789,* 2 vols. (Paris: Université de Paris, 1972).

20. Léo Elisabeth, *La société martiniquaise aux XVIIe et XVIIIe siècles (1664–1789)* (Paris: Karthala, 2003), 42.

21. "Ils se déterminèrent à l'abandonner et à passer aux isles voisines," ANOM FM C8B 9 N. 94, Mémoire sur la culture du café aux iles du Vent, 1731.

22. ANOM FM C8B 9 N. 94. Sainton dates the introduction of coffee to Martinique to 1721; by 1733, the colony exported 3,000 tonnes of coffee. Jean Pierre Sainton, ed. *Histoire et civilisation de la Caraïbe Tome II: Le temps des matrices* (Paris: Karthala, 2012), 135.

23. "Leur faciliter les moyens de réparer leurs pertes et les exciter à faire de nouvelles plantations." The exemption was offered for 1727, 1728, 1729, and 1730. ANOM FM A25 N. 87, Ordonnance qui accorde exemption de capitation pendant les années 1727–1730 aux habitants cacaoyers, 9 novembre 1728. In 1730, a two-year exemption from the capitation tax for themselves and their enslaved laborers was also afforded to any planter who established a new cacao plantation. *Code de la Martinique* (Saint-Pierre: Imprimerie P. Richard, 1767), 87.

24. On the structure and role of the Marine see Kenneth Banks, *Chasing Empire Across the Sea: Communications and the State in the French Atlantic, 1713–1763* (Toronto: McGill-Queen's University Press, 2002), 9.

25. For censuses of Dominica and St. Vincent see ANOM DPPC G1 498; for St. Lucia ANOM DPPC G1 506.

26. "Ils y ont passé en pirogues ou canots, au mépris des défences que j'en ay fais." ANOM FM C8A 54 F 181, M. de Champigny, May 18, 1742. On French subjects abandoning Guadeloupe for surrounding islands, ANOM FM C8A 54 F. 10, M. de Champigny, January 16, 1742.

27. "Le nombre d'habitants y augmente tous les jours et on peut dire qu'ils n'y sont attirés que pour l'amour de l'indépendance ou ils y vivent. . . . Celuy qui est etably à la Domi-nique nommé le Maus petit Marchand mis a son aise y a fait même la fonction de juge dans quelques occasions . . . il arrive fréquemment dans ces iles neutres des meurtres et des assassinats qui restent tous impunis." ANOM FM C8A 56 F. 143, Poinsable to Bochart, February 8, 1744.

28. "Le Sieur LeGrand qui les commande a scu s'en faire aimer et respecter . . . il y fait les fonctions de commandant, d'intendant, et de juge . . . il s'est attiré tant de confiance que les habitants se soumettent à ses decisions avec la meme resignation que s'il était revetu de pouvoir necessaire sans qu'il nous en revienne la moindre plainte . . . il a assez de désintéressement pour rendre tous ses services gratuitement sans rien exiger des habitants, et sans avoir aucuns appoin-tements." ANOM FM C8A 50 F.315, M. de la Croix, July 1, 1739.

29. Sieur Vernède began serving as Lieutenant Aide Major in Dominica in 1755 and was promoted to Capitaine Aide Major in 1757; see ANOM E 385, Vernède, habitant de la Domi-nique. The Sieur de Longueville was appointed Commander of St. Lucia in 1744, during the War of Jenkins' Ear, but was recalled, along with his detachment, in 1756. ANOM E 290, de Longueville.

30. "De faire entendre à des François, livrés à eux-mêmes, qu'ils ont une Religion, un Prince, et des loix . . . [il] ne doit durer que jusqu'au rétablissement du bon ordre, et que je l'ai chargé de m'indiquer celui des habitants qu'il jugera le plus capable de commander aux autres." ANOM COL E 342, Prevost Commandant à St. Vincent.

31. Dawdy, *Building the Devil's Empire*.

32. See Table 1. As discussed throughout this book, racial ascriptions varied according to context and census figures should therefore not be taken at face value. Nonetheless, the high percentage of people of color in the Creole Archipelago is significant.

33. On free people of color in Saint-Domingue see Garrigus, *Before Haiti*; for French Louisiana see Dawdy, *Building the Devil's Empire;* Johnson, *Wicked Flesh;* Jennifer Spear, *Race, Sex, and Social Order in Early New Orleans* (Baltimore: Johns Hopkins University Press, 2009), 79–99; Vidal, *Caribbean New Orleans*.

34. "Confisquées au profit des pauvres." ANOM FM C8B 19 N. 8, Ordonnance de M. de Baas, Gouverneur General des Iles, 1 aout 1669.

35. Louis XIV, *Le Code Noir ou recueil des règlements rendus jusqu'à présent* (Paris: Prault, 1767). Translated by John Garrigus. https://directory.vancouver.wsu.edu/sites/directory.vancouver .wsu.edu/files/inserted_files/webinterno2/code%20noir.pdf.

36. Cited in Abel A. Louis, *Les Libres de Couleur en Martinique, Tome 1: Des origines à la veille de la Révolution française 1635–1788* (Paris: L'Harmattan, 2012), 41. This observation is echoed in the correspondence of French officials in Martinique; ANOM FM F3 248 II N. 685, 3 xbre 1681, Blenac et Patoulet au Roi.

37. On attempts to associate Blackness with enslavement elsewhere in the Americas, Ale-jandro de la Fuente and Ariela J. Gross, *Becoming Free, Becoming Black: Race, Freedom, and Law in Cuba, Virginia, and Louisiana* (New York: Cambridge University Press, 2020).

38. "Les mulâtres qui tirent leur naissance du vice ne devraient pas recevoir d'exemptions." Quoted in Louis, *Les libres de couleur,* 140. Emphasis added.

39. On French opposition to *mésalliance,* see Aubert, "The Blood of France"; Doris Garraway, *The Libertine Colony: Creolization in the Early French Caribbean* (Durham: Duke University Press, 2005), especially 207–211.

40. "Nonobstant ce qui est porté par les articles 56, 57 & 59 dudit Edit du mois de mars 1685 . . . tous esclaves affranchis, ou negres libres, leurs enfans & descendans, soient incapables à l'avenir de recevoir des blancs aucune donation entre vifs, ou à cause de mort, ou autrement." *Code de la Martinique,* 281. This legislation echoes that found in the respective *Code Noirs* issued for Ile Bourbon (Article 51, 1723) and Louisiana (Article 52, 1724).

41. On the law in Louisiana, Johnson, *Wicked Flesh,* 132; in Saint-Domingue, Auguste Lebeau, *De la condition des gens de couleur libres sous l'Ancien Régime* (Poitiers: Masson, 1903), 114.

42. On the war as a turning point in Saint-Domingue, Garrigus, *Before Haiti.*

43. *Code de la Martinique,* 280–281.

44. Elisabeth, *La Société Martiniquaise,* 284.

45. For the 1671 exemption, see ANOM FM A 24 N. 824, Règlement de M. de Baas du 12 février 1671 pour les droits de capitation et exemptions des dits droits. For an example of the confusion, see ANOM FM A 25 N. 25 juillet 1724, Ordre qui assujettis les negres et mulatres libres au droit de capitation, which discusses an exemption afforded to "Magdeleine Berne negresse libre" in 1712. For an in-depth discussion of the tax see Louis, *Les Libres de couleur,* Vol. 1, 140–147.

46. On census taking in the French Caribbean, Jacques Petitjean Roget, *La Société d'habitation à la Martinique: Une demi-siècle de formation, 1635–1685* (Lille: H. Champion, 1980), 1198–1210.

47. Likely seeking to avoid further confusion, article I, section X of the 1730 code specified that "tous ceux qui ont ci-devant prétendu des exemptions de capitation, & qui ne sont point expressément dénommés dans ces présentes . . . seront tenues de payer la capitation en entier." *Code de la Martinique,* 87.

48. "Doivent s'estimer heureux de jouir de la liberté, sans ambitionner les mêmes prérogatives des créoles blancs." Cited in Christiane Duval née Mezin, "La condition juridique des hommes de couleur libres à la Martinique au temps de l'esclavage" (doctoral dissertation, Université de droit d'économie et de sciences sociales de Paris, Paris II, 1975), 177.

49. On narrowing horizons in late-eighteenth-century Saint-Domingue see Garrigus, *Before Haiti.*

50. Vidal defines racial formation, in contrast to racial hierarchies, as a process in which the meaning of race was constantly "re-instantiated and re-enacted." Vidal, *Caribbean New Orleans,* 27.

51. For a detailed discussion of Elisabeth's findings and methodology, Elisabeth, *La Société martiniquaise,* 304–311.

52. On "disappearing bodies in empirical archives" see Johnson, *Wicked Flesh,* 134–143.

53. Louis, *Les Libres de Couleur en Martinique,* 145. On free people of color being assimilated to the category of white, see Jessica Pierre-Louis, "Les libres de couleur face au préjugé: Franchir la barrière à la Martinique aux XVIIe–XVIIIe siècles" (doctoral dissertation, Université des Antilles et de la Guyane, 2015), especially 230–250. On race and censuses elsewhere in the French Atlantic see Johnson, *Wicked Flesh,* 134–143; Vidal, *Caribbean New Orleans,* 188–199.

54. "La distance de Ste. Lucie à la Martinique, qui n'est que de 7 lieues fait prendre le party à ceux qui veulent décamper de se servir de pirogues ou canots pour passer dans cette isle." ANOM FM C8A 55 F. 246, August 6, 1743.

55. See, for example, ADM Cote 2E2/1 page 128, Baptême du fils illégitime de Christophe, nègre libre demeurant à Sainte Lucie, et d'une Caraïbesse, 1722; ADM Cote 2E2/1 page 147,

Baptème d'Angelique petite nègresse née en légitime mariage de Marc et Magdeleine nègresse libre demeurant à Sainte Lucie.

56. ANOM, État Civil, Trois-Rivières Guadeloupe, September 17, 1735.

57. ADM Cote 2E2/1 July 21, 1734.

58. On the importance of documents attesting to free status in the Atlantic World, Rebecca J. Scott and Jean M. Hébrard, *Freedom Papers: An Atlantic Odyssey in the Age of Emancipation* (Cambridge, MA: Harvard University Press, 2014).

59. ANOM, État Civil, Basse-Pointe Martinique, July 14, 1742.

60. ADM Cote 2E2/1, October 26, 1734, Mariage Jean Cevet et Marie Rose.

61. For a free family of color who left northern Martinique to settle in St. Vincent see Jessica Pierre-Louis, "Les libres de couleur, à Basse-Point, au Macouba et au Prêcheur, de 1665 à 1774," *BSHG* 161 (2012: 77–102).

62. ANOM DPPC G1 506, Recensement de l'isle de Ste. Lucie de l'année 1730.

63. ANOM DPPC G1 498 N. 82.

64. ANOM DPPC G1 506 Recensement Ste. Lucie 1745; ANOM DPPC G1 498 Denombrement de l'isle Dominique pour l'année 1745. Unfortunately no contemporaneous population counts for St. Vincent are extant.

65. Ibid. Population counts for both islands also listed "elderly and infirm" settlers.

66. Children as a percentage of the free population of Martinique reached the highest point in 1694, at 40.9 percent. Boucher, *France and the American Tropics,* 258. Among Martinique's white population, children accounted for 36 percent of the population in 1738, and this proportion fell to 27 percent by 1751. Sainton, *Histoire et Civilisation* II, 243.

67. ANOM DPPC G1 506, Recensement de l'isle de Ste. Lucie de l'année 1730.

68. For censuses of Dominica, ANOM DPPC G1 498.

69. Similar practices persisted in Saint-Domingue's South province; Garrigus, *Before Haiti,* 45–50.

70. The phrase "hommes mariés et garcons portant armes, tant blancs que mulâtres et nègres libres" was used in all population counts for St. Lucia beginning in 1745. When St. Lucia became a French colony in 1763, census takers began distinguishing adult men based on race, suggesting that the decision not to do so earlier was deliberate. ANOM DPPC G1/506 Recensements St. Lucie.

71. Elisabeth, *La société martiniquaise,* 300. The same was not true for French colonial New Orleans, where census takers grouped together all free people without regard to race in the enumeration for 1721; parenthetical references to race were made in a household census of 1732. Dawdy, *Building the Devil's Empire,* 153–157.

72. A commander was established in St. Lucia in 1744. ANOM E 290, de Longueville.

73. ANOM DPPC G1 506, État des Compagnies, 1745.

74. ANOM DPPC G1 506, État des Compagnies, 1747.

75. On marriage between white women and Black men in metropolitan France, Jennifer Palmer, "What's in a name? Mixed race families and resistance to racial codification in Eighteenth-Century France," *FHS* 33, N. 3 (June 2010: 357–385). For the 1679 marriage between a white woman and a man of color in Martinique, Louis, *Les libres de couleur,* 52.

76. On the "normalcy of whiteness" in the French Caribbean see Laurent Dubois, "Inscribing Race in the Revolutionary French Antilles," in Sue Peabody and Tyler Stovall, eds., *The Color of Liberty: Histories of Race in France* (Durham: Duke University Press, 2003), 95–107.

77. ANOM DPPC G1 506, Compagnies de Ste. Lucie, 1747. Two men, Jacques Chantin and Jean Baptiste Champagne, are grouped with women of color and their children on the next line, suggesting relationships that were known but not legitimated by marriage. The wives

of twenty-six men noted to be people of color are simply listed as "sa femme," implying that they, like their husbands, were of African descent. On interracial marriage in Martinique see Houdaille, "Le metissage," 271, and Elisabeth, *La société martiniquaise*, 315–316.

78. Fuentes, *Dispossessed Lives,* 62.

79. On slave societies, see Moses Finley, *Ancient Slavery and Modern Ideology* (New York: Viking Press, 1980), 74–75; Ira Berlin, *Many Thousands Gone: The First Two Centuries of Slavery in North America* (Cambridge: Harvard University Press, 1998), 1–15.

80. Boucher, *France and the American Tropics,* 160. Emphasis in original.

81. "Les nègres sont toute la force d'un habitant, et par conséquent de toutes les colonies; ils sont très chers à la Grenade parce qu'il n'y va jamais de négrier: de sorte qu'on est obligé de les faire achetter à la Martinique, ou de la seconde main de ceux qui y en portent, et qui ne sont le plus souvent que le rebut d'une cargaison." HCL, Beinecke Collection MS 220, 4. Planters in Guadeloupe also complained about lack of access to the transatlantic slave trade, Laurent Dubois, *A Colony of Citizens: Revolution and Slave Emancipation in the French Caribbean, 1787–1804* (Chapel Hill: University of North Carolina Press for the Omohundro Institute of Early American History and Culture, 2004), 51.

82. I use 1760 rather than 1763 as the cutoff point for this trade because conquests during the Seven Years' War significantly altered the scale and nature of slave trading to the islands, resulting, for instance, in a marked increase in the number of Africans trafficked to British-occupied Guadeloupe.

83. Dutch planters ventured out from their colony on the island of St. Maarten in order to stake a claim to Tobago in the 1650s but were quickly repelled by Kalinagos as well as by English forces dispatched from Barbados. The failed Dutch settlement is briefly described in John Campbell, *Candid and Impartial Considerations on the nature of the sugar trade; the Comparative Importance of the British and French Islands in the West-Indies: with the value and consequence of St. Lucia and Granada, truly stated* (London: R. Baldwin, 1763), 121.

84. ANOM DPPC G1/498 N. 50, Grenada census 1745; N. 85, Dominica census 1745; ANOM DPPC G1/506 N. 4, St. Lucia census 1745.

85. James A. Rawley and Stephen D. Behrendt, *The Transatlantic Slave Trade: A History, Revised Edition* (Dexter, MI: Thomson-Shore, 2005), 114. Philip Curtin also suspects that many people were trafficked from Barbados to surrounding islands; Curtin, *The Atlantic Slave Trade: A Census* (Madison: University of Wisconsin, 1972), 67.

86. "Il est absolument impossible d'empescher ce commerce . . . à moins d'avoir une frégate armée qui roule perpetuellement dans les isles voisines. . . . L'interlope qui arrive avec les nègres, passe au large devant St. Pierre avec pavillon holandois, et cependant assés près pour pouvoir estre distingué et aperçeu par les negocians du bourg, et fait ensuite sa route pour la Dominique où il va mouiller. La nuit suivante tous les negocians qui ont coustume de faire ce commerce, envoyent avec leurs batteaux les uns de l'argent, les autres du sucre du cacao, et indigo pour traiter chacun suivant leurs forces les nègres qu'ils ont envie d'achetter, et les vont ensuite débarquer dans des ances ou ils ont leurs habitudes." ANOM FM C8A28 f. 15, de Feuquières, February 3, 1721.

87. A similar account of a ship from Nantes disembarking more than two hundred captives in St. Lucia can be found in ANOM C8A42 F.182, Correspondence of Jacques Pannier d'Orgeville, Intendant of the Windward Islands, March 15, 1731. On French officials' complicity in this trade, see Kenneth Banks, "Official Duplicity: The Illicit Slave Trade of Martinique, 1713–1763," in Peter Coclanis, ed., *The Atlantic Economic during the Seventeenth and Eighteenth Centuries* (Columbia: University of South Carolina Press, 2005), 229–251.

88. ANOM FM C8A 28 f. 15

89. Dominica had a total population of 4,690 people, of whom 1,160 were free and 3,530 were enslaved. ANOM DPPC G1 498, no number, Recensement général de l'isle de la Dominique pour l'année 1753. There were 1,019 free settlers and 4,020 enslaved people in St. Lucia, for a total population of 5,039. ANOM DPPC G1 506, Denombrement et ressencement [sic] général de l'isle Sainte Lucie le 15 janvier 1756.

90. Trevor Burnard and John Garrigus, *The Plantation Machine: Atlantic Capitalism in French Saint-Domingue and British Jamaica* (Philadelphia: University of Pennsylvania Press, 2016), 100. Grenada had 14,032 total inhabitants, of whom 12,608 were enslaved. ANOM DPPC G1 498 N. 52, Recensement général de l'isle de la Grenade pour l'année 1755.

91. Robin Blackburn, *The Making of New World Slavery: From the Baroque to the Modern* (New York: Verso, 1997), 410.

92. Tony Volpe, "Le logement des esclaves des plantations à la Martinique au XVIIIe siècle," in Jean-Marc Moriceau and Philippe Madeline, eds., *Les petites gens de la terre: Paysans, ouvriers et domestiques (Moyen Age–XXIe siècles)* (Caen: Presse Universitaires de Caen, 2017), 223–234.

93. ANOM DPPC G1/506, St. Lucia household enumeration 1760.

94. Between 1701 and 1809, 22.7 percent of people trafficked from Africa were children. David Eltis and Stanley Engerman, "Fluctuations in Sex and Age Ratios in the Transatlantic Slave Trade, 1663–1864," *Economic History Review*, 46, N. 2 (May 1993: 308–323), 301. In this respect, the Creole Archipelago mirrored enslaved populations in Martinique, where an estimated 30 percent of enslaved people were younger than fourteen in 1755. Sainton, *Histoire et Civilisation* Tome II, 245.

95. Gregory E. O'Malley, *Final Passages: The Intercolonial Slave Trade of British America, 1619–1807* (Chapel Hill: University of North Carolina Press for the Omohundro Institute of Early American History and Culture, 2014), 60.

96. DNA Deed Book B N. 1, 40. Translation of the list of souls &c upon the plantation of Lewis de la Ferriere Constance. For more on Bois Cotlette, see Tessa Murphy and Mark Hauser, "Dominica as an Evolving Landscape: Evidence of Changing Social, Political and Economic Organization in the Eighteenth Century," in Mark Hauser and Diane Wallman, eds., *Archaeology in Dominica: Everyday Ecologies and Economies at Morne Patate* (Gainesville: University of Florida Press, 2020). This degree of creolization among the enslaved population rivals that of Barbados, where by 1750 an estimated 45 percent of the enslaved population was island-born. Hilary McD. Beckles, "Creolisation in Action: The Slave Labour Elite and Anti-Slavery in Barbados," *Caribbean Quarterly* 44, N. 1/2 (March–June 1998), 108–128.

97. DNA Deed Book T N. 2, 120–122.

98. Du Tertre, *Histoire générale des Antilles* II, 504. On planters' attempts to encourage marriage and reproduction among enslaved people in early French colonies, Arlette Gautier, "Traite et politiques démographiques esclavagistes," *Population* 6 (November 1986: 1005–1024).

99. DNA Deed Book B N. 1, 40.

100. On absenteeism, Trevor Burnard, "A Failed Settler Society: Marriage and Demographic Failure in Early Jamaica," *Journal of Social History* 28, N. 1 (Autumn 1994: 63–82).

101. HCSP Vol. 71, page 196, Testimony of James Bailie.

102. "L'Habitant François . . . se familiarise plus avec ses Nègres, excite plus leur Émulation, leur Zele et leurs Talen, se confie à eux, et épargne les gages de plusieurs blancs." HCSP Vol. 70, page 335, Testimony of La Verge La Feuillée.

103. Wendy Warren, *New England Bound: Slavery and Colonization in Early America* (New York: Liveright, 2016), 145. On enslaved people's vulnerability to physical and sexual violence in small households, Block, *Ordinary Lives*, 38–50.

104. On the gang system, Burnard and Garrigus, *The Plantation Machine*, 4–8. On task versus gang labor, Philip D. Morgan, "Task and Gang Systems: The Organization of Labor on New World Plantations," in Stephen Innes, ed., *Work and Labor in Early America* (Chapel Hill: University of North Carolina Press for the Omohundro Institute of Early American History and Culture, 1988), 189–220.

105. On enslaved labor in non–sugar plantation contexts, Shepherd, ed., *Slavery Without Sugar*. On enslaved labor on coffee plantations, Michel-Rolph Trouillot, "Coffee Planters and Coffee Slaves in the Antilles: The impact of a Secondary Crop," in Berlin and Morgan, eds., *Cultivation and Culture*, 124–137.

106. Officials in Martinique complained that requiring or allowing enslaved people to grow their own food resulted in too much autonomy, as they traveled from place to place. ANOM FM C8A 58 F. 160, Marquis de Caylus, November 20, 1748.

107. Morgan, "Task and Gang Systems," 208.

108. Likely Arada, from the Bight of Benin.

109. Orlando Patterson, *Sociology of Slavery: An Analysis of the Origins, Development, and Structure of Negro Slave Society in Jamaica* (London: MacGibbon & Kee, 1967), especially 74. On violence in slave societies, Vincent Brown, *The Reaper's Garden: Death and Power in the World of Atlantic Slavery* (Cambridge, MA: Harvard University Press, 2008).

110. "Les contenir par la crainte d'un chatimen presen." ANOM FM C8 B 8 N.10, de Pradines, January 30, 1722. Planters in Martinique also complained about legal restraints on their punishment of enslaved people; see Rushforth, "The *Gaoulet*," 108.

111. ANOM FM C8A 50 F. 11, Champigny, February 11, 1743.

112. Anne Perotin-Dumon, "Cabotage, Contraband, and Corsairs: The Port Cities of Guadeloupe and Their Inhabitants, 1650–1800," in Franklin Knight and Peggy Liss, eds., *Atlantic Port Cities: Economy, Culture, and Society in the Atlantic World, 1650–1850* (Knoxville: University of Tennessee Press, 1991); Sainton, *Histoire et Civilisation de la Caraïbe* II: 112–119.

113. Casey Schmitt, "Virtue in Corruption: Privateers, Smugglers, and the Shape of Empire in the Eighteenth-Century Caribbean," *EAS* (Winter 2015: 80–110).

114. On food shortages caused by the turn to sugar production, Carl and Roberta Bridenbaugh, *No Peace Beyond the Line: The English in the Caribbean, 1624–1690* (New York: Oxford University Press, 1972), 43–51; Butel, *Histoire de Antilles françaises*, 29.

115. Sainton, *Histoire et Civilisation* II, 140.

116. "La Martinique et les autres isles de ce Gouvernement général tirent des isles neutres des secours infinis en magnoc, volailles, bœufs pour les boucheries &c, dont elles ne peuvent absolument se passer . . . interdire la communication entre les isles établies et les isles neutres ce servit non seulement réduire ces habitants au désespoir, mais encore à détruire une branche considérable de notre commerce." ANOM C8A59 f.158 M. de Bompar, November 14, 1751.

117. Gabriel Debien, "Les cultures à Sainte-Lucie à la fin du XVIIIe siècle," *Annales des Antilles* 13 (1966: 49–84), 62. The *quarré* was a unit of measure equal to one hundred surveyor's paces on each side of a square. In Guadeloupe and Saint-Domingue, where the surveyor's pace was just under one meter, the quarré equaled approximately 2.34 acres. In Martinique the pace was slightly longer; each Martiniquan quarré equals approximately 3.19 acres. Because both Grenada and St. Lucia were for a time administered as dependencies of Martinique, I use the Martiniquan quarré as the unit of measure for the Creole Archipelago.

118. ANOM DPPC G1/506 Recensements Ste. Lucie 1732, 1759. Total crop production in St. Lucia declined slightly from 1758 to 1759 and fell further still in 1760, likely due to the Seven Years' War.

119. ANOM DPPC G1/498, Recensement Dominica 1730, 1745, 1753.

120. ANOM DPPC G1/498, Recensement St. Vincent 1732.

121. ANOM DPPC G1/506, Recensement Ste. Lucie 1745; ANOM DPPC G1 498, Recensement Dominica 1745.

122. Trouillot, "Motion in the System."

123. Debien, "Les cultures à Sainte Lucie," 69.

124. The French pied was equal to approximately 1.065 English feet. Pritchard, *In Search of Empire*, xxiii.

125. ANOM DPPC G1/498, Recensement Dominica 1753.

126. ANOM DPPC G1/506, Recensement St. Lucia 1744, 1759.

127. Debien, "Les cultures à la Sainte Lucie," 73.

128. ANOM DPPC G1/506, Recensement St. Lucia 1747, 1748, 1756.

129. ANOM G1/498, Recensement Grenade 1755. Figures for Martinique sourced from Sainton, *Histoire et Civilisation* II: 128.

130. "Les charger entièrement de marchandises estrangeres qu'ils renversent ensuite ou dans leurs navires ou dans leurs magasins." ANOM C8A26 F.149, Marquis de Feuquières, March 18, 1719. French efforts to end this illicit trade continued in the ensuing decades; see, for example, ADM B8 1751 F161, Ordonnance du roi pour empêcher le commerce étranger illicite, pratiqué par les bâtiments qui abordent aux iles de St. Vincent, Tobago, la Dominique, 6 juillet 1751.

131. "Quelques recherches et quelques frais qu'on fasse on ne peut découvrir la contrebande faute de denonciateurs . . . sans un ou deux bateaux armez et commandez par des officiers de la Marine *qui ne soient point Creole* il est impossible d'empescher [ce] commerce." ANOM C8B6 N. 38, Vaultier de Moyencourt, Governor of Guadeloupe, to the Marquis de Feuquières, June 4, 1720. Emphasis added.

132. As a point of comparison, the French colony of Grenada exported 1,482,000 pounds of coffee, 51,919 pounds of cotton, and 84,932 pounds of cacao, along with 4,795 hogshead of sugar, 721 hogshead of molasses, and 17 hogshead of rum. TNA T1 423 N. 279, the amount of the produce of Grenada exported in 1762.

133. "Les Espagnols de la Marguerite, de Cumana, même des Caraques, viennent dans de petites barques enlever le cacao qu'ils payent, argent comptant 10s la livre. Les Hollandois prennent tout leur caffé, et il n'en vient que peu ou point à la Martinique." ANOM COL E 342, Prévost, commandant à Saint-Vincent, 1761.

134. Officials recognized that land scarcity drove some French subjects to the neighboring islands and offered land grants in exchange for returning to Martinique or Guadeloupe. ANOM C8A 28 F. 153, M. de Pas de Feuquières, November 15, 1721.

135. "Quel droit ont [les Anglais] sur la Dominique et sur St. Vincent ? N'ont-ils pas reconnu par les traités que ces isles appartiennent aux Caraïbes naturels du pais[?] . . . Mais si ces évacuations devaient absolument avoir lieu, que deviendraient tous de familles établies dans les quatre isles ou elles vivent dans l'aisance, et où elles ont la fortune de leurs enfants assurée? Que deviendraient elles si elles se perdaient les fonds qui les font subsister, ainsi que leurs esclaves? Il ne faudrait pas chercher à leur procurer des établissements dans les isles concédées, déjà trop petites pour les familles qui y résident. Ces pauvres gens périssaient donc de misère." ANOM F3 27 f. 553, Marquis de Caylus, March 17, 1750.

136. On the war in France's Windward Islands see Banks, *Chasing Empire*, 202–208.

137. Daniel Baugh, *The Global Seven Year's War, 1754–1763: Britain and France in a Great Power Contest* (New York: Pearson Longman, 2011), 321. On English conquest and occupation

of Guadeloupe see Lucien-René Abenon, *Petite histoire de la Guadeloupe* (Paris: Éditions L'Harmattan, 1992), 66–72.

138. "L'isle de St. Vincent est neutre . . . par conséquent . . . les Français qui s'y trouvent . . . doivent être regardés et traités comme neutres, c'est-à-dire y estre à labry de toute vexation et violence de la part des ennemis du Roi . . . serez regardé ipso facto comme désobéissant et rebelle." ANOM FM 3 58, Le Vassor de la Touche, June 6, 1761.

139. "Anglois étoient préalablement descendus à terre, et y avoient fait de ces propositions captieuses . . . les propos des Anglois avoient été écouté de la pluspart des habitans, même des principaux." ANOM FM C8A 63 N. 58, July 12, 1761, M. Levassor de Latouche.

140. ANOM FM C8A 63 N. 125, Copie et traduction d'une lettre de Lord Rollo au général Amherst, August 17, 1761.

141. Joseph Boromé, "The French and Dominica, 1699–1763" *Jamaican Historical Review* Vol. 7, N. 1 (January 1967: 9–39), 32–35.

142. CL, James Douglas Papers, Vol. N, Remarks &c on board the *Dublin*, June 1761.

143. "Cette isle étant très abondante en Bestiaux, volailles et légumes de toute espèce." ANOM C8A 64 N. 1, June 12, 1761, M. Levassor de Latouche and de la Rivière. On the conquest of Grenada, St. Lucia, and St. Vincent, ANOM C8A 64 N. 43, Analyze des lettres de M. Levassor de la Touche, May 15, 1762.

144. "Ste Lucie n'avoit que 37 soldats dont 4 ont déserté au moment de l'arrivée des Ennemis: un seul habitant se présenta et les autres restèrent chez eux. Celui de la Grenade avec encore moins de soldats . . . et un pareil abandon de la part des habitans." ANOM C8A 64 N. 43.

CHAPTER 3

1. ADM État Civil Le Prêcheur, Baptême La Verge La Feuillée, Novembre 1723. On Dominica as neutral, Edelson, *The New Map of Empire*, 199.

2. As of 1770 there were eighty-five people enslaved on the Desgommiers estate, forty-three of whom were identified as Creole. DNA Deed Book T2, pages 120–122. Belligny's name is spelled differently across different documents; for the sake of consistency, I have employed the spelling in his French colonial personnel file. See ANOM E 100, Crocquet de Belligny Nicolas.

3. On the Board of Trade's role in developing the Ceded Islands, Edelson, *The New Map*, 197–247.

4. On the consequences of the war, see Fred Anderson, *The Crucible of War: The Seven Years' War and the Fate of Empire in British North America, 1754–1766* (New York: Knopf, 2000); Mark Danky and Patrick J. Speelman, eds., *The Seven Years' War: Global Views* (Leiden: Brill, 2012).

5. On the British empire in the latter half of the eighteenth century, Edelson, *The New Map*; P. J. Marshall, *The Making and Unmaking of Empires: Britain, India, and America c. 1750–1783* (New York: Oxford University Press, 2005); on the French, Pernille Røge, *Economistes and the Reinvention of Empire: France in the Americas and Africa, c. 1750–1802* (New York: Cambridge University Press, 2019). On similarities between British and French territorial preoccupations at the end of the Seven Years' War, Paul Mapp, *The Elusive West and the Contest for Empire, 1713–1763* (Chapel Hill: University of North Carolina Press for the Omohundro Institute of Early American History and Culture, 2011), Chapter 15.

6. Distinguishing between what he terms first and second phase West Indian colonies, Barry Higman argues that Caribbean islands settled after sugar monoculture took root elsewhere in the Americas were able to borrow from existing patterns of plantation production, thereby

developing more quickly and efficiently. Barry Higman, *Slave Populations of the British Caribbean, 1807–1834* (Baltimore: Johns Hopkins University Press, 1984), 40–71.

7. On the British Ceded Islands as laboratories of empire see Edelson, *The New Map*, 198; this chapter builds on Edelson's work to emphasize how multiple empires simultaneously engaged in similar processes of reform and experimentation.

8. TNA CO 106/10 N. 67, An account of the French inhabitants of Dominica whose claims have been allowed by the commissioners and who paid their fines accordingly, February 1766.

9. On Bourbon Spain's promotion of the slave trade, Elena Schneider, "African Slavery and Spanish Empire: Imperial Imaginings and Bourbon Reform in Eighteenth-Century Cuba and Beyond," *JEAH* 5 (2015: 3–29).

10. https://slavevoyages.org/voyages/qakth28g.

11. On this "second Middle Passage" see O'Malley, *Final Passages*.

12. Although Choiseul was forced to resign as Secretary of the Marine in 1766, he is widely credited with shaping French military and economic policy in the wake of the Seven Years' War. John Fraser Ramsey, *Anglo-French Relations, 1763–1770: A Study of Choiseul's Foreign Policy* (Berkeley: University of California Press, 1939).

13. For these debates see Helen Dewar, "Canada or Guadeloupe?: French and British Perceptions of Empire, 1760–1763," *Canadian Historical Review* 91, N. 4 (December 2010: 637–660).

14. Although a discussion of the Bourbon Reforms is beyond the scope of this book, plans for developing Spanish Cuba bear many important resemblances to those for the Ceded Islands. See Elena Schneider, *The Occupation of Havana: War, Trade, and Slavery in the Atlantic World* (Chapel Hill: University of North Carolina Press for the Omohundro Institute of Early American History and Culture, 2018), especially Chapter 5.

15. On the debate over Canada see Anonymous, *Reasons for keeping Guadeloupe at a peace, preferable to Canada, explained in five letters from a gentleman in Guadeloupe, to his friend in London* (London: M. Cooper, 1761).

16. Røge, *Economistes*, 16–17. On French attempts to develop Guiana, Marion Godfroy, "La guerre de Sept ans et ses conséquences atlantiques: Kourou ou l'apparition d'un nouveau système colonial," *FHS* 32, N. 2 (Spring 2009: 167–191); Marion Godfroy, *Kourou and the Struggle for a French America* (New York: Palgrave Macmillan, 2015); François Regourd, *Sciences et colonisation sous l'Ancien Régime: le cas de la Guyane et des Antilles françaises, XVIIe-XVIIIe siècles* (Bordeaux: Presses Universitaires de France, 2000); Emma Rothschild, "A Horrible Tragedy in the French Atlantic," *Past and Present* 192 (August 2006: 67–108); Christopher Hodson, "A Bondage So Harsh: Acadian Labor in the French Caribbean, 1763–1766," *EAS* (Spring 2007: 96–131). On French proposals to settle West Africa, Pernille Røge, "'La clef de commerce'—The changing role of Africa in France's Atlantic empire ca. 1760–1797," *History of European Ideas* 34, N. 4 (Jan. 2012: 431–443), Røge, *Economistes*, Chapter 4.

17. Choiseul, quoted in Godfroy, *Kourou*, 24.

18. Etienne-François de Stainville, duc de Choiseul, *Mémoire Historique sur la négociation de la France et de l'Angleterre, depuis le 26 mars 1761 jusqu'au 20 septembre de la même année, avec les pièces justificatives* (Paris: Imprimerie Royale, 1761), 65.

19. On the role of "press propaganda as a political weapon" in the postwar era, John Brewer, *Party Ideology and Popular Politics at the Accession of George III* (New York: Cambridge University Press, 1976), 16.

20. Richard Sheridan, "Sir William Young: Planter and Politician, With Special Reference to Slavery in the British West Indies," *JCH* 33, N. 1 (January 1999: 1–26).

21. William Young, *Considerations which may tend to promote the settlement of our new West-India Colonies, by Encouraging Individuals to embark in the Undertaking* (London: James Robson, 1764).

22. For examples of these complaints, see "A planter at Barbados," *Reflections on the true interest of Great Britain with respect to the Caribbee islands, as well the old settlements as the neutral islands and the conquests. To which the importance of Martinique is particularly consider'd* (London: 1762); D. L. Niddrie, "Eighteenth-Century Settlement in the British Caribbean," *Transactions of the Institute of British Geographers* 40 (December 1966: 67–80), 78.

23. Young, *Considerations,* 23.

24. Young, *Considerations,* 47.

25. Røge, *Economistes,* 12; Hodson, "A Bondage So Harsh."

26. Røge, *Economistes,* 94. On these failed experiments, Godfroy, *Kourou,* 60–69; Hodson, "A Bondage So Harsh." For debates over slavery among Physiocrats, Røge, *Economistes,* 84–93.

27. On British abolitionism, Christopher Leslie Brown, *Moral Capital: Foundations of British Abolitionism* (Chapel Hill: University of North Carolina Press for the Omohundro Institute of Early American History and Culture, 2006).

28. On Spain's commitment to slavery in this era, Schneider, "African Slavery and Spanish Empire."

29. https://slavevoyages.org/voyages/Bg02xAy5

30. For Prime Minister Bute's role in the pamphlet, Brewer, *Party Ideology,* 225–226.

31. Campbell, *Candid & Impartial Considerations,* 21.

32. Vincent Brown, *Tacky's Revolt: The Story of an Atlantic Slave War* (Cambridge, MA: Harvard University Press, 2020).

33. On how land policy in the Ceded Islands differed from elsewhere in the British empire see Edelson, *The New Map,* 197–248; David H. Murdoch, "Land Policy in the Eighteenth-Century British Empire: The Sale of Crown Lands in the Ceded Islands, 1763–1783," *Historical Journal* 27, N. 3 (September 1984: 549–574); Niddrie, "Eighteenth-Century Settlement."

34. Edelson, *The New Map,* 202–203.

35. TNA 106/9 N. 166, Instructions to the Commissioners for disposing by sale or otherwise of certain lands in Grenada, the Grenadines, Tobago, St. Vincent and Dominica, July 26, 1764.

36. TNA CO 101/1 N. 279, Melvill to Higginson, October 22, 1765.

37. Young, *Considerations,* 31. The importance of preserving woodlands is also discussed in Campbell, *Candid and Impartial Considerations,* 129.

38. TNA CO 106/9 N. 166, Instruction 5.

39. On the preservation of woodlands in the Ceded Islands see Richard Grove, *Green Imperialism: Colonial Expansion, Tropical Island Edens, and the Origins of Environmentalism, 1600–1800* (New York: Cambridge University Press, 1995), 264–308.

40. On the origins and implications of this tale see Newton, "The Race Leapt."

41. On the symbolic role of mapping see J. B. Harley, *The New Nature of Maps: Essays in the History of Cartography* (Baltimore: Johns Hopkins University Press, 2001).

42. Mark Quintanilla, "The World of Alexander Campbell: An Eighteenth-Century Grenadian Planter," *Albion* 35, N. 2 (Summer 2003: 229–256), 236.

43. TNA CO 106/9 N. 166, Instructions to the Commissioners, July 26, 1764. As a point of comparison, when Barbados was first settled Governors Tufton and Hawley claimed 15,872 and 14,235 acres for themselves, respectively. Richard Pares, "Merchants and Planters," *Economic History Review Supplement* 4 (1960), 57, footnote 15.

44. TNA CO 106/9 N. 22, Abstract of the Terms and Conditions contained in His Majesty's Instructions. On the Dominica reserve see Lennox Honychurch, *In the Forests of Freedom: The Fighting Maroons of Dominica* (London: Papillote Press, 2017), 43.

45. Godfroy, *Kourou;* Rothschild, "A Horrible Tragedy." Colonists were lured to French Guiana with promises of free passage and two and a half years of provisions and lodging, as well as the tools necessary to cultivate the new lands. See Godfroy, "La guerre des Sept ans," 188, footnote 97.

46. As early as 1762, Choiseul suggested resettling Acadian refugees in St. Lucia; see Godfroy, "La guerre des sept ans," 172; St. Lucia parish registers show numerous "natives of Louisbourg" marrying in the islands from the 1760s onward. ANOM État Civil Ste. Lucie.

47. Monique Pelletier, "La Martinique et la Guadeloupe au lendemain du Traité de Paris (10 février 1763): L'œuvre des ingénieurs géographes," *Chronique d'Histoire Maritime* 9 (1984: 23–30).

48. BNF, Cartes et Plans, Section Hydrographique, portfolio 156, div. 2.

49. On Morancy, see ANOM E 316. The other surveyor appointed to St. Lucia, Sieur Lefort de Latour, finally succeeded in creating a survey and description of the island in 1787. A copy can be found in the St. Lucia National Archives, Castries. For Lefort de Latour's appointment, ADM CS B13 Fol. 96, September 6, 1774.

50. ANOM FM C10C 2 de Jumilhac, January 8, 1764.

51. François Regourd, "Coloniser les blancs de la carte" in Isabelle Laboulais-Lesage, ed., *Combler les Blancs de la Carte*, 221–242.

52. Marie Houllemare, "Seeing the Empire Through Lists and Charts: French Colonial Records in the Eighteenth Century," *Journal of Early Modern History* 22 (2018: 371–391); Edelson, *The New Map,* 204–205.

53. On contemporary attitudes to absenteeism see Edward Long, *History of Jamaica, Vol. I* (London: Frank Cass & Co., 1970 [1774]), especially 385–390.

54. On French settlement schemes in this era see Christopher Hodson, "Colonizing the *Patrie*: An Experiment Gone Wrong in Old Regime France," *FHS* 32, N. 2 (Spring 2009: 193–222); Røge, *Economistes.*

55. ANOM FM C10C 2, Liste des familles Françaises et étrangères venues avec passeports pour passer aux colonies . . . destinées pour la Sainte Lucie. October 24, 1764.

56. "N'étant point marier ils sont aussy point utiles à la population. . . . L'esprit de paresse et de fainéantise est leur partage . . . de 250 qui sont arrivés il n'y en a pas trente qui puissent nous être utiles." ANOM FM C10C 2, Chardon, August 1, 1763.

57. "Le système d'envoyer des passagers aux isles, était homicide en lui-même." ANOM C10C 2, Chardon, November 16, 1764.

58. ULL MS 522, William Hewitt papers, Sales of Land in St. Vincent, May 1765.

59. ANOM DPPC G1/506, Recensement Sainte Lucie 1764, and ANOM DPPC G1/506, Recensement 1765. No census is available for 1763. Before the Seven Years' War, St. Lucia counted 4,020 enslaved and 1,019 free people. ANOM DPPC G1/506, Recensement Sainte Lucie 1756.

60. "A avancé cette colonie de 10 ans," ANOM F3 57 N. 38, D'Ennery to Choiseul, May 27, 1765.

61. ANOM DPPC G1/506, Recensement 1765.

62. Trevor Burnard, *Jamaica in the Age of Revolution* (Philadelphia: University of Pennsylvania Press, 2020), 24.

63. TNA CO 262/1 N.87, "An Act for compelling owners and possessors of slaves, to keep proportionable numbers of white Protestant servants," October 7, 1767.

64. "An Act for increasing the Number of White Inhabitants on this Island," February 11, 1741. *The Laws of the Island of Antigua: Consisting of the Acts of the Leeward Islands, commencing 10ᵗʰ April 1668, ending 21ˢᵗ April 1798, and the Acts of Antigua, Commencing 10ᵗʰ April 1668, ending 7ᵗʰ May 1804* (London: Samuel Bagster, 1805), 271–280.

65. Young, *Considerations*, 26.

66. On family separation in the British Atlantic, Daniel Livesay, *Children of Uncertain Fortune: Mixed-Race Jamaicans in Britain and the Atlantic Family, 1733–1833* (Chapel Hill: University of North Carolina Press for the Omohundro Institute of Early American History and Culture, 2018); for the French Atlantic, Paul Cheney, *Cul de Sac: Patrimony, Capitalism, and Slavery in French Saint-Domingue* (Chicago: University of Chicago Press, 2017).

67. Edelson, *The New Map*, 208.

68. TNA CO 106/9 N. 166, Instructions to the Commissioners, July 26, 1764. The idea that absenteeism was detrimental continues to be espoused by historians; see, for example, Andrew Jackson O'Shaughnessy, *An Empire Divided: The American Revolution and the British Caribbean* (Philadelphia: University of Pennsylvania Press, 2000), 7–9; Lowell Ragatz, *The Fall of the Planter Class in the British Caribbean, 1763–1833* (New York: Century, 1928), 5. Trevor Burnard disputes this view, arguing that absentee planters provided important political and economic links between colony and metropole. Trevor Burnard, "Passengers Only: The Extent and Significance of Absenteeism in Eighteenth Century Jamaica," *Atlantic Studies: Global Currents* 1, N. 2 (2004: 178–195).

69. On Scottish sojourners see Alan L. Karras, *Sojourners in the Sun: Scottish Migrants in Jamaica and the Chesapeake, 1740–1800* (Ithaca: Cornell University Press, 1992); Douglas Hamilton, "Transatlantic Ties: Scottish Migrant Networks in the Caribbean, 1750–1800," in Angela Macarthy, ed., *A Global Clan: Scottish Migrant Networks and Identities Since the Eighteenth Century* (New York: Palgrave Macmillan, 2006); Quintanilla, "The World of Alexander Campbell."

70. Tobago also counted 417 white men and 10,613 enslaved people. TNA CO 285/1 N. 13, State of Tobago 1780.

71. TNA CO 106/9 N. 67, Minutes for the Sale and Disposal of Land, May 18, 1765.

72. TNA CO 106/9 N. 72, Commissioners for the Sale of Lands to the Treasury, May 12, 1765.

73. ULL MS 522, Hewitt Papers.

74. Mark Quintanilla, "Mercantile Communities in the Ceded Islands: The Alexander Bartlet and George Campbell Company," *International Social Science Review* 79, N. 1/2 (2004: 14–26), 20.

75. Murdoch, "Land Policy," 561.

76. Young, *Considerations*, 11.

77. Sheridan, "Sir William Young," 5.

78. TNA CO 106/9 N. 69, Minutes of the Commissioners, May 28, 1765.

79. While this river is often spelled Jambou in colonial records, I have elected to use the modern spelling.

80. Jeremiah Penniston purchased 197 cleared acres at a price of 59 pounds 10 shillings per acre. TNA CO 106/9 N. 33, An account of the first sale of land in the island of St. Vincent, June 1, 1765.

81. TNA CO 106/9 N. 72, Commissioners to Treasury, May 12, 1765.

82. TNA CO 106/9 N. 33.

83. Young, *Considerations*, 40.

84. Sheridan, "Sir William Young," 5.

85. ULL MS 522, William Hewitt papers, Sale of Lands in the Island of St. Vincent, May 31, 1765.

86. TNA CO 106/9 N. 72, Commissioners to Treasury, May 12, 1765.

87. TNA CO 106/10 N. 67, An Account of the French Inhabitants of Dominica, February 1766.

88. Mark Hauser notes that "people tend to build on slopes of 15 degrees or less, but in Dominica 44% of the land is on a slope between 20 and 90 degrees." Hauser and Wallman, eds., *Archaeology in Dominica*, 11.

89. Murdoch, "Land Policy," 560.

90. Young, *Considerations*, 40. Young purchased town plots 27, 28, and 30 on June 28, 1765.

91. UCL Legacies of British Slave Ownership, https://www.ucl.ac.uk/lbs/person/view /2146632173

92. ULL Manuscript 522, Hewitt papers 18, Sales of land in the island St. Vincent.

93. HCSP Vol. 71, page 135, Testimony of Alexander Campbell.

94. For records of ownership see UCL Legacies of British Slave Ownership Database, https://www.ucl.ac.uk/lbs/.

95. Murdoch, "Land Policy," 560.

96. As of 1779, officials counted no fewer than forty-nine estates in Grenada whose owners were absent in England. ANOM FM C10A 3 N. 124, Habitations dont les propriétaires sont à Londres, 6 septembre, 1779.

97. On the contemporary rationale for Britain's 1758 capture of Senegal, Malachy Postlethwayt, *The Importance of the African Expedition Considered* (London: C. Say, 1758).

98. *Voyages*, Voyage 91289.

99. *Voyages*, Voyage 91146.

100. *Voyages*, Voyage 91292. Another ship, the *Henry*, disembarked 117 people in Grenada on December 3, while the *London* disembarked 350 on November 26. Voyages 91081 and 77826.

101. https://slavevoyages.org/voyages/1wp7Sl9u.

102. On French slave trafficking in this era, Tarrade, *Le commerce colonial*, Vol. II, 759.

103. The database lists no ships with a primary port of disembarkation in St. Lucia during this period; instead, enslaved people were trafficked from surrounding islands as discussed in Chapters 2 and 5.

104. On slave trading from the Bight of Biafra, see Ugo H. Nwokeji, *The Slave Trade and Culture in the Bight of Biafra: An African Society in the Atlantic World* (New York: Cambridge University Press, 2010).

105. https://slavevoyages.org/voyages/qakth28g.

106. Alexander X. Byrd, *Captives and Voyagers: Black Migrants Across the Eighteenth Century British Atlantic World* (Baton Rouge: Louisiana State University Press, 2010), 11. More than 1.59 million captives, or just under 13 percent of the 12.5 million individuals trafficked from Africa between 1526 and 1850, embarked in the Bight of Biafra. Of these, more than 64 percent were trafficked by English merchants. Carolyn A. Brown and Paul E. Lovejoy, eds., *Repercussions of the Atlantic Slave Trade: The Interior of the Bight of Biafra and the African Diaspora* (Trenton: Africa World Press, 2011), 5.

107. On the Aro trade diaspora, Nwokeji, *The Slave Trade;* on Efik merchants, Stephen D. Behrendt, A. J. H. Latham, and David A. Northrup, eds., *The Diary of Antera Duke, an Eighteenth-Century African Slave Trader* (New York: Oxford University Press, 2010).

108. Behrendt et al., *The Diary*, 13, 56.

109. Dawson, *Undercurrents of Power*, 128.

110. For an account of two men captured and sold into slavery in Dominica following the 1767 conflict, see Randy Sparks, *The Two Princes of Calabar: An Eighteenth-Century Atlantic Odyssey* (Cambridge, MA: Harvard University Press, 2004).

111. Behrendt et al., *The Diary*, 22–26. A firsthand account of the conflict from an English perspective can be found in HCSP Vol. 73, pages 385–387, Testimony of George Millar.

112. On Aro trade diasporas, Nwokeji, *The Slave Trade*, 54–60.

113. Behrendt et al., *The Diary*, 59.

114. More than 68,000 people embarked at Bonny in this decade, compared to 38,000 at Calabar. https://slavevoyages.org/voyages/TdLXwcQD.

115. Byrd, *Captives and Voyagers*, 20.

116. HCSP Vol. 73, pages 124–125, Testimony of Isaac Parker. All House of Commons testimony cited in this chapter pertains only to voyages to the Ceded Islands in the period after the Treaty of Paris.

117. Nwokeji, 126; Brown and Lovejoy, *Repercussions*, 9–10; Sparks, *The Two Princes*, 50–51.

118. Brown and Lovejoy, eds., *Repercussions*, 8.

119. Byrd, *Captives and Voyagers*, 49–51. On the forging of Igbo identity in diaspora, Douglas B. Chambers, "Tracing Igbo into the African Diaspora," in Paul Lovejoy, ed., *Identity in the Shadow of Slavery* (New York: Continuum, 2000), 55–70.

120. The database lists no vessels whose primary place of disembarkation during this period was St. Lucia, though ships continued on to St. Lucia after first calling at another port. The smaller number of people trafficked to Martinique and Guadeloupe may be explained in part by demand, as planters in more established colonies had already amassed large numbers of enslaved laborers to work their estates.

121. On the trauma of enslavement and the Middle Passage, Byrd, *Captives and Voyagers*; Saidiya Hartman, *Lose your Mother: A Journey Along the Atlantic Slave Route* (New York: Farrar, Straus, and Giroux, 2007); Sowande' Mustakeem, *Slavery at Sea: Terror, Sex, and Sickness in the Middle Passage* (Champaign: University of Illinois Press, 2016).

122. Ottobah Cugoano, *The Negro's Memorial, or, Abolitionist's Catechism* (London: Hatchard and Co., 1825), 124.

123. Cugoano, *The Negro's Memorial*, 125.

124. HCSP Vol. 73, page 159, Testimony of James Morley.

125. HCSP Vol. 73, page 119, Testimony of Clement Noble. Of 81,284 enslaved Africans disembarked in the Ceded Islands between 1763 and 1773, 62.4 percent were male. https://slavevoyages.org/voyages/qakth28g.

126. HCSP Vol. 73, page 388, Testimony of George Millar.

127. HCSP Vol. 73, page 143, Testimony of Reverend John Newton.

128. This is slightly higher than the 14.7 percent estimated mortality rate for transatlantic slaving voyages during the eighteenth century as a whole. David Eltis and Paul Lachance, "The Demographic Decline of Caribbean Slave Populations," in David Eltis and David Richardson, eds., *Extending the Frontiers: Essays on the New Transatlantic Slave Trade Database* (New Haven: Yale University Press, 2008), 341.

129. HCSP Vol. 82, page 85, Testimony of Matthew Terry.

130. O'Malley, *Final Passages*, 320.

131. O'Malley, *Final Passages*, 371–374. Grenada later also obtained a free port from which enslaved people were trafficked to foreign colonies.

132. O'Malley notes that "these estimates significantly exceed those recorded in Dominica's port records, however, so the governor was either suggesting additional smuggling or simply exaggerating." O'Malley, *Final Passages*, 311.

133. "The number of Negroes imported between the years 1784 and 1788 amounted to 27,553, and the numbers exported in the same period amounted to only 15,781, and of course the number remaining in Dominique was 11,772." HCSP Vol. 72, page 67, Testimony of John Orde.

134. On Aro incorporation of captives, Nwokeji, *The Slave Trade*, 121–126.

135. On this process see Stephanie Smallwood, *Saltwater Slavery: A Middle Passage from Africa to American Diaspora* (Cambridge, MA: Harvard University Press, 2008), Chapter 2.

136. Selwyn H.H. Carrington, *The Sugar Industry and the Abolition of the Slave Trade, 1775–1810* (Gainesville: University Press of Florida, 2002), 18.

137. Richard Sheridan, *Sugar and Slavery: An Economic History of the British West Indies, 1623–1775* (Kingston: Canoe Press, 1994 [1974]), 489.

138. Pares, "Merchants and planters," 40.

139. Carrington, *The Sugar Industry,* 18.

140. ANOM FM C10C 8 N. 23, Relevé du produit de l'Isle Ste. Lucie pendant les années 1769, 1770, 1771 et 1772.

141. Carrington, *The Sugar Industry,* 18.

142. On Brunias see Mia Bagneris, *Colouring the Caribbean: Race and the Art of Agostino Brunias* (Manchester: Manchester University Press, 2017); Kay Dian Kriz, *Slavery, Sugar, and the Culture of Refinement: Picturing the British West Indies, 1700–1840* (New Haven: Yale University Press, 2008), 37–69; Sarah Thomas, "Envisaging a Future for Slavery: Agostino Brunias and the Imperial Politics of Labor and Reproduction," *Eighteenth Century Studies* 52, N. 1 (Fall 2018: 115–133).

143. As Thomas notes, such depictions differ markedly from images of slavery that show "brutality and coercion, and physical labor." Thomas, "Envisioning," 117.

CHAPTER 4

1. For Verger's baptism, ADM Cote 2E 2, November 2, 1710; for Victoire Auvray's baptism, ADM Cote 2E 2, May 28, 1719. For the couple's marriage record, ADM Cote 2E 2, May 22, 1736.

2. ADM Cote 2E 2, October 2, 1736.

3. ULL MS 522, William Hewitt papers, "Sales of land in St. Vincent on the 31st of May 1765 consists of plantation allotments in Rothia Quarter."

4. Owing primarily to interisland migration, St. Lucia's free population increased from 1,267 in 1764 to 2,391 in 1765, and rose to 3,159 one decade after the treaty. ANOM DPPC G1/506, Recensements Ste. Lucie 1764, 1765, and 1773.

5. Young, *Considerations*, 27.

6. Thomas Whately, *The Regulations lately made concerning the colonies, and the taxes imposed upon them, considered* (London: J. Wilkie, 1765), 31–32. Emphasis in original.

7. Marshall, *The Making and Unmaking of Empires*; Hannah Weiss Muller, *Subjects and Sovereign: Bonds of Belonging in the Eighteenth-Century British Empire* (New York: Oxford University Press, 2017); Aaron Willis, "The Standing of New Subjects: Grenada and the Protestant Constitution after the Treaty of Paris (1763)," *Journal of Imperial and Commonwealth History* 42, N. 1 (September 2013: 1–21).

8. Muller, *Subjects and Sovereign,* 121–165.

9. Muller, *Subjects and Sovereign,* 151.

10. Stephen Conway, "Quebec and British Politics," in Phillip Buckner and John G. Reid, eds., *Revisiting 1759: The Conquest of Canada in Historical Perspective* (Toronto: University of

Toronto Press, 2012), 141–165; on the decision to "shelve . . . representative government" in Quebec, Marshall, *The Making and Unmaking*, 184.

11. TNA CO 101/1 N. 5, Enquiry relating to the island of Grenada, May 15, 1763.

12. For Dominica TNA CO 101/1 N. 91, for St. Vincent TNA CO 101/1 N. 150.

13. TNA CO 101/1 N. 3, Ruffane to Board of Trade, May 3, 1763.

14. On civil rights, see Dominique Rogers, "On the Road to Citizenship: The Complex Route to Integration of the Free People of Color in the Two Capitals of Saint-Domingue," in David Geggus and Norman Fiering, eds., *The World of the Haitian Revolution* (Bloomington: Indiana University Press, 2008), 65–78.

15. Along with the population figures for Dominica, Grenada, and St. Vincent given above, as of 1760 St. Lucia counted 818 whites, 199 free people of color, 2,472 enslaved adults, and 1,340 enslaved children. ANOM DPPC G1/506, Dénombrement and Recensement générale de l'isle Sainte Lucie pour l'année 1760.

16. TNA CO 260/2, Morris to Germain, October 4, 1777.

17. "Outre qu'ils sont déjà acclimatés (ce qui est un grand avantage) c'est qu'ils connaissent mieux la culture des terres et l'exploitation d'une habitation," ANOM C10C 2 Chardon, March 22, 1764.

18. Treaty of Paris, http://avalon.law.yale.edu/18th_century/paris763.asp.

19. Whately, *The Regulations*, 32. Emphasis in original.

20. TNA CO 102/1 N. 7, Shelburne to Scott, August 5, 1763.

21. ULL MS 522, William Hewitt Papers. Twelve "former French possessors" relinquished fewer than ten acres of cleared land, while just two abandoned estates with more than one hundred acres of cleared land.

22. ANOM FM C8A67 F.221, Émigration des français des isles contentieuses dans les isles françaises du vent, February 21, 1765.

23. TNA CO 106/9 N. 53, Minutes of the Commissioners for the Sale and Disposal of Lands, April 2, 1765.

24. Whately, *The Regulations*, 32.

25. For terms in Grenada, see TNA CO 101/1 N. 105, Reports of His Majesty's Advocate and Attorney General, January 26, 1764.

26. TNA CO 106/9 N.166, Ninth Instruction of Instructions to the Commissioners for disposing by sale of otherwise of certain lands in Grenada, the Grenadines, Tobago, St. Vincent and Dominica, July 26, 1764.

27. Marshall, *The Making and Unmaking*, 186–187.

28. Christopher Hodson, *The Acadian Diaspora: An Eighteenth-Century History* (New York: Oxford University Press, 2012).

29. Ian R. Christie, "A Vision of Empire: Thomas Whately and the Regulations Lately made considering the Colonies," *EHR* 113, N. 451 (April 1998: 300–320).

30. Willis, "The Standing of New Subjects," 5.

31. HCL Beinecke Lesser Antilles Special Collection, MS 166.

32. TNA CO 106/10 N. 79, An account of the French inhabitants of St. Vincent whose claims have been allowed by the commissioners and who paid their fines accordingly, May 1766. On family agency in shaping broader Atlantic configurations see Julie Hardwick, Sarah M. S. Pearsall, and Karin Wulf, "Introduction: Centering Families in Atlantic Histories," *WMQ* 70, N. 2 (April 2013: 205–224), quotation on 206.

33. TNA CO 106/10 N. 79.

34. TNA CO 101/28 N. 123, State of Grenada.

35. TNA CO 101/1 N. 24, Extract from the capitation rolls for the quarter of Sauteurs for 1763.

36. TNA CO 101/10 N.1, Scott to Halifax, November 8, 1763.

37. TNA CO 101/18 Part II N. 57.

38. TNA CO 101/18 Part II N. 57.

39. TNA CO 101/18 Part II N. 57.

40. TNA CO 101/18 Part II N. 58–59. In St. Mark, the five planters of color listed in the nominative census brought the number of new subjects in the parish to 26, as compared to 13 old subjects. In the parishes of St. Andrew and St. David, French planters outnumbered their British counterparts even without the inclusion of planters of color, but the nominative census counted just one planter of color in each of the two parishes.

41. TNA CO 101/18 Part II N. 57.

42. TNA CO 101/18 Part II N. 57.

43. TNA CO 101/18 Part II N. 58–59.

44. Widow Herbert subsequently married English planter Michael Scott, who was also named guardian of her minor children, meaning that control of the plantation effectively transferred to him. ANOM C10A 4 N. 53, Lescallier, May 21, 1781.

45. TNA CO 101/18 Part II N. 60.

46. On landholding in Dominica in this era see Patrick Baker, *Centring the Periphery: Chaos, Order, and the Ethnohistory of Dominica* (Montreal: McGill-Queens University Press, 1994), 62–67.

47. For lists of owners and lessees in Dominica and St. Vincent, John Byres, *References to the Plan of the Island of Dominica as surveyed from the years 1765 to 1773* (London: S. Hooper, 1777); John Byres, *References to the Plan of the Island of St. Vincent as surveyed from the years 1765 to 1773* (London: S. Hooper, 1777).

48. On the effect of these debates in mainland North America and later in British India, Innes Keighren, "A Contested Vision of Empire: Anonymity, Authority and Mobility in the Reception of William Macintosh's *Travels in Europe, Asia, and Africa* (1782)," in David Lambert and Peter Merriman, eds., *Empire and Mobility in the Long Nineteenth Century* (Manchester: Manchester University Press, 2020), 50–68.

49. Muller, *Subjects and Sovereign*, 8; see also Willis, "The Standing."

50. Rogers, "On the Road," 66.

51. TNA CO 102/1 N. 238.

52. On British colonial councils and assemblies see Ian K. Steele, "The Anointed, the Appointed, and the Elected: Governance of the British Empire, 1689–1784," in P. J. Marshall, ed., *The Oxford History of the British Empire v. 2: The Eighteenth Century* (New York: Oxford University Press, 1998), 105–127; Frederick G. Spurdle, *Early West Indian Government: Showing the Progress of Government in Barbados, Jamaica and the Leeward Islands, 1660–1783* (Christchurch: Whitcombe & Tombs, 1962).

53. TNA CO 101/10 N. 292, Ordinance for regulating the elections for the General Assembly of Grenada, the Grenadines, Dominica, St. Vincent, and Tobago, February 10, 1766.

54. TNA CO 101/11 N. 106, Memorial of His Majesty's Adopted Subjects, February 14, 1766.

55. TNA CO 101/18 Part II N. 57.

56. TNA CO 101/11 N. 106.

57. Willis, "The Standing," 2–3.

58. Donald Akenson, *If the Irish Ran the World: Montserrat, 1630–1730* (Montreal: McGill-Queen's University Press, 1997), 161. In 1703, an attempt to exempt voters in the heavily Catholic

parish of St. Patrick, Montserrat, from taking the oaths was declared void. See Spurdle, *Early West Indian Government*, 73.

59. TNA CO 101/10 N. 292. Emphasis added.

60. TNA CO 101/11 N. 100, Memorial of the undersigned British Protestant Inhabitants of the Island of Grenada, February 14, 1766.

61. TNA CO 101/18 Part II, N. 60.

62. TNA CO 101/11 N. 102, Memorial of Several of His Majesty's Natural Born Subjects, Possessors of Property and Actually Residing in the Island of Grenada, February 14, 1766.

63. TNA CO 101/18 Part II, N. 60. For more on Macintosh see Keighren, "A Contested Vision."

64. TNA CO 101/11 N. 102.

65. TNA CO 101/11 N. 132, Melvill to Board of Trade, May 28, 1766. Conflicts over the privileges of elected officials also raged in Jamaica during this era. See Jack P. Greene, "The Jamaica Privilege Controversy, 1764–66," in *Negotiated Authorities: Essays in Colonial Political and Constitutional History* (Charlottesville: University of Virginia Press, 1994), 350–394.

66. TNA CO 101/11 N. 325, Votes of the Honorable General Assembly of Grenada and the Grenadines.

67. For the bills passed by the assembly during this period see TNA CO 101/11, N. 325–392.

68. TNA CO 101/11 N. 230, December 19, 1766.

69. TNA CO 101/12 N. 148, An Ordinance for Establishing an Assembly in the Island of St. Vincent's, February 25, 1767.

70. TNA CO 101/11 N. 423, Opinion of the Board of Trade, December 21, 1767.

71. TNA CO 101/12 N. 148.

72. Byers, *References to the Plan*.

73. TNA CO 101/12 N. 53, Melvill to Shelburne, December 27, 1767.

74. TNA CO 101/18 Part II N. 60.

75. TNA CO 101/12 N.121, Melvill to Hillsborough, May 1, 1768.

76. Donald Fyson, "The Conquered and the Conqueror: The Mutual Adaptation of the *Canadiens* and the British in Quebec, 1759–1775," in Buckner and Reid, eds., *Revisiting 1759*, 190–217.

77. TNA CO 101/3 N.1, September 7, 1768.

78. Fyson, "The Conquered," 190.

79. TNA CO 101/3 N. 112, Hillsborough to Fitzmaurice, May 13, 1769.

80. TNA CO 101/13 N. 157, Fitzmaurice to Hillsborough, August 26, 1769. Melvill sailed for England in July 1768 to cure his "West India disorder"; see TNA CO 101/12 N. 187–190.

81. TNA CO 101/18 Part II, N. 57.

82. TNA CO 101/13 N. 114, Fitzmaurice to Hillsborough, August 26, 1769.

83. TNA CO 101/13 N. 198, Minutes of the Grenada Council, September 25, 1769.

84. TNA CO 101/13 N. 204, Reasons for suspending and removing John Graham, William Lindow, Frederick Corsar, Thomas Townsend, John Melvill, and Thomas Williams from sitting, voting, or assisting in His Majesty's Council of Grenada, September 28, 1769.

85. TNA CO 101/5 N.166, Court of St. James, April 5, 1770.

86. TNA CO 101/3 N.140, Melvill to Hillsborough, July 5, 1770.

87. For complaints from British subjects in North America, Keighren, "A Contested Vision," 56.

88. TNA CO 101/5 N. 163, Court of St. James, February 11, 1771.

89. TNA CO 101/5 N. 90, Leyborne to Council and Assembly, March 14, 1772.

90. For discussion of these measures elsewhere, see Burnard, *Jamaica in the Age of Revolution*, 131–150; Garrigus, *Before Haiti*, 109–140; Sue Peabody, *There Are No Slaves in France: The Political Culture of Race and Slavery in the Ancien Régime* (New York: Oxford University Press, 1996); Jessica Pierre-Louis, "Fortune et catégorisation des Libres de couleur à la Martinique au XVIIIe siècle," in *Couleur et liberté dans l'espace colonial français (début XVIIIe–début XIXe siècle)* (Nantes: Les Anneaux de la Mémoire, 2017), 67–90.

91. On earlier laws regulating free people of color in the British West Indies see David Barry Gaspar, "A Mockery of Freedom: The Status of Freedmen in Antigua Slave Society Before 1760," *New West Indian Guide* 59, N. 3 (1985: 135–148); Brooke Newman, *A Dark Inheritance: Blood, Race, and Sex in Colonial Jamaica* (New Haven: Yale University Press, 2018), 61–67.

92. On privilege bills see Livesay, *Children of Uncertain Fortune*, especially 42–52.

93. Newman, *A Dark Inheritance*, 127.

94. Burnard, *Jamaica*, 140–144; Newman, *A Dark Inheritance*, 114–130.

95. On the 1726 law see Chapter 2. On inheritance as a civil right see Rogers, "On the Road," 66.

96. TNA CO 262/1 N. 53, Act for the making slaves real estate and for the better government of slaves and free negroes, July 13, 1767.

97. TNA CO 103/1 N. 43, Act to prevent the further sudden increase of free negroes and mulattoes, April 21, 1767.

98. TNA CO 106/10 N. 67.

99. TNA CO 101/18 Part II, N. 58.

100. TNA CO 73/1 N. 53, Act for regulation the manumission of slaves . . . and for punishing free negroes, free mulattoes, and mustees. September 7, 1774.

101. TNA PC 1/60/10 N. 30, Petition of the free negros, mulatto's [sic] and mustees in Dominica against an act passed there for regulating the manumission of slaves, July 20, 1777.

102. TNA PC1/60/10 N. 30.

103. TNA 106/10 N. 67.

104. On "mustees" see Livesay, *Children of Uncertain Fortune,* 93, footnote 3.

105. TNA CO 73/1 N. 53, clause 5. Emphasis added.

106. Melanie Newton, *The Children of Africa in the Colonies: Free People of Color in Barbados in the Age of Emancipation* (Baton Rouge: Louisiana State University Press, 2008), 59. In 1730, a bill in the Jamaica assembly forbid free people of color in Jamaica from giving testimony against whites, Livesay, *Children of Uncertain Fortune,* 34.

107. Free people of color in Dominica also gave testimony against whites before the island's cession to Great Britain; see ANOM E 159, Duplessis habitant à la Dominique, assassiné par Vernede habitant de la meme colonie, 1755.

108. Free people of color were denied the right to vote in Barbados and South Carolina in 1721, in Virginia in 1723, and in Jamaica in 1733. Newman, *A Dark Inheritance,* 271. While elite men of color in early colonial Jamaica exercised voting rights, in 1733 the island's assembly ruled that "mulattoes," defined as anyone with more than one-eighth African ancestry, were not entitled to vote. Livesay, *Children of Uncertain Fortune,* 32–38.

109. For an example of voter returns, see TNA CO 101/12 N.141, A list of polls taken for the assembly to be convened December 15, 1767.

110. TNA PC 1/60/10 N. 34, Further report of the Lords Commissioner for Trade and plantations upon an act passed in Dominica for regulating the manumission of slaves, June 8, 1778.

111. "Suivant le nombre des familles et les forces de chacun." ANOM FM C10C, Chardon, December 31, 1763.

112. ANOM C7A33, Noziere-Taschere, September 8, 1773. Exemption from the droit d'aubaine was also extended to foreigners residing in Tobago when France gained control of the
island in 1783, see *Edit du roi portant abolition du droit d'aubaine . . . juillet 1783*. For more on the
implementation and operation of the droit d'aubaine in continental France, see Peter Sahlins,
Unnaturally French: Foreign Citizens in the Old Regime and After (Ithaca: Cornell University
Press, 2004). Because he neglects to discuss the operation of the droit d'aubaine in France's
Lesser Antillean colonies, Sahlins states that it was first abolished during the French Revolution.

113. One quarré is approximately 3.2 acres. Pritchard, *In Search of Empire*, xxiv. For Verger's
holdings see Eugene and Raymond Bruneau-Latouche, *Sainte-Lucie fille de la Martinique* (Paris,
1989), 87.

114. ANOM DPPC État Civil Anse la Raye, Mariage Fournier Jean Baptiste et Verger
Françoise, July 14, 1767.

115. ULL MS 522, William Hewitt papers, "Sales of land in St. Vincent on the 30th of May
1765 consists of plantation allotments in Ouassigany quarter."

116. Bruneau-Latouche, *Sainte-Lucie,* 87.

117. ANOM DPPC État Civil Anse la Raye, Mariage Verger Pierre et Caumond Marianne,
October 12, 1772.

118. ULL MS 522, William Hewitt papers, "Sales of land in St. Vincent on the 30th of
May 1765."

119. Garrigus, *Before Haiti,* 113.

120. Legislation cited in Léo Elisabeth, "The French Antilles," in David W. Cohen and
Jack P. Green, eds., *Neither Slave Nor Free: The Freedman of African Descent in the Slave Soci-
eties of the New World* (Baltimore: Johns Hopkins University Press, 1972), 168. See also Pierre-
Francois-Régis Dessalles, *Les annales du Conseil Souverain de la Martinique, Tome II* (Bergerac:
J. B. Puynesge, 1786), 281.

121. ANOM DPPC État Civil, Anse la Raye, Enterrement Marie Françoise Fournier, October 15, 1772.

122. ANOM DPPC État Civil, Anse la Raye, Baptême Fournier Baptiste, June 18, 1768.

123. ANOM DPPC État Civil, Anse la Raye, Mariage Verger Jacques et Bernege Brigitte,
June 6, 1772.

124. ANOM DPPC État Civil, Anse la Raye, Mariage Caumont Louis et Verger Marie
Catherine, October 3, 1769; ANOM DPPC État Civil, Carenage, Mariage Claude Hiacinthe
Lalouette et Victoire Verger, January 29, 1771; ANOM DPPC État Civil, Carenage, Mariage
Louis Thomas Pilet et Rose Verger, February 11, 1771.

125. ANOM DPPC État Civil, Anse la Raye, Mariage Verger Pierre et Caumond Marianne,
October 12, 1772.

126. Émile Hayot, *Les Gens de couleur libres du Fort-Royal 1679–1823* (Paris: Publications de
la Société Française d'Histoire d'Outre-Mer Société d'Histoire de la Martinique, 2005).

127. ANOM DPPC État Civil, Carenage, January 29, 1771.

128. ANOM DPPC État Civil, Carenage, February 11, 1771.

129. ANOM DPPC État Civil, Anse la Raye, October 12, 1772.

130. ANOM DPPC État Civil, Anse la Raye, June 6, 1772.

131. In his late-eighteenth-century description of Saint-Domingue, Martinique-born Moreau
de Saint-Méry provides a detailed list of the racial assignations of people resulting from the union
of people of African and European ancestry. According to Saint-Méry, in Martinique a mestif/ve
was commonly classified as the offspring of a white person and a mulatto; the child of a mestive

and a white person was called a quarteron(ne) or carteron(ne). In a further testament to the variable nature of racial descriptors, Saint-Méry wrote that in Saint-Domingue the opposite was true: a mestif was thought to be the child of a white man and a quarteronne. Moreau de Saint-Méry, *Description topographique, physique, civile, politique et historique de la partie française de l'isle Saint-Domingue* (1797), Blanche Maurel and Étienne Taillemite, eds. (Paris: Larose, 1958), 86.

132. Garrigus, *Before Haiti*, 142.

133. Bruneau-Latouche, *Sainte-Lucie Fille de la Martinique*, 171–172.

134. ANOM DPPC NOT LCA 1 Boze, Vente d'habitation Fournier à ses frères, August 23, 1787. Boze used racial descriptors for other clients, suggesting that his decision not to attach them to the Fourniers was a conscious one.

135. ANOM DPPC NOT LCA 1 Boze, Vente d'esclaves par Louis Tiffaigne à Jean Baptiste Fournier, June 28, 1787.

136. ANOM DPPC NOT LCA 8 Marquis, October 7, 1778; ANOM DPPC NOT LCA 6 Foucard, February 18, 1784.

137. ANOM DPPC État Civil, Anse la Raye, Baptême Fournier Baptiste, June 18, 1768. On free people of color choosing more powerful (usually white) patrons to serve as godfathers to their children see Kimberley S. Hanger, *Bounded Lives, Bounded Places: Free Black Society in Colonial New Orleans, 1769–1803* (Durham: Duke University Press, 1997), 105–108. Historians of Europe also argue that vertical godparent relations were common; see Jean-Louis Flandrin, *Families in Former Times: Kinship, Household and Sexuality* (Cambridge: Cambridge University Press, 1979), 21. For a counterargument see Julie Hardwick, *The Practice of Patriarchy: Gender and the Politics of Household Authority in Early Modern France* (University Park: Pennsylvania State University Press, 1998), 169–171.

138. TNA PC1/60/10 N. 30, Petition of the free negros, mulatto's and mustees in Dominica against an act passed there for regulating the manumission of slaves, July 20, 1777.

CHAPTER 5

1. TNA CO 106/1 N. 5, A list of all ships which have entered inward in the island of Grenadoes between the 5th day of April 1765 and the 5th day of July following. See also Voyages, Voyage 101981.

2. On the "second middle passage" see O'Malley, *Final Passages*.

3. For works examining slavery through the lens of survival, Berlin and Morgan, eds., *Cultivation and Culture*; Randy M. Browne, *Surviving Slavery in the British Caribbean* (Philadelphia: University of Pennsylvania Press, 2017).

4. https://slavevoyages.org/voyages/ouJuCMQo.

5. Justin Roberts, "Surrendering Surinam: The Barbadian Diaspora and the Expansion of the English Sugar Frontier, 1650–75," *WMQ* 73 N. 2 (April 2016: 225–256).

6. HCSP Volumes 67–73 and Volume 82.

7. TNA CO 106/1 N. 5; Voyages, Voyage 101986.

8. Voyages, Voyages 102158 and 102152; Voyages 102197 and 102198.

9. https://slavevoyages.org/voyages/cPUtahJd.

10. TNA CO 101/1 N. 164, List of vessels cleared in the Custom House Fort Royal Grenada 20th January 1763 to 20 January 1764.

11. TNA CO 106/1 N. 24, List of Vessels entered inward, November 1764–October 1766.

12. TNA CO 71/4 N. 2, Memorial of the Commander in Chief and the Council and Assembly of Dominica to Lord North, March 6, 1773.

13. TNA CO 101/1 N. 164. At time of writing, there was no record of the *Royal Charlotte* in the Slave Voyages database.

14. TNA CO 71/4 N.2.

15. TNA CO 101/1 N. 164, no record in the database.

16. Young, *Considerations,* 45–46.

17. Thomas Atwood, *The History of the island of Dominica, containing a description of its situation, extent, climate, mountains, rivers, natural productions, &c. &c. together with an account of the civil government, trade, laws, customs, and manners of the different inhabitants of that island. Its conquest by the French, and restoration to the British Dominions* (London: J. Johnson, 1791), 224–225.

18. ANOM DPPC G1/506 Recensements Ste. Lucie.

19. Trans-Atlantic Slave Trade Database, Voyage 92315, and https://slavevoyages.org /voyages/NZVlZmSY.

20. "At the peak of black predominance in the 1720s and 1730s," South Carolina's Black majority outnumbered whites approximately 2 to 1. Peter Kolchin, *American Slavery, 1619–1877* (New York: Hill and Wang, 2003), 30. The ratio of white to enslaved people in Barbados in 1773 was 3.7:1. Watts, *The West Indies,* 311.

21. By the early 1770s, the ratio of white to enslaved people was 7.48:1 in Montserrat, 10.31:1 in Jamaica, 11:1 in Nevis, 12.35:1 in Saint Kitts, and 14.6:1 in Antigua. Watts, *The West Indies,* 311–313.

22. By 1789, enslaved people in Saint-Domingue outnumbered French colonists by 14 to 1, and this ratio falls when accounting for the island's 24,848 free people of color. Garrigus, *Before Haiti,* 2. This ratio pales in comparison to nineteenth century Berbice, where in the early nineteenth century "blacks outnumbered whites 46 to 1." Browne, *Surviving Slavery,* 31.

23. TNA CO 101/1 N. 315, Melvill, September 13, 1765.

24. See Chapter 2. On creolization among the enslaved population in Barbados see Simon P. Newman, *A New World of Labor: The Development of the Plantation in the British Atlantic* (Philadelphia: University of Pennsylvania Press, 2013), 237–238.

25. On enslaved people's vulnerability to physical and sexual violence in small households, Block, *Ordinary Lives,* 38–50.

26. On charter generations see Ira Berlin, *Generations of Captivity: A History of African-American Slaves* (Cambridge, MA: Harvard University Press, 2003), 23–50.

27. On sexual coercion in slave societies see Sharon Block, *Rape and Sexual Power in Early America* (Chapel Hill: University of North Carolina Press for the Omohundro Institute of Early American History and Culture, 2006).

28. Atwood, *The History,* 224.

29. HCSP Vol. 72, page 169, Testimony of John Orde.

30. HCSP Vol. 71, page 229, Testimony of James Bailie.

31. HCSP Vol. 71, page 194, Testimony of James Bailie. On the use of jobbing gangs for holing cane, see Justin Roberts and Nicholas Radburn, "Gold Versus Life: Jobbing Gangs and British Caribbean Slavery," *WMQ* 76, N. 2 (April 2019: 223–256).

32. On enslaved expertise, particularly among Creoles, Beckles, "Creolisation in action," 115; Jordan Smith, "The Invention of Rum," (PhD dissertation, Georgetown University, 2018), 238–244.

33. HCSP Vol. 71, page 206, Testimony of James Bailie.

34. HCSP Vol. 71, page 229, Testimony of John Greg.

35. HCSP Vol. 71, page 222, Testimony of John Castles.

36. HCSP Vol. 71, page 207, Testimony of John Castles.

37. HCSP Vol. 71, page 164, Testimony of Alexander Campbell. For Campbell's purchases, page 135.

38. HCSP Vol. 71, page 144–145, Testimony of Alexander Campbell.

39. Gordon Turnbull, *An Apology for Negro Slavery* (London: J. Stevenson, 1786), 25.

40. Young, *A Tour,* 268.

41. HCSP Vol. 71, page 153, Testimony of Alexander Campbell.

42. On relations and hierarchies among enslaved people on plantations, Browne, *Surviving Slavery,* 102–131; Justin Roberts, "The 'Better Sort' and the 'Poorer Sort': Wealth Inequalities, Family Formation and the Economy of Energy on British Caribbean Sugar Plantations, 1750–1800," *Slavery and Abolition* 35, N. 3 (458–473).

43. For examples of this "general opinion," HCSP Vol. 73, page 304, Testimony of Henry Hew Dalrymple; HCSP Vol. 72, page 135, Testimony of Lord Macartney; HCSP Vol. 82, page 84, Testimony of Matthew Terry.

44. Marshall, *Slavery, Law & Society in the British Windward Islands, 1763–1823: A Comparative Study* (Kingston: Arawak Publications, 2007), 101.

45. HCSP Vol. 71, page 101, Testimony of Ashton Warner Byam.

46. HCSP Vol. 71, page 90, Testimony of Gilbert Francklyn. This sentiment was echoed in contemporaneous French sugar colonies; see Arlette Gautier, *Les Soeurs de Solitude: La condition féminine dans l'esclavage aux Antilles du XVIIe au XIXe siècle* (Paris: Éditions Caribéennes, 1985), 95–98.

47. For similar changes in mainland America see Berlin, *Generations of Captivity,* 53–96.

48. TNA CO 262/1 N. 53, "An Act for the making slaves real estate and for the better government of slaves and free negroes," July 13, 1767.

49. "Act for the good order and government of slaves," Tobago, 1768, quoted in J. C. Nardin, *La mise en valeur de l'île de Tobago (1763–1783)* (Paris: Mouton & Co., 1969), 306–318.

50. On responses to the rise of sugar planting in the seventeenth- and early-eighteenth century Caribbean, see David Barry Gaspar, *Bondmen and Rebels: A Study of Master-Slave Relations in Antigua, with Implications for Colonial British America* (Baltimore: Johns Hopkins University Press, 1985); Rushforth, "The Gaoulet."

51. On marronage in the Americas, Sylviane Diouf, *Slavery's Exiles: The Story of the American Maroons* (New York: New York University Press, 2014).

52. Vincent Brown, "Spiritual Terror and Sacred Authority in Jamaican Slave Society," *Slavery and Abolition* 24, N. 1 (April 2003): 24–53.

53. Aline Helg, *Plus jamais esclaves! De l'insoumission à la révolte, le grand récit d'une émancipation (1492–1838)* (Paris: Éditions la Découverte, 2016), 138–146; Philip Morgan, "Conspiracy Scares," *WMQ* 59, N. 1 (January 2002: 159–166).

54. Quoted in Michael Craton, *Testing the Chains: Resistance to Slavery in the British West Indies* (Ithaca: Cornell University Press, 1982), 141.

55. Leblond, *Voyage aux Antilles: D'île en île, de la Martinique à Trinidad (1767–1773),* Monique Pouliquen, ed. (Paris: Karthala, 2000), 197.

56. Atwood, *The History,* 225–226.

57. Gaspar, *Bondmen and Rebels,* 174–184.

58. On Jamaica Maroons, Richard Hart, *Slaves Who Abolished Slavery: Blacks in Revolt* (Mona: University of the West Indies Press, 1985), 32–59; on Tacky's revolt, Vincent Brown, *Tacky's Revolt: The Story of an Atlantic Slave War* (Cambridge, MA: Harvard University Press, 2020).

59. TNA CO 101/1 N. 315, Melvill, September 13, 1765.

60. TNA CO 101/2 N. 3, Melvill, October 13 1766.

61. TNA CO 103/1 N. 95, Act for the better government of slaves, December 11, 1766, and N. 103, An Act for . . . the more speedy and effectual suppression of Run-away Slaves, December 3, 1766.

62. TNA CO 103/1 N. 95.

63. On subsistence crises associated with the turn to sugar see Carl and Roberta Bridenbaugh, *No Peace Beyond the Line: The English in the Caribbean, 1624–1690* (New York: Oxford University Press, 1972), 43–51; Bertie Mandelblatt, "A Land Where Hunger is in Gold and Famine is in Opulence: Plantation Slavery, Island Ecology, and the Fear of Famine in the French Caribbean," in Lauric Henneton and L. H. Roper, eds., *Fear and the Shaping of Early American Societies* (Leiden: Brill, 2016), 243–264.

64. HCSP Vol. 73, page 307, Testimony of Henry Hew Dalrymple.

65. Dunn, *Sugar and Slaves,* 256–257; Gaspar, *Bondmen and Rebels,* xi; Jerome Handler, "Slave Revolts and Conspiracies in Seventeenth-Century Barbados," *New West Indian Guide* 56 (1986: 5–42), 31.

66. On Creole participation in these conspiracies see Handler, "Slave Revolts," 24; Rushforth, "The *Gaoulet,*" 88; Craton, *Testing the Chains,* 120.

67. Jason T. Sharples, "Discovering Slave Conspiracies: New Fears of Rebellion and Old Paradigms of Plotting in Seventeenth-Century Barbados," *AHR* 120, N. 3 (June 2015: 811–843), 841.

68. Young, *Considerations,* 45. On problems associated with relocation, Roberts, "The Better Sort," 466–467.

69. TNA CO 73/1 N. 19. Act to prevent the importation of slaves who have been convicted, or known to have been guilty of murder or attempt to murder or poison, insurrection or other capital offences, June 26, 1769. Tobago passed a similar act in 1794; see Craton, *Testing the Chains,* 362.

70. TNA CO 101/4 N. 103, Stewart to Melvill, November 29, 1770.

71. Ibid. For an account of the insurrection see Nardin, *La Mise en Valeur,* 334–339.

72. Hart, *Slaves Who Abolished Slavery,* 9; Gaspar, *Bondmen and Rebels,* 234–238.

73. Walter C. Rucker, *Gold Coast Diasporas: Identity, Culture, and Power* (Bloomington: Indiana University Press, 2015).

74. Brown, *Tacky's Revolt,* especially Chapter 6.

75. TNA CO 101/16 N. 40, State of the island of Tobago, as had been sent in Returns to the Lieutenant Governor 25th June 1771, and TNA CO 101/16 N. 125, State of the Island of Tobago, April 1772. No such distinction was made in a census of the island created before the uprising, TNA CO 101/14 N. 126, Present State of the Plantations now Settling in Tobago, July 1770. On "internal turbulence" within Coromantee society see Brown, *Tacky's Revolt,* 10.

76. TNA CO 101/4 N. 99, Melvill to Hillsborough, December 3, 1770.

77. TNA CO 101/4 N. 120, Deposition of Valentine Joseph Piquery, December 11, 1770. On the role of drums and shells in announcing rebellion see Handler, "Slave Revolts," 17–18.

78. TNA CO 101/4 N. 119, Macintosh to Melvill, December 11, 1770.

79. TNA CO 101/4 N. 157, Address from proprietors, merchants, traders and other inhabitants of Grenada, January 23, 1771, and N. 159, Humble address and petition of the Council and Assembly of Tobago, January 23, 1771.

80. Leblond, *Voyage aux Antilles,* 209–214.

81. TNA CO 263/2, Address of the Assembly, December 17, 1770.

82. Newman, *A New World of Labor,* 237.

83. For example, in June 1771, Governor Melvill reported on "another rising of slaves in Tobago . . . in which a white overseer was murdered," TNA CO 101/5 N. 16, Melvill to Hillsborough, June 25, 1771, while Leblond reported that Maroons remained a problem in Grenada. See also Craton, *Testing the Chains,* 153–156.

84. Honychurch, *In the Forests of Freedom,* especially 75–90 and 165–185; Neil C. Vaz, "Maroon Emancipationists: Dominica's Africans and Igbos in the Age of Revolution, 1764–1814," *JCH* 53, N. 1 (2019: 27–59).

85. Cugoano, *The Negro's Memorial,* 126.

86. HCSP Vol. 82, page 83, Testimony of Matthew Terry; for other accounts of mutilation as punishment, HCSP Vol. 73, pages 299–300, Testimony of Henry Hew Dalrymple. On legal limits to dismemberment, HCSP Vol. 71, page 157, article LIV.

87. TNA CO 103/1 N. 103, An Act for the better government of slaves, and for the more speedy and effectual suppression of runaways.

88. TNA CO 73/1 N. 34, An act for punishing those who shall willfully and maliciously set fire.

89. Brown, *The Reaper's Garden,* especially Chapter 4.

90. Craton, *Testing the Chains,* 156.

91. HCSP Vol. 73, pages 234–239, Testimony of Ninian Jefferys. For West African beliefs about traveling home after death, Brown, *The Reaper's Garden,* especially Chapter 2.

92. Robin Fabel, *Colonial Challenges: Britons, Native Americans, and Caribs, 1759–1775* (Gainesville: University Press of Florida, 2000).

93. Young, *Considerations,* 10.

94. TNA CO 101/11 N. 428, Young to Treasury, April 11, 1767.

95. Newton, "The Race Leapt," 16–20; Neil L. Whitehead, "Black Read as Red: Ethnic Transgression and Hybridity in Northeastern South America and the Caribbean," in Restall, ed., *Beyond Black and Red,* 223–243.

96. On the Comte de Jumilhac, ANOM COL E 233, Chapelle de Jumilhac.

97. ANOM C10C 2, de Jumilhac, August 20, 1763.

98. TNA CO 106/10 N. 45, Minutes of the Board for Surveying and Disposing of Lands in St. Vincent, April 16, 1766.

99. CL, Thomas Townshend Papers, Box 7, Memorial of William Young, April 11, 1767.

100. Labat, *Nouveau Voyage,* 148.

101. *Cobbett's Parliamentary history of England. From the Norman conquest, in 1066. To the year, 1803,* Vol. 17 (London: T.C. Hansard, 1806), 619.

102. Brooke Newman, "Identity Articulated: British Settlers, Black Caribs, and the Politics of Indigeneity on St. Vincent, 1763–1797," in Gregory D. Smithers and Brooke N. Newman, eds., *Native Diasporas: Indigenous Identities and Settler Colonialism in the Americas* (Omaha: University Nebraska Press, 2014), 109–149, especially 133.

103. Julie Chun Kim, "The Caribs of St. Vincent and Indigenous Resistance During the Age of Revolutions," *EAS* (Winter 2013: 117–132); Newman, "Identity Articulated."

104. Between 1763 and 1773, fifty-one voyages disembarked more than 9,000 African captives in St. Vincent. https://slavevoyages.org/voyages/JBdHamzB.

105. TNA CO 101/11 N. 430, William Young to the Treasury, April 11, 1767.

106. The first European to note this practice was Columbus, on a visit to Hispaniola; it was also mentioned by historian Fernandez de Oviedo in the sixteenth century. Vera Tiesler, *The*

Bioarchaeology of Artificial Cranial Modifications: New Approaches to Head Shaping and its meanings in Pre-Columbian Mesoamerica and Beyond (New York: Springer, 2014), 101–102. For the Lesser Antilles, the practice was described by a French sailor who visited Martinique in 1618; see Jean-Pierre Moreau, ed. *Un flibustier français dans la mer des Antilles* (Paris: Payot, 2002), 95, and by Du Tertre, who lived in the region from 1640 to 1658. Du Tertre, *Histoire générale des isles*, 398.

107. Baptismal records served as another proof of freebirth; in the latter half of the eighteenth century, dozens of Kalinago mothers in St. Lucia brought their babies to be baptized. ANOM, État Civil Ste. Lucie.

108. TNA CO 101/13 N. 107, Fitzmaurice to Hillsborough, June 10, 1769.

109. CL, Thomas Gage Papers Vol. 22, ES, The report of the Commissioners . . . concerning the Charibbs of St. Vincent, October 16, 1771.

110. TNA CO 101/13 N.113, Fitzmaurice to Hillsborough, June 10, 1769.

111. *Authentic Papers,* 5–11.

112. TNA CO 106/9 N. 33, An account of the first sale of land in the island of St. Vincent, May 31, 1765.

113. TNA CO 106/9 N. 265, "Order of His Majesty the King of Great Britain for the more Effectual Establishing the Charibees of the Island of Saint Vincent," May 21, 1768.

114. TNA CO 106/9 N. 266, Minutes of the Board for Surveying and Disposing of Lands in St. Vincent, May 25, 1768.

115. TNA CO 106/9 N. 269, Minutes of the Board, May 31, 1768.

116. TNA CO 106/9 N. 263, Minutes of the Board, St. Vincent.

117. William Young, Jr., *An account of the Black Charaibs in the island of St. Vincent's: With the Charaib Treaty of 1773, and other original documents. Compiled from the papers of the late Sir William Young, bart.* (London: J. Sewell, 1795), 38.

118. Craton, *Testing the Chains,* 151.

119. *Cobbett's Parliamentary History*, Vol. 17, pages 569–573, December 9, 1772.

120. Jack P. Greene, *Evaluating Empire and Confronting Colonialism in Eighteenth-Century Britain* (New York: Cambridge University Press, 2013), 1–19.

121. Young Jr., *Account,* 45.

122. TNA CO 101/13 N.69, Copy of a letter from Harry Alexander to Lieutenant Governor Fitzmaurice, May 3, 1769.

123. TNA CO 106/11 N.11, Byres to Simpson.

124. TNA CO 101/13 N. 69, Alexander to Fitzmaurice, May 3, 1769.

125. TNA CO 263/1, Minutes of the St. Vincent Council and Assembly, May 10, 1769.

126. TNA CO 263/1, Minutes of the St. Vincent Council and Assembly, May 31, 1769. Emphasis added.

127. TNA CO 106/11 N. 32, June 7, 1769.

128. CL, Thomas Townshend Papers, Box 7, Melvill to Hillsborough, July 5, 1770.

129. TNA CO 101/14 N. 190, Opinion of Charles Payne Sharpe, September 11, 1770.

130. TNA CO 101/16 N. 9, Address from the Council of St. Vincent to His Majesty on the subject of the Charaibbs in that island, November 20, 1771. Also published in *Authentic Papers,* 49–52.

131. TNA CO 101/16 N. 11, Leyborne to Hillsborough, November 30, 1771.

132. TNA CO 101/16 N. 53, Memorial of the court in St. Vincent to Lord Hillsborough touching the Charibbs, April 4, 1772.

133. TNA CO 101/16 N. 63, Hillsborough to Leyborne, April 18, 1772, labeled "separate and secret." CL, Thomas Gage Papers, Vol. 22 ES, June 29, 1772.

134. CL, Thomas Gage Papers, Vol. 112 AS, Gage to Dalrymple, July 5, 1772.

135. Newton, "The Race Leapt," 20.

136. TNA CO 101/16 N. 63, Hillsborough to Leyborne, April 18, 1772.

137. TNA CO 101/16 N. 67, Copy of a Treaty with the Jamaica Maroons enclosed in Hillsborough to Leyborne, April 18, 1772.

138. For Parliament's February 1773 deliberations see *Cobbett's Parliamentary history* Vol. 17, 722–741. On the nature of the debate, Fabel, *Colonial Challenges,* 187–193; Heather Freund, "Who should be treated 'with every degree of humanity'? Debating rights for planters, soldiers, and Caribs/Kalinago on St. Vincent, 1763–1773," *Atlantic Studies* 13, N. 1 (2015: 125–143); Greene, *Evaluating Empire,* 6–15; Paul Thomas, "The Caribs of St. Vincent: A Study in Imperial Maladministration, 1763–73," *JCH* 18, N. 2 (1983): 60–73.

139. Thomas, "The Caribs," 61.

140. TNA CO 101/16 N. 201, Proclamation by His Excellency William Leyborne Esq., September 7, 1772.

141. For a narrative of the first Carib war see Christopher Taylor, *The Black Carib Wars: Freedom, Survival, and the Making of the Garifuna* (Jackson: University of Mississippi Press, 2012), 51–78; Bernard Marshall, "The Black Caribs: Native Resistance to British Penetration into the Windward Side of St. Vincent, 1763–1773," *Caribbean Quarterly* 19, N. 4 (December 1973: 4–20).

142. *Cobbett's Parliamentary History,* Vol. 17, 722, February 10, 1773.

143. TNA CO 101/17 N. 72, Return of the Casualties of the several Regiments of St. Vincents from the time of their taking the Field against the Charibbee Indians in September 72 to the Conclusion of the Campaign the 20th of February 73.

144. *Cobbett's Parliamentary History,* Vol. 17, 741.

145. TNA CO 101/17 N. 68, A Treaty of Peace and Friendship, concluded by His Excellency Major General Dalrymple on the part of His British Majesty, and the Chiefs of the Charibbs in St. Vincent here mentioned, for themselves and the rest of their people, February 17, 1773.

146. TNA CO 101/17 N.149, Leyborne to Dartmouth, May 10, 1773.

147. TNA CO 101/17 N.154, William Young, John Hunt, Robert Stewart, and Robert Wynne, May 13, 1773.

148. Fabel, *Colonial Challenges,* 197.

149. For more on Brunias's role in shaping metropolitan understandings of life in the West Indies see Kriz, *Slavery, Sugar, and the Culture of Refinement,* 37–69.

150. Bagneris, *Colouring the Caribbean,* 36.

151. Ibid., 39.

152. On Indigenous dispossession and the expansion of slavery in the United States, see Claudio Saunt, *Unworthy Republic: The Dispossession of Native Americans and the Road to Indian Territory* (New York: Norton, 2020).

CHAPTER 6

1. TNA CO 260/2, Morris to Germain, January 1, 1779.

2. TNA CO 260/2, Morris to Germain, December 1, 1778.

3. TNA CO 260/2, Morris to Germain, January 1, 1779.

4. TNA CO 101/23 N. 58, Macartney to Germain, January 10, 1779.

5. Historians have explored African American and Native American participation in the revolution in mainland North America, but little attention has been paid to the experiences of the demographic majority in the Caribbean. See Colin Calloway, *The American Revolution in Indian Country: Crisis and Diversity in Native American Communities* (New York: Cambridge University Press, 1995); Kathleen DuVal, *Independence Lost: Lives on the Edge of the American Revolution* (New York: Random House, 2015); Sylvia R. Frey, *Water from the Rock: Black Resistance in a Revolutionary Age* (Princeton: Princeton University Press, 1991); Alan Gilbert, *Black Patriots and Loyalists: Fighting for Emancipation in the War for Independence* (Chicago: University of Chicago Press, 2012).

6. To date, one book-length study focuses specifically on Jamaica during this era, while two more examine events throughout the British West Indies. Burnard, *Jamaica in the Age of Revolution*; Selwyn H. H. Carrington, *The British West Indies During the American Revolution* (Providence: Foris Publications, 1988); Andrew Jackson O'Shaughnessy, *An Empire Divided: The American Revolution and the British Caribbean* (Philadelphia: University of Pennsylvania Press, 2000). See also Burnard and Garrigus, *The Plantation Machine*, 192–218.

7. O'Shaughnessy, *An Empire Divided*, 9, 34.

8. T. R. Clayton, "Sophistry, Security, and Socio-Political Structures in the American Revolution; or, Why Jamaica Did Not Rebel," *Historical Journal* 29, N. 2 (June 1986: 319–344).

9. On the development of distinct institutions in mainland North America in the century preceding the revolution see Jon Butler, *Becoming America: The Revolution Before 1776* (Cambridge, MA: Harvard University Press, 2000). Brathwaite argues that Creole nationalism existed in colonial Jamaica but that loyalties to Great Britain ultimately proved more important. Kamau Brathwaite, *The Development of Creole Society in Jamaica, 1770–1820* (New York: Oxford University Press, 1971).

10. Burnard, *Jamaica*, 206.

11. O'Shaughnessy, *An Empire Divided*, 62–69.

12. TNA CO 71/6 N. 85, Stuart to Germain, September 29, 1779

13. TNA CO 101/18 N. 179, Address of the Council and Assembly of Grenada, June 25, 1775. Emphasis in original.

14. TNA CO 260/4 N. 40, Morris to Germain, September 19, 1776.

15. Chief Justice Mansfield, *Genuine Speech from the Lord's Bench, on Monday, November 28, 1774, in the cause of Campbell against Hall* (London: G. Kearly, 1774), 1.

16. TNA CO 101/18 Part II, N. 60. For more on Campbell see Quintanilla, "The World of Alexander Campbell."

17. Mansfield, *Genuine Speech*, 23. Emphasis added.

18. Carrington, *The British West Indies*, 142. O'Shaughnessy agrees, stating that the "judgment had far-reaching constitutional implications," O'Shaughnessy, *An Empire Divided*, 132.

19. Planters in Barbados were particularly resentful; see O'Shaughnessy, *An Empire Divided*, 195.

20. In 1772 alone, Dominica, Grenada, St. Vincent, and Tobago collectively imported 15,777 barrels of salt fish, 43,880 bushels of peas and corn, 5,372 barrels of rice, 479 horses, and 2,215 sheep and hogs from the mainland colonies. Carrington, *The British West Indies*, 40.

21. Richard Sheridan, "The Crisis of Slave Subsistence in the British West Indies During and After the American Revolution," *WMQ* 33, N. 4 (October 1976: 615–641).

22. TNA CO 101/22 N. 139, Macartney to Germain, October 10, 1778.

23. TNA CO 101/22 N. 155, Macartney to Germain, October 25, 1778.

24. TNA CO 71/6 N. 22, Shirley to Germain, February 17, 1776.

25. TNA CO 71/6 N. 99, Petition of the merchants and other inhabitants of Roseau, Dominica, February 11, 1777. See also Carrington, *The British West Indies*, 95.

26. TNA CO 101/20 N. 242, Memorial of the Proprietors and Merchants concerned in the island of Tobago. For Tobago's population, TNA CO 101/24 N. 45, A state of the Island of Tobago taken in April 1780.

27. TNA CO 101/20 N. 239, Macartney to Germain, July 23, 1777.

28. TNA CO 260/4 N. 98, Morris to Germain, March 5, 1777.

29. "Envoier deux ou trois petites goelettes ou Batteaux Croisés, ils leurs auroient couler chacun 15 ou plus de leurs pirogues, et qu'il se seroient noyés de 2 à 300 de leurs meilleurs hommes. C'est un moyen dont je ne manquerai pas de faire usage s'ils persistent dans cet espèce de commerce." ANOM FM C7A 56 F. 109, Copy of a letter from Morris to Micoud, June 7, 1777.

30. Margaret L. Brown, "William Bingham, Agent of the Continental Congress at Martinique," *Pennsylvania Magazine of History and Biography* 61, N. 1 (January 1937: 54–87).

31. TNA CO 260/5 N. 203, Morris to Germain, June 30, 1778.

32. TNA CO 101/22 N. 126, *Gazette de la Martinique* September 10, 1778. On Dominica during the war see Baker, *Centering the Periphery*, 69–71; Joseph Boromé, "Dominica during French Occupation, 1778–1784," *EHR* 84, N. 330 (January 1969: 36–58).

33. Atwood, *History of Dominica*, 115.

34. TNA CO 71/7 N. 76, Stuart to Germain, September 9, 1778.

35. Atwood, *History*, 112. The sabotage is also related in Baker, *Centering the Periphery*, 69, and Boromé, "Dominica," 38.

36. TNA CO 71/6 N. 85, Stuart to Germain, September 29, 1778.

37. DNA PC, Translation of a Speech by the Marquis Duchilleau to the Privy Council, September 14, 1778.

38. DNA PC, Articles of Capitulation, September 14, 1778.

39. TNA CO 253/1 N. 435, Grant to Germain May 1779.

40. TNA CO 253/1 N. 332, Grant to Germain, December 31, 1778.

41. TNA CO 253/1 N. 435, Grant to Germain, May 1779.

42. TNA CO 260/2 Morris to Germain, December 1, 1778.

43. TNA CO 253/1 N. 429, Grant to Germain April 4, 1779.

44. TNA CO 253/1 N. 349, Articles of Capitulation, December 30, 1778.

45. Valentine Morris, *A Narrative of the Official Conduct of Valentine Morris, Esq.* (London: J. Walker, 1787), 117.

46. ANOM FM F3 58, *Supplément à la Gazette de la Martinique, du jeudi 24 juin 1779*; Chris Taylor, *The Black Carib Wars: Freedom, Survival, and the Making of the Garifuna* (Jackson: University Press of Mississippi, 2012), 91–95.

47. TNA CO 260/4 N. 128, Morris to Germain, May 20, 1777.

48. TNA CO 260/5 N. 244, Morris to Germain, August 24, 1778.

49. TNA CO 260/5 N. 292, Morris to Germain, September 17, 1778.

50. TNA CO 260/5 N. 276, Morris to Germain, September 11, 1778.

51. Taylor, *The Black Carib*, 92.

52. TNA CO 101/23 N. 256, *Supplément à la Gazette Royale de la Grenade*, July 24, 1779.

53. TNA CO 101/21 N. 226, State of Grenada 1779. Members of the latter groups were much more likely to have wives and children in the island, resulting in larger populations of new subjects and people of color.

54. TNA CO 101/23 N. 58, Macartney to Germain, January 10, 1779.

55. TNA CO 101/23 N. 218, Macartney to Germain, July 5, 1779.

56. "Pillèrent sa maison enlevèrent tous les meuble Bestiaux et autres effets transportable, endommagèrent ses Batiments." ANOM E Staunton, January 27, 1780.

57. TNA CO 71/7 N. 76, Stuart to Germain, September 9, 1778.

58. ANOM FM C10E 1 Dossier 9, Projet d'attaque de l'ile Tabago et sa prise.

59. TNA CO 101/24 N. 99, Ferguson to Germain, June 5, 1781. For the terms, which actually mirrored those for Dominica and St. Vincent, see ANOM FM C10E 1 Dossier 9 N. 1.

60. For examples, see EAP 688/1/1/29, St. Vincent Deed Book 1778–1781.

61. CL, Charles Winstone Letterbook, April 8, 1780.

62. Atwood, *History,* 146–151.

63. Atwood, *History,* 152.

64. ANOM E, Brevet de Conseiller au Conseil de la Dominique pour le Sieur Nicolas Crocquet de Belligny, February 28, 1779. For more on the family see Chapter 3.

65. ANOM E, Brevet de Conseiller au Conseil de la Dominique pour le Sieur Colas Dauchamps, June 8, 1779; Brevet de Conseiller au Conseil de la Dominique pour le Sieur Fournier Desravineres. Two more French planters became councilors; see ANOM E Brevet de Conseiller au Conseil de la Dominique pour le Sieur Edme Desabye, January 17, 1780; Brevet de Conseiller au Conseil de la Dominique pour le Sieur Cane, December 7, 1781.

66. John Byres, *References to the Plan of the Island of Dominica* (London: S. Hooper, 1776), 9.

67. ANOM E, Colas Dauchamps, commandant les milices de la Dominique, 1781.

68. TNA CO 260/6 N. 59, January 20, 1779, Proclamation by Governor Morris dissolving Assembly of St. Vincent.

69. ANOM FM C10D 2 N. 6, October 10, 1779; for examples of French planters purchasing land in St. Vincent during the occupation see EAP 688/1/29, page 240. St. Vincent Deed Book 1778–1781, William Fitzgerald to James Questell, Release of Land, March 17, 1781. French subjects who settled in Grenada before 1763 also capitalized on the return of their former crown in order to reestablish title to plantations they claimed had been forcibly appropriated during British rule, see ANOM C10A 3 N. 291, Memoire sur la possession des habitations, 23 decembre 1779; ANOM C10A 4 N. 53, May 21, 1781.

70. TNA CO 260/3, Ordonnance of Dumontet and de la Mothe, October 10, 1779.

71. HCL Beinecke MS 328, *Arrêt du Conseil d'État du Roi, qui fixe les règles, les époques et la forme de la distribution de la Justice en l'ile de la Grenade et dépendances* (Paris, 1779), 2.

72. TNA CO 101/24 N. 5, Arret of the King's Council of State, December 12, 1779. Emphasis added.

73. On *Conseil Superieurs* see Laurie Wood, *Archipelago of Justice: Law in France's Early Modern Empire* (New Haven: Yale University Press, 2020).

74. ANOM FM C10A 3 N. 47, July 20, 1779. For a list of those appointed, ANOM FM C10A 3 N. 217, Procès Verbal de l'installation du Conseil Superieur de la Grenade, 1 mai 1780.

75. TNA CO 101/18 Part II N. 57, State of the parish of St. George; ANOM E 314, Molenier.

76. ANOM FM C10A 3 N. 125, Relève général des rôles de capitation, 1779.

77. ANOM FM C10A 4 N. 233, Tableau de la Population, Grenade, 1783.

78. On Kalinagos during the war see Taylor, *The Black Carib,* Chapter 4.

79. TNA CO 260/5 N. 292, Morris to Germain, September 17, 1778.

80. TNA CO 260/2, Morris to Germain, December 1, 1778.

81. Taylor, *The Black Carib,* 92.

82. Morris, *A Narrative of the Official Conduct of Valentine Morris,* 174.

83. ANOM FM C8A 79 F. 189, Peynier to Bouillé, December 22, 1780.

84. TNA CO 260/3, Lincoln to North, April 6, 1783.

85. TNA CO 260/2, Morris to Germain, January 1, 1779.

86. Morris, *A Narrative*, 174–175.

87. ANOM FM C8A 80 N. 139, Ordonnance de M. de Bouillé en faveur des Caraïbes de l'ile de St. Vincent, September 25, 1781.

88. The Awara Waqeri are the Indigenous inhabitants of Trinidad. ANOM FM C8A 79 F. 212, Mémoire adressé à Bouillé par les chef Caraïbes, September 21, 1781.

89. Brown, *Tacky's Revolt*, 237–239; Craton, *Testing the Chains*, 172–179.

90. Sharples, *The World That Fear Made*, 226–236.

91. TNA CO 260/4 N. 98, Morris to Germain, March 5, 1777.

92. TNA CO 260/4 N. 189, Morris to Germain, September 6, 1777.

93. TNA CO 260/4 N. 126, Morris to Germain, May 14, 1777.

94. DNA PC May 30, 1781.

95. DNA PC June 1, 1781.

96. Atwood, *History*, 230.

97. Atwood, *History*, 228.

98. DNA PC, June 1, 1781.

99. DNA PC, June 1, 1781. Emphasis added.

100. Boromé, "Dominica," 55.

101. Honychurch, *In the Forests of Freedom*, 71. For Honychurch's detailed account of Maroon activity during the American War, 64–74.

102. DNA PC, June 1, 1781.

103. Boromé, "Dominica," 50.

104. "Leur faisant des chasses très meurtriers qui ont nécessairement diminué le nombre des bras dont la culture avait si grand besoin." ANOM FM C10C 3, January 9, 1784.

105. TNA CO 101/25 N. 153, Mathew to Sydney, June 22, 1784.

106. https://slavevoyages.org/voyages/7kfworyk.

107. Voyages, Voyage 83594.

108. In 1781, French forces conquered St. Martin, Saba, and St. Kitts before being defeated at the Battle of the Saintes, just north of Dominica, in April 1782. O'Shaughnessy, *An Empire Divided*, 232–237.

109. DNA PC, February 15, 1781.

110. Carrington, *The British West Indies*, 59.

111. TNA CO 101/25 N. 156, Lincoln to Mathew, May 31, 1784.

112. Burnard, *Jamaica*, 213.

113. C. R. Ottley, *The Complete History of the Island of Tobago in the West Indies* (Port-of-Spain: Guardian Printery, 1972), 43–56.

114. P. J. Marshall, *Remaking the British Atlantic: The United States and the British Empire After American Independence* (New York: Oxford University Press, 2012), 185.

115. Willis, "The Standing," 5.

116. TNA CO 101/26 N. 423, Byam et al. to Charles Spooner, March 1, 1786.

117. On Britain's commitment to plantation colonies in this era, Burnard, *Jamaica*, 210–216.

118. Baillie and Hamilton to Davenport, May 24, 1784, Manuscript D_Dav_13, Adam Mathew Slavery, Abolition, and Social Justice Digital Collection.

119. TNA CO 260/9, Slaves imported into and exported from St. Vincent, January 1784–July 1789.

120. Baillie and Hamilton to Davenport, May 15, 1784, Manuscript D_Dav_13.

121. TNA CO 71/8 N. 65, Proclamation by Governor John Orde, January 28, 1784.

122. TNA CO 102/3 Instructions to Governor Mathew, March 2, 1784.

123. TNA CO 101/28 N. 228, Mathew to Sydney, August 25, 1788.

124. TNA CO 101/29 N. 28, Mathew to Sydney, May 30, 1789.

125. TNA CO 101/27 N. 175, An Act for Regulating Elections.

126. TNA CO 101/30 N. 6, Petition of freeholders enclosed in Mathew to Grenville, February 27, 1790.

127. TNA CO 101/26 N. 423, Byam et al. to Spooner, March 1, 1786.

128. ANOM FM C10D 2, Recensement général, 1782.

129. ANOM FM C10E 7, Recensement général, 1782.

130. TNA CO 101/28 N. 123, State of Grenada.

131. ANOM FM C10A 4 N. 233, Tableau de la Population, Grenade, 1783.

132. TNA CO 71/8 N. 190, A Sketch of the State of this Island.

133. TNA CO 101/23 N. 218, Macartney to Germain, July 5, 1779.

134. DNA Deed Book H N. 55, January 1784–September 1784.

135. TNA CO 103/8 An Act. . . for repealing the first, second, and third clauses of an act, intitled, Act to prevent the further sudden increase of free negroes and mulattoes, November 3, 1788.

136. Frey, *Water from the Rock,* 182.

137. Wallace Brown, "The Governorship of John Orde, 1783–1793: The Loyalist Period in Dominica," *JCH* 24, N. 2 (January 1990), 160.

138. TNA CO 71/8 N. 317, Committee of Dominica Proprietors Assembled in London, November 25, 1783.

139. TNA CO 73/1 N. 107–112, An Act to exempt for the term of fifteen years from the payment of public taxes all such of His Majesty's Loyal subjects as are arrived at this island from East Florida, September 30, 1785.

140. TNA CO 71/9 N. 178, Orde to Sydney, June 20, 1785.

141. TNA CO 71/13, No pagination, Orde to Sydney, September 23, 1787. For an example of such petitions, see TNA CO 71/10 N. 29, Petition of His Majesty's Faithfull American Subjects, who have taken refuge in this island, to Governor Orde, April 5, 1786.

142. Maya Jasanoff, *Liberty's Exiles: American Loyalists in the Revolutionary World* (New York: Knopf, 2011), 245–277.

143. Jasanoff, *Liberty's Exiles,* 261.

144. TNA CO 260/7 Lincoln to Sydney, May 2, 1784.

145. ANOM FM C10E 4, Comte de Dillon and Roume de St. Laurent, September 25, 1787.

146. Young, *Considerations,* 30.

147. TNA CO 101/24 N. 423, Byam et al. to Spooner, March 1, 1786.

148. "Nous attendions avec impatience une révolution qui nous remit sous les loix d'un souverain que nous avions apris depuis notre existence à aimer et à respecter. " ANOM FM C10D2 N. 23, Marquis de Bouille, September 21, 1781.

CHAPTER 7

1. All quotations from Alexandre Moreau de Jonnès, *Aventures de guerre aux temps de la République et du consulat* (Paris: Pagnerre, 1852), 156–159.

2. On revolutionary contests in the Lesser Antilles in the 1790s, William S. Cormack, *Patriots, Royalists, and Terrorists in the West Indies: The French Revolution in Martinique and Guadeloupe, 1789–1802* (Toronto: University of Toronto Press, 2019); Laurent Dubois, *A Colony of Citizens: Revolution and Slave Emancipation in the French Caribbean, 1787–1804* (Chapel Hill: University of North Carolina Press for the Omohundro Institute of Early American History and Culture, 2004); Michael Duffy, *Soldiers, Sugar and Seapower: The British Expeditions to the West Indies and the War Against Revolutionary France* (New York: Oxford University Press, 1987).

3. On unrest in these and other Windward Islands during this era, Craton, *Testing the Chains,* 180–210, 224–239; Paul Friedland, "Every Island Is Not Haiti: The French Revolution in the Windward Islands," in David A. Bell and Yair Mintzker, eds., *Rethinking the Age of Revolutions: France and the Birth of the Modern World* (New York: Oxford University Press, 2018); David Barry Gaspar, "La Guerre des Bois: Revolution, War, and Slavery in St. Lucia, 1793–1838," in David Barry Gaspar and David Patrick Geggus, eds., *A Turbulent Time: The French Revolution and the Greater Caribbean* (Bloomington: Indiana University Press, 1997), 120–130.

4. Craton, *Testing the Chains,* 195.

5. Damages in Grenada were estimated at £2 million to £2.5 million, while in St. Vincent colonial officials reported more than £815,000 in lost crops, buildings, and enslaved laborers. See Duffy, *Soldiers,* 156, and TNA CO 260/14, no pagination, Report of the Committee of the Legislature appointed by both Houses in November last to investigate and ascertain losses suffered in consequence of the rebellion and invasion of the Charaibs and French.

6. On the transatlantic dimensions of events in the Ceded Islands, Edward L. Cox, "Fedon's Rebellion 1795–1796: Causes and Consequences," *Journal of Negro History* 67, N. 1 (Spring 1982: 7–19); Cox, *Free Coloreds in the Slave Societies of St. Kitts and Grenada, 1763–1833* (Knoxville: University of Tennessee Press, 1984), 76–91; Dubois, *A Colony of Citizens,* Chapter 8; Friedland, "Every Island Is Not Haiti."

7. ANOM FM C8A 90 F. 245, Laumoy to Viomenil, September 7, 1789. On the role of rumors in shaping events in the colonies, Cormack, *Patriots,* Chapter 2.

8. Cormack, *Patriots,* 44–47; David Patrick Geggus, "The Slaves and Free Coloreds of Martinique During the Age of the French and Haitian Revolutions: Three Moments of Resistance," in Robert Paquette and Stanley Engerman, eds., *The Lesser Antilles in the Age of European Expansion* (Gainesville: University Press of Florida, 1996), 280–301. See also Dubois, *A Colony of Citizens,* 85–89.

9. On the role of rumors that monarchs had issued decrees for the amelioration or abolition of slavery in prompting revolts see Wim Klooster, "Slave Revolts, Royal Justice, and a Ubiquitous Rumor in the Age of Revolutions," *WMQ* 71, N. 3 (July 2014: 401–424).

10. Dubois, *A Colony of Citizens,* 87. Another letter, signed "nous, les negres," can be found in FM C8A 89 F.68, Copie d'une letter anonyme addressée a N. Mollerat, August 28, 1789.

11. Dubois, *A Colony of Citizens,* 85–87. See also Léo Elisabeth, "Gens de couleur et révolution dans les iles du Vent (1789–janvier 1793)," *RFHOM* 76, N. 282 (1989: 75–95).

12. ANOM FM C8A 89 f. 57, Vioménil, September 14, 1789.

13. ANOM FM C8A 89 f. 81, Vioménil, October 17, 1789.

14. "Le dangereux, l'exécrable exemple," *Gazette de Sainte-Lucie, Nationale et Politique,* Vol. IV, N. 11, January 11, 1791, page 10. Subsequent enslaved insurgencies in the eastern Caribbean are traced in Yves Benot, "La Chaine des Insurrections d'esclaves dans les Caraïbes de 1789 à 1791," in Marcel Dorigny, ed., *Les Abolitions de l'esclavage: De L.F. Sonthonax à V. Schoelcher* (Paris: Presses Universitaires de Vincennes), 179–186.

15. For a firsthand account see Anonymous, *Révolution de la Martinique, Depuis le premier septembre 1790 jusqu'au 10 mars 1791* (Fort-de-France: Société d'Histoire de la Martinique, 1982). For a historical analysis, Liliane Chauleau, "La Ville de Saint-Pierre sous la Révolution Française," in Roger Toumson and Charles Porset, eds., *La période révolutionnaire aux Antilles: Images et Résonnances* (Paris: Groupe de Recherche et d'Étude des Littératures et Civilisations de la Caraïbe et des Amériques Noires, 1986), 115–135; Cormack, *Patriots,* Chapter 3.

16. On French refugees in Dominica, TNA CO 101/23, Orde to Dundas, June 13, 1792; in St. Vincent, TNA CO 260/12, Seton to Dundas, July 1, 1793.

17. Dubois, *A Colony of Citizens,* Chapter 7.

18. Dubois, *A Colony of Citizens,* 193.

19. TNA CO 101/33 N. 26, A Proclamation by the King, January 29, 1793; DNA PC 1 Vol. 3, January 7, 1793; TNA CO 260/12 N. 6.

20. TNA CO 101/33 N. 26.

21. DNA PC 1 Vol. 3, March 7, 1793.

22. On the 1792 declaration and its effects see Garrigus, *Before Haiti,* 268.

23. TNA CO 101/32 N. 95, Enclosed in Mathew to Dundas, January 10, 1792.

24. TNA CO 260/12, Minutes of the Privy Council, March 23, 1793.

25. TNA CO 260/12, Minutes of the Privy Council, March 27, 1793.

26. Murphy, "A Reassertion of Rights."

27. For the will of Raymond's brother, a wealthy Grenada planter named Joseph, see ANOM E 357, Ronzier Joseph.

28. LDS Microfilm 1563516. My deepest thanks to Peter Redhead for sharing this document with me. The record specifies, "Les futurs époux ont dit qu'il est né d'eux six enfants, nommé Marie, Jean, Scolastique, Etienne, Julien et Marie Louise, agée présentement la dite Marie d'environ douze ans, et la dite Marie Louise de quatorze mois, lesquels enfants ils entendent reconnaitre en légitime, et du fait, ils ont dit reconnaitre en légitimes les dites Marie et Marie Louise mulatresses, pour leurs enfans."

29. HCL Beinecke MS 166, Oaths of Allegiance, Grand Pauvre.

30. For a state of the parish under French rule, ANOM DPPC G1 496 N. 55, 1755.

31. TNA CO 101/1 N. 26. Extract from the capitation rolls of the quarter of Grand Pauvre for 1763.

32. For the marriages, Kit Candlin and Cassandra Pybus, *Enterprising Women: Race, Gender, and Power in the Revolutionary Atlantic* (Athens, GA: University of Georgia Press, 2015), 23; on "networking," Garrigus, *Before Haiti,* 172–173.

33. EAP 295/2/3/1 Gouvaye Register of Baptisms, marriages and burials, 12, 21.

34. TNA CO 101/18 Part II N. 58. No Fedons appear on the list, suggesting that they owned fewer that the minimum ten acres of land necessary to be counted, or that they did not live in Grenada at the time.

35. EAP 295/2/3/1 page 12, March 12, 1780. "Marie Rose Cablant [Cavelan], épouse de Julien Fedon selon la coutume Angloise . . . mais à présent épouse légitime, ayant revalidé le mariage, selon les rites de l'église Catholique Romaine le 7 février dernier et légitimé la dite fille."

36. Following British occupation of St. Lucia during the American War of Independence, residents of the island also deliberately revalidated marriages contracted in the Anglican church. See ANOM État Civil Dennery, Mariage Prevert et Garnier, 1784.

37. ANOM F5A 7/7, Instructions pour les desservans des paroisses, dans les colonies, dans la tenue des registres de baptêmes, mariages et sépultures, 1777.

38. On civil rights in the French Atlantic see Rogers, "On the Road to Citizenship."

39. TNA CO 101/30 N. 6, Mathew to Grenville, February 27, 1790.

40. TNA CO 101/33 N. 174, Humble Petition of His Majesty's Most Loyal and Dutiful Subjects, April 1785.

41. TNA CO 101/26 N. 294, Petition of New Adopted Subjects, February 27, 1786. On religious motivations for Fedon's Rebellion see Curtis Jacobs, "Revolutionary Priest: Pascal Mardel of Grenada," *Catholic Historical Review* 101, N. 2 (2015): 317–341.

42. TNA CO 101/30 N. 275, Mathew to Grenville, October 30, 1790.

43. TNA CO 103/8, Act to require all Free Mestives, Cabres, Negroes, and other Coloured Free Persons . . . to register their names, December 28, 1786.

44. TNA CO 103/1 N. 43, Act to prevent the further sudden increase of free negroes and mulattoes, April 21, 1767.

45. Kit Candlin, *The Last Caribbean Frontier, 1795–1815* (New York: Palgrave MacMillan, 2012), 12; Candlin and Pybus, *Enterprising Women,* 21–23.

46. TNA CO 101/26 N. 96, Marquis de Cazeau, March 28, 1785.

47. TNA CO 101/30 N. 6, Mathew to Grenville, February 27, 1790.

48. Gordon Turnbull, *Revolt in Grenada: A Narrative of the Revolt and Insurrection of the French Inhabitants in the Island of Grenada. By an eye-witness* (London: Vernor and Hood, 1795); Anonymous [Thomas Turner Wise], *A Review of the Events which have happened in Grenada, from the commencement of the insurrection to the 1st of May: By a sincere wellwisher to the colony* (Grenada: Printed for the author in St. George's, 1795); Henry Thornhill, *A Narrative of the Insurrection and Rebellion in the Island of Grenada from the Commencement to the Conclusion* (Barbados: Gilbert Ripnel, 1798).

49. John Hay, *Narrative of the Insurrection in the Island of Grenada, which took place in 1795* (London: J. Ridgway, 1823); Francis McMahon, *A Narrative of the Insurrection in the Island of Grenada, in the year 1795* (Grenada: John Spahn, 1823); D. G. Garraway, *A Short Account of the Insurrection of 1795–96* (London: Wells, 1877).

50. TNA CO 101/34 N. 22, Mackenzie to Portland, March 22, 1795. The estimate of 7,200 insurgents is provided in Wise and echoed by historians; see Cox, "Fedon's Rebellion," 8.

51. Kit Candlin, "The Role of the Enslaved in the 'Fedon Rebellion' of 1795," *Slavery and Abolition* 39 N. 4 (April 2018: 685–707).

52. Caitlin Anderson, "Old Subjects, New Subjects and Non-Subjects: Silences and Subjecthood in Fédon's Rebellion, Grenada, 1795–96," in Richard Bessel, Nicholas Guyatt, and Jane Rendall, eds., *War, Empire and Slavery, 1770–1830* (New York: Palgrave MacMillan, 2010), 201–217.

53. Thornhill, 2.

54. McMahon, 26.

55. TNA CO 101/34 N. 39, List of the several white inhabitants of landed property who have joined in the insurrection, March 28, 1795; Turnbull, Revolt in Grenada, 160–161.

56. TNA CO 106/12 N. 70, Return of the estates slaves &c forfeited by persons attainted by an Act of this Island.

57. In addition to contemporary narratives of Fedon's Rebellion, historical analyses can be found in Candlin, *The Last Caribbean Frontier,* 1–23; Craton, *Testing the Chains,* 180–210; Cox, "Fedon's Rebellion"; Cox, *Free Coloreds;* Jacobs, "Pascal Mardel."

58. Duffy, *Soldiers,* 143.

59. Wise, *Review,* 4. The figure of four survivors is corroborated in Turnbull, *Revolt,* 18.

60. On their opposition, see Chapter 4.

61. Hay, *Narrative,* 34–35.

62. GRO, Book L3, 282–293, April 26, 1786.

63. The sale is listed in GRO, index of deeds, and described in greater detail in Curtis Jacobs, "The Fedons of Grenada, 1763–1814," http://www.open.uwi.edu/sites/default/files/bnccde /grenada/conference/papers/Jacobsc.html, no pagination. Jacobs also comments on the suspect terms of sale.

64. TNA CO 106/12 N. 73, Return of the estates slaves &c forfeited. Emphasis added.

65. Candlin and Pybus, *Enterprising Women,* 72–75.

66. Turnbull identifies Besson as "a mulatto silver-smith [from] Grenville." Turnbull, *Revolt,* 16.

67. "Tous individus de . . . vous soumettre dans le délai de <u>deux heures</u> aux forces de la République sous nos Ordres . . . éprouverez tous les Fléaux d'une Guerre Désastreuse." TNA CO 101/34 N. 29, Fedon to Council, March 4, 1795.

68. TNA CO 101/34 N. 31, Declaration of the Commissioners delegated by the National Convention of France.

69. TNA CO 101/34 N. 29.

70. ANOM FM C7A 49 N. 138, Coup d'œil sur la Guadeloupe et dépendances en 1797.

71. TNA CO 101/34 N. 36, Council to Fedon, March 6, 1795.

72. Wise, *Review,* 43–44.

73. TNA CO 101/34 N. 45, MacKenzie to Portland, April 24, 1795.

74. TNA CO 101/34 N. 45. Hay speculates that sixty-seven to one hundred British soldiers were killed in the attack. Hay, *Narrative,* 78–80.

75. For a list of the 48 hostages killed see Hay, *Narrative,* 83.

76. McMahon, 130.

77. Wise, *Review,* 100–101.

78. Turnbull, *Revolt,* 103.

79. Wise *Review,* 108; Turnbull, *Revolt,* 133.

80. On Dominica, Robert Brown, *A Diary of the Defence of the Island of Dominica, against the Invasion of the French Republicans, & the Revolt of the Dominicans of the Quarter of Colyhaut, in June 1795* (No publication information, item held in the John Carter Brown Library); on St. Lucia, Gaspar, "La Guerre des Bois."

81. Hay, 125.

82. For accounts of the ensuing battles see Thornhill, *Narrative,* 30–49.

83. Candlin, "The Role of the Enslaved."

84. Julie Chun Kim, "The Caribs of St. Vincent and Indigenous Resistance during the Age of Revolutions," *EAS* (Winter 2013: 117–132).

85. Charles Shephard, *An Historical Account of the Island of St. Vincent* (London: W. Nichol, 1831), 66–68.

86. TNA CO 260/13 N. 13, Seton to Portland, March 16, 1795.

87. "Quel est le Français qui ne se réunisse à ses frères dans un moment où le cri de la Liberté se fait entendre à Cœur. . . . Mais s'il existait encor des hommes timides, des Français retenus par la crainte, nous leur déclarons au nom de la Loi, que ceux qui ne seront pas rassemblés dans la journée à l'entour de nous, seront regardés comme Traitre a la Patrie, et traités comme Ennemis. Nous leur jurons que le Fer et le Feu vont être employés contre eux, que nous allons incendier leurs biens et que nous égorgerons leurs femmes et leurs enfants pour anéantir leur Race." TNA CO 260/13 N. 16, Declaration de Joseph Chatoyer General. On similarities with *La Marseillaise,* Taylor, *The Black Carib,* 116.

88. Shephard, *Historical Account,* 160.

89. Chun Kim, "The Caribs," 119.

90. "Afin de pousser les Caraïbes, Victor Hugues martelait la haine des Anglais." Gérard Lafleur, *Les Caraïbes des Petites Antilles* (Paris: Éditions Karthala, 1992), 210.

91. "Chef d'un nation libre . . . la nation Française en combattant le Despotisme, s'est allié à tous les Peuples Libres . . . attaquez exterminez . . . tout ce qui est Anglais, mais donnez les moyens aux Français de vous seconder. " ANOM FM C10D 2, 23 Ventôse 3eme année.

92. TNA CO 260/13 N. 13, Seton to Portland, March 16, 1795.

93. Shephard, *Historical Account,* 75.

94. TNA CO 260/13 N. 20, A Proclamation by His Excellency James Seton, March 20, 1795.

95. TNA CO 260/13 N. 59, Seton to Portland, May 8, 1795.

96. TNA CO 260/13 N. 64, Seton to Portland, May 14, 1795.

97. Shephard, *Historical Account,* 104.

98. TNA CO 260/13 N. 80, Seton to Portland, July 10, 1795.

99. Shephard, *Historical Account,* 92–93. In September 1795, "about five hundred men" landed from St. Lucia, Shephard, 120.

100. Shephard, *Historical Account,* 92, 117, 136.

101. "Mes jours furent tissus de soie et d'or. C'était bien là l'Eden." Jonnès, 176.

102. Lafleur, *Les Caraïbes,* 207.

103. Jonnès, *Aventures,* 134.

104. "Mit à profit la haine nationale que les Caraïbes portaient aux Anglais," Jonnès, *Aventures,* 136.

105. "Ces sauvages, il faut bien l'avouer, étaient les hommes les plus civilisés de l'armée, et ceux qui avaient le moindre penchant pour le pillage, l'incendie et la dévastation." Jonnès, *Aventures,* 180.

106. Shephard, *Historical Account,* 77–174; Taylor, *The Black Carib,* Chapter 6; Craton, *Testing the Chains,* 180—94.

107. TNA CO 260/13 N. 137, Seton to Portland, March 29, 1796.

108. On Abercromby's campaigns see Duffy, *Soldiers,* 160–198; Craton, *Testing the Chains,* 195–210.

109. TNA 260/13 N. 153, Articles of Capitulation, June 11, 1796.

110. Dubois, *A Colony of Citizens,* 296–297.

111. Chun Kim, "The Caribs," 130–132.

112. ANOM C10D 2, Hugues to Audibert, 12 prairal An III.

113. For Hugues' promise of reinforcements, see ANOM FM C10D 2 23 prairial an IV.

114. For a list of the regiments that participated in combat, Shephard, *Historical Account,* 151–152.

115. Shephard, *Historical Account,* 166–167.

116. "J'eus le courage d'examiner tous ces corps dont la terre était jonchées. . . . Il ne restait plus de ce carbet que des cendres." Jonnès, *Aventures,* 212.

117. "Si jamais la Providence a protégé le faible contre l'iniquité, elle doit assurément donner la victoire aux Caraibes et garantir d'une subversion fatale le dernier peuple aborigène de ce vaste archipel." Jonnès, *Aventures,* 212. Reports of scattered insurgency on the part of "Brigands or Caribs" persisted after the mass exile, see for example TNA CO 260/15 N. 57, Bentich to Portland, July 20, 1798.

118. Thornhill, *Narrative,* 48.

119. TNA CO 101/34 N. 230, Houston to Portland, July 4, 1796.

120. TNA CO 106/12 N. 80, Return of houses and lots of land forfeited.

121. Duffy, *Soldiers*, 162.

122. TNA CO 101/34 N. 230, Houston to Portland, July 4, 1796.

123. On Acts of Attainder, see Thomas Bartlett, "Clemency and Compensation: The Treatment of Defeated Rebels and Suffering Loyalists After the 1798 Rebellion," in Jim Smyth, ed., *Revolution, Counter-Revolution and Union: Ireland in the 1790s* (New York: Cambridge University Press, 2000), 99–127.

124. Anderson, "Old Subjects," 209; on the United Irish Rebellion see Bartlett, "Clemency."

125. Turnbull, *Revolt*, 6; Wise, *Review*, 5. For a transcript of court proceedings, see EAP 295/2/6/1.

126. TNA CO 101/34 N. 245, Houston to Portland, July 30, 1796.

127. TNA CO 103/19 N. 42, An act to secure and detain such persons as shall be suspected of conspiring against His Majesty and His Government within these Islands . . . and for the more speedy trial and punishment of slaves charged with the said offences.

128. Benton, *A Search for Sovereignty*, 64.

129. TNA WO 1/82 N. 383, Houston, July 4, 1796.

130. TNA CO 101/35 N. 107, Statement of some circumstances, relative to the forfeited estates in the island of Grenada. For a list of those sold, EAP 295/2/1, Sale of Forfeited Slaves, 1797.

131. Turnbull, *Revolt*, 11–12. Emphasis in original.

132. *The St. George's Chronicle & Grenada Gazette* n. 387, Saturday July 30, 1796, in TNA CO 101/36 N. 38.

133. Craton, *Testing the Chains*, 208.

134. EAP 295/2/6/1, 69–71.

135. Hay, *Narrative*, 62, 24, 76.

136. McMahon, *Narrative*, 79–80.

137. Brown, *Diary of the Defence*, 72.

138. In some respects, this mirrors the relationship between Indigenous removal and the rise of plantations in the U.S. South. See Claudio Saunt, *Unworthy Republic: The Dispossession of Native Americans and the Road to Indian Territory* (New York: Norton, 2020).

139. In much eighteenth-century correspondence the island is spelled "Baliseau"; I have elected to use the modern spelling.

140. TNA WO 1/82 N. 658, Return of the Charaibs landed at Baliseau. For a detailed narrative of these surrenders see Shephard, *An Historical Account*, 164–174.

141. Taylor, *The Black Carib*, 165–166. In total 1,002 men, 1,779 women, and 1,555 children described as "black Carib" were landed at Baliceaux, as well as 102 individuals described as "Yellow Caribs" and 41 "Negroes the property of the Black Caribs."

142. Taylor, *The Black Carib*, 141–142; Shephard, *An Historical Account*, 172.

143. A discussion of the epidemic can be found in TNA WO 1/82 N. 661, "History of the Causes of a Malignant Pestilential Disease, Introduced into the Island of Baliseau, by the Black Charaibs from Saint Vincent." Nancie Solien Gonzalez speculates that the disease was either typhus or yellow fever but concludes that "we shall probably never know for sure." Nancie Solien Gonzalez, *Sojourners of the Caribbean: Ethnogenesis and Ethnohistory of the Garifuna* (Champaign: University of Illinois Press, 1988), 22.

144. TNA WO 1/82 N. 647–651. Of those embarked at Baliceaux, 2,026 arrived at Roatán.

145. For an account of the Caribs' landing at Roatán and subsequent migrations along the Central American coast see Solien Gonzalez, *Sojourners*, 39–50. Officials in St. Vincent continued to offer rewards for the capture or killing of any Kalinago found to be in the island into the early

nineteenth century; the last mention of "Caribs" in the colony dates to 1812, when several were reported to have left the island after the eruption of the Soufrière volcano. See Charles J. M. R. Gullick, "The Black Caribs in St. Vincent: The Carib War and Aftermath," *Actes du XLIIe Congrès International des Américanistes* (Paris: Société des Américanistes, 1975): 451–465.

146. https://slavevoyages.org/voyages/iZMDOCqK.

147. TNA CO 260/15 N. 57, Bentich to Portland, July 20, 1798

148. Joseph Spinelli, "Land Use and Population in St. Vincent, 1763–1960" (doctoral dissertation, University of Florida, 1973), 76–77.

149. TNA CO 260/15 N. 125, Minutes of the Privy Council, St. Vincent, February 21, 1797.

CONCLUSION

1. Alex Tyrell, "Joseph Sturge," *Oxford Dictionary of National Biography*, https://doi.org/10.1093/ref:odnb/26746; A. C. Bickley, "Thomas Harvey," *Oxford Dictionary of National Biography*, https://doi.org/10.1093/ref:odnb/12529.

2. Joseph Sturge and Thomas Harvey, *The West Indies in 1837: Being the Journal of a Visit to Antigua, Montserrat, Dominica, St. Lucia, Barbados, and Jamaica; undertaken for the purpose of ascertaining the actual condition of the Negro population of those islands.* (London: Frank Cass & Co., 1968), 11.

3. Sturge and Harvey, *The West Indies*, 94.

4. Ibid., 120–121.

5. Ibid., 161.

6. Ibid., 2, 120.

7. Ibid., 91.

8. Ibid., 116. On apprenticeship, see W. L. Burn, *Emancipation and Apprenticeship in the British West Indies* (London: Jonathan Cape, 1970 [1937]); for a firsthand account of apprenticeship in the eastern Caribbean, Roderick A. McDonald, ed., *Between Slavery and Freedom: Special Magistrate John Anderson's Journal of St. Vincent during the Apprenticeship* (Philadelphia: University of Pennsylvania Press, 2001).

9. Sturge and Harvey, *The West Indies*, 115.

10. On emancipation in the French Caribbean, Rebecca Hartkopff-Schloss, *Sweet Liberty: The Final Days of Slavery in Martinique* (Philadelphia: University of Pennsylvania Press, 2009).

11. Sturge and Harvey, *The West Indies*, 11.

12. On intercolonial marronage elsewhere in the Caribbean see Rupert, "Seeking the Waters of Baptism"; Hall, "Maritime Maroons."

13. Dator, "Search for a New Land," 42; Dator addresses interisland and interimperial mobility throughout his dissertation.

14. On maritime connections, see especially Julius Scott, *The Common Wind: Afro-American Currents in the Age of the Haitian Revolution* (New York: Verso, 2018).

15. See, among others, Bassi, *An Aqueous Territory*; Jarvis, *In the Eye of all Trade*; Schneider, *The Occupation of Havana*; Warsh, *American Baroque*; Wheat, *Atlantic Africa*.

16. Johnson, *Wicked Flesh*, 230.

17. On Indigenous erasure see Newton, "The Race Leapt"; O'Brien, *Firsting and Lasting*.

18. On the importance of families see Julie Hardwick, Sarah M. S. Pearsall, and Karin Wulf, "Introduction: Centering Families in Atlantic Histories," *WMQ* 70, N. 2 (April 2013: 205–224).

19. For another counterpoint see Ada Ferrer, *Freedom's Mirror: Cuba and Haiti in the Age of Revolution* (New York: Cambridge University Press, 2014).

20. DuVal, *Independence Lost*, especially part IV.

21. Dale Tomich and Michael Zeuske, "The Second Slavery: Mass Slavery, World Economy and Comparative Microhistories," *Review: A Journal of the Fernand Braudel Center* 31, N. 3 (2008): 91–100.

22. Schneider, *The Occupation of Havana*, chapter 6. On experimentation in the British Ceded Islands, Edelson, *The New Map*, Chapter 5.

23. Marshall, *The Making and Unmaking*; Muller, *Subjects and Sovereign*.

24. TNA PC1/60/10 N. 30.

25. For an example of how the Ceded Islands directly influenced debates over governance in India, see Kreighen, "A Contested Vision"; Keighren's analysis tackles questions of religion but not of race.

26. On these features see Candlin, *The Last Caribbean Frontier*. While Candlin analyzes Grenada as part of the southern Caribbean rather than the Ceded Islands, he notes that "many of the features that marked the society on Grenada would be repeated elsewhere," 23.

27. James Epstein, *Scandal of Colonial Rule: Power and Subversion in the British Atlantic during the Age of Revolution* (New York: Cambridge University Press, 2012), 6.

28. For an account of some of the free migrants see Candlin and Pybus, *Enterprising Women*. For a general history of Trinidad, see Bridget Brereton, *A History of Modern Trinidad, 1783–1962* (London: Heineman, 1985).

29. TNA T 71/501, Plantation Slaves, Trinidad, 21.

30. TNA T 71/437, Personal Slaves, Berbice, 23.

31. Sturge & Harvey, *The West Indies*, 103.

32. Ibid., 106.

33. https://slavevoyages.org/voyages/KQfbTy2S.

34. Sturge and Harvey, *The West Indies*, 106.

35. TNA T 71/346, page 593, Morne Rouge Estate, St. Mark.

36. TNA T 71/346.

37. TNA T 71/346, page 593.

38. Sturge and Harvey, *The West Indies*, 111.

39. For an innovative attempt to recover how people in Jamaica experienced their world see Simon Newman, "Hidden in Plain Sight: Escaped Slaves in Late Eighteenth- and Early Nineteenth-Century Jamaica," *WMQ* OI Reader (June 2018): 1–53.

40. Sturge and Harvey, *The West Indies*, 106. The possibility that this patriarch had in fact fathered some of these children went unmentioned.

41. For emancipation-era debates over labor see Epstein, *Scandal*, 184–221.

42. Sturge and Harvey, *The West Indies*, 106.

Index

Acknowledgments

In the course of researching and writing this project I incurred many debts, but I also built a community. Dr. Melanie Newton first introduced me to Caribbean history when I was an undergraduate at the University of Toronto, and she has remained a source of support and inspiration in the years since. At the University of Chicago, I was privileged to be mentored by Dr. Julie Saville. Julie's ability to put people at the center of her research, writing, and teaching is an example to aspire to, even if it's sometimes difficult to emulate. I am thankful for her mentorship but even more so for her friendship. Professors Dain Borges and Paul Cheney were ideal complements to Julie. I particularly appreciate Paul's expansive perspective on the French Atlantic and his keen attention to writing, and Dain's seemingly encyclopedic knowledge and good humor. Many other faculty, including Professors Tom Holt, Matt Briones, Rachel Jean-Baptiste, Leora Auslander, Emilio Kourí, and Emily Osborn, made UChicago a wonderful place to earn a PhD. Brett Baker, David Goodwine, and Sonja Rusnak are indispensable in helping students navigate university bureaucracy, and I am grateful for their knowledge and support.

At UChicago, I was fortunate to join a cohort of scholars who also became my friends. Among them are C. J. Alvarez, Natalie Belsky, Ramaesh Bhagirat-Rivera, Maura Capps, Enrique Dávila, Emilio de Antuñano, Chris Dingwall, Bethany Eiffert, Ashley Finigan, Korey Garibaldi, Keith Hernandez, Elisa Jones, Patrick Kelly, Aiala Levy, Emily Lord Fransee, Casey Lurtz, Deirdre Lyons, Semyon Khokhlov, Emily Marker, José Juan Pérez Meléndez, Eleanor Rivera, Basil Salem, Jackie Sumner, Jenna Timmons, Dan Webb, and Sarah Weicksel. Nate Leidholm joined me on many of the research trips that informed this book. Diana, Luis, Joaquín, and Lúcio Schwartz Francisco became my Chicago family, while John McCluskey and Dugan Hayes were the best things to ever come out of a grad school party.

As this project transitioned to its present form, Nadine Zimmerli invited me to workshop the entire manuscript at the Omohundro Institute of Early

American History and Culture (OI). I am deeply thankful to Carolyn Arena, Guillaume Aubert, Cathy Kelly, Paul Mapp, Simon Middleton, Josh Piker, Nick Popper, Fabricio Prado, Shauna Sweeney, and Karin Wulf, who took the time to read and provide feedback on the project at this critical juncture, and to Max Edelson and Brett Rushforth, who each provided a detailed written report that pushed me to refine and restructure my work. The final product is considerably stronger because of the OI's investment in an early-career scholar. I am also indebted to the organizers of and participants in the many other fora where I presented work in progress, including the Association of Caribbean Historians, the Early Modern Global Caribbean Symposium at the John Carter Brown Library, the Porter Fortune Symposium at the University of Mississippi, the McNeil Center for Early American Studies, the American Historical Association, the Neubauer Collegium, the Lees Seminar at Rutgers University, and several OI conferences including the Region and Nation in American Histories of Race and Slavery Conference at Mount Vernon.

Many other historians I call friends provided crucial feedback and support throughout this process. Jordan Smith, Hayley Negrin, and Scott Cave all read countless chapter drafts, and Scott later lent his extraordinary attention to detail to the index. Flavio Eichmann and Casey Schmitt were always willing to read and discuss all things Caribbean, and their enthusiasm and expertise carried the work forward at many points. I am also grateful for the advice and camaraderie of Kristen Block, Trevor Burnard, Natalie Cobo, Juan Cobo Betancourt, Linford Fisher, Norah Gharala, Jared Hardesty, Mark Hauser, Bertie Mandelblatt, Jennifer Palmer, Catie Peters, Pernille Røge, Greg O'Malley, Franco Rossi, Miriam Rothenberg, Neil Safier, Yevan Terrien, and Laurie Wood. Peter Redhead's willingness to share research about his family in Grenada greatly enriched this book.

I am fortunate to have joined Syracuse University, where students and colleagues in the history department and beyond provide a wonderful intellectual home. I am particularly thankful to department chairs Michael Ebner, Norman Kutcher, and Susan Branson for shepherding me through my first years as a professor; Junko Takeda, Gladys McCormick, Amy Kallander, and Samantha Kahn Herrick for their advice and support; my fellow junior faculty members, especially participants in the Moynihan Research Workshop, for their collegiality; and Faye Morse for fielding my many administrative questions and requests.

Researching this book gave me the opportunity to access libraries and archives across the United States, Europe, and the Caribbean. I greatly appreciate the support of staff at the Archives Nationales d'Outre Mer, the National Archives, Kew, the Archives Départmentales de la Martinique, the Grenada Registry Office, the Dominica National Archives, the St. Lucia National Archives, Special Collections at Hamilton College Library, the Clements Library, the David Library of the American Revolution, and the John Carter Brown Library, among others.

This book would not have been possible without the financial support provided by long-term fellowships from the National Endowment for the Humanities, the Social Sciences and Humanities Research Council of Canada, the Quinn Foundation, and France's Institut National d'Études Démographiques (INED), as well as short-term fellowships from the David Library of the American Revolution, Hamilton College Library, the Clements Library at the University of Michigan, the John Carter Brown Library, the Tinker Foundation, and the University of Chicago's France-Chicago Center and Nicholson Center for British Studies. At INED, Loïc Charles, Christine Théré, and members of Research Unit II, "Histoire et Populations," provided a warm welcome to an interloper in the field of historical demography.

Since our first conversation many years ago, Bob Lockhart has had a clear understanding of—and enthusiasm for—the story I want to tell. I thank him, and the team at Penn Press, for their support of this project and for shepherding it to completion. Anonymous reviewers, who later revealed themselves to be Randy Browne and Brett Rushforth, engaged with the manuscript with an exemplary level of detail and generosity. I thank them for pushing me to clarify the stakes of my work and for modeling the kind of mentorship that makes the field of Caribbean-Atlantic history such a wonderful one in which to work.

Portions of the book appeared in L. H. Roper, ed., *The Torrid Zone* and in *La Révolution Française* and are here reprinted with permission.

Perhaps my most important sources of community were the many friends and family who supported and distracted me throughout this lengthy process. From the moment I arrived to begin research on this project in Martinique, Betty, Dee Dee Joy, and the entire Manscour family welcomed me into their home, and Betty has offered a warm home base in my trips since then. Alice, Perrine, and the Billaux family made research in Aix-en-Provence even more enjoyable than it is already. The extended Murphy, Bildfell, O'Brien, and O'Beirne families in Canada and Ireland provided excellent reasons to take breaks from research and writing, while friends from a tiny island far from the Caribbean (the Sherkin crew) managed to reunite in many far-flung locations. Mikkel Dack, Engda Temesgen, Lindsay Bell, Manan and Retika Desai, and many other friends helped us make a home in Syracuse, while my dad, Brendan, siblings Ciara and Nick, and sister-in-law Taylor Townsend have had to make far too many trips across the border. Dipankar Rai's drive, enthusiasm, and constant desire to do better in all areas of his life motivated me to keep chipping away at this project, even during a pandemic. There's no one I would rather spend a year house-bound with.

Communities are also shaped by those they lose. In the course of writing this book, I said goodbye to my much-loved grandfather, Torfi Bildfell, the matriarch of the Canadian branch of our family, Dr. Betty O'Brien, and uncles Diarmuid Murphy and Ron Bildfell. I thought a lot about their lives and legacies as I tried to tease out the experiences of the people who fill these pages. My mother, Laurie Bildfell, died long before I realized that "historian" was a job, but I hope she had some inkling that I, like her, would someday tell people's stories. This is for her.